COUNTRY DRIVING

ALSO BY PETER HESSLER

River Town

Oracle Bones

Peter Hessler
COUNTRY DRIVING

A Chinese Road Trip
寻路中国

CANONGATE

Edinburgh · London · New York · Melbourne

Published by Canongate Books in 2010

1

Copyright © Peter Hessler, 2010

The moral right of the author has been asserted

First published in the United States of America in 2010 by HarperCollins Publishers,
10 East 53rd Street, New York, NY 10022

First published in Great Britain in 2010 by Canongate Books Ltd, 14 High Street,
Edinburgh EH1 1TE

www.meetatthegate.com

British Library Cataloguing-in-Publication Data
A catalogue record for this book is available on
request from the British Library

ISBN 978 1 84767 436 4

Book design: Emily Cavett Taff

Printed and bound in Great Britain by CPI Mackays, Chatham ME5 8TD

This book is printed on FSC certified paper

Mixed Sources
Product group from well-managed
forests and other controlled sources
www.fsc.org Cert no. TT-COC-002341
© 1996 Forest Stewardship Council
FSC

for Leslie

CONTENTS

BOOK I

THE WALL

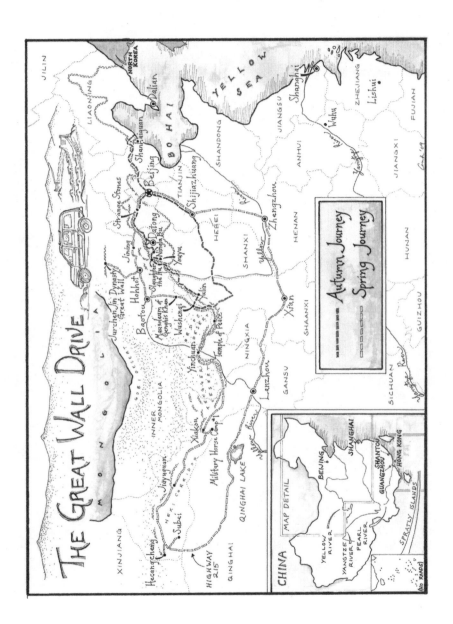

I
——

THERE ARE STILL EMPTY ROADS IN CHINA, ESPECIALLY
on the western steppes, where the highways to the Himalayas carry little
traffic other than dust and wind. Even the boomtowns of the coast have
their share of vacant streets. They lead to half-built factory districts and
planned apartment complexes; they wind through terraced fields that
are destined to become the suburbs of tomorrow. They connect villages
whose residents traveled by foot less than a generation ago. It was the
thought of all that fleeting open space—the new roads to old places,
the landscapes on the verge of change—that finally inspired me to get a
Chinese driver's license.

By the summer of 2001, when I applied to the Beijing Public Safety
Traffic Bureau, I had lived in China for five years. During that time I had
traveled passively by bus and plane, boat and train; I dozed across provinces and slept through towns. But sitting behind the wheel woke me
up. That was happening everywhere: in Beijing alone, almost a thousand
new drivers registered on average each day, the pioneers of a nationwide auto boom. Most of them came from the growing middle class,
for whom a car represented mobility, prosperity, modernity. For me, it
meant adventure. The questions of the written driver's exam suggested a
world where nothing could be taken for granted:

> 223. *If you come to a road that has been flooded, you should*
>
>   *a) accelerate, so the motor doesn't flood.*
>   *b) stop, examine the water to make sure it's shallow, and drive*
>   *across slowly.*
>   *c) find a pedestrian and make him cross ahead of you.*

282. When approaching a railroad crossing, you should

    a) accelerate and cross.
    b) accelerate only if you see a train approaching.
    c) slow down and make sure it's safe before crossing.

Chinese applicants for a license were required to have a medical checkup, take the written exam, enroll in a technical course, and then complete a two-day driving test; but the process had been pared down for people who already held overseas certification. I took the foreigner's test on a gray, muggy morning, the sky draped low over the city like a shroud of wet silk. The examiner was in his forties, and he wore white cotton driving gloves, the fingers stained by Red Pagoda Mountain cigarettes. He lit one up as soon as I entered the automobile. It was a Volkswagen Santana, the nation's most popular passenger vehicle. When I touched the steering wheel my hands felt slick with sweat.

"Start the car," the examiner said, and I turned the key. "Drive forward."

A block of streets had been cordoned off expressly for the purpose of testing new drivers. It felt like a neighborhood waiting for life to begin: there weren't any other cars, or bicycles, or people; not a single shop or makeshift stand lined the sidewalk. No tricycles loaded down with goods, no flatbed carts puttering behind two-stroke engines, no cabs darting like fish for a fare. Nobody was turning without signaling; nobody was stepping off a curb without looking. I had never seen such a peaceful street in Beijing, and in the years that followed I sometimes wished I had had time to savor it. But after I had gone about fifty yards the examiner spoke again.

"Pull over," he said. "You can turn off the car."

The examiner filled out forms, his pen moving efficiently. He had barely burned through a quarter of a Red Pagoda Mountain. One of the last things he said to me was, "You're a very good driver."

The license was registered under my Chinese name, Ho Wei. It was valid for six years, and to protect against counterfeiters, the document featured a hologram of a man standing atop an ancient horse-drawn carriage. The figure was dressed in flowing robes, like portraits of the

Daoist philosopher Lao Tzu, with an upraised arm pointing into the distance. Later that year I set out to drive across China.

WHEN I BEGAN PLANNING my trip, a Beijing driver recommended *The Chinese Automobile Driver's Book of Maps*. A company called Sinomaps published the book, which divided the nation into 158 separate diagrams. There was even a road map of Taiwan, which has to be included in any mainland atlas for political reasons, despite the fact that nobody using Sinomaps will be driving to Taipei. It's even less likely that a Chinese motorist will find himself on the Spratly Islands, in the middle of the South China Sea, territory currently disputed by five different nations. The Spratlys have no civilian inhabitants but the Chinese swear by their claim, so the *Automobile Driver's Book of Maps* included a page for the island chain. That was the only map without any roads.

Studying the book made me want to go west. The charts of the east and south looked busy—countless cities, endless tangled roads. Since the beginning of "Reform and Opening," the period of free-market economic changes initiated by Deng Xiaoping in 1978, development has been most intense in the coastal regions. The whole country is moving in that direction: at the time of my journey, approximately ninety million people had already left the farms, mostly bound for the southeast, and the routines of rural life were steadily giving way to the rush of factory towns. But the north and the west were still home to vast stretches of agricultural land, and the maps of those regions had a sense of space that appealed to me. Roads were fewer, and so were towns. Sometimes half a page was filled by nothing but sprinkled dots, which represented desert. And the western maps covered more space—in northern Tibet, a single page represented about one-fifteenth of China's landmass. In the book it looked the same size as Taiwan. None of the Sinomaps had a marked scale. Occasionally, tiny numbers identified the distance in kilometers between towns, but otherwise it was anybody's guess.

Most roads were also unlabeled. Expressways appeared as thick purple arteries, while national highways were red veins coursing between the bigger cities. Provincial roads were a thinner red, and county and local roads were smaller yet—tiny capillaries squiggling through remote areas. I liked the idea of following these little red roads, but not a single one had a name. The page for the Beijing region included seven expressways, ten highways, and over one hundred minor roads—but only the highways were numbered. I asked the Beijing driver about the capillaries.

"They don't name roads like that," he said.

"So how do you know where you are?"

"Sometimes there are signs that give the name of the next town," he said. "If there isn't a sign, then you can stop and ask somebody how to get to wherever you want to go."

The driver's exam touched on this too:

> 352. *If another motorist stops you to ask directions, you should*
>
> > a) *not tell him.*
> > b) *reply patiently and accurately.*
> > c) *tell him the wrong way.*

Thousands of nameless roads webbed the Sinomaps, and it was impossible to find one clear route across the west. But another symbol was less confusing: ⎍⎍⎍⎍⎍⎍⎍ . This marking appeared on the northeastern coast, at the city of Shanhaiguan, and from there it ran westward through Hebei Province. It continued into Shanxi, Shaanxi, and Inner Mongolia. In the deserts of Ningxia and Gansu, where dotted sands lay thick as stars, neat lines of ⎍⎍⎍⎍⎍⎍⎍ pierced the galaxy. That was one part of a Sinomap that was easy to understand: even as a boy I would have recognized it as the Great Wall. Throughout my childhood, whenever I looked at a map of China I thought: Imagine following a wall across a whole country!

At one point the Chinese had even considered converting the Great Wall into a highway. During the 1920s, intellectuals in China began to look to the example of the United States, where the automobile was already transforming the landscape. Chinese urban planners, some of whom had been educated in the States, encouraged cities to demolish their ancient defensive walls and use the material to build loop roads suitable for cars. By 1931 more than two dozen places had adopted this strategy, including the southern city of Guangzhou, which tore down structures that were over eight hundred years old. Inevitably, modernizers turned their attention to the Great Wall itself. In 1923, the Shanghai newspaper *Shenbao* published an article titled "Using Waste Material to Build a Road on the Great Wall." The author, Lei Sheng, supported a recent government proposal to modernize the structure; in Lei's opinion it represented "a very good opportunity." He wrote: "The Great Wall runs from Shanhaiguan to Yumenguan; it's continuous for thousands of *li*, and it's a straight line. To convert it into a road would link Beijing, Shanxi, Shaanxi, and Gansu; it would make it easier to do business. . . ." The proposal bounced around for a while—in 1931, the influential *Students' Magazine* supported it. Their article explained that with all the stones in the wall, "not so much capital will be required, with the result being that we'll fill a big gap in transportation infrastructure, going from the east to the west, from the ocean to the interior. . . ."

Nobody ever acted on this plan, undoubtedly because Great Wall regions are so rugged and remote. But seventy years later the general route appealed to me as a driver. East to west, from the ocean to the interior—I had always wanted to take such a road trip in China. In my *Book of Maps*, the ⊓⊔⊓⊔⊓⊔⊓ were often paralleled and intersected by roads, usually of the capillary type; sometimes these small routes ran for miles alongside the ruins. And the crenallated symbol still inspired the same reaction I'd had as a child: Imagine following a wall across a whole country! It could guide me through small-town China; I could chase the Great Wall all the way to the edge of the Tibetan plateau. Once I had the idea, I couldn't shake it, although friends cautioned me about taking a long car journey alone. But that was also covered on the written driver's exam:

> *347. If another driver, with good intentions, warns you about something, you should*
>
> > *a) be open-minded and listen carefully.*
> > *b) not listen.*
> > *c) listen and then don't pay attention to the advice.*

⊙ ⊙ ⊙

IN BEIJING, I RENTED a car and headed to Shanhaiguan, a city on the coast where the Great Wall meets the Bohai Sea. From there I drove west through the harvest of Hebei Province. It was mid-autumn and most crops had already been cut down; only the corn still stood tall in the fields. Everything else lay out in the road—mottled lines of peanuts, scattered piles of sunflower seeds, bright swaths of red pepper. The farmers carefully arranged the vegetables on the side of the asphalt, because that was the best surface for drying and sorting. They tossed the chaff crops into the middle of the road itself, where vehicles would be sure to hit them. This was illegal—there's no other act that so publicly violates both traffic safety and food hygiene. In rural China, though, it's still widely tolerated, because threshing is easiest when somebody else's tires do the work.

Initially I found it hard to drive over food. On the first day of my journey, I screeched to a halt before every pile, rolling down the window: "Is it OK for me to go through?" The farmers shouted back impatiently: "Go, go, go!" And so I went—millet, sorghum, and wheat cracking beneath me. By the second day I no longer asked; by the third day I learned to accelerate at the sight of grain. Approaching a pile, I'd hit the gas—*crash! crunch!*—and then in the rearview mirror I'd see people dart into the road, carrying rakes and brooms. That was my share of the autumn work—a drive-through harvest.

The Hebei hills are steep, marked by faces of open rock, and I drove through villages with rugged names: Ox Heart Mountain, Double Peak Village, Mountain Spirit Temple. The Great Wall shadowed these red-tiled towns. Usually the fortifications followed the ridgeline, high above the fields, and I'd catch glimpses as I wound through the hills. The Ming dynasty built these structures, mostly during the sixteenth century, and they had done their work well—the stone foundation and gray brick walls still clung firmly to the ridge. Sometimes a wall dipped into a valley, and in these low places the structure had been harvested as clean as the fields. The brick facing was completely gone: all that remained was the foundation and the hard-tamped earth interior, pockmarked and crumbling from the elements. This naked wall crossed the valley floor and climbed once more into the hills, until finally, after it reached a certain elevation, the bricks reappeared. The line of destruction was level on opposite sides of the valley, as if marking the tide of some great torrent that had swept through Hebei. But this flood had been human, and the watermark was one of motivation. It measured exactly how high people were willing to climb for free bricks.

In the village of Yingfang, I stopped to examine one of these bare sections, and a farmer named Wang Guo'an joined me in the road. "It was in better shape when I was young," he said. "A lot of it got torn down during the Cultural Revolution."

He was referring to the political campaigns that lasted from 1966 to 1976, when Mao Zedong encouraged the Chinese to attack anything traditional and "feudal." Some sections of the Great Wall were damaged during this period, and Wang could remember villagers in Yingfang tearing down their local fortifications and using the materials for other building projects.

He took me behind his home, where old bricks had been piled into neat four-foot-tall stacks. "Those are from the Great Wall," he said. "You can tell from the mortar—that's the kind they used in the old days. They came from a big tower in the village."

I asked if people still ripped up the wall, and he shook his head. "The government around here won't let you do it anymore," he said. "These bricks were first taken forty years ago. People used them to build a house, which was recently demolished. Now we'll use them to build something else."

In these crowded landscapes, everything was a potential resource. Hebei is about the same size as the state of Washington, but the population is more than eleven times higher—sixty-eight million people total. Hills have been carved into crop terraces; roads serve to dry vegetables; passing cars double as threshers. If there's wall within reach, it's used, sometimes twice. Able-bodied people often lead double lives—they might farm for a while and then head to the cities. They serve on construction crews; they do roadwork; they spend time on factory assembly lines. The most jobs I saw listed on a single business card was twenty-seven. That was in Shanxi Province, just beyond the Hebei border, and I met the man at a funeral.

In this part of China, even funerals have a bustling air, and I stopped for processions all across the north. They took place in the road, as public as the threshing, and usually the participants invited me to the banquet that followed. It was possible to drive from funeral to funeral all the way across Hebei and Shanxi, and in fact there were people who lived this way—an endless road trip where every stop represented somebody else's final terminus. In the town of Xinrong, I met Wei Fu and his wife, who specialized in performing traditional Shanxi opera at memorial services. They drove an old Beijing-brand flatbed truck, and they had customized the back for performances. In Xinrong they parked on the main street, set the brake, removed the railings, and erected an awning and two huge Peavey speakers. Within half an hour they had a stage, and hundreds of people gathered in the street to watch. The funeral was a seven-day event; it was especially elaborate because the dead man had owned the biggest shop in Xinrong, the Prosperous Fountainhead Store. The family arranged the man's coffin right at the entrance, and even in death he was doing good business—the street crowd overflowed into the shop, where people bumped past the coffin and bought snacks to eat while listening to opera.

A day later I stopped at another funeral just after the grave had been filled. It was in the countryside, on an open plain marked by a huge Great Wall signal tower. There weren't any cities nearby—in China, where the law requires most citizens to be cremated, only outlying rural regions are allowed to conduct burials. Near the tower, twenty men and women had gathered, wearing white sackcloth tied at the waist with red rope. In the distance a massive government propaganda sign read: "Protecting the Arable Earth Means Protecting Our Line of Life."

I was greeted by the only attendant not dressed in mourning white. He was sixty-nine years old, a pudgy man in a blue suit and cap; his round moon face shone with sweat. He wore the biggest smile I'd seen since yesterday's funeral, when I'd chatted with Wei Fu, the leader of the opera troupe. There's always at least one happy person at a Chinese funeral.

"Come over, come over!" the pudgy man said, pulling at my arm. "We're almost finished!"

He gave me a laminated name card. The front featured a picture of two hands clasped in a businessman's shake, along with the words:

Zhang Baolong
Feng Shui Master
Services for the Entire Length of the Dragon,
From Beginning to End

Traditionally, feng shui masters evaluate the relationship between buildings and landscapes, trying to create harmony between what is natural and what is manmade. In ancient times, these beliefs often influenced military and political affairs. Northwest of Beijing, the Ming dynasty avoided building the Great Wall along a twenty-mile-long ridge because of its proximity to the imperial tombs. From a strategic point of view, the ridge was perfect for defenseworks, but feng shui masters believed it represented a *longmai*, or "dragon vein." Any construction that violated the vein could bring bad fortune to the Ming, and so the ridge was left alone. The emperor went to the trouble of building walls farther to the north, where the terrain was less defensible and required more extensive fortifications.

After the Communists came to power in 1949, they attacked many cultural traditions as superstitious, including religion, fortune-telling, and feng shui analysis. Even when the reforms of Deng Xiaoping introduced greater tolerance, some practices never recovered—Taoism, for example, attracts few believers in today's China. But faith in feng shui has proven to be resilient, largely because it's connected to business. Good feng shui means good fortune, and people are willing to pay for expert analysis. Zhang Baolong was one of the new masters—he negotiated the market economy as skillfully as he did the geography. His business card listed twenty-seven separate services, ranging from "selecting marriage partners" to "choosing grave sites"—this was the "length of the dragon, from beginning to end." He also offered to install wood beams for houses, determine locations for mining, and treat "unusual diseases." He built coffins. ("You must supply your own wood.") He assisted in the carrying of wedding sedans. On the card, service number twenty-one involved moving bones to a new grave site—a common task in a nation undergoing a construction boom.

"I chose this site!" Zhang said proudly, pointing at the patch of recently dug earth. In front of the tomb, mourners took turns kowtowing: each person knelt, burned a stack of paper grave money, and wailed as he knocked his head against the ground. Nobody seemed to mind my presence. In northern China, I had learned that funerals are almost always welcoming, in part because people rarely see foreigners. Nevertheless, I dropped my voice to a whisper: "Who's the funeral for?"

But Zhang Baolong didn't seem to hear my question; he was still talking about feng shui. "It's arranged east-west," he continued, pointing at the patch of earth. "The head faces west, and the feet are to the east. And that tree I planted is a poplar. We plant poplars for men and willows for women; the purpose is to tell the soul where the grave is. This particular place is good for a lot of reasons. The position of that signal tower is very important, for example. You see, this place is good because it's high, and there's water in that stream to the east. And you have the signal tower above, which serves to protect the tomb. A person buried in this location will have many wealthy descendants, who will rise to high civil, military, and scholarly positions."

The men had finished kowtowing and now it was the women's turn: one by one, they touched their heads to the ground. The women were louder and their cries echoed across the valley.

"My father and grandfather were both feng shui masters," Zhang continued. "We've always done this in my family. And everybody in my family lives for a long time! My father lived to be ninety-five, and my mother was ninety-eight when she died. My grandmother lived to be ninety-nine!"

The keening rose another pitch. I wondered if a conversation about longevity might be more appropriate at another time, but Zhang kept talking. "I have three sons and three daughters," he said. "My sons are feng shui masters, too! And one of my daughters"—he beamed, perhaps at the thought of security in this world and the next—"is a nurse!"

❖   ❖   ❖

THE WEATHER HELD PERFECT across Hebei and Shanxi—cool, crisp mornings, the sunlight falling sharp across terraced fields. Usually I awoke early, but there was never any schedule or plan. I tried to keep the Great Wall in sight, and I stopped whenever something interested me. I figured out the route as I went; on many days I traveled less than one hundred miles. Rural driving tended to be slow, because often something was happening in the street—a crop threshing, a sheep crossing, a funeral procession. The roads themselves were completely unpredictable. A thin red line on my Sinomap might represent a brand-new asphalt road, but it could also be a dirt track or even a dry creekbed. Quite often the routes were in the process of being improved. Beginning in 1998, the government had invested heavily in rural roads, partly as a response to the Asian financial crisis, and this project was still under way when I took my journey.

In modern China, road building has often been a strategy for dealing with poverty or crisis. The first major construction campaign of motor roads began in 1920, when a drought resulted in a terrible famine across the north. It was hard to transport food to people who were starving—China's road system, which dated to imperial times, had been designed for horse-drawn carts. The American Red Cross sponsored a project to build modern roads suitable for trucks and automobiles, and in October of 1920 they began construction in Shandong Province. They hired local farmers, many of whom had been close to starvation, and the new roads allowed relief trucks to arrive. Oliver J. Todd, an American engineer who directed the Shandong project, estimated that it provided food and fuel, directly or indirectly, to half a million people.

The Red Cross eventually built roads in four northern provinces, and their work was so successful that Todd was hired by the Chinese government. He stayed for eighteen years, supervising highway construction all across the country. On a single road-building project in 1928, he had a crew of two hundred thousand laborers—more people than were employed by the entire U.S. road system at that time. The number of passenger cars in China remained low—in 1922, Beijing had approximately 1,500—but interest was intense. Chinese cities held car shows; the Shanghai newspaper *Shenbao* ran a weekly "Automobile Supplement." By 1935, China had fifty thousand miles of good earthen motor roads, and it seemed only a matter of time before the nation would experience an auto boom.

In the end, that boom was postponed for more than half a century. The Japanese invaded northern China in 1937, and the war crippled the young auto market. After Mao came to power, decades of Communist economics made it impossible for people to buy cars. The road system of rural China languished, and it wasn't until the Reform years that the government could improve such infrastructure on a major scale. In 1998, the Asian financial crisis provided motivation, somewhat like the famines of old. The government wanted to offset the economic threat, and it also saw an opportunity to finally inspire the long-delayed auto boom. History was being repeated: this was China's second wave of car pioneers, and they were essentially starting over. In 2001, the year that I got my license, the country had a population of over 1.2 billion, but there were fewer than ten million passenger vehicles. The ratio was 128 people for every vehicle, similar to the United States in 1911.

For my road trip, I rented a Chinese-made Jeep Cherokee from a Beijing company called Capital Motors. It was a new industry—even five years earlier, almost nobody would have thought of renting a car for a weekend trip. But now the business had started to develop, and my local Capital Motors branch had a fleet of about fifty vehicles, mostly Chinese-made Volkswagen Santanas and Jettas. They were small sedans, built on the same basic model as the VW Fox that was once sold in the States. At Capital Motors, I often rented Jettas for weekend trips, and there was an elaborate ritual to these transactions. First, I paid my twenty-five dollars per day and filled out a mountain of paperwork. Next, the head mechanic opened the trunk to prove that there was a spare tire and a jack. Finally we toured the Jetta's exterior, recording dents and scratches onto a diagram that represented the shape of a car. This often took a while—Beijing traffic is not gentle, and it was my responsibility to sketch every door ding and bumper dent. After we documented the prenuptial damage, the mechanic turned the ignition and showed me the gas gauge. Sometimes it was half full; sometimes there was a quarter tank. Occasionally he studied it and announced: "Three-eighths." It was my responsibility to return the car with exactly the same amount of fuel. Week to week, it was never the same, and one day I decided to make my own contribution to the fledgling industry.

"You know," I said, "you should rent out all the cars with a full tank, and then require the customer to bring it back full. That's how rental companies do it in America. It's much simpler."

"That would never work here," said Mr. Wang, who usually handled my paperwork. He was the friendliest of the three men who sat in the Capital Motors front office, where they smoked cigarettes like it was a competition. Behind their veil of smoke, a company evaluation sign hung on the wall:

CUSTOMER SATISFACTION RATING: 90%
EFFICIENCY RATING: 97%
APPROPRIATE SERVICE DICTION RATING: 98%
SERVICE ATTITUDE RATING: 99%

"That might work in America, but it wouldn't work here," Mr. Wang continued. "People in China would return the car empty."

"Then you charge them a lot extra to refill it," I explained. "Make it a standard rule. Charge extra if people don't obey and they'll learn to follow it."

"Chinese people would never do that!"

"I'm sure they would," I said.

"You don't understand Chinese people!" Mr. Wang said, laughing, and the other men nodded their heads in agreement. As a foreigner, I often heard that, and it had a way of ending discussion. The Chinese people had invented the compass, paper, the printing press, gunpowder, the seismograph, the crossbow, and the umbrella; they had sailed to Africa in the fifteenth century; they had constructed the Great Wall; over the past decade they had built their economy at a rate never before seen in the developing world. They could return a rental car with exactly three-eighths of a tank of gas, but filling it was apparently beyond the realm of cultural possibility. We had a couple more conversations about this, but finally I dropped the subject. It was impossible to argue with somebody as friendly as Mr. Wang.

He seemed especially cheerful whenever I returned a freshly damaged car. In the States, I had never had an accident, but Beijing was a different story. When I first came to the capital and walked around, I was impressed by the physicality of pedestrians—I was constantly getting bumped and pushed. In a city of thirteen million you learn to expect contact, and after I got my license I realized that driving works the same way. The first couple of times I dented a Jetta, I felt terrible; after the fourth or fifth time, it became routine. I bumped other cars; other cars bumped me. If there was a dent, we settled it in the street, the way everybody does in China.

Once, a driver backed into my rental car near the Lama Temple in downtown Beijing. I got out to inspect the dent; the other motorist, by way of introduction, immediately said, "One hundred yuan." It was the equivalent of about twelve dollars, which was generally the starting point for a midsize Beijing dent. When this offer was relayed by telephone to Mr. Wang, his response was also immediate: "Ask for two hundred." I bargained for five minutes, until the other driver finally agreed to one hundred and fifty. Mr. Wang was satisfied; he knew you never get what you ask for. And every accident had a silver lining—dents were good business. There wasn't any paperwork for these exchanges, and I suspected that the desk men at Capital Motors sometimes kept the cash.

Another time I hit a dog while driving in the countryside north of Beijing. The animal darted out from behind a house and lunged at the front of my Jetta; I swerved, but it was too late. That was a common problem—Chinese dogs, like everybody else in the country, weren't quite accustomed to having automobiles around. When I returned the car, Mr. Wang seemed pleased to see that the plastic cover for the right signal light had been smashed. He asked me what I had hit.

"A dog," I said.

"*Gou mei wenti?*" he said. "The dog didn't have a problem, did it?"

"The dog had a problem," I said. "It died."

Mr. Wang's smile got bigger. "Did you eat it?"

"It wasn't that kind of dog," I said. "It was one of those tiny little dogs."

"Well, sometimes if a driver hits a big dog," Mr. Wang said, "he just throws it in the trunk, takes it home, and cooks it." I couldn't tell if he was joking; he was a dog owner himself, but in China that doesn't necessarily involve dietary restrictions. He charged me twelve bucks for the light cover—the same price as a midsize dent.

They never asked where I was taking the Jeep Cherokee. The rental contract specifically forbade drivers from leaving the Beijing region, but I decided to ignore this rule—they wouldn't figure it out until I returned the Jeep with a loaded odometer. In China, much of life involves skirting regulations, and one of the basic truths is that forgiveness comes easier than permission. The Jeep was the biggest vehicle on the lot, a Cherokee 7250, and they gave me a special price of thirty dollars a day. It was white, with purple detailing along the sides; the doors were decorated with the English words "City Special." The name was accurate—the thing would be worthless in rough terrain, because it was strictly rear-wheel drive. I was certain that at some point on my journey I'd get stuck in mud or sand or snow, but there was no point in worrying about that now, because Capital Motors had nothing better to offer. At any rate, if things got bad in the west I could always call Mr. Zhang, the feng shui master. On his business card he offered to "tow cars and trucks"—service number twenty-two, listed between "collecting bones" and "playing horns and drums."

DRIVING WEST, I HAD climbed steadily, until now in northern Shanxi the elevation was over four thousand feet. This was a dry, dusty landscape, with low brown peaks scarred by creekbeds that had burrowed into their flanks. It was as if the mountains had been bled of all brightness, the color running down the hillsides and pooling in fields where farmers harvested sweet oats. Only these valleys were vivid: the deep green of the crops, the dark shimmer of irrigation channels, the bright blue of the cotton jackets that were still common among elderly Chinese in the countryside. But the landscape had a stark, simple beauty, and for the first time it felt open—a foreshadowing of the great steppes of Central Asia.

Everywhere the valley floor was broken by the remnants of signal towers. They were made of tamped earth, the same dusty brown color as the hills, and they rose more than twenty feet tall. Some villages were entirely surrounded by ancient defenseworks. To the north, Inner Mongolia lay less than twenty miles away, and on my map this provincial boundary was marked by a familiar symbol: ⌐⎍⌐⎍⌐⎍⌐⎍ .

I pulled over at the last village before the border. The place was called Ninglu Bu—many town names in this region include the character *bu*, which means "fortress," because they're located on the sites of former Ming-dynasty garrisons. In Ninglu an old fort stood in the middle of town, and the village was surrounded by walls of packed earth. These fortifications completely dwarfed the simple homes of today's residents, who numbered only one hundred and twenty.

When I stopped in villages with ancient ruins, I often asked locals if anybody knew the history. In Ninglu, a group of elderly people in the village square responded immediately. "Talk to Old Chen," somebody said, and another man shuffled off to find him. Five minutes later, Chen Zhen appeared. He was fifty-three years old, with sun-lined skin and gray hair that had been cropped close. He wore dark policeman's pants, a green shirt that bore the gold buttons of the People's Liberation Army, and a blue military jacket with epaulets on the shoulders and stripes across the cuffs. In the Chinese countryside, men often wear surplus army and police gear, because the cheap garments are practical. Invariably these clothes are mismatched and oversized; Old Chen's sleeves hung to his fingertips. He looked as if he had inherited the outfit, much as Ninglu had inherited its earthen walls—all of it, from the baggy jackets to the crumbling fortifications, could have been the castoffs of some defeated army that had abandoned everything and fled south.

He stood ramrod straight while I introduced myself. I explained that I had come from Beijing and was interested in the Great Wall; I asked if he knew anything about the history of this village. Old Chen listened carefully and then he cleared his throat. "Come with me," he said. "I have information."

I followed him down a dirt path that led to a series of mud-walled houses. At the largest one, he opened the door. Most of the room was occupied by the *kang*, the brick bed that's traditionally used in northern China. During winter a *kang* can be heated from beneath with a wood fire, but in Ninglu it was still autumn, and Old Chen was saving his fuel. The room was cold; he poured me a cup of tea to warm my hands. He opened a drawer in a cabinet, removed a sheaf of thin rice paper, and proudly handed it over. The front cover featured a handwritten title:

The Annals of Ninglu Bu
Research Established January 22, 1992

On page one, Old Chen's careful script read: "The town wall was built in the 22nd year of the Jiajing emperor (in 1543), and encased in kiln-fired brick in the first year of the Wanli emperor (in 1573)." I flipped through the book—dozens of pages, hundreds of dates. There were maps: one page had been labeled "Great Wall," and it was criss-crossed with thick blue lines and circles.

"There are thirty-three signal towers in this region," Old Chen explained, pointing at the circles on the map. "Those are from the Ming. The Ming wall is along the Inner Mongolian border. But there are other walls also going through this region, from other dynasties."

He opened a second drawer and took out a gray shard of pottery. When he handed it over, the hardened clay felt cool in my palm. "What dynasty do you think this is from?" he asked.

I told him that I had no idea, and Old Chen looked disappointed.

"Well, if you ever come back here, maybe you can bring an archaeologist," he said. "I know where a lot of this pottery can be found, but I don't know which dynasty it is." He told me that treasure seekers had found intact pottery and bronze artifacts in this area. "All of the good ones have been sold," he said. "Nobody regulates it."

The research was his hobby—he was a farmer, and in the past he had also served as Party Secretary, the highest Communist Party position in the village. Now he was retired from local politics but he still worked two acres of land, where he grew potatoes. He owned five sheep. He told me that his annual income was around two hundred dollars, and he had only a sixth-grade education, but he had done his best to educate himself in history. Since retiring, he had made frequent trips to the government archives of Zuoyun County, fifteen miles away. He tracked down information about local fortifications, and he surveyed the region, trying to match ruins with historical descriptions. He had also interviewed Ninglu's elderly residents, some of whom remembered the war against the Japanese, when bricks from the Ming garrison wall had been harvested to build houses. I asked why he had undertaken the research. "Because nobody else was doing it," he said. "If nobody studies it, then nobody's going to know the past."

In terms of academia, Old Chen was right: there isn't a single scholar at any university in the world who specializes in the Great Wall. Chinese historians focus on textual research, and usually they study political institutions that can be traced through the records of a dynasty or a government. In the field, archaeologists tend to excavate ancient tombs. The Great Wall fits into neither tradition: it's not underground, and it's not strictly on the printed page; a researcher needs to combine both fieldwork and reading. Even if a scholar were interested, he'd have trouble defining his subject, because there are hundreds of walls across the north. In the past, this was the most problematic region for Chinese empires, which enjoyed natural boundaries in other directions: ocean to the east, jungle to the south, the Himalayas to the west. But the northern steppes are wide open, and in ancient times this landscape was populated by nomadic tribes who raided their more sedentary neighbors. In response, the Chinese often built walls—the earliest known historical reference to such defenseworks dates to 656 BC. Over the next two millennia, many dynasties constructed fortifications, but they did so in different ways and used different terms to describe their defenseworks. At least ten distinct words were used for what we now think of as "Great Wall."

Two dynasties became especially famous for wall building. In 221 BC, Qin Shihuang declared himself emperor, and during his reign he commanded the construction of three thousand miles of barriers of tamped earth and fieldstone. His dynasty, the Qin, became notorious for such forced labor projects, and popular songs and legends outlasted most of the earthen walls themselves, which gradually deteriorated over the centuries. Whereas the Qin walls survive primarily in the popular imagination, the Ming dynasty built structures that have lasted by virtue of their materials. The Ming came to power in 1368, and in the Beijing region they eventually constructed fortifications of quarried stone and brick. They were the only dynasty to build extensively with such durable materials—these are the impressive walls I'd seen in Hebei Province. But the Ming defenseworks are a network rather than a single structure, and some regions have as many as four distinct barriers.

In the eighteenth century, Western explorers and missionaries began to visit China in greater numbers. They heard the Qin stories, and they saw the Ming walls; inevitably they connected the two in their minds. This imaginative line from the Qin to the Ming became what we now think of as the Great Wall: supposedly, a single structure of brick and stone, two thousand years old, that stretches across China as neatly as a marking on a map— ⌐⌐⌐⌐⌐⌐⌐ . In 1793, an Englishman named Sir John Barrow visited the wall near Beijing, extrapolated from what he saw, and declared that the nationwide structure contained enough stone to build two smaller walls around the equator. (He didn't realize that walls in the west are smaller and made of tamped earth.) In 1923, *National Geographic Magazine* claimed that the Great Wall is visible to the human eye from the moon. (In truth, nobody on the moon could see it in 1923, and they still can't.) For a while, Chinese intellectuals tried to resist such exaggerations, believing rightly that the foreigners had confused both history and geography. But eventually the myths proved appealing to nationalists like Mao Zedong, who used the Great Wall in propaganda, recognizing the symbolic value of a unified barrier. In any case, it was hard to set the record straight in a country with no academic tradition of studying the ancient structures. Finally it was as if the Chinese threw up their hands and accepted the foreign notion: nowadays there's even a single term, *Changcheng*, literally "long wall," which has been adopted as the catchall equivalent of "Great Wall."

The only Chinese studying the Great Wall do so outside of academia. In Beijing, small communities of amateur historians try to combine fieldwork with textual research, and occasionally in the provinces there's somebody like Old Chen. He told me that eventually he hoped to find a provincial publisher for his book. After he showed me his writings, and the artifacts that he had collected, he offered to take me out to see the local walls.

We climbed into the City Special and drove north along a dirt road. A couple of miles outside the village, we stopped and Old Chen led me through a high valley of scrub grass. He walked slowly, with the thoughtful pose that's common among men in the countryside: head down, hands clasped behind his back. He stopped at a distinct grass-covered ridge.

"That's from the Northern Wei," he said, referring to a dynasty that ruled this region from AD 386 to 534. Over the centuries the structure had been worn down by wind and rain, until now it was nothing more than a two-foot-tall bump stretching northeast across the hills. It was intersected by another ridge so faint that I wouldn't have seen it without his help. "That's the Han wall," he said. It was even older: the Han ruled from 206 BC to AD 220. High in the hills, a third wall dated to the Ming. The Ming fortifications were six feet tall and ran clear to both horizons, east and west. In this landscape of ancient barriers, the Ming wall was a relative newcomer—only four centuries old.

"Over the years, I saw these things so many times, until I finally got curious," Old Chen explained. "Where did they come from? What was the system behind it? That was my main reason for starting the research."

I drove him back to his home, where we had another cup of tea. He explained that the village name had been shortened from Ningxi Hulu, which means "Pacify the Hu." In ancient times, *hu* was a term used by the Chinese to describe the nomadic peoples of the north. It wasn't specific to a certain tribe or ethnicity, and it was derogatory—a slur that encompassed all outsiders. The final character, *lu*, was even blunter: "barbarians."

"Basically, the name of our village means 'Kill the Foreigners,'" Old Chen said with a smile. "Look at this." He opened my book of Sino-maps and pointed out another village ten miles to the east: Weilu, or "Overawe the Barbarians." Nearby was the town of Pohu: "Smash the

Hu." Other villages were called "Overawe the Hu," "Suppress the Barbarians," and "Slaughter the Hu." Modern maps use the character for *hu*
that means "tiger"—a substitution first made during the Qing dynasty,
whose Manchu rulers were sensitive to the portrayal of people from
outside the walls. But the change was cosmetic, and the original meaning is still as obvious as the old forts that tower over the village.

I left Ninglu in late afternoon, when the sun began to fall low over
the fields. Old Chen escorted me to the City Special, and a dozen locals
followed out of curiosity. Many of the men wore military castoffs, and
the collected uniforms—worn, dirty, ill-fitting—made me feel if I were
being sent on some desperate mission. My next destination lay to the
north, where hills loomed high along the borderlands, a line of dry
peaks that seemed to have been bled of all color. Old Chen shook my
hand and wished me good luck. "Next time you come," he reminded
me, "try to bring an archaeologist."

I drove past neat lines of poplars turning gold with the season, and
then the road began to climb through the bare mountains. There weren't
any other cars. At an elevation of six thousand feet, the pavement pierced
the Ming wall, which represented the Shanxi provincial boundary. The
ancient structure had been broken to make room for the roadway, and
a cement pillar marked the entrance to Inner Mongolia. This is the last
region in north-central China, and it was the least populated place I had
visited thus far.

I continued driving until I reached a pass, where I found a dirt track
branching off the main road. The track ran along the ridge for a few
hundred yards, and then I pulled over. In the back of the Jeep, I carried
a tent and sleeping bag. It was a perfect night for camping—the air was
so clear that the stars seemed to pulse above the valley. In the tent, I fell
asleep thinking about the border towns that I intended to visit the next
day. Smash the Hu, Slaughter the Hu: just another quiet drive in the
countryside.

At midnight the tent was suddenly bathed in light. Startled, I awoke
and sat bolt upright, thinking that it was the headlights of an approaching car. Fumbling with the tent flap, I looked outside and realized that
the full moon had just broken the horizon. Everything else was normal:

the empty dirt track, the parked City Special. Down below, the lights of Ninglu village had been extinguished, and the rising moon cast shadows across the steppe. For a moment I sat still, waiting for my fear to settle, hearing nothing but the wind and the pounding of my heart.

IN THE EVENINGS I worried about visitors, especially the police. There wasn't yet a tradition of cross-country driving in China, and rules were strict for foreigners. I wasn't supposed to take the City Special outside of Beijing, and some parts of the west were closed completely to outsiders, because of poverty, ethnic tensions, or military installations. And a foreign journalist was technically required to apply to local authorities before traveling anywhere in the country. That was one reason I brought my tent—I hoped to avoid small-town hotels, which hand over their guest lists to the police.

On the road I followed my own set of guidelines. I waited until sunset to pitch my tent, and I left at first light; I never started a campfire. If I needed to stay in a small town, I looked for a truckers' dorm, where foreign guests are so rare that they usually don't have police registration forms. I carried enough water to last for days. I generally drove under the influence of caffeine and sugar—the City Special was fully stocked with Coca-Cola, Gatorade, Oreo cookies, and candy bars. If I traveled for a few days without a shower, I stopped at a barbershop and paid somebody to wash my hair. Every small town in China has at least one barbershop, and a standard service is the wash and head massage, usually for about a dollar. At noon I often pulled off the road to take a nap. I never drove at night. Fatigue is such a factor on Chinese roads that it appears on the driver's exam:

> *133. If you drive for four hours, you must stop the car and take a mandatory rest of at least*
>
> *a) 10 minutes.*
> *b) 20 minutes.*
> *c) 15 minutes.*

The correct answer is B—if you rest for a quarter hour, you're still five minutes short of legal. Chinese driving is a physical endeavor, or at least that's how it's portrayed in the rulebook. According to law, a truck driver must be at least 155 centimeters tall, whereas the driver of a passenger car has to be 150 (four feet eleven inches). In order to get a license, you need to have at least three normal fingers on each hand. Thumbs are nonnegotiable. Each ear must be capable of distinguishing the sound of a tuning fork at a distance of fifty centimeters. You can't be red-green color-blind. You can't suffer from epilepsy, congenital heart disease, vertigo, or Ménière's syndrome. The law explicitly forbids any driver stricken by "hysteria." If your legs happen to be of different lengths, and the difference exceeds five centimeters, you are legally banned from operating a standard transmission vehicle.

The driving law spells out such physical requirements in detail, as if sound health and body are critical to road safety, which clearly is not the case. The issue isn't traffic volume, either—in 2001, when I drove across the north, China had about one-fifth the number of cars and buses as the United States. But there were more than twice as many traffic fatalities, and the government reported a total of 750,000 road accidents. It was a nation of new drivers, most of them negotiating new cities, and the combination was lethal. People might have done better if surroundings had remained familiar—in Beijing, drivers tended to be brilliant in old parts of town. Traditionally, Beijing is composed of *hutong* neighborhoods, networks of narrow brick-walled alleyways that had originally been laid out in the thirteenth century. Every time I drove into a *hutong*, the walls pressed close and I broke out in a sweat, but everybody else seemed unfazed. They were patient and they were skilled: a Beijing *hutong* driver could dodge an oncoming Santana, cruise cleanly through a pack of schoolchildren, and park his car within inches of a Ming-dynasty brick wall. If the nation's road system somehow could have channeled the *hutong* mentality, maybe all of us would have been fine.

But people didn't respond as well to the open space of a new road. Some of it was poor planning: by 2001, Beijing had suddenly become home to over one million vehicles, and the city's infrastructure struggled to catch up. South of the *hutong* where I lived, old neighborhoods had been cleared out for bigger roads, but traffic rules were often bizarre. At one major intersection, some genius urban planner had located the left turn lane on the far right side of the road, which meant that anybody heading in that direction had to cut across five lanes of traffic. If he successfully made the turn and continued straight for another mile, he reached another intersection where the traffic signals had been mistimed so badly that lights were green in all directions for a good five seconds. Elsewhere in the city, entire districts were under construction. Roads were half built; signs were poorly planned; unmarked ramps led to mystery thoroughfares. Beijing maps featured cloverleaf exchanges that could have been designed by M. C. Escher:

Even today, when some of the road problems have been improved, city driving is an adventure. And trouble is inevitable in a place where most drivers are rookies. In China, the transition has been so abrupt that many traffic patterns come directly from pedestrian life—people drive the way they walk. They like to move in packs, and they tailgate whenever possible. They rarely use turn signals. Instead they rely on automobile body language: if a car edges to the left, you can guess that he's about to make a turn. And they are brilliant at improvising. They convert sidewalks into passing lanes, and they'll approach a roundabout in reverse direction if it seems faster. If they miss an exit on a highway, they simply pull onto the shoulder, shift into reverse, and get it right the second time. They curb-sneak in traffic jams, the same way Chinese people do in ticket lines. Tollbooths can be hazardous, because a history of long queues has conditioned people into quickly evaluating options and making snap decisions. When approaching a toll, drivers like to switch lanes at the last possible instant; it's common to see an accident right in front of a booth. Drivers rarely check their rearview mirrors. Windshield wipers are considered a distraction, and so are headlights.

In fact, the use of headlights was banned in Beijing until the late 1970s, when the nation's leaders began going overseas in increasing numbers. During the early Reform years, these trips were encouraged by governments in Europe and the United States, who hoped that glimpses of democracy would convince Chinese officials to rethink their policies. In 1983 Chen Xitong, the mayor of Beijing, made one such visit to New York. On the way to and from his meetings with Mayor Ed Koch and other dignitaries, Chen made a crucial road observation: Manhattan drivers turn on their lights at night. When Chen returned to China, he decreed that Beijing motorists do the same. It's unclear what conclusions he drew from his encounters with American democracy (eventually he ended up in prison for corruption), but at least he did his part for traffic safety.

Nevertheless, Chinese drivers haven't grasped the subtleties of headlight use. Most people keep their lights off until it's pitch-dark, and then they flip on the brights. Almost nobody uses headlights in rain, fog, snow, or twilight conditions—in fact, this is one of the few acts guaranteed to annoy a Chinese driver. They don't mind if you tailgate, or pass on the right, or drive on the sidewalk. You can back down a highway entrance ramp without anybody batting an eyelash. But if you switch on your lights during a rainstorm, approaching drivers will invariably flash their brights in annoyance.

For the most part, though, they're unflappable, and it's hard to imagine another place where people take such joy in driving so badly. On the open road it feels like everybody has just been unleashed from a *hutong*—there's a sudden rush of speed and competition, and the greatest thrill comes from passing other motorists. People pass on hills; they pass on turns; they pass in tunnels. If they get passed themselves, they immediately try to pass the other vehicle back, as if it were a game. From what I can tell, that's the only question on the written driver's exam with three correct answers:

77. *When overtaking another car, a driver should pass*

    a) on the left.

    b) on the right.

    c) wherever, depending on the situation.

On the exam, questions are taken directly from government-published study materials, and the Public Safety License Bureau provided me with a booklet that contained 429 multiple-choice questions and 256 true-false queries. Often these questions capture the spirit of the road ("True/False: In a taxi, it's fine to carry a small amount of explosive material"), but it's less obvious how they prepare people for driving in China. In fact the trick is to study the wrong answers. They describe common traffic maneuvers with such vividness that you can practically see the faces behind the wheel:

81. *After passing another vehicle, you should*

    a) wait until there is a safe distance between the two vehicles, make a right-turn signal, and return to the original lane.

    b) cut in front of the other car as quickly as possible.

    c) cut in front of the other car and then slow down.

117. *When approaching a marked pedestrian crossing, you should*

    a) slow down and stop if there are pedestrians.

    b) accelerate in order to catch up with the car directly in front of you, and then cross closely behind him.

    c) drive straight through, because pedestrians should give vehicles the right of way.

80. *If, while preparing to pass a car, you notice that it is turning left, making a U-turn, or passing another vehicle, you should*

    a) pass on the right.

    b) not pass.

    c) honk, accelerate, and pass on the left.

Lots of answers involve honking. In a Chinese automobile, the horn is essentially neurological—it channels the driver's reflexes. People honk constantly, and at first all horns sound the same, but over time you learn to interpret them. In this sense it's as complicated as the language. Spoken Chinese is tonal, which means that a single sound like *ma* has different meanings depending on whether it's flat, rising, falling and rising, or falling sharply. A single Chinese horn, on the other hand, can mean at least ten distinct things. A solid *hooooonnnnkkkkk* is intended to attract attention. A double sound—*hooooonnnnkkkkk, hooooonnnnkkkkk*—indicates irritation. There's a particularly long *hooooooooonnnnnnnnnkkkkkk* that means that the driver is stuck in bad traffic, has exhausted curb-sneaking options, and would like everybody else on the road to disappear. A responding *hoooooooooooonnnnnnnnnnnnnnnkkkkkkkkkkkk* proves they aren't going anywhere. There's a stuttering, staggering *honk honk hnk hnk hnk hnk hnk hnk* that represents pure panic. There's the afterthought *honk*—the one that rookie drivers make if they were too slow to hit the button before a situation resolved itself. And there's a short basic *honk* that simply says: My hands are still on the wheel, and this horn continues to serve as an extension of my nervous system. Other honks appear on the exam:

> *353. When passing an elderly person or a child, you should*
>
> > *a) slow down and make sure you pass safely.*
> > *b) continue at the same speed.*
> > *c) honk the horn to tell them to watch out.*

> *269. When you enter a tunnel, you should*
>
> > *a) honk and accelerate.*
> > *b) slow down and turn on your lights.*
> > *c) honk and maintain speed.*

> *355. When driving through a residential area, you should*
>
> > *a) honk like normal.*
> > *b) honk more than normal, in order to alert residents.*
> > *c) avoid honking, in order to avoid disturbing residents.*

◦ ◦ ◦

I PICKED UP MY first hitchhiker on the way to Smash the Hu. At sunrise I had taken down my tent, and after studying the map I decided to try a route that paralleled the north side of the Ming wall. This turned out to be the worst road thus far—it began as a dirt track, high on the mountain, and then it descended steeply. Water runoff had badly rutted the surface; the City Special lurched and groaned. To my left, the Great Wall perched neatly atop a ridgeline—it seemed to float effortlessly while I banged down the broken road. Halfway to the valley floor, a young woman stood beside the dirt track, waving madly. I rolled down the window.

"Where are you going?" she asked.

"Smash the Hu, then Slaughter the Hu," I said. In Chinese those village names really roll off the tongue.

"Can I get a ride to Smash the Hu?"

"No problem," I said, pushing open the door. The woman carried a sack of fresh pork, the fatty meat glistening white and pink against the plastic. She set it on the floor and hesitated before entering.

"How much is it?" she said.

"How much is what?" For a moment I thought she was talking about the pork.

"To Smash the Hu," she said. "How much?"

Good question—how can anybody put a price on destroying indeterminate nomadic tribes? "Don't worry about it," I said. "I'm going there anyway."

Her name was Gao Linfeng, and she was twenty-seven years old. She told me that she had grown up in Smash the Hu but now she worked in a factory in Hohhot, the capital of Inner Mongolia. She was traveling home in order to see her grandmother—the pork was a gift. In these parts, transport was rare; she had caught a ride on the Ninglu bus, which only took her as far as the pass. From there she had planned to continue on foot until a ride came along. She wore a new gray business suit and fresh makeup, and her hair was neatly styled. How was it possible to look so good on a dirt road in Inner Mongolia? I was dressed in an old gray T-shirt and dirty trousers; it had been two days since somebody last washed my hair.

Like many rural Chinese, Gao had left home to find work in the city. In 1978, at the beginning of Reform and Opening, approximately 80 percent of the population lived in the countryside. As the economy boomed, it created an increasing demand for construction workers and factory staff, most of whom came from rural regions. Chinese farms had always been overpopulated, and young people were glad to leave; by 2001, an estimated ninety million had already left home. To drive across China was to find yourself in the middle of the largest migration in human history—nearly one-tenth of the population was on the road, finding new lives away from home.

Most migrants went to coastal regions, but there were also opportunities in provincial cities like Hohhot. Gao told me that she had started on the assembly line but worked her way up, and now she was in management. Her factory produced wool sweaters for export. She had a three-year-old son in Hohhot, and they rarely returned to Smash the Hu. "It's so poor here," she said. "Farming is hard, because of the elevation and the dryness. Look at that corn." She pointed outside, where a field of dusty green stalks bordered the road. "In most places it's already been harvested, but everything happens so late here, because it's so high."

After we chatted for a while, she said, politely, "You're not from our China, are you?"

"No."

"Which country are you from?"

It was tempting to say that I was Hu, but I told the truth.

"My factory exports sweaters to your country!" she said happily.

Like many young people in the factory towns, she had studied some English on her own, although she was too shy to practice it with me. She was curious about life in America—she asked how many people were in my family, and if farmers lived in my hometown. "Do you drive on the same side of the road as in China?" she asked. I said yes, although at the moment it was irrelevant, because our route had deteriorated to a single pair of tire ruts. And if there was any irony in having a friendly conversation with a foreigner just beyond the Great Wall, on the way to Smash the Hu, Gao Linfeng didn't show it. I dropped her off at the town's massive entrance gate, which had been built by the Ming; she thanked me and waved as I headed off toward Slaughter the Hu.

The towns along this road were heavily fortified, and they were also emptying fast. Everywhere I stopped, residents told me that most young people were already gone. Life here had never been easy—there was a long history of instability, and for centuries these remote areas had been shaped by the impersonal and sometimes violent demands of the outside world. In the old days, these were the borderlands: places like Smash the Hu could engage in Chinese-style agriculture, sometimes marginally, but north of here the land was suitable only for grazing. Herdsmen naturally developed a high degree of mobility, whereas the Chinese were rooted to their farms. They made for good targets, and the clash of cultures was often vicious. "They come like hurricanes and disappear like lightning," a Chinese minister wrote during the second century BC, describing the nomads. "Moving with no constant settlement is their way of life, which makes it difficult to control them." One emperor said that fighting the herdsmen "is like attacking a shadow." Another official described them as "covetous for grain, human-faced but animal-hearted."

Most nomads weren't invaders—generally they had no interest in occupying land. They wanted Chinese goods, not Chinese culture; and this perplexed emperor after emperor, dynasty after dynasty. It wasn't like that in the south, where the empire spread largely through cultural impact rather than military force. The American historian Arthur Waldron has written a book called *The Great Wall of China*, in which he describes some of the clashes in the north during the Ming dynasty. He told me that it's critical to understand the Chinese perspective. "To them, it wasn't Chinese civilization," he said. "It *was* civilization. It would naturally appeal to anybody, regardless of their ethnicity, in the same way that dentistry with Novocain would appeal to anybody. And by and large that was the case. As the empire expanded to the south, it wasn't that Chinese people moved in, but that locals changed their customs. They cooked up phony family trees, they built shrines—they did the same thing that anybody does when they're trying to enter a new culture. To this day, this is the strength of the Chinese. It's not force. It's not that they've got spies or secret police. It's that there is something about being a part of this Chinese world that is appealing to the people around it."

"The horse nomads are the first people to whom this has no appeal at all," Waldron continued. "And this baffles the Chinese, because they've always banked on any outsider getting hooked on the culture. But the horse nomads don't do it. They just come in and they rape and they pillage and burn. It posed the same problem for the Chinese as Americans have with al Qaeda, with the people who just hate us. Americans often feel like they just need to know us better. Give them a good old American barbecue, show them what life here is like; they're bound to like it! But it just doesn't work. There was a similar fault line in Chinese culture. There was a fault line between a tremendous confidence in the strength of the culture and an awareness that force may have to be invoked."

Over the centuries, the Chinese response fell on both sides of this line. Sometimes they attacked the nomads, and their methods could be just as brutal as anything done by the "barbarians." Chinese soldiers searched out camps, and they slaughtered women and children. They engaged in ecological warfare—they set fire to miles of pastureland, to prevent nomads from feeding their horses. And the Chinese prepared defenseworks, building miles of walls across the north. This tactic was especially important to the Ming, who were often too weak to take the offensive.

The problem of the nomads was complex, and so was the Chinese solution. A dynasty like the Ming combined strategies: they tried offensive maneuvers; they built walls for defense; and they also relied on trade and diplomacy. Ming emperors sometimes gave goods and official titles to Mongol leaders, and they sponsored trade fairs at key points along the border. Slaughter the Hu was one such site—during the Ming it became a famous market where people from beyond the wall could exchange goods with the Chinese. But trade was always imbalanced, because nomads had few products that the Chinese wanted, apart from horses. And the government administered such sites closely, in part because they didn't want Mongols to trade for metal that could be used to make weapons. In the end, the cultural divide was insurmountable.

The Chinese were good at producing grain and goods, and they controlled the trade fairs; the Mongols didn't have the administrative capabilities but they were brilliant raiders. Sooner or later, the conjunction of these two very different groups always resulted in violence.

Nowadays, foreigners still wanted Chinese goods, but they didn't have to go all the way to Slaughter the Hu to find them. And once again the demands of the outside world had changed this remote place. The Great Wall still ran through the middle of town, which had high garrison walls, and ruined towers rose throughout the valley. It was the most fortified part of the north that I had visited thus far, and it was also the quietest. The main street was little more than a truck stop—a sleepy row of cheap restaurants and auto repair shops that served people going somewhere else. That was all that remained of the local economy; the lure of southern factory jobs had defeated this place in a way the nomads never had. Slaughter the Hu was dying—I didn't see a single young person out on its dusty streets.

DRIVING SOUTH AND WEST, I followed a long line of signal towers that paralleled the Cangtou River. Ever since I had left Hebei, the land had been getting steadily poorer, and now I reached the highlands of north-central China. The people here live atop loess—thin, dry soil that was originally blown south from the Gobi and other deserts of the northwest. Over millennia, wind redeposited layers in this part of China, where the yellow earth can be as deep as six hundred feet. The soil is fragile but fertile, and at one time the region was forested, but centuries of overpopulation stripped it bare. After the trees were gone, people began carving the hills into terraces, until the landscape acquired the look of a desperate human construction: a layered cake of dust. Rainfall is rare—around ten inches annually—but even such small amounts of water can tear through the brittle soil. Creekbeds disappear into gullies; sometimes a tiny stream burrows its way hundreds of feet below the surrounding hillsides. Most peasants live in *yaodong*, simple cave homes that have been dug out of the loess. The caves are cool in summer, warm in winter, and disastrous in an earthquake. Ming dynasty texts report that a major tremor in 1556 killed hundreds of thousands of people.

The Great Wall wasn't a primary reason for the environmental degradation, but undoubtedly it contributed. Everywhere the wall went, it swallowed resources, and the Ming administrators documented the costs of construction. In recent years, an American historian named David Spindler has analyzed the figures for one wall-building project, estimating that for each brick that was fired and set in the wall, soldiers had to burn sixteen and a half pounds of wood. Even in areas where they built the structure out of tamped earth or unquarried stones, they needed wood for cooking fires, and garrison income depended heavily on logging. Spindler's research shows that during the Ming, only 60 to 70 percent of the wall's operating budget came from the state, and the rest was made up for by soldiers, often through logging. Some officials complained that this was counterproductive—by stripping the land bare, they only made it easier for horseback raiders.

Four centuries later, the tamped-earth structures seem like the only permanent features on this fluid landscape. I drove past hillsides that had collapsed into ravines, and crop terraces that seemed likely to crumble away tomorrow—but the signal towers still looked ready for war. Their square forms were visible for miles, riding the tops of the terraced hills. Beside the road, one tower had been decorated with a single character: 土. The word was twenty feet tall, painted in white, and it means "Earth." Not long after that, I saw another: 水, "Water." If the signal towers were sending a message, I wasn't getting it, so I parked the City Special. Scanning the horizon, I realized that four consecutive towers had been inscribed with characters. Together they created a single sentence that spanned a mile, leaping across rivers and valleys and broken hillsides:

PROTECT WATER, SOLIDIFY EARTH

The line of inscribed towers ended at a huge Ming fort atop a mountain. I followed a side road up to the fort, where the view was stunning. It overlooked a half-dozen valleys, and most hillsides had been pockmarked with thousands of holes that had been dug in order to plant trees. Each pit was two feet across and a few inches deep; depending on the angle of the hillside, they had been carved into squares or crescents. The pits were empty, and they continued as far as the eye could see—a galaxy of holes waiting for new saplings. Another message had been whitewashed across the walls of the Ming fort:

USE THE WORLD BANK'S OPPORTUNITY WISELY
HELP THE MOUNTAINOUS AREA ESCAPE FROM POVERTY

Having been constructed to keep the barbarians out, the Great Wall was now welcoming the World Bank. I contacted the local government, to see if somebody could give an introduction to the project, and a cadre agreed to meet me. He was the director of the Youyu County tax bureau, and he told me that over the past two years the local government had received nearly three million dollars in loans from the World Bank. It was one of many projects that the organization sponsored on the loess plateau. Over the years, World Bank loans had funded the construction of mini-dams that conserved water, and their tree-planting campaigns had successfully reduced erosion in many areas. Here in Youyu, they intended to plant pines—all told, the county's project would cover an area of two hundred and seventy square miles. The director escorted me to a village where earlier antierosion campaigns had been successful. The local Communist Party Secretary told me that now almost every family could afford a tractor; we met a villager who had just purchased a motorized cart to use for trade. Nearby, two observation stations had been specially built on hilltops to provide clear views of the project.

Everywhere we were chauffeured in a black Volkswagen Santana. After weeks of driving, it felt strange to sit passively in a car, but the routine of the official tour was familiar from my work as a journalist. In the provinces, the government cars were always black, with heavily tinted windows, and there was always a driver. If an area was wealthier, you rode in an Audi; poorer regions had Santanas and Jettas. At every stop you were served tea and statistics. Here in Youyu County, the government was proud of their World Bank project, and figures piled up in my notebook. They intended to plant 1,400 hectares of trees around the Ming fort; currently Youyu County had successfully controlled erosion in 28 percent of their target region; their final goal was 53 percent. The Chinese government is amazing with numbers, and it always has been. Even in the days of empire, the bureaucracy churned out statistics— during the Ming, wall-building projects were sometimes measured and documented down to the inch. Since the Reform years began, this age-old tradition has helped make China an ideal client for the World Bank. The government can mobilize labor; it can produce statistics; and it can pay loans back.

It's also good at banquets, which was how my tour ended. We ate in a private room at a local restaurant, and the courses appeared, one after another: pork, chicken, fish, Shanxi-style noodles. A half dozen officials accompanied me, and they drank *baijiu*, clear grain alcohol. One by one, they raised their glasses.

"I'm sorry, but I have to drink tea today," I said. "I'm driving this afternoon, so I can't drink *baijiu*."

"How about beer?"

That was actually the subject of a trick question on the driver's exam:

212. *Before driving, a person can*

 a) *drink a little alcohol.*
 b) *not drink alcohol.*
 c) *drink beer but not other types of alcohol.*

"I can't drink beer, either," I said. "I can't drink any alcohol if I'm driving."

"Certainly you can drink a little bit!"

"I'm sorry, but I can't."

"Sure you can—just a glass or two!"

The cadres weren't nearly as persistent as others I met on my journey. When it came to drinking-and-driving peer pressure, weddings were the worst occasions, followed closely by funerals. That was another challenge of being on the road—if I attended any kind of banquet during the day,

I had to find a way to be polite but firm, and accepting one drink only opened the floodgates. In America it's enough to say, "I'm driving"— after that, the subject is closed. In China, though, that statement simply opens new avenues of logic, some of which are hard to refute. On my journey, the first reason to drink was usually the fait accompli. "You have to drink it now," people said, holding up a full glass. "It's already been poured. You can't turn it down." The second reason was that I had come so far and must be tired. The third reason was that after the banquet I could drive very slowly. They also pointed out that Americans use the right side of the road, so Chinese driving is natural; a couple of drinks won't matter. Anyway—reason number five—the glass had already been poured. Sometimes people said the police would be so shocked to see a foreigner behind the wheel that they'd never think of arresting me for driving while intoxicated. Once, a banquet host asked, "When did you first learn how to drive?"

"About twenty years ago."

"See? Most people here have only been driving for a year or two. With so much experience, of course you can drink something!"

His logic made sense: I couldn't imagine how much I'd have to drink before feeling inspired to go backward down the on-ramp of an express-way. In Youyu, though, the cadres were on their best behavior, and I was able to fend off the *baijiu* and beer. After the banquet I thanked them for the tour and drove out of town. Two miles later, I turned around, skirted the city center, and headed back toward the line of signal towers. I was curious to see if villagers said the same things when I arrived in a City Special instead of a chauffeured Santana. Near the Ming fort, I saw a group of people high on a mountainside, working with shovels, and I followed a dirt track to the site.

There were ten men and women digging crescent-shaped holes into the loess. All of them wore surplus army jackets, and they gathered around my Jeep. They lived in a nearby village called Dingjia; like most settlements in this area, it was composed of cave homes. When I said that I was a journalist, they gathered closer.

"They've been doing this kind of thing since I was young," one man said. "In the past it wasn't the World Bank, but there have been other campaigns. You see all of these holes? They're empty. For two or three generations people have been digging these holes, and you still don't see any trees here. Why not? Because our labor is free, but they'd have to pay money for the trees. It doesn't cost anything to have us dig. They do it so that when the leaders come past, they see the holes and they believe that trees are being planted. The local officials embezzle the money instead."

He was only twenty-eight years old, but the others in the group seem to defer to him as a spokesman. In the countryside, I sometimes met ranters—people who couldn't stop complaining angrily about government corruption. But this man was soft-spoken; he chose his words carefully, and there was a certain sadness in his eyes. He wore an especially big military jacket—another member of rural China's great castoff army. I asked how much they were paid for the digging.

"We get five bowls of instant noodles every day," he said.

I couldn't believe that I'd heard correctly, so I asked him to repeat it. "Five bowls," he said. "If you stick around, you'll see them deliver it."

"Why do you do the work?"

"Otherwise we don't get government relief," he said. "We've had a drought, and this year it was too dry for corn. We didn't even plant it. All we have this autumn are potatoes. The government gives us corn for relief, but they won't give it unless we do the digging." He continued: "Most people in our village are opposed to this project, because we've lost three-fourths of our land. We'd like to graze animals in places like this, but the government says they need to protect it. Protect, protect, protect—that's all we hear, a bunch of slogans."

The others murmured in agreement. "You know the saying: The mountains are high and the emperor is far away," the young farmer said. "The country's leaders are sitting in a high place, and they have no idea what's really going on. And the people don't know what the country's leaders really say. Local leaders are the biggest problem—the county officials are the ones who embezzle everything." He pointed at the Ming fort, with its World Bank slogan. "We see the World Bank officials in their cars, when they have inspections, but we can't talk to them. The county leaders don't let us. Actually, I don't even know what

'World Bank' means. All I know is that it has something to do with investment. They come by in their cars, and we've tried to get them to stop, but they never do. They just tell us slogans: Protect the Land, Turn the Land into Forest."

The phrase he used—*Shan gao huangdi yuan*, The mountains are high, the emperor far away—is common in rural China. People invariably believe that problems are local, and that higher-ranked leaders are honest and decent; it's rare to meet somebody who is cynical about the system to its core. And it's hard for them to grasp the inevitability of bad geography. For a village like Dingjia, the mountains are high and the factories far away—there was no way they could compete with the coastal economy, and even the best-run tree-planting campaign would have a limited impact on a place like this. The man told me that when he was a child, Dingjia had a population of two hundred; now there were only eighty people left. I'd heard the same thing at all the stops along my drive—every village had a declining population. "I should go out to look for work, too," the farmer said. "But I have a small child and both my parents are still in the village. I'll probably go eventually, but I'd rather be able to stay a little longer."

I told him that I'd been escorted to other villages where people praised the World Bank project.

"Maybe there are some places where they get the money and they plant the trees and things improve," he said. "But not around here. Look at this hillside—nothing good is going to grow here, because they already removed most of the topsoil. They put it in places near the road, so they can plant things there and it will look good. It's just for show."

While we were talking, a two-stroke engine echoed from down in the valley. The puttering grew louder, and then a tiny blue tractor appeared on the road. It looked like a cartoon vehicle hacking and coughing its way up the steep hillside. When it finally gasped to a stop I saw that the back was loaded with bags of instant noodles. Silently the driver distributed five packages to every worker. In China, people often eat instant noodles dry, as a snack, and the workers tore open their packages. The brand name said "Islamic Beef Noodles."

"Are you Islamic?" I asked.

"No," the young farmer said, laughing. "But these are the cheapest brand—no pork. A nickel each!"

He opened a bag and handed it to me. That was even worse than the poured drink: the last thing I wanted to do on this hillside was eat dry halal instant noodles that represented one-fifth of a laborer's day wage. After some polite arguing, I convinced him to keep it, along with a pack of Oreos from my stash in the City Special. Later, when I contacted a World Bank official, he insisted that the farmers were wrong, and he noted that the bank's projects on the loess plateau had already benefited over one million people. But it was just another statistic: the only thing I knew for certain was that those million beneficiaries did not include the individuals I had spoken with. And I had always been wary of development work that was administered from the capital, with little local contact. The mountains are high, the NGOs far away—that was how you ended up with people digging holes in exchange for Islamic Beef Noodles. It also seemed like a bad idea to paint World Bank slogans onto Ming dynasty ruins. But the Great Wall had already survived countless invasions, and undoubtedly it would still be there, high on the ridgeline, whenever this latest wave of barbarians disappeared.

FOR THE NEXT HUNDRED miles I followed the border between Shanxi and Inner Mongolia. The Ming wall remained the boundary, and the fortifications were still impressive; but these regions were poor and the roads deteriorated fast. At the village of Shirenwan, I saw a peasant following a camel that had been hitched to a plow. Nothing about that scene looked promising: the animal had stopped dead in its tracks; the peasant was shouting; the soil had the hard yellow color of clay brick. An hour later I stopped for two young women who were hitchhiking. They insisted on sitting together in the backseat, and when I asked questions they responded in voices so quiet that they were almost whispers. After ten minutes they told me that I was the first foreigner they had ever seen.

There were more hitchers now, and picking up passengers became part of my typical routine. Motor traffic was light, but it wasn't uncommon to see somebody beside the road, making the Chinese hitchhiking gesture: arm extended, palm down, hand bouncing as if petting an invisible dog. To me, this was new—Beijing pedestrians don't flag down random rides, and nobody had asked me to stop in Hebei. The driver's exam provides little guidance with regard to passengers, apart from a single question:

> *356. If you give somebody a ride and realize that he left something in your car, you should*
>
> a) *keep it for yourself.*
> b) *return it to the person or his place of work as quickly as possible.*
> c) *call him and offer to return it for a reward.*

I rarely saw a farmer looking for a ride. Locals typically didn't travel much, apart from trips to market centers where they knew the regular transport schedule. Most people I picked up were women who looked almost as out of place as I did. They tended to be of a distinct type: small-town sophisticates, girls who had left the village and were on their way to becoming something else. They were well dressed, often in skirts and heels, and their hair was dyed unsubtle shades of red. They wore lots of makeup and cheap perfume. They sat stiffly, backs not touching the seat, as if riding in the City Special were a formal experience. They rarely made eye contact. They were unfailingly polite, and they answered all my questions, but they were reluctant to initiate conversation. Once I picked up three young people, two women and a man, and we chatted for half an hour; during that time they didn't ask me a single question. Often it took ten minutes before a passenger inquired where I was from. This was strange, because usually it's the first order of business in a Chinese conversation—people always wanted to know my nationality. But something about the interaction changed when the foreigner sat in the driver's seat. People tried to be courteous, and they weren't sure what to make of me. Several asked if I were Chinese, which had never happened anywhere else in the country. A couple of passengers guessed that I was Uighur, a Turkic minority from the west; others thought I might be Hui, a Muslim Chinese. One woman, after watching me battle a rutted road for ten miles, finally said, "Are you Mongolian?"

Invariably they were migrants on a home visit. They worked in factories, in restaurants, in hair salons, and they didn't say much about these jobs. At first, I couldn't figure out why there were so many women, because in fact the majority of Chinese migrants are male. But this wasn't a peak travel season—in China, most migrants go home only once a year, during the Spring Festival, and this is especially true for those who find jobs far away. The people I met generally worked closer to home, in provincial cities or good-sized townships. For them, village trips were feasible, and women were more likely to make the effort, because they were attentive to parents and grandparents. When I asked about their packages, they said: "Gifts."

They were curious about the City Special—they couldn't imagine why a solitary traveler needed such a big vehicle. Sometimes a woman told me shyly that she was hoping to learn to drive herself. Near a place called Clifftop Temple, I gave a ride to a pretty young woman who had just visited her parents. She wore a red silk dress and matching lipstick, and she filled the Jeep with a cloud of sickly-sweet perfume. After picking up so many hitchers, I had come to associate that scent with the steppes: Eau de Inner Mongolia.

The young woman worked in a restaurant in a small city called Clearwater River. The farthest she had ever been was the provincial capital of Baotou, but she told me that she dreamed of buying a car of her own. "If you could go anywhere in the world," I asked, "where would you go?" The woman smiled at the thought, and said: "Beijing." When I asked about her hometown, she shook her head. "Most people in the village raise sheep," she said. "It's too dry for good corn and potatoes and millet, but they still try. What else can they do?"

She was right: What were the options? People either fought the land or they left, and in this part of the country it was hard to imagine why any young person would stay. Only the Sinomaps still reflected the optimism of the past: I drove through places with names like Yellow Dragon Spring, Three-Forks River, and the Well of the Yang. But the landscape had turned brittle and now these names were nothing but ironies scattered across the steppes. White Orchid Valley bloomed with dust; Fountain Village was dry as a bone. A place called Defeat the Hu might have won the battle, but it had lost the war. In these regions there was often more wall than road—my maps were crisscrossed with crenellations, but the red capillaries grew fewer with every mile.

Sometimes they disappeared entirely. My atlases became less reliable, until two or three times a day I'd find myself Sinomapped: Sinomapped onto dead ends, Sinomapped onto washouts, Sinomapped onto grass tracks that led nowhere. In Inner Mongolia, lulled by a pastoral-sounding place called the Village of Chives, I got Sinomapped onto a creekbed. In the book it looked promising, a thin red line that paralleled the Ming wall, but after a few miles the dirt surface became nothing more than the jumbled rocks of a dry stream. I tried to follow the riverbed, which braided across the valley floor; I took a few turns and then I was lost. Other freelance drivers had left tracks in all directions, and the familiar form of the Great Wall was no longer in sight. When I stopped to ask directions at a village of cave homes, the people just gaped at me, because their dialect was so far removed from Mandarin. The day was growing late; I was exhausted; I feared that a tire would blow any minute. Finally, bouncing over the rocks, I turned a corner and saw a hitchhiker.

She could have been a mirage: high heels, short skirt, pale tights. The City Special must have looked the same way to her, because she started petting the invisible dog, waving like crazy for me to stop. I rolled down the window.

"Where are you going?" she said.

"I want to go to North Fortress and then Fountain Village," I said. "Is this the right way?" The name of Fountain Village represented another sad irony in this desolate valley, but the woman told me I was still on the right track. "I'm going to North Fortress," she said. "Can I get a ride?"

"Sure." She put one foot in the Jeep, ducked her head, and for the first time got a good look at me. She froze and finally said, "Where did you come from?"

"Beijing."

"Are you alone?"

"Yes."

"Why are you here?" she asked.

"*Wanr*," I said. In Chinese the phrase is so common that it comes out automatically: For fun. But it's probably the wrong thing to say on a creekbed in Inner Mongolia. The woman removed her foot from the car.

"I think I'll wait," she said. And that was where I left her, standing on the broken rocks—the only hitcher I met who turned down the City Special.

IN CHINA, IT'S NOT such a terrible thing to be lost, because nobody else knows exactly where they're going, either. In the summer of 1996, when I first arrived in the country as a Peace Corps volunteer, I was immediately impressed by my own ignorance. Language, customs, history—all of it had to be learned, and the task seemed insurmountable. From my perspective, everybody else had a head start of three thousand years, and I felt desperate to catch up.

Over time my learning curve never really flattened out. China is the kind of country where you constantly discover something new, and revelations occur on a daily basis. One of the most important discoveries is the fact that the Chinese share this sensation. The place changes too fast; nobody can afford to be overconfident in his knowledge, and there's always some new situation to figure out. How does a peasant leave the farm and find a factory job? Who teaches people how to start businesses? Where do they learn how to make cars, and how do they figure out how to drive them? Who shows the small-town sophisticates how to dress and put on makeup? It was appropriate that they hitched rides on a City Special driven by an American with a book of Sinomaps. We were all out of place; nobody has today's China figured out.

Most learning is informal, although there are plenty of private courses. Young Chinese often enroll in classes for English, typing, computers, accounting; in factory towns they sometimes pay for specialized courses that teach them how to behave like educated urbanites. And there are driving classes—that's one type of training that's regulated by the government. National law requires every Chinese driver to enroll in a certified course, at his own expense, for a total of fifty-eight hours of practice. In China, you can't just go to a parking lot with your father and learn how to drive. Anyway, there aren't many parking lots yet, and most fathers don't have licenses.

One month I observed a driving course in Lishui, a small city in southeastern China. It's located in the factory belt, where the boom economy produces a lot of new motorists. The institution was called the Public Safety Driving School, and I sat in on a course taught by Coach Tang. In China, all driving instructors are addressed as Jiaolian, "Coach." It's the same word you use for a basketball coach or a drill instructor, and it carries connotations of a training regimen. That's the essence of Chinese driving—a physical endeavor.

The course began with the most basic kinds of touch. On the first day, Coach Tang raised the hood of a red Volkswagen Santana, and six students huddled close. He pointed out the engine, the radiator, the fan belt. They walked around to the back, where he opened the trunk. He showed them how to unscrew the gas cap. The next step involved the driver's door. "Pull it like this," he said, and then each student practiced opening and closing the door. Next, Coach Tang identified the panel instruments, as well as the clutch, the brake, and the gas pedal. After an hour the students finally entered the vehicle. Each took turns sitting in the driver's seat, where they practiced shifting from first to fifth gear. The motor wasn't on, but they worked the clutch and moved the gear-shift. Watching this made me wince, and finally I had to say something. "Isn't that bad for the car?"

"No," Coach Tang said. "It's fine."

"I think it might be bad if the motor's off," I said.

"It's completely fine," Coach Tang said. "We do it all the time." In China, instructors are traditionally respected without question, and Coach Tang had been kind enough to allow me to observe his class, so I decided to hold my tongue. But it wasn't always easy. For the next step, they learned to use the clutch by setting the parking brake, starting the engine, shifting into first gear, and then releasing the clutch while flooring the accelerator. The motor whined against the force of the brake; the hood kowtowed with torque. One by one, students entered the driver's seat, gunning the engine and going nowhere. By the end of the day you could have fried an egg on the Santana's hood, and my palms broke into a sweat every time another driver hit the gas. I could practically hear my father's voice—he's a good amateur mechanic, and few things anger him more than mindless abuse of an automobile.

Nobody was allowed to move a car until the second day of class. From the beginning, the students had circled the Santana warily, like the blind men and the elephant: they peered in the hood, they worked the doors, they fiddled with the gas cap. There were four men and two women, all of them under the age of forty. Each had paid over three hundred dollars for the course, which was a lot of money in a city where the monthly minimum wage was roughly seventy-five dollars. Only one person came from a household that currently owned an automobile. The others told me that someday they might buy one, and the college students—there were four of them—believed that a driver's license looked good on a résumé. "It's something you should be able to do, like swimming," one young man named Wang Yanheng said. He was a college senior majoring in information technology. "In the future, so many people in China are going to have cars," Wang said. "It's going to be important to know how to drive." The only student from a home with automobiles was a nineteen-year-old sociology major named Liang Yanfang. Her father owned a plastics factory, and he had three cars. When I asked what kind of plastics the family factory produced, the woman ran her finger along the rubber lining of the Santana's window. "This is one of the things we make," she said.

The first ten days of class focused on what they called the "parking range," and during that time they performed exactly three movements. They practiced a ninety-degree turn into a parking space, moving forward, and then they did the same thing in reverse. The third skill was parallel parking. Every day, for a total of six hours, they performed these three movements repeatedly. Like any good Chinese instructor, Coach Tang was strict. "What are you doing?" he said, when one student brushed a pole during the reverse parking. "You must have forgotten your brain today!" "Don't hold the gearshift loosely like that!" he yelled at another man. "If you do, your father will curse you!" Sometimes he slapped a student's hand. Whenever somebody turned his head, he shouted, "Stop looking behind you!" There was a strict rule against head turns. When reversing, you were supposed to rely on the mirrors only; the blind spot didn't exist, at least not in Coach Tang's eyes. Nobody ever wore a seat belt. I never saw a turn signal flash on the parking range at the Public Safety Driving School.

The next step was the "driving range," where students practiced an obstacle course of tight turns and learned how to stop within twenty-five centimeters of a painted line. The most challenging skill was known as the "single-plank bridge." This consisted of a long concrete riser, slightly wider than a tire; students had to aim the car perfectly so that two wheels perched atop the riser. First they did the left tires, then the right; if a wheel slipped, they failed the exam. Students told me that they spent the majority of their road range time practicing the single-plank bridge. I asked the coach why it was so important.

"Because it's very difficult," he said.

That's the underlying philosophy of Chinese driving courses: if something is technically difficult, then it must be useful. But the details of this challenge shift from place to place, coach to coach. There isn't much standardization, apart from the required fifty-eight hours; sometimes a school emphasizes the single-plank bridge and sometimes they've developed some other obstacle. In this sense, coaches are like the martial-arts masters of old, developing individual regimens. Times have changed—instead of journeying to a mountaintop monastery, where a student might punch a tree a thousand times a day, he now joins the Public Safety Driving School and spends two weeks trying to park a Santana onto a single-plank bridge.

The Lishui courses concluded with a week and a half on the road, and I accompanied one group on their final day before the exam. With the coach in the passenger seat, students took turns driving a Santana along a two-lane rural road, where they performed set movements. They shifted from first to fifth; they downshifted back to first; they stopped within twenty-five centimeters of a marker. They made a U-turn and braked at an imitation traffic light. The course was three kilometers long and it had not changed at all during the ten days of practice; there were no intersections and very little traffic. Students had been instructed to honk when pulling out, as well as before performing turns. They honked whenever they encountered anything in the road—a car, a tractor, a donkey cart. They honked at every pedestrian. Sometimes they passed another car from the driving school, and then both vehicles honked happily, as if recognizing an old friend. At noon, the class took a break for lunch at a local restaurant, where everybody drank beer, including the coach. They told me that a day earlier they had gotten so drunk that they canceled afternoon class.

Later that day, the students returned to the road range for more practice, and one of them begged me to let him drive my rental car along the way. In a moment of extremely poor judgment, I decided to see what he had learned in a month of training. The moment the driver hit the open road, he became obsessed with passing other vehicles, but he had no idea how this was done; twice I had to yell to keep him from swinging wide on blind turns. Another time I grabbed the wheel to prevent him from veering into another car that was pulling up on our left. He never checked the rearview or side mirrors; he had no idea that there's a blind spot. He honked at everything that moved. The complete absence of turn signals was the least of our problems. He came within inches of hitting a parked tractor, and he almost nailed a cement wall. When we finally made it to the driving range, I felt like falling on my knees to kiss the single-plank bridge.

Foreigners in Beijing often said to me, I can't believe you're driving in this country. To which I responded: I can't believe you get into cabs and buses driven by graduates of Chinese driving courses. Out on the road, everybody was lost—*une génération perdue*—but it felt a little better to be the one behind the wheel.

IN NORTHWESTERN SHANXI PROVINCE, sections of Great Wall run alongside the Yellow River, and for nearly one hundred miles I followed the high loess banks. The driving here was easy, because the government infrastructure campaign had recently improved local roads. Propaganda signs celebrated the construction: "A Smooth Road Brings Prosperity and Drives Away Poverty"; "To Protect the Road Brings Prosperity, To Destroy the Road Brings Shame." In rural China there was still so little traffic that private advertisers had yet to sponsor billboards, which meant that a driver wasn't bombarded with images of things to eat or drink or buy. Instead there were government slogans, whose language had distinctive qualities: simple but forceful, direct but strangely obscure. "People Embrace Soldiers"—a sign like that on an empty road gave my imagination somewhere to roam. In rural Shanxi I passed a billboard that simply said: "Self-Reliance, Struggle, Persistence, Unreserved Devotion." There were no further details—and in the end, what more could you ask for? In Inner Mongolia, a local power plant slogan was so charged with wordplay that I had to pull over to figure it out: "Everybody Use Electricity; Use Electricity Well; Electricity Is Good to Use." (My delayed response: "Yes!") Often I passed billboards dedicated to the planned-birth policy, whose catchphrases ranged from tautology ("Daughters Also Count as Descendants") to unsolicited advice ("Marry Late and Have Children Late") to outright lies ("Having a Son or a Daughter Is Exactly the Same"). As I drove west, the messages became bigger, until barren hillsides were covered with slogans, as if words had swelled to fill the empty steppes. "Everybody Work to Make the Green Mountain Greener"—this in forty-foot-tall characters across an Inner Mongolian mountain that was neither green nor the site of a single working person. Across another particularly desolate stretch of wasteland, a poem had been spelled out in painted rocks:

> *Plant grass and trees here in the mountains,*
> *Build flourishing agriculture,*
> *Build homes, raise sheep,*
> *Create a beautiful land of mountains and rivers.*

Above the Yellow River, signs warned farmers not to thresh crops in the road. For a while I wondered if this local campaign had been effective: the City Special hadn't smashed a pile of grain since entering western Shanxi. But then I visited Sigou, a village high atop the eastern bank, where locals told me that they hadn't harvested any grain crops at all this year because of drought. They were surviving on potatoes and government grain. While I was talking to a farmer in his cave home, the village chief stopped by with a sheaf of relief applications. The forms were entitled "The Two Lacks and the One Without." The village chief explained the phrase: the people in Sigou lacked money and food, and they were without the ability to support themselves. Of all the slogans I had seen, that was the most brutally honest, and it marked a grim end to the north-central farmland—the last gasp of the loess plateau.

Across the river lay the Ordos Desert and the beginning of western China. In ancient times, the Ordos represented one of the most troubling regions for the empire, and there is no other part of the steppes that played such a major role in the inspiration of the Great Wall. The Ordos is expansive—roughly the size of New England—and it's defined by the great northern loop of the Yellow River. Within this loop, the loess plateau gives way to sand and scrubland, and in ancient times there was never enough water to support traditional Chinese agriculture. But resources were adequate for nomads, for whom the Ordos represented a perfect base: remote enough to avoid control by Chinese settlements, but within range for raiding trips. Some dynasties, like the Tang, were able to staff garrisons across the desert, but the Ming became too weak to fight in the region.

Instead they constructed the Great Wall across the southern borderlands of the Ordos, in what is now Shaanxi Province. Driving west from the Yellow River, I searched for traces of fortifications that had been marked on my map. The pages had suddenly emptied: there were few villages and almost no roads. On the atlas, the white space was occasionally interrupted by short-lived streams—anonymous streaks of blue that came out of nowhere, flowed for a dozen miles, and then vanished back into the sand. Outside my windows the landscape was featureless. I drove through a town called Divine Tree, and then I continued to Yulin, which means "Elm Forest"—another hopeful name in this barren place.

North of town the Great Wall was in the process of being buried. A huge Ming fort called Zhenbeitai stood stark against the horizon, and the wall ran southwest into the desert. It was made of tamped earth, a slightly darker shade than the sand that piled against its base. Sometimes the structure disappeared entirely beneath a dune. In the east, where I had started my journey, the wall had often accentuated the permanence of the Hebei landscape. Those had been rocky, solid mountains, and the structures of brick and stone seemed secure atop high ridgelines. Westward, Chinese geography became less stable with every mile, until from a driver's perspective it felt as if the land itself was collapsing. I had moved from the stony peaks to the dry steppes, and then to the crumbling hills of the loess plateau, and now at last I had arrived in shifting desert sands. The Great Wall was still here, but it no longer spoke of permanence. The Ordos was creeping south, and even the most impressive Ming fortifications were nothing more than lines in the sand.

Beyond the wall, people were trying to reform the barren landscape. This battle is common in the north—more than one-fourth of China's land suffers from desertification, and the total area of stricken regions expands by an estimated 1,300 square miles every year. According to the United Nations, four hundred million Chinese live in places threatened by desertification. Various government projects attempt to make northern life more sustainable, and they range from local tree planting to major irrigation programs. The most ambitious is the Yangtze diversion. Realizing that parts of the south have plenty of water, the government has initiated a ten-billion-dollar project designed to rechannel some of these resources to the north. But it's unclear how effective this solution will be, and in the end it may be pointless to bring water north while most young people are heading south.

The Ordos is one part of northern China that never should have been settled by farmers in the first place. In ancient times only nomads inhabited this region, but during the nineteenth century Chinese pioneers began to move north, driven by poverty and war. After the revolution of 1949, the Communists encouraged mass settlement beyond the Great Wall, hoping that Chinese-style agriculture would flourish in the desert north of Yulin. They sponsored periodic campaigns to plant trees, grass, and even rice; the few local streams and lakes were diverted for irrigation. The natives, who were mostly Mongol herdsmen, invariably resisted these projects, telling officials that they wouldn't work, but politics had a way of overwhelming experience. During the 1960s and 1970s, in the heat of the Cultural Revolution, one local township called Wushenqi became celebrated nationwide as a model commune. Other desert regions were instructed to follow its lead, digging irrigation channels and planting grain. But by the 1980s it was clear that Wushenqi's efforts had been disastrous—the combination of increased population and non-native crops had destroyed precious water resources.

In recent years the local government had adopted a new strategy. Instead of planting rice or grain, they seeded willow trees, and then they used the leaves to feed sheep. They called it "the pasture in the sky"— they plucked the sheep fodder straight from the willow branches, and the trees were also intended to halt the desert's expansion. In some ways this worked: the township's agricultural territory was holding steady at 10 percent of the total land, and locals had been able to expand their herds. I visited the home of one Mongolian family that cared for two hundred head of sheep. "Everything is better now," the patriarch told me. "It's easier to get food, easier to get clothes." He spoke halting Mandarin, and he told me that he had grown up in a traditional Mongol *ger*, or tent. Now he lived in a brick home, where the walls were decorated with one poster of a Ferrari Mondial and another of a Harley Davidson motorcycle. There was also a map of China, two portraits of Genghis Khan, and a shrine dedicated to Mao Zedong. When I asked about the shrine, the man said, "Mao was a liberator, a great leader, and a good man." He added that all true Mongols keep portraits of Genghis Khan. On another wall hung a framed government prize that the man had received for paying his taxes on March 20, 1997. In rural homes I often saw prizes like this—sometimes people got awards for keeping their houses clean.

In Wushenqi, though, it seemed that any benefits of willow planting would be short-lived. A Chinese-born geographer named Jiang Hong was conducting research in the region, and she told me that the groundwater was dropping. The desert simply couldn't support any additional agriculture, not even the willow trees. But Jiang Hong had also noticed that locals remained supportive of the planting project, despite the fact that they knew about the dwindling groundwater. This was different from the past, when there had always been resistance to heavy-handed government campaigns. Back then, projects tended to be abstract and collective: Mao would declare that China's productivity needed to surpass that of Great Britain or the United States, and a herdsman in a place like Wushenqi was reluctant to destroy his environment for such goals. But ever since Deng Xiaoping, the economy had been driven primarily by individual motivation, and rewards were suddenly tangible. And the new mobility meant that many people had caught a glimpse of a better life.

"They see more of the outside world now," Jiang Hong said. "They can visit the cities, and they see things on television. They want to have more of the material benefits that they see." In a sense, people had become more worldly, but this contact with the outside was disorienting. The frame of reference no longer consisted of the limited resources available in Wushenqi, but rather the infinite products available in the city. By learning more about other places, residents had lost touch with their immediate environment.

And decades of political instability had warped people's mindsets. "When things change so quickly, people don't have time to gain information about their environment," Jiang Hong said. "If you look back at Chinese history from 1949, policies have changed so often. When the reforms took hold in the 1980s, people saw that as an opportunity—and you have to take the opportunity now because it won't last. People tend to have a short-term view of development."

For this generation, the economic landscape had become as unstable as the Ordos sands. Everything shifted: the rules, the business practices, the challenges of daily life. There was always some new situation to figure out, and it was hard for people to get their bearings. Often the ones who reacted quickly without thinking were the most successful. Sustainability was a luxury that few could afford to worry about, especially in places where young people were likely to leave anyway. Long-term planning made no sense: the goal was gain some profit today before you found yourself overwhelmed by the next wave of change.

⊙   ⊙   ⊙

AFTER LEAVING WUSHENQI, I returned across the Great Wall and headed south back to Yulin. I wasn't sure how much longer I wanted to stay on the road; the nights were growing cold and I could feel a fatigue settling in. From the beginning I had planned to divide my journey into two parts, so I could see the countryside in both autumn and spring. In Yulin I intended to rest—I hoped to spend a couple of nights in a bed, eat good meals, and decide how much farther to chase the wall. But in the end the local government made the decision for me.

It was the first city I had seen in weeks. The population was about one hundred thousand, small by Chinese standards, and the town had a pleasant, sleepy air. An old city wall still surrounded the downtown, where streets were narrow; the auto boom hadn't yet touched this place. I checked into the best hotel, took a shower, and lay down for a nap. Almost immediately the telephone rang. It was the hotel receptionist, and she told me that there was somebody in the lobby who wanted to see me.

"He's from the government," she said.

Of all the ways to get woken up, that was one of the worst. I dressed and went downstairs. The man was in his thirties, dressed in a dark suit, and his face wore a tight thin smile that said: Trouble.

"I understand that you're a journalist," he said.

He asked to see my passport, residence permit, and journalist accreditation, so I handed them over. He studied the documents in silence, jotting notes onto a pad of paper. At last he looked up. "You know, in China we have a law that requires a journalist to apply to a place before he does any reporting," he said. "You've broken this law."

"I'm just here to see the Great Wall," I said. "I don't need to talk to anybody in the government. I'm not planning to interview anybody here in Yulin."

"I'm afraid it doesn't matter. You still need to apply."

I apologized and told him that in the future I'd be sure to apply in advance. "I'll leave tomorrow if you want," I said.

The man's smile tightened a little more. "I'm afraid you'll have to leave now," he said.

"Can I have lunch?"

"I'm sorry," he said. "But you have to go immediately."

He waited in the lobby while I packed, and then he followed me all the way to the City Special. He was accompanied by a cop, to make sure I left town. From Yulin I drove south to Yan'an, six hours away; it was a cradle of the Chinese Communist Revolution, where Mao and other leaders had built their base in the late 1930s. Nowadays, Yan'an had become a tourist destination, and I hoped to check into a hotel without attracting attention. But this time the police appeared before I had even finished unpacking. They already knew where I had come from, and what kind of car I was driving; a warning must have been sent out across the province. The Yan'an cops told me to keep moving, and that was when I decided to abandon the Great Wall until spring.

I took the highway back to Beijing. A new toll expressway had just been built across Shanxi Province, and after weeks of rural roads it felt like flying. The surface was perfect; there was almost no traffic; I flashed past miles of harvested corn. At Capital Motors I returned the City Special with exactly one-eighth of a tank of gas, no new dents, and a backseat full of empty Coke bottles. In the office Mr. Wang was smoking a cigarette beneath the performance ratings sign:

CUSTOMER SATISFACTION RATING: 90%
EFFICIENCY RATING: 97%
APPROPRIATE SERVICE DICTION RATING: 98%
SERVICE ATTITUDE RATING: 99%

He studied my rental papers, checking off items and entering them into a computer. When he came to the mileage, he put the cigarette down.

"Look how far this is!" he said. "Where did you go?"

I could have claimed that all my driving had been within the Beijing city limits, but it would have been a shameless lie: the City Special had accumulated over 2,200 miles. At first I tried to be vague—I told Mr. Wang that I had driven west.

"Where exactly?" he said.

"Hebei, Shanxi," I said.

"That's all?"

"Well, Shaanxi, too," I said. "And Inner Mongolia. But not too far in Inner Mongolia. Mostly along the Shanxi border."

"*Waah!*" Mr. Wang exclaimed. "Did you go by yourself?"

"Yes."

"Do you know that you're not supposed to leave Beijing?"

"I thought it would be OK as long as I was careful."

"Did you stay on paved roads?"

"Most of the time."

"You're not supposed to drive off the pavement," Mr. Wang said.

"I know," I said. "But some parts of Inner Mongolia don't have paved roads. I drove really slowly."

Mr. Wang seemed nearly as thrilled as he did whenever I returned a damaged car. "That's great!" he said, beaming. "All the way to Inner Mongolia!" He called over the other workers and showed them the mileage; everybody laughed and lit cigarettes in celebration. I picked up my deposit and headed to the door. They were still talking about it when I left: "All the way to Inner Mongolia!"

AFTER THAT FIRST LONG TRIP I NEVER WORRIED ABOUT where I took a car from Capital Motors. I usually rented Jettas or Santanas, and I made weekend jaunts all around the north—to the Eastern Qing tombs, to the old imperial summer resort at Chengde. A couple of times I drove the new expressway to the coast. It took less than two hours to reach the beach resort of Beidaihe, and there wasn't much traffic. In China, city people were buying automobiles, but they still weren't taking many long journeys, because tolls were high and drivers were inexperienced. The expressways were empty, and they were beautiful: four lanes, wide shoulders, perfect landscaping.

You could drive for hours without seeing a cop. It was strange, because police are prominent in other parts of Chinese life, and as a journalist I had been detained a number of times. And like any American from the Midwest, I hit an open road and instinctively kept an eye out for police. But China had yet to develop a functioning highway patrol, and the few cops I saw were simply on their way to some other destination. They always flashed their rack lights, probably because they'd seen it in American movies, but they weren't patrolling and they weren't in a hurry. In fact they tended to be among the slowest vehicles on the expressway. At first it felt strange to fly past a policeman flashing his lights, but after a while I learned to ignore them, like everybody else. The only drivers who had to worry were freight truckers. Cops sometimes stationed themselves at tollbooths, where they fined and extorted truck drivers who had overloaded their vehicles. But nobody paid any mind to passenger cars—it was the golden age of highway driving in China.

The only problem consisted of other motorists, but even amid the chaos of Chinese traffic there was a degree of predictability. Certain car models tended to attract certain character types, and on the road I learned to profile accordingly. The highest risks usually clustered at both ends of the spectrum. If somebody had a Mercedes or a top-end Buick, he was probably a businessman in the first flush of success; these people drove recklessly. And I was wary of the cheapest cars, the battered Xialis and Chang'ans whose drivers had nothing to lose. In the countryside, black Santanas with heavily tinted windows were trouble. They were cadre cars, usually from places where the local government was either too poor or too unskilled at embezzlement to afford an Audi. Black Santanas cruised around like small-town bullies: blaring their horns, passing on the right, cutting people off. In a big city like Beijing, corrupt cadres bought black Audi A6s and A8s, and those were also vehicles to avoid, especially if you were on a bike. Subcompacts like the Alto City Baby were scary for a different reason. They usually represented a first car for lower-middle-class people, who combined inexperience with extreme tentativeness. As for the Jeep Cherokee, there wasn't a stereotype associated with the City Special. This was the problem for American Motors, a brand that never found its niche in the new economy. They were simply the latest example in a long history of missed opportunities for American automakers, who had always found China a complicated place to do business.

In a sense, foreign trade had been tough ever since the days of the Great Wall. Back then, the Chinese had closest contact with northern nomads, and the experience convinced the empire that outsiders had little to offer. This worldview survived until the nineteenth century, when it was shattered by the opium trade. In southern China, British merchants found a booming market for the drug, and at last the Qing dynasty tried to end the trade by force; the result was the Opium War of 1839–1842. Suddenly the technological superiority of the West became apparent: British warships easily defeated the Qing, who were forced to give up Hong Kong and access to other treaty ports. Over the following decades, the British and other foreigners expanded their presence in

China, usually by force. For a civilization that once believed it needed nothing from outsiders, it was a traumatic introduction to the world of modern trade.

At the beginning of the twentieth century, many Chinese remained deeply suspicious of anything foreign. Initially, the automobile was criticized as yet another tool of the imperialists, but attitudes began to change as people realized the benefits of better transport. The American Red Cross road-building campaigns of the 1920s were enormously successful, and intellectuals were more inclined to welcome brands from America than Britain, whose image remained tainted by the history of opium trade. In 1924, Sun Yat-sen, the founder of the Republic of China, wrote a letter to Henry Ford, praising his company and inviting him to Asia. "I think you can do similar work in China on a much vaster and more significant scale," Sun wrote. Ford Motors responded with a form letter— apparently Sun's note never made it to Henry. Despite this brush-off, and despite the fact that the Chinese drove on the left side of the road, the Ford Company quickly dominated the market. By the early 1930s there were two dozen Ford dealers in China, and the company considered opening an assembly line in Shanghai.

The Japanese invasion put an end to these plans, but war presented other opportunities. In the early 1940s, when the U.S. Army sent jeeps and trucks to southwestern China in support of the Republic, they suffered an inordinate number of traffic accidents. Vehicles had been designed for the right side of the road, and American drivers had trouble making the adjustment. U.S. Army General Albert C. Wedemeyer proposed a simple solution: the whole nation of China should switch over to the American way of driving. Chiang Kai-shek, who had always depended heavily on U.S. support, agreed. The change finally took place on January 31, 1945, after the Japanese had already surrendered.

At that time, it seemed like American automakers were well positioned for China, but the Communist Revolution changed everything. Mao was aligned with the Soviets, and the United States imposed a trade embargo after the start of the Korean War. In any case, the Communist planned economy didn't create private consumers. There was virtually no market for sedans; Chinese factories turned out trucks and buses.

When Deng came to power, China's auto industry faced the same basic challenge that characterized so much of the Reform period: How do people learn to do something completely new? From the government's perspective, it was critical to learn from foreign automakers, but nobody wanted to relinquish profits and control of the industry to outsiders. As a result, Deng invited foreign manufacturers to set up shop under strict regulations. In order to produce cars in China, a foreign company had to find a state-owned partner, and outside ownership was limited to 50 percent.

The American Motors Company jumped at the opportunity. In January of 1979, less than a week after President Jimmy Carter formally recognized the government of the People's Republic, AMC was already sending a delegation to work out a deal. Over the next decade they learned to regret their pioneering status. While other companies such as Toyota stayed out of China, biding their time, AMC forged ahead and got nowhere. The partnership structure was awkward: two sets of management, each with its own culture, goals, and values. The AMC experience became so notorious that it eventually inspired a book called *Beijing Jeep* by the journalist Jim Mann. It's a story of one misunderstanding after another; the chapter titles include "Getting Nowhere," "A Very Long Haul," and "An Outpouring of Grievances." Even the index conveys a sort of taut frustration—it begins with "Absenteeism" and continues through "Xenophobia," an alphabetized testimony to cultural differences of the 1980s:

> *Beatrice Companies, Inc., 236–238*
> *Bechtel Corporation, 65, 105, 299*
> *Beds in Chinese offices, 127*
> *Beijing Automotive Industrial Corporation (BAIC),*
> *   91, 254, 263*

The Beijing Jeep became a symbol for the problems that beset foreign partnerships in the early Reform years. During that period the Chinese were still figuring out how to do business, and it wasn't until the 1990s that the economy really took off. American Motors never recovered; their experience was a classic case of being in the right place at the wrong time. And the Jeep Cherokee represented one of their worst miscalculations. They started producing Chinese Cherokees in 1985, which was far too early for a sport-utility vehicle; most customers were still businesses or government bureaus that preferred sedans. When private consumers finally began to appear, AMC tried to target new city buyers by abandoning the Cherokee's four-wheel-drive feature. They painted a sporty line along the doors, added some purple detailing, and tacked on an urban name: the City Special. This resulted in a cheaper price but a much less useful and distinctive vehicle. Not long after that, China developed a class of moneyed people with outdoor interests, but in their eyes the Cherokee was already outdated and useless. Yuppie adventurers were far more likely to splurge on a Toyota Land Cruiser or a Mitsubishi Pajero. The only reason I drove a City Special was because I had no other option—that was all I could find on the Capital Motors lot.

Unlike AMC, other foreign companies survived the hard years in China, and by the end of the 1990s some of them began to enjoy major profits. The strict industry rules limited competition, and prices could be kept artificially high. Chinese consumers lagged several generations behind other countries, which allowed automakers to bring in outdated technology from overseas. In the 1990s, Volkswagen took a failed plant from Westmoreland, Pennsylvania, where they had formerly manufactured the VW Fox, and moved the main equipment to northeastern China. The car they produced, the Jetta, eventually surpassed the Santana to become the nation's best-selling passenger vehicle. Margins were huge: in 2001 and 2002, on a per-car basis, Volkswagen and General Motors made more profits in China than anywhere else in the world. When a Buick Regal sold in China, it generated as much as double the profit made on the same car in America. Michael Dunne, an analyst who specializes in the Chinese auto market, told me that during this period he once asked a General Motors executive about profits in China. "We are making more money than God," said the GM executive.

But the whole system was ripe for change. If a Chinese company could find a way to use foreign technology without getting saddled with a partnership, they could create a more efficient management structure.

And there was enormous opportunity in the low-end market, because the expensive joint-venture products had never targeted the fledgling middle class. At the end of the 1990s, the government of Wuhu, a city in eastern China's Anhui Province, decided to set up a car company of their own. They hired an engineer named Yin Tongyao, who had previously been a star at Volkswagen. Yin had distinguished himself during the transfer of the VW Fox, when he helped move manufacturing equipment from Westmoreland, Pennsylvania, to northeastern China.

At his new job in Wuhu, Yin immediately put this international experience to good use. He first went to England, where he bought equipment from an outdated Ford engine factory. Then he traveled to Spain, where he acquired manufacturing blueprints from a struggling Volkswagen subsidiary that formerly made a car called the Toledo. The Toledo shared the same platform—the basic frame and components—as the Jetta. In secret, Yin moved the British Ford engine factory to Wuhu, incorporated the Spanish blueprints, and set up an assembly line. Strict national regulations forbade new auto manufacturers from entering the market, so the officials in Wuhu simply called it an "automotive components" company. The factory produced its first engine in May of 1999. Seven months later it turned out a car. It had a Ford-designed engine, a body that came from Volkswagen via Spanish blueprints, and many authentic Jetta accessories. The folks in Wuhu had simply tracked down Chinese parts suppliers who were supposedly exclusive to Volkswagen, and then they worked out deals on the side. Volkswagen was furious, and so were people in the central government.

But everybody knew the basic principle of the Reform years: It's easier to ask forgiveness than permission. For more than a year, Wuhu's leaders negotiated with the central government, and in 2001 they finally received permission to sell their cars nationwide. (Reportedly, they paid a financial settlement to Volkswagen, which decided not to sue.) They named their company Qirui, two Chinese characters that have connotations of good fortune. It sounds a little like "cheery," but the English name was Chery. Chery officials said the name was missing one *e* because the company would always be one step away from the complacency that comes with happiness. Almost immediately they began to transform the market, producing cheap cars that contributed to a price drop across the industry. It wasn't long before Chery declared their ultimate goal: to become the first Chinese car company to export to the United States.

EVER SINCE I HAD started driving in China, I was curious to know where the cars came from, and one year I went to Wuhu and accompanied some engineers on a Chery test-drive. They were working on two prototypes, the T-11 and the B-14, neither of which had been given a proper model name yet. The vehicles were top-secret—they had taped plastic wrapping along the sides, to foil any industry photographers who might be looking for a surreptitious shot. The B-14 was a crossover, and the T-11 was a small sport-utility vehicle that bore a remarkably close resemblance to the Toyota RAV4. That had become Chery's specialty: they were notorious for making cars that were suspiciously similar to market leaders. The T-11 wasn't destined for American consumers— Chery's quality still wasn't up to U.S. standards—but the vehicle was supposed to represent a step in that direction. They were aiming for the new Chinese middle class, the people with outdoor interests who hadn't been around when AMC first developed the City Special.

An American engineer named John Dinkel had been brought in as a consultant, and his specialty was test-driving. "You find out how good a car is when you do bad things," he explained as he guided a T–11 out of the main Chery factory. I sat in the front seat, serving as translator; three young Chinese engineers were in the back. None of them wore a seat belt.

Outside the plant, a big transporter truck was loading stacks of new Chery sedans. Dinkel drove the T-11 past the truck, and after he reached an open road he ran through a series of tests: accelerating, braking, turning. "It's picking up a wheel," he said in the middle of a tight turn. "The wheel is spinning. You need a limited slip differential for that." He accelerated to ninety miles per hour, cruising through the industrial district where Chery was located, and glimpses of the factory world flashed past: a tractor cart full of bricks, the gate of a new air-conditioner plant, a row of temporary shacks for construction workers. A boy stood beside the road, pissing in the grass; his head swung to look when we flew by. Dinkel braked suddenly and a bus honked. I turned to the three engineers in the back.

"What if the police see us?" I said. "He doesn't have a Chinese license."

"There aren't any police around here," one engineer said. "Even if there were, they'd understand what we're doing."

The three engineers were all in their early twenties, dressed in blue company jumpsuits, and they watched intently, hoping to pick up tips from the American test driver. Dinkel embarked on another series of maneuvers, shifting fast and then braking; he switched lanes rapidly. The three engineers clutched at the ceiling. Outside, we zipped past a truck loaded with construction materials, and finally one of the Chery employees asked me to relay a request: "Do you think we could go to a place without any other cars?"

He suggested that we head north, where Wuhu was in the process of building a new factory zone. The construction crews were still at work, and Dinkel dodged materials along the way; he swerved around an earthmover and he steered between piles of bricks. A big construction truck made a left turn across our lane without signaling. "That in America would be called an idiot," Dinkel muttered, and I left that remark untranslated. He drove by a complex of half-built apartment blocks, their frames skeletal in the misty morning. He said, "Tell them the gearbox is very notchy from second to third, and from fourth to fifth."

Dinkel was sixty years old, and he lived in Orange County. When I asked where he was originally from, he said, "What's it to you?" which meant Long Island. He was alert, good-humored, and small-framed—he weighed only 140 pounds. He told me that as a graduate student at the University of Michigan at Dearborn, back in the late 1960s, he was the only guy in the emissions laboratory who could fit into the driver's seat of a Mazda Cosmo. He had never had any particular interest in becoming an engineer. When I asked him why he'd originally taken that path, he said, "I didn't have a very bright guidance counselor." Dinkel had graduated from high school in 1962, during the heat of the space race and the boom years of American industry, when people believed that anybody with good math scores should automatically become an engineer. He worked briefly at Chrysler and then switched to journalism. He was at *Road & Track* for twenty years, including two as editor in chief. "I've tested cars for thirty years," he said. "I've driven practically every car that's ever been on the road." He told me that Wuhu's empty streets reminded him of the old days in California, when they could still test cars in the beanfields of Orange County.

Wuhu is located on the banks of the Yangtze River, about five hours from Shanghai, and it's one of the new frontiers of the southern economic boom. When we drove through the city's industrial zone, it was still in the early stages: roads had curbs, sidewalks, and even street signs, but few people were outside. Most factories were still half-built shells behind high walls and impressive gates, all of them waiting for the machinery to be installed. In an odd way, it reminded me of the villages I'd driven through in northern China. In places like Smash the Hu and Slaughter the Hu, everything had been surrounded by massive fortifications, but most residents had already left. Here in the development zone it felt similar: big walls and gates, lots of structures, few people. If you were transported directly from a northern village to a fledgling factory strip, you'd wonder, Where is everybody? But that's the nature of a country in transition: something is always being abandoned while something else is always being built. The people are in constant motion—they're on trains, in buses, on boats. They stand beside rural roads, petting the invisible dog, looking for a ride south. In half a year this Wuhu factory strip would be finished, and after that the young people would arrive in droves.

In the T-11, we reached a roundabout that was still under construction. To John Dinkel, it looked a lot like a skid pad. He accelerated to forty miles an hour, and we flew past a pile of dirt, a half-dozen bags of cement, and a stack of bamboo that would someday be used to scaffold another building project. Dinkel held the turn, tires squealing; we spun around again and again. Construction materials flashed by: dirt, cement, bamboo; dirt, cement, bamboo. In the back of the T-11, the three Chinese engineers were thrown against the side of the car. They still weren't wearing seat belts.

The one in the middle was named Qi Haibo. He was twenty-two years old, and he could have fit into the driver's seat of a Mazda Cosmo, along with a sack of groceries. He'd grown up just beyond the Great Wall in Inner Mongolia, in the Ordos Desert; his home was the region where the government was trying to plant willow trees in an attempt to support local herdsmen. Qi Haibo was ethnic Chinese and he told me that his grandfather had originally moved to the Ordos from Shaanxi Province. ("Probably because of famine or war.") In the desert, the grandfather had scraped by as a farmer raising wheat, sunflowers, and corn. Qi's father attended school for only five years; his mother had even less education, giving up after the first grade. In the 1980s the family tried to grow watermelons, but they never moved beyond a state of subsistence farming. Qi could still remember the day they first got electricity. But his parents encouraged him to focus on his studies, and at the local school he became the top pupil. He always knew that some-day he'd head south, across the Great Wall, and he didn't plan on coming back.

After high school he tested into Wuhan Polytechnic University, a good institution in Hubei Province. He had never had any particular interest in engineering, but like John Dinkel he happened to come of age at a time when his nation was at a critical moment. "I wanted to go to a good university," Qi said, "and I heard that computers and elec-tronics were the best subjects for careers nowadays. So I chose those specialties when I took the entrance examination." At university, he was assigned to an engineering department that focused on transport vehi-cles, because that's the fastest-growing market in China. As a senior he attended a job fair and met some Chery recruiters. "They offered me a job, and people at the school said it was a new company, a company that was developing fast. So the next day I signed a contract. I figured that a young person could learn a lot there."

By Chery standards, Qi wasn't particularly young—the average age of a company employee was twenty-four. Qi worked six days a week, for a salary of less than two hundred dollars per month, and he lived in a factory dormitory. There were four engineers in his room; they shared a bathroom with dozens of others who lived along the hallway. Qi would have preferred his own space, but the dorm conditions were a lot better than anything he'd known in the Ordos. He hoped for a long-term future at Chery. "I also like the fact that it's not a joint venture," he said. "It's China's own auto company."

After the test-drive, I asked Qi Haibo what he had learned from John Dinkel. Qi said the T-11 had a slight problem with driveshaft length, which meant that the outside wheel slipped on tight turns. The rear end of the B-14 floated a bit at high speeds. In particular Qi admired Dinkel's skills behind the wheel. The Chinese engineer, whose job involved quality control and test-driving, had received his license only one month earlier.

DRIVING IN CHINA OFTEN made me feel old. So much of the nation's energy comes from the very young, the recent migrants and the fresh-faced college grads, and new companies like Chery constantly shift the economic landscape. On the road, most people are in their thirties or forties—anybody much older encounters legal restrictions. By law, an applicant for a truck or bus driver's license must be younger than fifty. Nobody over the age of seventy can operate a passenger car. Only the young have the fortitude for Chinese traffic, and time seems to accelerate once you begin to drive. After I got my license, I understood how fast roads are being built, and the flood of new car models caught my eye. That's part of the rush of the open road—a sense that the crowds are close behind.

I liked Beijing's Capital Motors for the opposite reason, because the rental company felt slow. It was still state-owned, a throwback to the old Communist economy, and its corporate culture was a world apart from a place like Chery. At Capital Motors most workers were middle-aged men who sat around smoking cigarettes and reading newspapers. Despite having been among the first to enter a promising market, they did virtually nothing to take advantage of their position. Eventually, Avis and others set up shop in Beijing, but my local Capital Motors branch never responded to the new competition. They didn't upgrade their fleet of cars, and they didn't streamline the paperwork. They didn't get rid of the Jeep Cherokee, which nobody ever rented, and which sat sulking in the lot like a retired racehorse whose record is too bad to stud. Capital Motors never improved the gas-refill policy or bothered to enforce even the most basic rental guidelines. Their Appropriate Service Diction Rating held steady at 98 percent. And I kept coming back—I couldn't imagine renting from anybody else in Beijing.

Six months after my first drive across the north, I returned to Capital Motors and put down a deposit on the City Special. The mechanic showed me the spare, marked the gas gauge, and toured the exterior. There weren't any new dents; the odometer had hardly budged since I dropped off the Jeep last autumn. In the office, Mr. Wang signed off on the papers with a smile and wished me good luck. He didn't ask where I was going. The man was so unfailingly kind and polite that it seemed a form of discretion—as far as he was concerned, it was my own private business what I decided to do with a vehicle from Capital Motors.

This time I intended to drive all the way to the edge of the Tibetan plateau. The last lines of the Great Wall are located in the high desert of Gansu Province, along the ancient Silk Road, and I hoped to get there in a month. I scheduled the trip for late April, when the weather is usually good; I stocked the City Special full of Coke, Gatorade, Oreos, and Dove chocolate bars. In Beijing I picked up a foreign hitchhiker: Mike Goettig, a friend from my Peace Corps days who was looking for a ride to the capital of Inner Mongolia. I figured it would take us a day at the most, and then I'd resume last year's route along the trail of the Great Wall.

On the morning of departure, a storm swept south from Siberia and cold rain pounded the capital. Downtown traffic slowed to a crawl; it took nearly an hour to escape the city. I headed northwest on Highway 110, a worn two-lane road that would soon be obsolete, because an expressway was being built. Bulldozers and cement mixers had been abandoned beside the new road—you know it's bad weather when Chinese construction crews stop working. At the moment it was rain but I could see clearly what lay ahead; that forecast had been frozen atop the oncoming traffic. Most vehicles were big Liberation-brand trucks carrying freight south from Inner Mongolia, and their stacks of boxes and crates were covered with ice. The trucks had fought a crosswind on the steppes and now their frozen loads listed to the right, like ships on a rough sea.

In Hebei Province we began to see advertisements for "Strange Stones." The landscape was desolate, low rocky hills where the farming was bad, and the only color came from the red banners that had been posted beside the road. Each sign had big characters promising Qi Shi—literally, Strange Stones—and the banners had been tattered and torn by the wind. The air had grown colder and now bits of ice and snow began to pelt the windshield. We passed a half dozen signs before either of us spoke.

"What's up with this?" Goettig said at last.

"I have no idea," I said. "I haven't driven this road before."

The banners stood before cheaply built shops of cement and white tile. *Strange stones* is the Chinese term for any rock whose shape resembles something else. It's an obsession at scenic destinations across the country; in the Yellow Mountains you can seek out natural formations with names like Immortal Playing Chess and Rhinoceros Watching Moon. Collectors buy smaller rocks: sometimes they've been carved into a certain shape, or maybe they contain a mineral pattern with an uncannily familiar form. I had never understood this particular obsession, and the sudden proliferation of Strange Stones in this forgotten corner of Hebei mystified me. Who was buying all this stuff? Finally, after about twenty banners, I pulled over.

Inside the shop, the first thing I noticed was that the arrangement seemed odd. The lighting was bad, and display tables completely encircled the room, leaving only a narrow gap for entry. A shopkeeper stood beside the gap, smiling. With Goettig behind me, I squeezed past the tables, and then I heard a tremendous crash.

I spun around. Goettig stood frozen; shards of green lay strewn across the concrete floor. "What happened?" I asked.

"He knocked it off!" the shopkeeper said. He grabbed the hem of Goettig's coat. "Your jacket brushed it."

Goettig and I stared at the scattered shards. Finally I asked, "What is it?"

"It's jade," the man said. "It's a jade ship."

Now I recognized pieces: a corner of a smashed sail, a strand of broken rigging. It was the kind of model ship that Chinese business-men display in their offices for good luck. The material looked like the cheap artificial jade that comes out of factories, and it had absolutely exploded—there were more than fifty pieces.

"Don't worry about it," the shopkeeper said brightly. "Go ahead and look around. Maybe there's something else you'll want to buy."

We stood in the center of the room, surrounded by the ring of tables like animals in a pen. Goettig's hand was shaking. "Did you really knock it over?" I said.

"I don't know," he said. "I didn't feel anything, but I'm not sure. It fell down behind me."

I had never seen a Chinese shopkeeper react so calmly when goods were broken. Now a second man emerged from a side room, carrying a broom. He swept the shipwreck into a neat pile, but he left it lying on the floor. Silently, other men appeared, until three more of them stood near the door. In the past I had heard about antique shops where owners broke a vase and blamed a customer, and now I wondered if this technique had been adopted as a roadside scam. It made sense: so many motorists in China are rookies with money to burn.

"What do we do now?" Goettig said.

"I don't know," I said. "Maybe we just buy something."

A few Strange Stones looked like food. For some reason this has always been a popular Chinese artistic motif, and I recognized old favor-ites: a rock-hard head of cabbage, a stony strip of bacon. Other stones had been polished to reveal some miraculous mineral pattern, but in my nervousness most of the shapes looked the same to me. I selected a smaller one and asked the price.

"Two thousand yuan," the shopkeeper said. He saw me recoil; it was nearly two hundred and fifty dollars. "But we can go cheaper," he said quickly.

"You know," Goettig said, in English, "nothing else in here would break if it fell."

He was right—it was all Strange in a strictly solid sense. And why had a jade ship been there in the first place? As a last resort, I hoped that maybe Goettig's size would discourage violence. He was six feet one and well built, with close-cropped hair and a sharp Germanic nose that the Chinese found striking. But in truth I had never known anybody gentler, and we shuffled meekly toward the door. The men were still standing there.

"I'm sorry," I said. "But I don't think we want to buy anything."

"*Zenmeban?*" the shopkeeper said softly. He had stopped smiling, and now he pointed at the shards on the floor. "What are you going to do about this?"

In hushed voices, Goettig and I conferred and decided to start at fifty yuan. He took the bill out of his wallet—the equivalent of about six dollars. He handed it to the shopkeeper, who accepted it without a word. All the way across the parking lot I expected to feel a hand on my shoulder. I started the City Special, spun the tires, and roared back onto Highway 110. I was still shaking when we reached the city of Zhangjiakou. We pulled over at a truck stop for lunch; I guzzled tea to calm my nerves. The waitress became excited when she learned we were Americans.

"Our boss has been to America!" she said. "I'll go get her!"

The boss was in her fifties, with dyed hair the color of shoeblack. She came to our table and presented a business card with a flourish. One side of the card was Chinese, the other English:

> *United Sources of America, Inc.*
> *Jin Fang Liu*
> *Deputy Director of Operations*
> *China*

Embossed in gold was a knockoff of the Presidential Seal of the United States. It looked a lot like the original, except the eagle was fatter: the Zhangjiakou breed had pudgy wings, a thick neck, and round legs like drumsticks. Even if it dropped the shield and arrows, I doubted this bird would be capable of flight. The corner of the card said, in small print:

President Gerald R. Ford
Honorary Chairman

"What kind of company is this?" I asked

"We're in the restaurant business here in Zhangjiakou," Ms. Jin said. She told me her daughter ran another restaurant in Roanoke, Virginia. I pointed at the name in the corner of the business card. "Do you know who that is?"

"Fu Te," Ms. Jin said proudly. "He used to be president of the United States!"

"What does he have to do with your company?"

"It's just an honorary position," Ms. Jin said. She waved her hand in a way that suggested: *No need to tell Mr. Fu Te about our little truck stop in Zhangjiakou!* She gave us a discount and told us to come back any time. A couple hours later, near the Inner Mongolian border, I pulled over on the side of the road and got the City Special stuck in snow. It took us a while to find a farmer with a tractor that could pull us out, and by now I wondered if I'd ever make it back to the Great Wall. The snow was falling harder, and things were getting Stranger; that evening, in the town of Jining, we checked into a hotel called the Ulanqab that had a bowling alley in the lobby. We registered at the front desk, surrounded by the crash of balls and pins.

Early the next morning we set off determined to make it to Hohhot. At the entrance to Highway 110, the local government had erected a sign with changeable numbers, like the scoreboard at Fenway Park:

AS OF THIS MONTH,

THIS STRETCH OF ROAD

HAS HAD **65** ACCIDENTS AND **31** FATALITIES

The snow had stopped falling, but the temperature was brutally cold. From Jining to Hohhot there was nothing but empty steppe—low snow-covered hills huddled beneath the howling north wind. We passed Liberation trucks that were stopped dead on the road; their fuel lines had frozen, probably because of water in their tanks. After fifteen miles we crested a hill and saw a line of hundreds of vehicles stretching all the way to the horizon—Jeeps, Jettas, Santanas, Liberation trucks. Nobody was moving, and everybody was honking; an orchestra of horns blared into the wind. Never had I imagined that a traffic jam could occur in such a desolate place.

We parked the City Special and continued on foot to the gridlock, where drivers explained what had happened. It all started with a few trucks whose fuel lines had frozen. The trucks stalled, and then other vehicles began to pass them on the two-lane road. While passing, they occasionally encountered an oncoming car whose driver didn't want to budge. People faced off, honking angrily while more vehicles backed up; eventually it became impossible to move in any direction. Potential escape routes along the shoulder were quickly jammed by curb-sneaking drivers. A couple of motorists with Jeep Cherokees had taken advantage of their rear-wheel drive by embarking off-road; usually they made it about fifty yards before getting stuck. Men in loafers slipped in the snow, trying to dig out City Specials with their bare hands. The wind was so cold it hurt just to stand there. Meanwhile, truckers had crawled beneath their rigs, where they lit road flares and held them up to frozen fuel lines. The tableau had a certain beauty: the stark snow-covered steppes, the endless line of black Santanas, the orange fires dancing beneath blue Liberation trucks.

"You should go up there and get a picture of those truckers," Goettig said.

"*You* should get a picture," I said. "I'm not going anywhere near those guys."

At last, here on the unmarked Mongolian plains, we had crossed the shadowy line that divides Strange from Stupid. There was no sign of police or traffic control, so Goettig and I watched the flares for a while and then turned around. This time the Sinomaps came through—I leafed through the book and found a back route to Hohhot. The moment we arrived, the City Special celebrated by breaking down. The vehicle wouldn't start, and finally I called Mr. Wang at Capital Motors. "No problem!" he said. "We can come get you."

"Umm, I don't think that's possible," I said.

"Where are you?" he said.

"In Hohhot."

"Where?"

"Hohhot. The capital of Inner Mongolia."

"*Waah!*" he said, and I could hear the smile in his voice. "All the way to Hohhot! Not bad!"

As always, Mr. Wang took everything in stride. He told me to find a mechanic, do whatever was necessary, and save the receipt. Goettig planned to catch a train out of Hohhot, but he hung around long enough to help get the City Special working. We push-started the Jeep and drove it to a garage, where they replaced the starter for a little more than a hundred bucks. The mechanic chain-smoked State Express 555 cigarettes the whole time he worked on the engine, but after Highway 110 it seemed as harmless as a sparkler on the Fourth of July.

WHEN THE CITY SPECIAL returned to working order, and the weather improved, I finally found the walls again. There were plenty of them out here—of all the places I'd been, Inner Mongolia most belied the singular nature of the term *Great Wall*. On my first journey I had followed the Ming wall along the southern border, and now I drove nearly two hundred miles northward to another barrier. It was over eight hundred years old, dating to the Jurchen Jin dynasty, and the thing was so weathered that it had faded into the steppes: a long grass-covered bump, thirty feet wide and three feet tall, heading straight as an arrow to the horizon. I couldn't have found it without a local resident, who sat in the passenger's seat and directed me across a stretch of grassland. After he told me to stop, and we got out of the City Special, I realized that I had parked atop the relic itself. "It's not a problem," the man said. "They just don't want people to drive on it for long distances." Another hundred miles to the west, outside the city of Baotou, I stopped at a barrier that dated to the Warring States period, which had ended in 221 BC. It was the oldest wall I ever saw—after more than twenty-two centuries the structure was still impressive, as tall as a man and visible for miles.

In this featureless landscape the barriers seemed quixotic, the markings of lost empires that had vanished into the steppes. Even modern buildings looked temporary, especially in the north, where sheepherders' shacks were constructed with their backs to the northwest, because of the relentless wind. They were low structures, crouching behind curved walls of mud that had been designed to shed the grit that blows off the Gobi Desert. Apart from herdsmen, few people live in this region, and there are almost no shops. One afternoon I drove for a hundred miles, and the sole indication of commerce was a hunchbacked shack with a lonely sign in front. It advertised an Inner Mongolian two-for-one: "Car Repair/Medical Clinic."

The biggest city in Inner Mongolia is Baotou, and the sudden size of the place, surrounded by empty steppe, feels surreal. The population is over a million and growing rapidly, mostly because of new money from the central government's Develop the West campaign. The Party is attempting to counterbalance the growing economies of the coast, but for the most part investment in the west has been a failure: these regions simply don't have the necessary resources and proximity to foreign trade. Nevertheless, money flows into certain designated cities, and when I drove through Baotou the place was in the midst of an artificial boom. City planners had turned it into a frenzy of detours and road construction, and everything was clogged with automobiles; I had never heard such honking. Throughout the city, in hopes of managing the new traffic in the way that scarecrows manage birds, the government had erected fiberglass statues of police officers. These figures were located at major intersections and roundabouts, where they stood at attention atop pedestals. They portrayed officers in full uniform, complete with necktie, visored cap, and white gloves. Each statue even wore an ID tag with a number. In Baotou I never saw a live cop.

Driving south of the city, I crossed the Yellow River and entered the Ordos Desert once more. The land became flat and desolate, with the washed-out color of a dead creekbed, and periodically a policeman statue loomed beside the road. There was something eerie about these figures: they were wind-swept and dust-covered, and the surrounding desert emphasized their pointlessness. But their posture remained ramrod straight, arms at attention, with a sort of Ozymandian grandeur—terracotta cops. After an hour of driving I came upon the aftermath of the most spectacular tollbooth accident I ever saw in China. A trucker obviously had been moving at a high rate of speed, and his angle also must have been perfect; he'd wedged his vehicle sideways into the tollbooth. It reminded me of those Chinese jade carvings in which a dragon curls within an egg, and you wonder: How did they ever do that?

For most of the journey I had followed small roads, but now I picked up Highway 210 toward the Mausoleum of Genghis Khan. One of the mysteries of traveling through Inner Mongolia is that there are virtually no signs of the greatest empire to ever rule these steppes. There are walls everywhere, but all of them were built against the nomads; the Mongols themselves left virtually nothing. They were never great builders, and their origins could hardly have been more humble. In AD 1162, when Genghis Khan was born, Mongol society was illiterate, nomadic, and structured narrowly around ties to kin and tribe. The great leader rose to power by overcoming these weaknesses; he united tribes, and he created systems. In Genghis Khan's military, squads were organized in units of ten, and officers gave orders in set rhymes and songs that were easily remembered by illiterate soldiers. The Mongols had no army, no columns, no defensive fortifications. There was no supply train. They were strictly cavalry: on the average, each soldier had five horses. When it came time to advance, they spread out across the steppes to ensure that animals could graze, and they milked their mares along the way. Mostly they moved fast: in the span of twenty-five years, the Mongols conquered more lands and people than the Romans did in four centuries.

In *Genghis Khan and the Making of the Modern World*, the historian Jack Weatherford describes the Mongol strategies and their impact on other cultures. Some Mongol characteristics are surprising—for all their fearsome reputation, they were remarkably squeamish about the sight of blood. They despised hand-to-hand combat; bows and arrows were the preferred weapons. In battle, they liked to keep their distance, and they became so skilled at siege warfare that they essentially rendered walled cities obsolete. Diplomacy was another strong suit. Genghis Khan banned torture and looting, believing them to be counterproductive, and he established the concept of diplomatic immunity. He granted religious freedom to the lands he conquered. His genius was essentially one of recruitment: he was willing to accept anybody with skills to offer. Strategies of siege warfare were incorporated from the Chinese; knowledge of astronomy came from the Persians; a new Mongol alphabet was adopted from the script of the Uighurs. German miners came to work in China; Chinese doctors went to Persia. Genghis Khan's court included Buddhists, Daoists, Muslims, and Nestorian Christians. By the time he died, in AD 1227, his empire was twice as large as that of any other individual in history. His grandson, Kublai Khan, completed the Mongol conquest of China, founding the Yuan dynasty in 1279. The Yuan became the first non-Han dynasty to rule all of China, with territory stretching all the way from northern Vietnam to Siberia.

But it was also extremely short-lived. The Mongol rise had depended primarily on Genghis Khan's vision, and they never again produced such a brilliant leader. Within a century, the Yuan was overthrown by the Chinese founders of the Ming, who drove the Mongols back to the north. Once they were gone, they didn't leave much behind. Unlike other empires, the Mongols didn't spread a dominant religion, or a form of writing, or a political system. They didn't create technological innovations, and one of their few building specialties consisted of bridges, because they were always on the move. The sense of movement became their most lasting legacy—new trade and cultural exchanges that continued after the brief empire.

The Mongols wrote little, and we don't know much about how they viewed themselves. Most contemporary accounts come from the people they defeated—a rare instance in which history was written primarily by the conquered. After the Mongol empire collapsed, its descendants were tracked most closely by the Ming, who had to deal with the periodic attacks of nomadic raiders. Some Chinese military officers wrote about these encounters, including a man named Yin Geng, who served in a Ministry of Defense department that dealt with border issues. The historian David Spindler has translated Yin Geng's words, which are as vivid and detailed as if he were still standing on the Great Wall today. Like most Chinese of the mid-1500s, he refers to the northerners as simply "barbarians." "Barbarian women have buxom figures," Yin Geng writes. "Because they eat meat and cheese and wear skins, their flesh is tender and white. They like to fornicate, paying little attention to whether it's day or night or whether there's anyone watching." Mongol males, according to Yin Geng, have similar interests. ("Young barbarian men like to abduct women, carry them away on horseback, and copulate with them.") He describes Mongols as smelling *shan*— "muttonlike"—and they possess other animal qualities. ("Every barbarian family brews alcohol, and all of them like to drink; the barbarians drink like cattle, not even stopping to breathe in the process.") Lest the reader get the impression that Mongols are only interested in sex and alcohol, Yin Geng describes other pastimes. ("Barbarians like to spear babies for sport.")

By the time of Yin Geng, the Mongols had lost the unity of Genghis Khan's reign, but they were still brilliant raiders. They traveled on horseback, usually in small groups, and they liked to come at night. They followed ridgelines, because they feared ambushes. They communicated through smoke signals. They developed a nomadic version of microcredit—this system allowed a poor Mongol to borrow a horse from a wealthier person, embark on a raid, and pay the owner a percentage of spoils. Generally the Mongols did not linger in Chinese territory. They penetrated defenses, gathered booty, and returned home as quickly as possible. (The Great Wall around Beijing and other regions has crenellations and arrow holes on both sides because soldiers sometimes attacked Mongols heading back north after a successful raid.) In China, the Mongols liked to steal livestock, household goods, and even Chinese people. They carried the Chinese men and women back to the steppes, where they forced them to form families. Then they turned the men, and sometimes the women, into spies—a Chinese could be sent south to gather military intelligence, with his or her family essentially held in Mongolia as hostages.

Sometimes these captives adapted so well to life in the north that they seemed happy to stay there. It's a type of pragmatism that's still recognizable in modern times—Chinese who leave home learn to make the best of their new environment, whether they've gone south during the Reform years or north during the Ming dynasty. One text from the early sixteenth century, translated by David Spindler, describes an encounter between a group of nomads and some soldiers who were guarding the Great Wall. The nomads are accompanied by a Chinese man, originally from a town in Ningxia Province, and he makes no pretenses about his group's desire to gather information. The Ming report reads:

> *One morning, a party of five Mongols approached a signal tower and addressed the soldiers guarding it, saying, "I've been sent here by the Mongol leadership to find out the reason for all of the movement of oxen and carts on your side of the wall." The soldier replied, "The Governor-General is using thousands of men to haul grain in preparation for an attack on you Mongols inside the bend of the Yellow River." The Mongol: "There are lots of us in this area—you don't want to attack us. I'm actually [a Chinese person] from Weizhou and I've come to trade a bow with you as a sign of my sincerity." The soldier retorted, "Well, if you're from Weizhou, why don't you just surrender and come home?" The other man replied: "Things are bad in Weizhou and good out here on the grasslands. Why should I come back?" He handed the bow up to the soldier, but the soldier didn't give him a bow in return. The "Mongol" then sped away on his horse.*

Officers like Yin Geng described methods of identifying these turncoat Chinese. Their hair tended to be short, like the Mongols, and they often had visible scars. They smelled *shan*. If you asked them the year of the emperor's reign, they sometimes couldn't answer correctly, because they had lost track of time. They often referred to China as *nan chao*, the "southern dynasty." In one battle, Chinese soldiers captured a man named Puning, a Chinese who had been kidnapped by the Mongols. An officer described the man: "Puning had been living among the barbarians for so long and eating meat and cheese that his frame was stocky and his face was like that of a lion." The officer continued, "He was fat, his hair was short, and he walked like a duck." In ancient China, race was essentially cultural, and a person who lived among barbarians could lose his "Chineseness."

For Mongols, though, political legitimacy ultimately depended on genetics. Leadership was supposed to be confined to the direct heirs of Genghis Khan, and anybody outside this line had few ways of improving his standing. One common solution was to try to gain goods and titles from the Chinese, and David Spindler has researched a number of instances in which this strategy culminated in attacks across the Great Wall. During the 1540s, Altan Khan rose as a capable Mongol leader, eventually founding the city of Hohhot. But he found himself limited by genealogy—he was the second son of a third son. In 1550, in an attempt to gain wealth and status among his Mongol peers, he turned southward, leading tens of thousands of Mongols on a surprise attack northeast of Beijing. At that time, the Ming fortifications consisted mostly of crude stone walls, which the Mongols easily penetrated. They pillaged for two weeks, killing and capturing thousands of Chinese. After that, the Ming began using mortar on a large scale to improve fortifications around the capital.

Altan Khan's oldest son, known as the Imperial Prince, tried another strategy for dealing with genealogical shortcomings. He married dozens of women from important Mongol families, hoping to solidify alliances. But he ran into financial problems, which he solved in the simplest way possible: he sent the women back. Lacking money and accompanied by their families, the ex-wives began visiting Chinese wall garrisons, demanding gifts from the Chinese. In 1576, after one such appeal was rejected, some Mongols formed a raiding party and penetrated a gap in a remote part of the defense network. The region was so rugged that the Ming hadn't seen a need for extensive walls, but the Mongols got through, killing twenty-nine Chinese. The Ming responded with another major wall-building campaign, this time using brick, which allowed construction on even the steepest terrain.

Nowadays, outside of Beijing, brick walls still cling to sheer cliffs, and tourists often wonder: Was it really necessary to build defenseworks in a place like this? But Mongols were indeed capable of attacking such remote regions, and sometimes a leader's position on Genghis Khan's family tree was a major factor. Low genealogical status could initiate a chain of events that swept southward, resulting in violence against the Ming. Spindler calls the incident of 1576 "the Raid of the Scorned Mongol Women"—a failed harem that eventually inspired the stunning Great Wall of Beijing.

THE PARKING LOT AT the Mausoleum of Genghis Khan was full of black Santanas with tinted windows. My heart always sank at such a sight—it was like watching a flock of crows settle into a quiet forest. In rural China, black Santanas are cadre cars, and if they show up en masse at a tourist destination it usually means that a junket is in full swing. When I arrived at the mausoleum, it was early afternoon but many of the cadres were drunk from their lunchtime banquets. They stumbled out of Santanas, shouting and laughing in the parking lot. I followed a group of three Chinese men as they staggered up the steps to the entrance, where they initiated an argument with the attendant. He was Mongolian, and he asked them for the standard admission price of thirty-five yuan per ticket. It was less than five dollars.

"How 'bout this," slurred one of the cadres. "I'll give you a hundred for three."

"Three tickets cost one hundred and five," the Mongolian said.

"Special price," the cadre said. "Give special price. One hundred."

"We can't do that. It's thirty-five each. One hundred and five."

"How 'bout this," the cadre said. "I give you one hundred."

"One hundred and five."

"One hundred."

Each man spoke very slowly, and they continued this inane conversation for several minutes. In China, admissions to state-run tourist sites are nonnegotiable, and I couldn't figure out why the attendant remained so patient, until I realized that he was also intoxicated. He slumped against his desk; the ticket booth reeked of grain alcohol. Inside the gate, three buildings were shaped like massive *ger*, traditional Mongol tents, their roofs decorated in tile of burnt orange and deep blue. Everywhere

I saw drunk cadres: they staggered through hallways; they tripped down steps; they sat red-faced in the shade, heads in their hands. They wobbled in front of exhibits, trying to read inscriptions about the history of Genghis Khan and the Yuan dynasty.

Exhibits appeared in Chinese, Mongolian, and English. As in many Chinese museums, there were subtle shifts between languages. One English sign read:

GENGHIS KHAN IS CONSIDERED BY THE WORLD AS A GREAT STRATEGIST AND STATESMAN.

The Chinese version said:

IN THE HISTORY OF THE CHINESE PEOPLE, GENGHIS KHAN WAS A GREAT STRATEGIST AND STATESMAN.

In China, people often speak of Genghis Khan as if he were Chinese, at least in the cultural sense, because he founded a dynasty that ruled China. And from the Chinese perspective, Mongolia was a natural part of the empire—it had been ruled by the Qing dynasty until their collapse in 1912. During the twentieth century, Mongolia proper became a Soviet satellite and then an independent nation, but Inner Mongolia remained under Chinese rule. After Mao Zedong came to power, he encouraged Han Chinese settlement in the region, and nowadays the population is over 80 percent Chinese.

The Chinese have also occupied the history just as efficiently. At the Mausoleum of Genghis Khan, there is no body; the true burial place of the great leader is unknown, although historians believe it's located in independent Mongolia. The Chinese built the mausoleum in the mid-1950s, as a way of symbolizing their authority in Inner Mongolia. The exhibits put a Chinese spin on Mongol history:

> Kublai Khan, one of Genghis Khan's grandchildren, founded the Yuan dynasty, which was a united multinational state with extensive territory. He carried forward the traditions of the central

plains of China. He encouraged the development of agriculture, handicraft, and textile industries by improving productive means as well as science and technology. Trade and navigation were well developed, which promoted the cultural communication with western countries.

The mausoleum's central room features a row of coffins, supposedly belonging to Genghis Khan and his closest relatives. Outside the room, a Mongolian tour guide approached me, speaking Chinese. She asked where I was from, and when I answered, she smiled wistfully. "The Great America," she said. "It's like Genghis Khan used to be."

I didn't know exactly how to respond to that. Among the flocks of cadres she looked as out of place as many of my hitchhikers—dyed-red hair, silver earrings, tight jeans. She was twenty-four years old, with high cheekbones and the long thin eyes of the steppe people. I was still thinking about the Great America when she spoke again.

"This isn't really Genghis Khan's tomb," she said. "I work here, but I want you to know that this place is fake. Those coffins are empty, and nobody knows where his tomb really is. Anyway, according to tradition there were special ceremonial objects that contained his soul."

She mentioned the names of the objects, but the words were unfamiliar; I asked her to write them in my notebook. For a moment she stared helplessly at the pen and paper. "I'm sorry," she said at last. "I'm too drunk to write."

She gave me an impromptu tour of the exhibits, pointing out mistakes and exaggerations. She told me that Genghis Khan had been born in what is now independent Mongolia—that detail was important to her. She believed that Inner Mongolia had become an ecological disaster, because of all the Chinese-style farming in the region. "That's why you have dust storms in Beijing every spring," she said. "Anyway, we're a fallen race. We used to be great, but now we're nothing. We don't have a united country—there's Mongolia, Inner Mongolia, and then the Buryats in Russia. And yet at one point we were the greatest race in the world. We're not the same as the Chinese; those are two totally different races. Mongolians like freedom, but that doesn't matter to the Chinese. Have you noticed that Mongolians drink a lot?"

I said yes, this was something I had noticed.

"It's because of the psychology," she said. "It's bad for your psychology to fall so far. And there isn't anything for Mongolians to do about it, so we drink."

We walked outside into the blazing sunshine. Beyond the mausoleum walls I could see flat dry scrubland, and the wind blew the woman's hair around her face. "Of course the Mongols killed a lot of people in the old days," she said. "But they also had great advances in culture and religion. It's like Hitler—people might say that he's bad, but at least he was capable of leading a country. You can't deny that."

"Do you think Hitler was bad or good?" I said.

"It doesn't matter," she said. "That's not important for me to decide. What matters is that he left his name for history. You can call him fascist or anything else you want to, but he succeeded in leaving his name. The same is true for Genghis Khan. The whole world knew him and they still know him. Osama bin Laden is the same. When he attacked America, I was happy for him and the Afghans. Nothing against America, but the Taliban were a small race of people and they wanted to get noticed. Now everybody knows Osama bin Laden. He left his name for history, and I respect that."

She wavered unsteadily in the wind and asked if we could sit down. We found a bench outside the museum entrance and she rested, closing her eyes in the sunshine. "I like to talk to strangers," she said. "Sometimes it's easier to talk with somebody I don't know. And today it's easier because I'm drunk. Usually I'm not as drunk as this, and usually I don't talk so freely. But there are many things in China that I don't like. You go to this museum and they say that Genghis Khan was a Chinese hero, and it's nonsense. He fought against the Chinese. This museum is all garbage."

Periodically other employees walked past, along with groups of drunken cadres, and everybody grinned when they saw us together. The woman didn't seem to mind. "When I first started giving tours," she said, "people complained because I talked about the Mongols—the Mongol leader, the Mongol victories, the Mongol empire. They wanted me to say it was all Chinese. So the leaders criticized me and now I have to say that it's Chinese, but I don't believe it. Even so, the way that I tell the stories isn't the same as other tour guides. People tell me it's different. I don't know exactly how, but it's different in some way."

"Maybe it's different because you say the museum is all garbage," I said, and she laughed.

"It's different because I'm different from other people," she said. "I talk with strangers, and women aren't supposed to do that. My boyfriend doesn't like that."

On the bench she had edged closer, and now I could feel her leg against my thigh. Her breath came strong—the sickly-sweet smell of *baijiu*.

"Actually," she said, "I don't like my boyfriend very much."

It seemed like a good time to change the subject, but I couldn't think of anything to say. She studied my face closely, looking into my eyes, and finally she spoke. "Are you a spy?" she said.

"No," I said. "I'm a writer. I told you, I write articles and books."

She pressed closer. "If you're a spy, you can tell me," she said in a low voice. "I promise I won't tell anybody."

"Honest, I'm not."

"Come on!" Her tone was pleading. "You're here alone, you speak Chinese, you're in Inner Mongolia, you drove your own car. Of course you're a spy! Can't you just tell me the truth?"

"I *am* telling you the truth," I said. "I'm not a spy. Anyway, why would a spy go to Genghis Khan's mausoleum?"

She pondered this and looked crestfallen. "I've always wanted to meet a spy," she said in a small voice. "I wish you really were one."

The woman seemed less drunk now and she asked to write her name and phone number in my notebook, in case I ever returned. She wrote the words carefully, in both Chinese and Mongolian, and then she sketched a picture. It was the sun—childlike rays around a ball of flame.

◉　◉　◉

FOR THREE HUNDRED MILES I followed small roads through the southern borderlands of the Ordos. Usually the Great Wall was nearby, marked on my Sinomaps, but from the roads it was rarely visible. Sometimes I drove for an hour without seeing another car; when I turned on the radio, all I heard was Mongolian. Occasionally the wind picked up and a small sandstorm swept across the blacktop, the grit moving in waves like it was liquid. Near the Shaanxi border I saw two hitchhikers petting the invisible dog. One of them was an old man, and he shouted when I pulled over: "How much to Jingbian?"

I told him I was heading in that direction anyway. Jingbian is a small city near the Great Wall; the name means "Pacify the Border."

"No money?" the man said in surprise. He asked where I had come from, and I said Beijing. He seemed slightly deaf—he leaned forward and shouted every time he spoke. "Can we bring these bags?" he yelled.

"Of course," I said. "What's in them?"

"Salt! It's from my daughter's farm!"

I opened the back of the City Special and helped the man lift the bags—they were fifty pounds each. That was the only major food group I had been missing; now the Jeep was fully stocked with Coke, Gatorade, Oreos, Dove bars, and Ordos salt. The old man planned to sell the salt in Jingbian. The moment he got inside the vehicle he shouted another question. "Do you know Han Heliu?"

"Who?"

"Han Heliu! Do you know Han Heliu?"

"No," I said, confused. "Who is Han Heliu?"

"He's from our village!" the old man shouted. "He's gone to Beijing to work! I was wondering if you had met him!"

I told him I'd keep an eye out. The old man wore a weathered cap and rough blue cotton clothes. He was mostly toothless; a wispy beard hung from his chin. His traveling companion was the most strikingly pretty woman I ever saw in the north. She was twenty years old, with hair that had been dyed a light red; her lipstick was bright pink and a tiny beauty mark had been tattooed between her eyebrows. She wore a red silk jacket, tailored tight at the waist, with gold flowers embroidered across the front. She was small-boned, with a birdlike name—Wang Yan, which means "Swallow." In this hard landscape she seemed completely out of place, like an exotic that had been blown off course and then alighted in the City Special. She perched stiffly in front, her back not touching the seat.

"He's my grandfather," she said. "We live together in Jingbian."

In the backseat, the old man leaned forward. "Are you sure you're not going to charge us?" he shouted. "It's usually five yuan to Jingbian! We can't pay more than that!"

We drove south past rows of willows that had been planted in the sandy soil. Wang Yan was shy—she stared straight ahead, eyes on the road, and she answered my questions in a soft voice. She had just visited her parents at their farm; a few years ago she had migrated to Jingbian, which was the nearest township, and recently her grandfather had joined her in the small city. "All of the young people leave our village," she said. "Nobody stays there anymore. I'm not planning to go back." In Jingbian she worked in a beauty parlor. Among uneducated female migrants, jobs tend to be sharply divided according to looks. A pretty woman is more likely to find work in a barbershop or as a restaurant hostess; the plainer girls end up as waitresses or factory workers. Jobs are easier for women who are good looking, but there are also pitfalls. Most beauty parlors offer the basics—hair styling, makeup, hair-washing, and simple massages—but there are also shops that double as fronts for prostitution. It occurred to me that Wang Yan's family had probably sent the grandfather to live with her to make sure she didn't get into trouble.

After twenty minutes the old man leaned forward once more. "Are you Chinese?" he shouted.

"No. I'm American."

"I thought you weren't Chinese!" he said, with a big smile. "You're the first foreigner I've ever met!"

In Jingbian I dropped them off at the beauty parlor. It was called the Jian Hua—"Build China"—and we carried the bags of salt inside.

Four young men and women were working, and they greeted Wang Yan warmly. The men had the look of small-town hipsters; their hair was long and they wore leather jackets covered with zippers. It was too early for customers and they put a Madonna disk in the video player. A full-length mirror ran along one wall, and the employees pushed aside the barber chairs and practiced dance moves. They were focused on their reflections, repeating the steps over and over, trying to get it right. At the far end of the shop, Wang Yan leaned close to another mirror, fixing her road-worn hair and makeup. The grandfather stood alone near the door. Upon entering the shop he had fallen silent, and now he watched the young people intently, his face expressionless. In a room full of mirrors he was the only person not staring at himself.

THE FARTHER I DROVE across northern China, the more I wondered what would become of all of the villages. The cities were easy to predict, at least in terms of growth—their trajectory was already laid out in tracks of cement and steel. In the countryside, though, it was impossible to imagine who would be living here in a generation. Often I stopped in a village and saw only the very old, the disabled, and the very young, because migrants left their children behind to be raised by grandparents. Workers still didn't feel settled in the cities, although inevitably that was bound to change; it seemed likely that in the future they'd find some way to have their families closer to work. For many of the northern villages this might be the last generation where a significant number of children were still growing up in the countryside.

An hour west of Jingbian, I stopped to visit the Great Wall near the village of Ansi. This region had been a major defense point for the Ming, and people told me that there were particularly impressive ruins near Ansi. The name means "Temple of Peace," and when I pulled over in the village I saw only one adult. He was disabled, with a pair of rough-hewn wooden crutches, and he was minding a flock of children. In rural China, that's become an archetypal scene: little kids dancing around somebody who can hardly walk.

The old man told me that the Wall wasn't far away, but his directions weren't clear. Finally he pointed at the oldest boy. "Just take him," the man said. "He knows the way."

In a flash, the child was inside the City Special. Before he could close the door, four others piled in. They successfully slammed the door in the face of a nine-year-old girl, who stood forlornly in the dust, her face a taut little frown between pigtails. I looked at the old man, expecting him to call the children back out, but he didn't say a word. He wore the slightly dazed expression that you find among people who have lived through war and revolution and famine and now, in their twilight years, have been assigned the task of raising young children.

"OK," I said. "If all of you are coming, she gets to come, too."

Sighing, one of the boys opened the door and the girl clambered in. We drove west along a loose dirt track; periodically I had to accelerate in order to plow through a patch of drifted sand. I heard the children whispering, and then I realized that I had told the old man virtually nothing about myself. They didn't know where I was from, or what I was doing; all I had asked for were directions to the ruins. I pulled over and faced the children.

"I drove here from Beijing," I said. "That's where I live. But I'm an American. I'm visiting a lot of areas with the Great Wall, and that's why I came here."

The children listened intently. In the front seat there was a boy and a girl, and three more boys sat in the back. The oldest boy was twelve and in his lap he carried a two-year-old girl. All six were extremely serious, especially the baby—a look of worry creased her pudgy face. It occurred to me that this was a situation for chocolate. I divided and distributed three Dove bars, and then we headed off for the Great Wall. I felt like the Pied Piper—for all I knew, these kids represented the entire future of Temple of Peace.

Here in the southern Ordos, the elevation was nearly five thousand feet, and hills of sand had crept to the very edge of town. The Great Wall ran through the dunes, ten feet tall and made of tamped earth. "You could walk along it for a year and still not reach Beijing!" one of the boys announced as he jumped out of the City Special. The children scampered across a dune and I followed, great sheets of sand sliding away beneath our feet. The wall led to a fort—it was square in shape and also made of tamped earth; there were turrets at every corner and a massive signal tower in the center. The tower was shaped like a pyramid, with a tiny hole at the base, like the entrance to some pharaoh's tomb. One by one the boys vanished inside.

Following them, I crawled on hands and knees. The tunnel turned to the left; pale walls disappeared into darkness. I groped forward, scrambling across the dirt, and then a spot of light appeared. It opened into a shaft—a narrow chimney that rose straight up for fifty feet. In Ming times, soldiers would have used a ladder here, but the boys simply wedged their legs across the shaft and shimmied up. Grit rained down below; I covered my eyes. "Maybe you shouldn't climb up here!" I shouted. "It's too dangerous!"

"It's fine!" one of them sang out. "We've done it before!"

I backtracked through the tunnel and rejoined the girl, who had been left holding the baby. By the time I emerged, the boys were already at the top, whooping triumphantly. After they descended I noticed that one of them had a filthy plaster cast on his arm. He told me that he had broken the bone at school, playing leapfrog. The youngest boy, who was seven, had an ugly bruise on his head from some other misadventure. If this was indeed the last generation of countryside children, at least these boys were making the most of it. Three of them were brothers, look-alikes with crew-cut heads. I never saw kids like this in Beijing—in the capital, nearly everybody is an only child, coddled and spoiled from birth.

When we returned to Temple of Peace, the old man on crutches was waiting patiently. I learned that he was the grandfather of the three brothers; he told me that in this particular region the planned birth policy hadn't been strictly enforced. "People just pay a fine and have more kids," he said with a smile. He still wasn't the slightest bit concerned about who I was or what I was doing. In northern villages, people were rarely suspicious, and it was standard for them to invite me in for tea or a meal. I had no illusions about the toughness of rural life, and my time in the Peace Corps had taught me not to romanticize poverty. But nevertheless there was something poignant about driving through the dying villages. These were last glimpses—the end of small

towns and rural childhoods; perhaps even the end of families with siblings. And rural traditions of honesty and trust wouldn't survive the shift
to city life. There aren't many parts of the world where a stranger is welcomed without question, and entrusted with children, and it made me
sad to drive away from Temple of Peace.

FOR A WEEK I followed the Great Wall until I reached the far edge
of the Ordos, and then the earthen barriers headed northwest into the
Tengger Desert. The Tengger is known for the fineness of its sand, which
leaves the dunes gracefully shaped, their tops curved like the arabesques
of the Sahara. This is desert, pure and simple: not even nomads live in
the heart of the Tengger. In the evenings I pulled over and pitched my
tent in the dunes. There's no better sleeping surface than sand, at least
on a calm night, and I was lucky with the spring weather. Skies were
clear and the dunes glowed pale beneath the light of the moon.

Whenever I passed a town of any size, I stopped for a meal and
a hair-washing. These were odd, forgotten places, so remote that they
received only the scattered leavings of China's economic boom. I began
to see motorcyclists who had attached computer discs to their back
mudflaps, because they made good reflectors. In a place called Xingwuying, locals climbed the Great Wall whenever they wanted to receive
a cell phone signal. Xingwuying means "Prosperous Military Camp,"
because the Ming had built huge fortifications in this place; now the
village was poor and remote, but the people still made use of the wall.
They stood along the ramparts, phones pressed to their faces, sentries
of the digital age. What does it mean when the Great Wall becomes a
cell phone accessory? Or when computer discs are most useful because
they bounce light? Everything was tangled in these parts; there was no
distinction between progress and improvisation.

In the town of Yanchi, I got my hair washed and went for a stroll
along the main street. It was another dry, forgotten place, located six miles
within the wall; the name means "Salt Pool." While I was walking, a
motorcyclist drove past slowly, and then he hit a curb and pitched forward
into the dust. A few people gathered and at first the man didn't move.

"He's drunk," somebody said. They stood there staring, until finally the motorcyclist rolled over—he was so intoxicated he couldn't speak. Somebody helped him stand, and the drunk man tried to make his way to the bike. "You shouldn't ride," the bystander said gently, holding him back. But the motorcyclist kept trying to push past, and soon thirty people had collected around him.

Chinese crowds behave in unpredictable ways, especially in remote places like Yanchi. There isn't much to do, and even a minor incident in the street draws attention. Most onlookers are passive, at least in the beginning—they simply want to see what's happening. But as more people show up, and the crowd swells, it can develop its own momentum. They might encourage a disagreement to develop into a full-fledged fight, or they might turn suddenly against an individual. The final direction is never easy to anticipate, because it depends largely on whether some dominant personality emerges within the group. A single outspoken person can sway an entire incident, inspiring the crowd to action.

In Yanchi, if a strong-willed individual had stepped forward and criticized the motorcyclist for being so drunk, or warned him shrilly against causing an accident, the others probably would have followed suit. But in this particular crowd the most powerful force happened to be the drunk man's desire to mount his motorcycle. Every fiber of his being was directed at that bike—he was mute, and he couldn't stand without assistance, but he angrily tried to push past anybody who held him back. After a while, his sheer willpower seemed to earn the crowd's respect, and the bystanders stopped resisting. At last they even helped. One person guided the drunk man onto the bike; somebody else got the starter going. A third person gave a push. The motorcyclist wobbled off and abruptly made a U-turn—gasps from the onlookers—but somehow he maintained balance and disappeared into the night. The crowd waited for half a minute, listening intently, faces eager. But that was it—no crash. At last the people dispersed, chattering happily as they wandered off to find some other entertainment in Yanchi.

The desert had a way of sharpening scenes: everything stood out against this blurred background. One afternoon, driving through a desolate stretch of sand dunes along the border between Inner Mongolia and Ningxia Province, I saw a solitary figure walking beside the road. I pulled over and called out: "Where are you going?"

"Where are *you* going?" the man said.

Both questions were moot: this road had no turnoffs for forty miles. I asked if he wanted a ride, and he shrugged and got in. He was twenty-five years old, with a thin crooked mustache that crossed his lip like a calligrapher's mistake. He was dressed neatly, in a blue button-down shirt, and he said he lived in Yinchuan, the provincial capital. I asked if he had had some kind of trouble on the road.

"No," he said. "I come here every month, just to walk. There are three daily buses that follow this road. Nine thirty, twelve thirty, and two thirty. The early one drops me off and then I walk for a while. I usually catch one of the other two back to Yinchuan."

He had a strange, spasmodic way of speaking—words piled fast in jerky sentences, like he was trying to fill all the space that surrounded us. He wouldn't tell me his full name; all he said was that his family name was Zhen. But he answered at length when I asked why he came to the Tengger Desert.

"I used to be in the military," Zhen said. "I was a soldier in the 1990s, and I was stationed in Shaanxi, in the Qinling Mountains. Every day we were in the wilderness, and now sometimes I miss it. I don't know exactly how to say it, but that was a very happy time. It was difficult, of course, but there was honor and pride to the job. And it didn't have anything to do with me—everything was about the squadron. The group was more important than the person. That's what I really liked about it. We got to know each other and depend on each other, and eventually it's like your individual self isn't so significant anymore. That's why I come here every month. It's very empty in the desert and it reminds me of the way I used to feel."

Zhen told me frankly that he didn't like the United States—in particular he blamed the Americans for NATO's bombing of the Chinese embassy in Belgrade in 1999. After completing his military service, he had received a government-assigned job in a grain company in Yinchuan. He was single, and he intended to never marry.

"Part of it is money," he said. "If you don't have much money, it's hard to get married. But the main reason is that I believe people should be more united, and marriage has a way of breaking that up. Right now I have good friends and we get together to eat and drink and talk. It's a little like the times I remember in the military. But once you marry you can't do that anymore. You spend all your time with your family. That sense of togetherness is gone, and I don't want that to happen."

I asked if he had any hobbies apart from walking alone across the Tengger.

"I really like driving," he said. "That's my favorite thing to do. I can't wait to get my license."

He had nearly finished a driving course, and eventually he hoped to become a cabbie. If possible, he would buy his own car, but in the meantime he practiced with friends every chance he got. He asked me when I had learned to drive—it amazed him that I had started at sixteen, like many Americans. In China, the minimum driving age is eighteen, but the important issue is financial. By the time people are able to pay for a driving course, and consider buying a car, they're often already in their thirties.

"Is driving this Jeep much different from a Santana?" he asked.

"No," I said. "It's five speeds, basically the same. It's easy. If you can drive a Santana, you can drive this Jeep."

"I've never driven a Jeep before," he said. "That's something I'd really like to do." He was silent for a moment, watching the desert flash by. Somewhere to our left, the Great Wall was lost amid the dunes. Zhen said, "Would you let me drive a little bit?"

I pulled to the side of the road, got out, and walked around the front of the City Special. Zhen slid over and settled behind the steering wheel. He pointed at the pedals. "This is the gas, right?" he said. "And aren't those the brake and the clutch?" I had no idea why I let him drive; maybe it had something to do with the long desert days, the vacant roads and the landscapes that seemed unreal. I put on the safety belt. It was the first time I had ever sat in the passenger seat of the City Special.

He started the engine, ran it in neutral for a few seconds, and began to drive. He leaned forward, peering intently through the windshield, his knuckles white around the wheel. Whenever an oncoming car approached, he slowed dramatically. This happened five times in half an hour. Otherwise the road was vacant and it ran straight as an arrow; there was wasteland in all directions. After Zhen began to feel more comfortable, he accelerated to forty miles an hour, and a look of bliss appeared behind the miswritten mustache. There were no turns along the way, but he tried the blinkers, just to see how they worked. Right, left, right, left. He switched on the lights. He fiddled with the windshield wipers. He pressed the horn, twice, and the sound was swallowed by the empty road.

LATER THAT DAY, AFTER dropping off Zhen at a truck stop, I got Sinomapped onto sand. The Great Wall was still marked clearly on my atlas, a neat line of crenellations that ran westward across the desert, but roads in this region were sparse. I tried an anonymous capillary that ran to the north of the ruins; the surface was paved, but periodically it disappeared beneath wind-blown sand. Every once in a while I had to accelerate and slide through a bad patch, and finally the City Special hit a big dune and spun to a halt, wheels buried to the hubcaps. I tried unsuccessfully to dig it out, and I was about to release air from the tires to get more traction when a man showed up in a four-wheel-drive Jeep. He gave me a tow, and I turned back—it was hopeless to continue along this road.

The day was growing late, and I came to an unmarked intersection. There was nobody around to ask for directions, so I relied on the compass and just headed south. Thirty miles later the road passed a small memorial tablet. Sand had piled against the base, but the inscription was still clear:

AUGUST 1991
ALL OF THE FACTORY'S WORKERS WON'T FORGET YOU

There were no other details on this odd monument. What factory? Which workers? Who wasn't being forgotten? A few miles later I pulled off onto a dirt track, drove for a few minutes, and pitched my tent in the dunes. I enjoyed an Ordos dinner—Oreo cookies, Dove bars, and Gatorade. The sky was calm and I slept with the tent open, looking up at the Milky Way.

By that point in the journey I was accustomed to falling asleep without knowing where I was. In the morning I could usually figure it out, and I stocked plenty of water in case the City Special broke down. For the most part I had good cell phone coverage—the Chinese system consists of a handful of state-owned companies, and they've installed towers with amazing thoroughness. The government also controls the fuel industry, which means that even in remote areas you can find a gas station. I never came close to running out, and price controls kept gas cheap: in the spring of 2002, I paid the same amount all across China, the equivalent of $1.20 per gallon. There were no self-service stations. In over three thousand miles of driving across western China, from Inner Mongolia to the Tibetan plateau, the City Special's fuel cap was hardly touched by a man. Pumping gas was women's work, at least in the west, where stations were staffed by young girls who had recently left their home villages. Usually these migrants were in their teens, with brand-new uniforms, neat haircuts, and makeup—small-town sophisticates taking their first step on the road to success.

The gas-station girls were attentive, polite, and friendly, but they were hopeless when it came to directions. This was a common problem—I spent an enormous amount of time trying to find people who could give reliable information. Dialects were sometimes hard to understand, but the biggest problem was simply that few Chinese had traveled. Even fewer had driven. They knew little about roads, even around their homes, and they were terrible at explaining how to get someplace. It was best to structure any query as a yes/no proposition: "Is this the road to Zhongwei?" The absolute worst thing that a driver could do was open a map. It was like handing over a puzzle to a child—people's faces went from confusion to fascination as they turned the map this way and that, tracing lines across the page. One of the first things I learned on the road was to keep the Sinomaps out of sight while asking directions.

It wasn't surprising that rural people had little understanding of maps, but this was also true for educated Chinese. Even professional drivers with years of experience could be hopelessly confused by a simple atlas. Maps simply aren't part of modern culture, despite the fact that the Chinese have an impressive ancient history of cartography. The earliest known maps date to the second century BC; these documents are printed on silk and were excavated from tombs in Hunan Province. They are contemporary with the maps of ancient Greeks and Romans, and the Chinese diagrams are technically quite advanced. They were developed for use by military and government, and they are abstract, viewing landscapes as if from above. The sense of scale is remarkably good. They use consistent symbols for key features, and they show rivers getting progressively wider downstream—a critical detail for any army commander who needed to stage a troop crossing. By the third century AD, an official named Pei Xiu outlined many principles of surveying and mapmaking, and the Chinese had a good technical foundation for cartography.

These early Chinese maps were well drawn, but the fundamental approach was narrowly practical rather than scientific. In ancient Greece, cartography developed out of astronomy, as people applied principles from tracking the stars. This is how Western thinkers came up with the concepts of longitude and latitude, which were missing from ancient Chinese cartography. And over the centuries the Chinese began to ignore even Pei Xiu's guidelines, until maps became less analytical and more descriptive. They relied heavily on words rather than symbols. Landscapes were warped to emphasize whatever happened to be of prime interest. On Ming maps of the Great Wall, for example, huge towers loom atop steep cartoonish peaks, whereas the surroundings lack detail or scale. These diagrams represent a step backward from what the Chinese had been doing sixteen centuries earlier.

There are a number of reasons why cartography developed in this manner, and the most important factor was a lack of government interest in exploration and trade. Chinese emperors rarely encouraged expeditions, and officials traditionally disdained the merchant class. In contrast, the greatest advances in European and Arabic cartography were tied to trade. During the thirteenth century AD, the introduction of the compass—originally a Chinese invention—allowed merchants to create meticulously detailed charts of the Mediterranean. Two hundred years later, as the Portuguese tried to open southern trade routes, they mapped the coast of Africa with remarkable accuracy. This project depended on both government and private merchants—Portuguese princes coordinated the surveying efforts of traders, until finally they created a diagram of the African coastline.

But there weren't any equivalent breakthroughs in Chinese cartography, which developed out of very different motivations. In ancient China, maps served military needs, and the army had little incentive to create detailed diagrams of the interior and the coastline. Wars tended to be fought in the north and the west, in the regions of the Great Wall, where geography is vast and often featureless. For an army in such a landscape, specific points matter more than context, and Chinese maps usually focused on key passes or important forts. In the end, any map describes not only a region but also the key interests of the mapmakers themselves. During the same century that the Portuguese were trying to access the gold trade of East Africa, the Ming dynasty was protecting itself against northern nomads, and these very different goals created very different schematic views of the world.

In China, where maps developed primarily as tools of the government and military, there isn't a tradition of emphasizing their use by private individuals. Atlases play little role in Chinese education: open an elementary school geography textbook and you see mostly words. Students might be encouraged to write about their environment, but they never sketch it. Like many practical skills of the new economy, map reading hasn't yet become part of the curriculum, and people can spend years in school without learning how to handle an atlas. Often the first time they wrestle with one is when they start to drive. Even if a Chinese person is interested in highly detailed maps, he has trouble finding them, because the government is wary about such diagrams. There's still a tendency to associate any mapmaking with military interests, especially in the far west, where it's impossible to find good atlases of places such as Tibet and Xinjiang. Even in nonsensitive parts of China, topographic maps are classified and unavailable on the market. For my driving trip, I didn't bother to bring a GPS device. It would have been all but worthless without good maps, but my main concern was that such equipment might make me look like a foreigner engaged in surveying the remote west.

And so I relied on the Sinomaps, which were still the best thing available on the market. The state-owned company was founded in 1954, not long after the Communists came to power, and for decades Sinomaps continued to follow the traditional goal of serving the government and military. Their headquarters are located in downtown Beijing, near Tiananmen Square, and once I stopped by for a visit. The place had the feel of an old-school *danwei*, or work unit: badly lit hallways, big meeting rooms, lots of people wandering around without much obvious purpose. They currently had 480 employees, which must have been enough, because workers played Ping-Pong in the hallway throughout my meeting with the deputy editor in chief. His name was Xu Gencai; he greeted me warmly and an assistant served us tea. We sat side by side, teacups between us, like Mao and Nixon. Out in the hallway we were apparently missing a great game—I could hear the pitter-patter of the ball interrupted occasionally by muffled cheers.

Xu told me that China's pace of change represented Sinomaps' biggest challenge. They had to update Beijing city maps every three months, because of all the new construction, and the auto boom was creating a type of private market that had never existed. During the 1990s, Sinomaps published only five simple road maps for motorists; now they had more than twenty. Their target market was shifting away from government and military, but they still had an idiosyncratic notion of the private consumer. "We publish many maps of things that people need because of economic development," Xu said. He meant this literally—the company was attempting to map the things that Chinese people buy. "We publish a Restaurant Map, which shows all the places where you can eat in Beijing," Xu said. "And we make a Special Tourist Map, which shows not just the famous museums, but also places like Bar Street and Silk Alley."

I mentioned that the old Silk Alley, which had been a popular clothes market, had recently been demolished and moved to a new location.

"See what I mean?" Xu said. "Now we have to change that one, too!"

Proudly, he showed off other specialty maps. The Xiaodian Wuyu Amazing Shopping Map featured malls and stores. The School Map of Beijing identified every educational institution in the capital. The Chinese City Real Estate Map was designed for investors, and it listed estimated apartment prices in cities across the country. If you were looking for something that would go out of date quickly, the Chinese City Real Estate Map was a good bet. There was also a Medical Map of Beijing—a hypochondriac's dream, marking the locations of hundreds of hospitals, clinics, and pharmacies. It occurred to me that Sinomaps, which had spent so many years focused on government and military, still hadn't quite grasped the concept of creating an open-ended tool for the private individual. In their eyes, people need direction; it's not enough to give them the best possible Beijing atlas and let them figure out for themselves whether they want to find a restaurant, or a pharmacy, or a six-month-old real estate price. At the end of our conversation, after sitting side by side for an hour, Xu and I rose simultaneously and shook hands, as if marking the end of our diplomatic summit. He wished me good luck on my travels; he told me to come back any time. Out in the hallway, that Ping-Pong ball was still zinging when I left.

FROM THE TENGGER DESERT I drove west into Gansu Province. The road was unnamed, too small to qualify as a national highway, but recently it had been paved as part of the government's infrastructure project. Truckers were already using the route, and billboards lined the way: "The Road Police Patrol Wishes You a Safe Journey"; "The Silk Road's New Face: The Road Patrol Protects Safety." But there still weren't any law officials to be seen, and it was just another version of the terra-cotta cop strategy—policework by allusion. Outside the village of Hongshui, a truck had broken down beside the road. Three men stood beside the vehicle, petting the invisible dog with an unusual degree of urgency. Cars and trucks flashed by, just like the question on the driving exam:

344. If you see an accident and the people need help, you should

    a) continue driving.
    b) stop, do what you can to help, and contact the police.
    c) stop, see if the people offer a reward, and then help.

I pulled over and the truckers told me that their oil pump had failed. It was a big Liberation truck, the model known as Ju Neng Wang: "The All-Powerful King." They had been petting the dog for an hour and a half before I stopped. They asked if I could give one man a ride to Anyuan, the nearest town with a train station, and I agreed. They put the old oil pump in a burlap sack and dropped it in the back of the City Special.

The trucker was named Li Changjie, and he was a southerner, a native of a village in Jiangsu Province. His wife still farmed, but he had left the land to do business. He was short, gaunt, and quick-eyed—he had the hungry look that you often saw among former peasants who had succeeded in the new economy. Li first started trucking in 1993, when he bought a secondhand vehicle with loans from relatives; over time he had steadily improved his rigs. Last year he had purchased the All-Powerful King for thirty-two thousand dollars. In China, that's a huge amount of money, and Li was furious about the oil pump.

"I checked and nobody has it stocked in this entire province," he said. "I have to go all the way back to Xuzhou to get a replacement. I can't find a reliable way to get one sent here fast, so I have to go myself. It's a two-day train trip to Xuzhou, and then two days back. You're a writer—you know what you should write about? You should write about Liberation trucks and how hard it is to get parts for them. It's ridiculous. Something else you should write about is the low quality of Chinese products. Everything made in this country breaks."

I always liked talking to Chinese truckers, who are among the purest entrepreneurs in the country. They generally own their rigs, often in partnership; usually they travel in pairs, so one can drive while the other sleeps. Of all the professional drivers in China, they're the most skilled.

Cabbies are too aggressive, because stakes are low: city traffic moves slowly and nobody cares much about dents. And long-distance bus drivers are the worst. They never own the buses, and their pay depends on a percentage of ticket sales. This gives them incentive to speed, especially in a country where the highway patrol consists of signs and statues. Whenever I read about a terrible accident, it usually involves a long-distance bus.

But truckers rarely make me nervous. Most are too overloaded to drive fast, and they don't take risks, because they own their vehicles. They tend to follow set routes where they know the roads, and they're smart about adjusting for bad weather. They're interesting to talk to. I once spent a night at a truck stop in Shandong Province, on the east coast, asking drivers about what they carried. Two men had a truck full of bamboo whisk brooms; they had just dropped off a shipment of nonferrous metal. Another pair had unloaded color televisions and picked up processed wheat. Others had gone from chemical materials to radiators, from tennis shoes to dynamos. They were the alchemists of the new economy, at the center of every mysterious exchange that occurs along the Chinese road system. One truck had just dropped off computerized mah-jongg sets and picked up elementary school textbooks; somebody else had carried leather loafers one way and recycled plastic the other.

During that same trip, on an expressway near the city of Tianjin, I drove in the wake of a truck that just had come unlatched. It carried foreign paper imported to China for recycling, and after the door opened the printed materials were strewn across the highway. Hundreds of pamphlets flapped low to the road like dying birds; I pulled over and caught one. It was in English: a fourteen-page mortgage application from a financial services company called Woolwich, which was located in Dartford, Kent. When I contacted Woolwich, they didn't have the faintest idea how a flock of mortgage forms ended up on a Tianjin highway. But that's true for almost any product you buy in the developed world: it's probably already spent time on a Chinese road, and someday it may return there to be recycled.

In Gansu Province, Driver Li's All-Powerful King had failed while carrying raw cotton. His standard route ran from Xinjiang to Jiangsu, a distance of over two thousand miles. In the northwest he followed the route known as the Silk Road, passing through the Hexi Corridor of Gansu and the oasis towns of central Xinjiang. Usually he carried cotton east, dropped it off in a factory town, and picked up finished clothing—that was his particular alchemy. "They're cheap clothes," he said. "The kind that are exported to poor countries in Central Asia." He earned more than six thousand dollars a year, an excellent income in China, and currently he traveled with two other drivers, one of whom was an apprentice. The others would spend the next four days sitting atop the All-Powerful King, waiting for Driver Li to return. Apart from police fines, theft is a trucker's biggest concern. "People jump onto the back and steal whatever you're carrying, sometimes even when you're moving," he said. "The worst place is Henan Province. In Henan if there's a thief and you call the police, they won't even bother to come. I hate driving through Henan."

At the Anyuan train station, I dropped off Driver Li and his fuel pump, which had leaked oil all over the floor of the City Special. He apologized profusely; I channeled Mr. Wang at Capital Motors and said, "*Mei wenti!*"—No problem! After that I continued into the Hexi Corridor. This narrow stretch of Gansu is bordered by harsh terrain: desert to the east, mountains to the west. But the heart of the corridor is fertile enough to be inhabited, because of the snowmelt of the western peaks, and in ancient times it represented a natural trade route. Caravans coursed throughout the region; some of the goods that passed this way eventually reached the Middle East and Europe. In the nineteenth century, Western geographers and historians began to refer to this series of trade routes as the Silk Road. In fact it consisted of dozens of braided routes, connecting many destinations and carrying many types of products, but the term stuck. It's similar to the Great Wall: a foreign simplification that appeals to the imagination, like a branding of history. And in the same way that the Great Wall became *Changcheng*, the foreign notion of the Silk Road eventually returned to China, until now it's a term that any Chinese recognizes: *Sichouzhilu*.

In Gansu these two ideas intersect along Highway 312. The modern road follows the heart of the corridor, and driving northwest I began to see stretches of Ming wall off to the right. They were barriers of tamped earth, as tall as a man and running unbroken for miles; occasionally a village was nestled within the ramparts. At one point I turned off the highway and followed a dirt road for a couple of miles, until it ended at a place called Xiakou. The village had been built just within the wall, and locals still made good use of it. Rows of sheep pens lined one stretch of fortifications, the animals pawing at the Ming relic. On the outskirts of town, homes without running water had dug their outhouses straight into the barrier. So much for the glorious idea of the Great Wall: in Xiakou it smelled like shit.

In ancient times this place had been a military outpost, and the administrative region is still called "Old Soldiers' Township." At one time it served to protect the caravans that passed this way. "Even when I was a boy, camel trains were still coming through," an old man told me. "I can remember them. They were going to Xinjiang." His companion nodded. "One trader would have ten or more camels, all of them loaded down," the other man said. "There were Chinese and also Uighurs, although it was mostly Chinese. After Liberation the camels didn't come through as much. They started using trucks about then."

A half dozen men sat in the sunshine, smoking Golden City cigarettes at the foot of an ancient tower. At one time this building must have been beautiful: it stood two stories tall, and each level had a four-cornered roof and painted eaves. Graceful calligraphy spelled out a message along the top, "With Power Control the Heaven and the Earth." It marked the town's central intersection, where camel trains used to pass. Nowadays, when the weather was good, old folks liked to gather at the tower, but it had fallen into disrepair. The paint was cracked and holes had rotted in the wooden roof; bricks from the base had been cannibalized for local construction. The old men said that two massive iron lions once decorated the entrance, but they were melted down for scrap during a Mao Zedong campaign for increased industrial production. Iron bells had been salvaged during the Cultural Revolution. "The bells used to ring whenever the wind blew," one man remembered. "There were eight of them. They hung on the corners—four on the first level, and four more on the second level."

They talked about other buildings that had disappeared, remembering the names and the locations around Xiakou. Most were temples from the days when religion was still common, and they had been torn down during the anti-superstition campaigns of the Cultural Revolution. "People used to go the Temple of the Goddess of Fertility if they wanted to have children," one man said. "Old people would go to the temple called the Three Highest Manifestations of the Dao. The God of Literature Temple was where scholars went before taking the imperial examinations. Farmers went to the Dragon King Temple if they wanted rain."

Nowadays these places were nothing but remembered names. Even the crossroads at the ruined tower had become meaningless, because the modern Silk Road had shifted away from Xiakou. The new Highway 312 had been built two miles to the west, which represented the final blow for the town, because travelers no longer stopped here. The population had dwindled to four hundred, less than half of what it was at the beginning of the Reform period. Everybody said young people left as soon as they finished middle school. That was the last building in town that seemed to be well kept—when I asked where I could stay for the night, people immediately directed me to the school.

The day had grown too cold and windy for camping, and there wasn't enough time to drive to the next town before dark. At the Xiakou school, teachers welcomed me warmly; they said that occasionally a visitor spent the night after seeing the local ruins of the Great Wall. The teachers pulled out a cot, and I slept in the fourth-grade classroom. Like most rural Chinese schools, it was neat but sparsely decorated, and the bare surroundings made it feel like a traveler's quarters. I was just passing through, and so were the students; eventually the new Silk Road would take almost all of them away. The walls were decorated with quotes from the former premier Zhou Enlai, Karl Marx, and the revolutionary general Zhu De—inspirational words for children destined to make their way to the factory towns of the south:

STUDY HARD SO CHINA CAN RISE UP

A MAN WITH KNOWLEDGE TURNS INTO
THREE HEADS AND SIX ARMS

MEN AND MACHINES ARE THE SAME:
IF THEY KEEP MOVING, THEY DON'T RUST

IN THIS PART OF Gansu, the Sinomaps bristled with military names: Dragon's Head Fort, Old Soldiers' Stockade, Plentiful Fort. West of Xiakou, a string of places had been named after horses: Horseshoe Temple, Big Horse Camp, Military Horse Camp One, Military Horse Camp Two, Military Horse Camp Three. All of them were located within striking range of the Great Wall, on the nearby slope of the Tibetan Plateau, and I decided to detour in that direction.

Xiakou was dry and dusty, like most places that lay on the eastern edge of the Hexi Corridor. That was the desert side, but as I drove west the landscape changed. I started at an elevation of seven thousand feet, in near-barren scrubland, and in the span of an hour I climbed to a lush plateau that was almost two miles high. These regions benefited from snowmelt; in the distance I could see the white-capped peaks of the Himalayas. And all at once the desert drabness gave way to brilliant color: the hard blue of the springtime sky, the deep green of the grasslands. Animals grazed in open pastures, and streams ran fast beside the fields. It was ranchland—as wide and welcoming as the high plains of Montana.

At Military Horse Camp One, cowboys were herding hundreds of animals into a pen. The horses were low-shouldered and stocky, with powerful legs; their hooves thundered as they charged in front of the men. The cowboys wore Chinese military uniforms: short-brimmed caps, camouflaged jackets, fatigues, big military boots. When I got out of the City Special, one man on horseback trotted over, dismounted smartly, and introduced himself with an army title—Squad Leader Wang Jiayi.

"This breed is known as the Shandan horse," he said, when I asked about it. "They aren't tall or fast, but they're known for endurance. They're good at pulling things."

Shandan is a nearby town, and Squad Leader Wang said that locals first started raising horses for the Chinese military during the Han dynasty, over two thousand years ago. Back then, the empire's main adversary was the Xiongnu, a nomadic people who terrorized the Chinese for generations. The only way to effectively fight this enemy was on horseback, and the empire set up breeding grounds in this part of the Hexi Corridor. In the old days, they called the region the Imperial Horse Camp, and over the centuries this tradition had survived. The Communists renamed the camps, giving each of them a number, but they still bred the Shandan horse, and the animal remained useful in the rugged lands of the west. Out in Xinjiang, China's remote national borders are still patrolled on horseback. Locals told me that during the 1980s, when the Chinese aided the Taliban in their war against the Soviet Union, they sent large numbers of Shandan horses to Afghanistan.

But even a remote place like this wasn't immune to the changes of the Reform period. The name remained Military Horse Camp Number One, and they still cared for over two thousand animals, but Squad Leader Wang told me they were in the process of privatizing. "We're not technically under the army anymore," he said. "The military stopped requesting horses from us a couple of years ago; they have enough for the time being. We sell to other companies now, especially ones that do tourism. And some of our leaders say that we're going to start doing tourism, too."

That seemed the most likely future for Military Horse Camp Number One—someday it would be a dude ranch for urban Chinese. In the meantime, the place still had a military feel; everybody wore uniforms and there was little sign of civilian life. When I stopped at the headquarters, the director became extremely nervous and asked to see my passport and journalist accreditation. But he didn't seem to know what to do after that, and he let me drive away in the City Special.

In recent weeks, as I approached the far west, I had sensed that local authorities were becoming more alert about foreigners. At one tollbooth I had been stopped by a cop, who inspected the City Special thoroughly—he even opened the hood and jotted down the serial number. He never said why he was concerned, but I knew that there were some military installations in the region. And ethnic tensions could have been a factor, as Gansu is home to large Tibetan communities.

I knew it was best to keep moving, and after visiting Military Horse Camp Number One, I decided to get out of the county, in case the police had been alerted. I drove north until almost midnight, when I finally arrived at a small place called Gaotai. The settlement had sprung up along Highway 312, a strip of auto repair shops, cheap restaurants, and truckers' dorms. At one of the low-end places I found a bed for two dollars a night. They didn't have the police registration forms; all I had to do was hand over the cash. The room contained four beds, a window that overlooked the highway, and a poster of a Dutch windmill.

A pair of Sichuanese truckers already occupied two other beds. The men came from Neijiang, a town I knew from my days in the Peace Corps, and their Liberation truck carried a load of children's clothes to be exported to Kazakhstan. They had stopped to make repairs on their vehicle—another All-Powerful King humbled in Gansu Province. The truckers became excited when I showed up.

"Did you come to see the other foreigner?" one of them said.

"What other foreigner?"

"The Russian woman."

"I don't know any Russians," I said. "I'm American."

"Oh, I thought you knew her. She works upstairs."

"What does she do upstairs?"

His companion laughed and said, "She's a prostitute!"

Oh God, I said to myself. If there was anything more depressing than a four-bed room in a Gansu truckers' dorm, it was the knowledge that a Russian woman was turning tricks upstairs.

"Do you want to go see her?" the man said.

"No," I said. "I'm tired. I just drove for five hours without stopping."

"Come on, let's go! She's a foreigner, too. You guys can talk!"

I'm sure she had a story—probably some terrifying post-Soviet version of *Sister Carrie* that began in Vladivostok and ended in the Hexi Corridor. But I couldn't bring myself to hear it, or gawk at the woman; and finally the Sichuanese truckers gave up. Sometimes all you want from a two-dollar bed is a little sleep.

◈   ◈   ◈

I RAN OUT OF Gatorade in Gansu Province. I had finished the last Dove bar in Ningxia, and all my Coke was long gone; in these small towns you couldn't find such foreign products. I restocked my soda supply with syrupy Feichang Cola, whose slogan—"China's Own Cola!"—was both boast and warning. For weeks I had buzzed westward on a cloud of sugar and caffeine, but here in the Hexi Corridor the fatigue brought me back to earth. Mornings were ragged; at night I fought to keep my eyes open. I was filthy—even the most thorough hair washing didn't seem to take anymore. The City Special's starter had been replaced; the interior was full of sand; there was a huge stain on the carpet from the All-Powerful King's oil pump. I couldn't blame hitchers for keeping their backs off the seat—the car was becoming a wreck.

The Great Wall was still there, right outside the window, and it still looked stunning. The farther I drove, the more the structures impressed me, as much for their beauty as for their persistence. They had a remarkable chameleon quality—the walls always followed the lines of the landscape, clinging atop ridges, and they even acquired the earth's color, because of age and the use of local building materials. In Hebei the structures had been steep and jagged, like local mountains, and sometimes on a hill you could hardly distinguish between native rock and Ming brick. On the loess plateau, where mountains fell away into terraced gullies, the Great Wall forts were as angular as the rest of the broken landscape. On the edge of the Ordos the barriers looked like piled sand. Here in the Hexi Corridor the Ming wall sprawled pale in the sunshine like a springtime snake. If its construction had originally damaged the environment, the passage of centuries had blunted that edge, until now it looked almost natural. It was amazing that people once believed the Great Wall was visible from the moon—I had never seen another man-made object that fit so subtly within its natural surroundings. There were places where you could stand atop the thing and not even know it.

The Great Wall's meaning is also chameleon-like, and interpretations have a way of shifting across time and perspective. Early in the twentieth century, the revolutionary and nationalist Sun Yat-sen celebrated it as the greatest engineering feat in Chinese history. Mao portrayed it as a forerunner of modern national defense. For Lu Xun, the great author of the 1920s and 1930s, the wall represented everything bad about Chinese culture. He described it as "a wonder and a curse," writing, "I have always felt hemmed in on all sides by the Great Wall; that wall of ancient bricks which is constantly being reinforced. The old and the new conspire to confine us all." When the Japanese occupied the north during World War II, the invaders photographed their soldiers beside the wall, in an attempt to gain credibility for their territorial claim. Jorge Luis Borges wrote a story about the Great Wall, as did Franz Kafka. To foreign writers, it usually represents xenophobia, whereas Chinese see it as evidence of cultural greatness. The government-run journal *China Today* even portrayed it as a symbol of multiethnic unity—"more like a river than a barrier." The significance of the Great Wall is so fluid that it can mean virtually anything, even cooperation between Chinese and Mongols.

In academia, historians have generally described the structure as a defensive failure. The American scholar Arthur Waldron studied certain periods of Ming construction, and in his book he concludes that it was "useless militarily even when it was first built." But his research was limited to specific periods and wall locations, and no other university scholar has pursued the history in real depth. Nowadays the most significant research on the Great Wall is being conducted by people outside of academia. Their backgrounds range widely, from village historians like Old Chen, the farmer I met in Shanxi, to foreigners with graduate degrees, but often they share certain characteristics. Usually they are male, and they tend to be athletic. Traditionally that's a rare quality among the Chinese intelligentsia, but it's necessary for anybody planning to explore wall regions. The Great Wall also attracts obsessives. Independent researchers have to be tenacious hikers, and they also must be resourceful enough to support their own study. In that sense, it's the perfect historical topic for the new economy. Ignored by the government and neglected by academia, the field of Great Wall studies depends entirely on private individuals: history as free market.

Nearly all of them eventually find their way to Beijing. In 1984, a utility line worker named Dong Yaohui quit his job and, along with two companions, spent sixteen months doggedly following wall sections on foot all the way across China. After writing a book about the experience, he moved to the capital, where he enrolled in courses in classical Chinese. Eventually he helped found the Great Wall Society of China, which now publishes two journals and advocates preservation. Another self-made expert is Cheng Dalin, who was originally educated at a sports academy. After graduating, he became a photographer, and his news agency frequently sent him to the wall because he was strong enough to climb the structure. On his own, he studied Ming history, finally publishing eight books that combine photographs and research. William Lindesay, a British geologist and marathoner, came to China on a whim in 1986 and spent nine months running and hiking along the walls all the way from Gansu to the ocean. He eventually settled in Beijing, published four wall-related books, and founded International Friends of the Great Wall, an organization that focuses on conservation.

At Peking University, China's most famous institution, the top Great Wall researcher is a cop named Hong Feng. As a child, Hong also attended a sports school—he was a sprinter and a long jumper—but he always enjoyed reading history. After barely missing the cutoff for college admission, he became a policeman, eventually getting assigned to the unit at Peking University. In his spare time he studies Ming texts in the library and hikes to remote wall sections. He publishes articles on a Web site devoted to wall enthusiasts, and he's made some significant discoveries. (For example, Hong found Ming texts that explained how ideas about feng shui influenced wall construction outside of Beijing.) When I met Hong, he told me that despite working at Peking University, he had never discussed his research with a professor. "Scholars in the archaeology and history departments just aren't interested in the Great Wall," he said.

The most thorough researcher of all is David Spindler. Like the others, he's athletic—at Dartmouth he rowed varsity crew and was on the cross-country ski team. In 1990, he came to China in order to study for a master's degree in history at Peking University, where he wrote a thesis in Chinese about a philosopher in the Western Han dynasty. Afterward, Spindler decided against pursuing a career in academia; he attended Harvard Law School and became a China-based consultant. For years he hiked the Great Wall as a hobby, and soon after leaving his job, he decided to devote himself to full-time research. His goals are ambitious: he plans to hike every section of Ming wall in the Beijing region, and to read everything about the defenseworks that was published during that dynasty. He funds his research entirely on his own, through lectures and guided tours of the wall.

Unlike other foreign scholars, Spindler has found evidence that the Ming Great Wall actually worked as a defensive structure. One such incident occurred in 1555, when thousands of Mongols attacked at Shuitou, a village northwest of Beijing. The Ming had recently improved the Shuitou walls, which held firm, turning back the raiders. Throughout the years, there were many other such instances of successful defense. In one account from the late sixteenth century, a Chinese officer describes the aftermath of a victory:

> On the day when we stuck the severed heads of the barbarians on poles, there was a soldier named Zhan Yu who cut off a piece of barbarian flesh, walked over to his comrades, and said, "Anyone who raids us deserves this fate." There was another soldier named Zhao Pian who cut off two pieces of flesh from the neck of a dead raider and ate them raw, telling his comrades, "I hate anyone who harasses our civilians and causes trouble for us soldiers and will eat their flesh!" As their commander, I was pleased to have such brave and loyal soldiers.

Nobody in the world knows the Ming Great Wall as thoroughly as Spindler, and once I asked him what the structures say about China. "When I give lectures, people always ask me that," he said. "What does this say about China, that China built these walls? My answer is basically: Nothing. It's very disappointing to them. But it's just one manifestation of what China has done. It's just a way they defended themselves."

Spindler hates any symbolic use of the Great Wall. In his view, it's become such an easy metaphor that people are more inclined to interpret than they are to research. And he believes that it's unfair to take such a specific structure and use it to explain something as complex as Chinese civilization. "The way I look at it, this was a boundary that was often attacked," he said. "They had to have some kind of border-defense system. And it was combined with diplomacy, with trade, with raids into Mongol territory."

For the Ming, walls were simply one part of a complex, multipronged strategy, but nowadays it's easy to take the fortifications out of context. They are still impressive, and any tourist can take a walk along the ramparts, whereas the Ming archives, and their details about other aspects of foreign policy, are much more difficult to access and understand.

Spindler continued: "People say, Was it worth it? But I don't think that's how they thought at the time. You don't get a nation-state saying, 'We're going to give up this terrain' or 'We're going to sacrifice x number of citizens and soldiers.' That's not a calculus they used. An empire is always going to try to protect itself."

I FOLLOWED THE MING walls northwest to Jiayuguan, the fort at the end of the Hexi Corridor, and then I drove to Dunhuang. The town is famous for the Buddhist art of its caves, and for the massive sand dunes that stand nearby. But I kept driving—after so much time on the road I couldn't bear to linger at tourist sites. I was heading to a place called Subei when the police stopped me at a checkpoint. The roadblock had been set up at a desolate intersection, not far from the border of Qinghai Province.

"License," an officer said sternly, and then he looked inside. "*Waah!* Where did you come from?"

"Beijing," I said.

"You're not from Beijing!"

"I'm American, but I live in Beijing."

"Look at this!" he called to the other officers, grinning. "This guy's a foreigner!"

Three of them huddled around the City Special. They seemed barely more than children—skinny guys in their twenties dressed in oversize uniforms. The first cop studied my document and exclaimed, "It looks just like a Chinese license!"

"It *is* a Chinese license," I said. "I couldn't drive here if I only had an American license."

"Do you have your American license?"

I handed it over, and the cops passed it around—undoubtedly the first time that a Missouri driver's license had ever been inspected in Gansu Province. "So why are you here?" one officer said.

"I'm just driving around. Tourism."

"How did you learn Chinese?"

"I've lived here for years."

"You must be a spy!" he said. The others picked up the refrain, laughing. "He's a spy! He's driving around, he speaks Chinese—he must be a spy! A spy! A spy!"

Shaking with laughter, the cop returned both my licenses. It took me a while to find my voice. "Is it OK if I continue?" I said.

"Of course!"

Driving away, looking through the rearview mirror, I could see them roughhousing on the side of the road. The cops punched each other and laughed, "A spy! A spy!"

IT TOOK MORE THAN an hour to reach Subei. There was nothing along the way but white herdsman tents, home to Mongol and Kazakh nomads, and the town itself was a low line of buildings that ran across a dry valley. I stopped at a public toilet; when I exited, a man was waiting for me. He said one word: "Identification."

He was short, dark-skinned, and wore a sparse mustache—ethnic Mongolian, I guessed. His request took me by surprise, and when I hesitated he flashed a badge: Public Security. He inspected my passport and put it in his pocket. "This district isn't open to foreigners," he said.

"I'm sorry, I didn't know," I said. "Nobody told me that."

"It doesn't matter whether somebody tells you. It's not open."

"I'm just traveling," I said. "I'll be happy to leave right now. I don't want to cause any problem."

"You've already caused a problem," he said. "We have to go to the station now."

We left the City Special parked beside the road. I had a sinking feeling that the car would be impounded—I knew this had happened to other foreigners who had driven illegally into restricted areas. But there's never any way to predict the outcome of a Chinese detention, which depends entirely on the place and the people you happen to be dealing with.

At the station a woman officer was waiting, and they seated me behind a desk. The male cop mentioned that recently they had detained another foreigner. "He came here on a bus," he said.

"What happened to him?" I asked.

"He was punished according to law."

"How was he punished?"

The cop ignored the question. The two of them rooted through file cabinets, pulling out papers; they moved efficiently, like this was a familiar routine. I decided to make one last play for leniency. "There were policemen at the highway turnoff," I said. "They checked all my documents. They didn't tell me Subei was closed, and they said it's fine to come here."

"Of course they did!" the Mongolian cop retorted. "What do those guys know about anything? They're just road police! They're worthless!"

It was hard to argue with that. The police began the interrogation: the Mongolian cop asked questions, and the woman wrote. Where did you come from today? Is this your correct passport? Residence card? Is this your current address in Beijing? How long have you lived there? What's your education level? Do you have a receipt for renting the car? How much was it? Where is the rental company? Where did you stay last night? How much did it cost? Did you register? What's the name of your work unit? Is this the correct way to write it? Do you have a doctorate?

For some reason they kept returning to my education level. It baffled me—what exactly was the link between degree status and wandering into a closed town on the edge of the Tibetan plateau? But then it dawned on me that they were simply filling out forms. There were dozens of blanks, and many of them overlapped; sometimes I answered the same question three times. The queries were so specific and detailed that they essentially prevented effective interrogation. Neither officer seemed the least bit suspicious, and they never asked any open-ended questions, like where I planned to go or what I was doing so far from home. They didn't so much as glance at the City Special. It was strictly a matter of paperwork, and afterward they sat back, looking relieved.

"You've broken our national law regarding aliens in China," the female cop announced. She pulled out a rule book and pointed to number forty-six. "We have to punish you."

"What's the punishment?"

"You will be fined," the male cop said, and both of them suddenly grinned. It was a certain Chinese smile that masks embarrassment, and I found myself grinning, too.

"By law, we can fine you five hundred," she said. "But since this is your first time, we'll only fine you one hundred."

It was the equivalent of twelve dollars. "Thanks," I said, and put the money on the table. The moment they saw the bill they became nervous, and neither would touch it. "I'm going to have to call our supervisor," the female cop said, and she left the room. A few minutes later she returned: "We can't take cash."

"Why not?"

"Because of corruption. If it's cash, there's no proof of the amount. So you're going to have to mail it."

Periodically, anticorruption campaigns sweep through the Communist Party; invariably they fail to make much difference. But in this forgotten part of Gansu the cops were taking it seriously. The woman escorted me outside, and we crossed the street to the Agricultural Bank of China. It was Sunday, so she contacted a manager, who opened the place especially for us. I filled out a form with the address of the police station, wrote the woman's name, and handed over the money. The bank manager said, "It'll arrive by Tuesday." He seemed pleased by the efficiency—it would take only two days for the money to reach the woman who stood immediately beside me. She was happy too; on the street she shook my hand and wished me a good journey. I started the City Special, turned around, and drove back to the checkpoint. The road cops were still there, goofing around in their baggy uniforms, and they shouted happily when I cruised past.

FOR FORTY MILES I followed a small road into the Gobi. This was the blankest Sinomap yet: only ten place-names marked the page. One was Yumenguan, the Jade Gate, a military structure that had been built by the Han dynasty, and that was where the pavement ended.

A rough dirt track continued farther into the desert. I was off the map now, in unmarked territory; the City Special bounced over low rocky hills. After ten miles the track terminated at the ruins of Hecangcheng. It's an ancient fortified granary, built over two thousand years ago to serve the Han soldiers who were stationed here. In this part of the desert, on the western edge of the empire, the Chinese had constructed forts instead of a wall. The land is so flat and barren that I could see the next one in the distance, three miles away. I had reached the end of the line—the stream of continuous walls had given way to scattered forts, like final drops from a spigot that had been shut off.

There was nobody else at Hecangcheng. The government planned to build a paved road to the site, but the modern construction had yet to begin and the place remained isolated. The old granary was massive, more than two hundred feet long, with ten-foot walls that rose stark above the scrubland. There were pillars of tamped earth, and gaping holes that showed the sky; in the mud walls I could see the matted straw that had been used for construction. This part of Gansu is so dry that the straw still looked fresh; in truth it had been here for more than twenty centuries. This granary, like all the forts in the region, was surveyed in the early 1900s by Aurel Stein, the great Hungarian-British explorer and archaeologist. He made two trips here, spending months with camel trains in the desert. On his second journey he literally retraced his steps. At one point he stumbled upon two sets of tracks, the prints of a man accompanied by a dog, and he realized they were his own—seven years earlier he had wandered here with his faithful dog Dash II. He wrote,

"Time seems to have lost all power of destruction on this ever-dry ground which knows no drift sand nor erosion."

I pitched my tent in the shadow of the fort. A small stream ran in the distance, surrounded by marshland, like a thin ribbon of green tied taut across this parched landscape. The sky was restless—fugitive clouds scattering across a dome of blue. At midnight the gusting wind shook me awake. It hummed across the Gobi, and whistled through the ruins, and I lay there listening to the same song that stirred soldiers in the days of the Han.

AFTER HECANGCHENG I TURNED for home. Highway 215 heads south out of Gansu, and I followed the road to the border of Qinghai Province. At the boundary, a pass stood at an elevation of twelve thousand feet, and after that I was in the high country of the Tibetan Plateau. There were no more forts, no more signal towers, no more Great Wall—all of it had been left behind.

The road was newly built. It consisted of two lanes, surrounded by high desert landscapes of rock and dirt, and periodically the monotony was broken by a sign: "Danger! On This Slope It's Easy to Fall Asleep!" At one location the government had suspended a small sedan above the highway. It was smashed almost beyond recognition; the front end was crumpled flat and the remains of a door dangled in strips of steel. Painted across the back end were the words: "Four People Died." The whole thing had been erected on spindly poles, fifteen feet off the ground, like some gruesome version of a children's treat: a Carsicle.

At the next bend in the road, a sign noted that fifty-three people had died here. A billboard presented the speed limit like options on a menu:

40 KM/HR IS THE SAFEST
80 KM/HR IS DANGEROUS
100 KM/HR IS BOUND FOR THE HOSPITAL

Along that road I saw two truckers who had broken down. Both stood beside All-Powerful Kings, waiting for their partners to return, and both refused a ride. One trucker had already been there for two days. He asked if I had any food or water, and I gave him two bottles and the last Oreos from my stash. Other than that the road was empty. To the west, snow-covered peaks rose to over eighteen thousand feet.

For one hundred and fifty miles I saw almost no signs of human habitation. There weren't any gas stations or shops; the landscape was so barren that nobody had bothered to carve propaganda into the mountains. The first town I passed had been recently razed. It had the look of a former military installation; the buildings were arranged in neat rows, and at one point there must have been a couple hundred people living there. But now it was abandoned—roofless walls stood stark on the plateau, lonely as the traces of some lost empire. Not far beyond that, a pair of empty dirt roads branched off the highway. One headed east, the other west; a signpost gave the names of military-sounding destinations. A left turn led to a place called "Build." A right turn went to "Unite." I took a deep breath and drove straight through.

BOOK II

THE VILLAGE

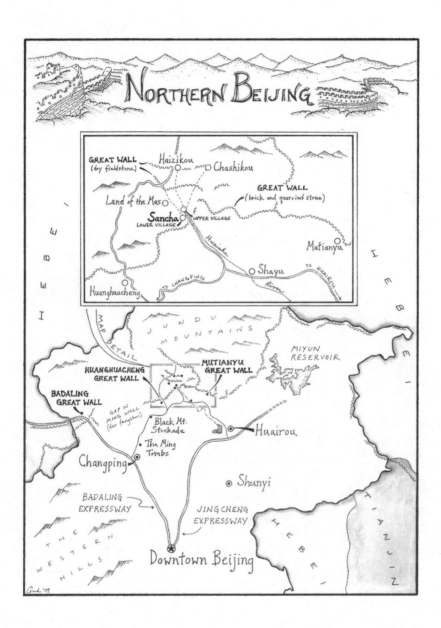

I

———

THE YEAR THAT I RECEIVED MY DRIVER'S LICENSE, I BEGAN
searching for a second home in the countryside north of Beijing. Empty
houses weren't hard to find—occasionally I came across whole villages
that had been abandoned. They were scattered across the front range of
the Jundu Mountains, in the shadow of the Great Wall, where the farming had always been tough and the lure of migration was all but irresist-
ible. Sometimes it felt as though people had left in a rush. Millstones
lay toppled over; trash was strewn across dirt floors; house frames stood
with the numb silence of tombstones. Mud walls had already begun to
crumble—these buildings were even more broken-down than the Ming
fortifications. Whenever I saw an empty village, I thought: Too late.

I hoped to find a place where people still farmed, their lives tuned
to the rhythms of the fields. I had a vague idea of a writer's retreat—
somewhere I could escape the city and work in silence. For a while I
searched near the Hebei border, on the far side of the Miyun reservoir,
where the roads were still dirt and most vehicles were two-stroke tractors. Sometimes I traveled by car, sometimes by foot; I carried my tent
and sleeping bag. I used the Sinomaps to track roads that ran alongside
the crenellated symbol of the Great Wall.

One day in early spring of 2002, I went for a drive with Mimi Kuo-
Deemer, an American friend who was also looking for a place in the
countryside. We passed through Huairou, a small city at the northern
edge of the Beijing plain, and then we entered the foothills of the Jundu
Mountains. On a rural road we picked up a hitchhiker. The old man

wore an army surplus jacket, and he was headed home from market. He didn't hesitate when we asked what was the most beautiful stretch of wall in these parts.

"Tianhua Cave," he said. "That's where you should go."

The region had been named after a fissure in the limestone cliffs. Locals had turned it into a shrine—there were two statues of Buddha, a quiver of burned-out incense, and a plate of rotting fruit offerings. Above the cave, a section of the Great Wall led to a massive tower atop the ridgeline's highest peak. This was the first row of mountains north of Beijing, rising more than three thousand feet above the plains, and the view from the tower was stunning: the mist-covered fields on one side, the blue-gray peaks on the other. But it was a tiny cluster of buildings to the northwest that caught our eyes. They perched high on a hillside, in complete isolation—there were no other settlements for miles.

We climbed down from the wall, got back in the car, and found the village at the end of a dirt road. The place was called Sancha, and within an hour some locals had shown us two empty houses; by the end of that month we had signed a lease for one of them. The home had three rooms, a wood-fired *kang*, and mud walls that had been papered with old copies of the *People's Daily*. There was an outhouse nearby. We had electricity and a phone line; water came straight from a spring in the mountains. Rent was three hundred and sixty yuan a month—for each of us, a twenty-dollar time-share. From the front door, where a broad dirt platform had been laid out for threshing crops, I could see the Great Wall. The brick towers rose from the valley floor, snaked their way along the folded peaks, and disappeared over the western horizon—headed toward the loess plateau, the Ordos Desert, the Hexi Corridor. In the past, a glimpse of the Great Wall had always made me think about traveling, but when I saw it from Sancha I said to myself: This is where I'll stay.

SANCHA HAD ALWAYS BEEN a small village, and in recent years it had become even smaller. In the 1970s the population had been around three hundred; now there were fewer than one hundred fifty people left.

Most of them lived in the lower part of the village, although there was another cluster of homes up in the hills, at the end of a winding dirt road, which was where we found our house. The government called this upper settlement Spring Valley, but to locals it was all Sancha—they made no distinction between the two parts. And the whole place had been fading for decades. The local Buddhist temple had been demolished during the Cultural Revolution, along with smaller shrines that were scattered throughout the hills, and nobody had bothered to rebuild them. The school shut down in the early 1990s. None of the villagers owned a car; nobody had a cell phone. There were no restaurants, no shops—not a single place where a person could spend money. Three or four times a week, a peddler's flatbed truck puttered up from the valley, loaded with rice, noodles, meat, and simple household goods. During autumn other trucks appeared to buy the villagers' harvested crops. In the upper settlement, all vehicles parked at the top of the dead-end road, where the dirt surface had been widened. That patch of earth represented the full range of local commerce—it was a parking-lot economy.

The average resident's annual income was around two hundred and fifty dollars. Almost all of it came from orchards: walnuts, chestnuts, and apricot seeds that were grown high in the mountains. They sold most of these nuts, but everything else was raised for food. They kept chickens and pigs, and they grew corn, soybeans, and vegetables. It was far too dry for rice; even wheat grew poorly in these parts. Occasionally, if a villager was lucky, he trapped a badger or a pheasant in the hills. There were feral pigs, too—wild animals with big tusks and matted hair.

Beijing wasn't too far away, only a couple of hours by car, but back then it was still unusual for city residents to visit the countryside. The auto boom was already growing—in 2001, Beijing issued over three hundred thousand new driver's licenses, a 50 percent increase over the previous year. But people rarely took long road trips for pleasure. Occasionally an adventurous driver found his way to Sancha, and sometimes a group of serious hikers came to climb the unrestored Great Wall. But on most weekends Mimi and I were the only outsiders in the village. Locals didn't know what to make of us—they knew I was a writer who had lived in China for years, and Mimi was a Chinese-American photographer; but there was no precedent for young city people spending time in rural conditions. Neighbors often wandered over to get a better look, and like anybody in the Chinese countryside, they didn't bother to knock before entering our house. They inspected our threshing platform, and peered into the windows, and fiddled with our belongings. Sometimes I walked to the dirt lot and found two or three villagers huddled around the rental car that I had driven out from the city. They stared with a sort of benign intensity: faces calm, hands clasped behind the back, heads bowed as if in prayer—homage to a Jetta.

Once I went to the village alone, and while writing at my desk I had the sensation that I was being watched. I turned around and almost yelped—a man was standing in the middle of the room. He was one of the neighbors, a white-haired man in his sixties; his cloth shoes hadn't made a sound when he entered. He was smiling softly, with the blank-eyed expression of somebody watching television—he hardly blinked when I turned around. That was the saving grace of Chinese staring: people never glanced away in embarrassment when you caught them looking, and it was hard not to respect such open curiosity. For a few seconds neither of us spoke.

"Hello," I finally said.

"Hello," he said.

"Have you eaten yet?" I said. That was a traditional Chinese greeting, often left unanswered.

"Have you eaten yet?" he said. "What time is it in your country?"

"It's night there," I said. "There's a difference of twelve hours."

He beamed—rural people are often fascinated by the time zones. There was another long pause and then he gestured to the far room. "You have a *kang*," he said.

"That's right."

"You have a desk," he said. I stood up and gave him a tour; he made approving comments along the way. ("You have a kitchen. You have a stove. You have a table.") In fact Mimi and I had hardly touched the place since we moved in. The previous residents had been a young couple who had recently left the village for city jobs, and their decorations still marked the walls. They must have been fans of the costume drama *Princess Pearl*, because they had hung a poster of the TV show's starlets in their silk and brocade Qing dynasty gowns. Another wall featured a photograph of twin baby boys, a common decoration in the countryside, especially for newlyweds. Twins represent a kind of lottery prize—for most people in China, that's the only legal way to have two sons. The previous residents of my house hadn't been quite that lucky, but they had given birth to a healthy boy, which was as much as anybody could ask for. Even the poster didn't show real twins. When I looked closely, I realized that it was the same baby twice: the photograph had simply been duplicated and reversed. When I woke up every morning, that's what I saw: an anonymous Photoshopped baby, abandoned by yet another young couple who had left the countryside.

I didn't take down the poster, because Mimi and I had decided not to change the place, at least in the beginning. The floor was naked cement; the ceiling had holes. In the outhouse, the squat toilet consisted of a slit between two slabs of slate. At night I was often wakened by rats in the walls. They were particularly active whenever the moon was full; on those nights I heard them rolling walnuts to hidden stashes in the ceiling. But Mimi and I didn't want to appear to be the rich foreigners, so we left everything the same. That was our plan: keep a low profile. It took us by surprise the first time a police car rolled up the dead-end road.

There were two officers in uniform. They had come from the nearest station in Shayu, a bigger village six miles away in the valley. Cops never visit a remote place like Sancha unless there's a problem, and these two knew exactly where to go—they made their way directly to our house. They asked to see our passports, and wrote down our Beijing addresses, and then one of them gave the bad news.

"You can't stay here at night," the officer said. "It's fine to come here during the day, but at night you have to go back to Beijing."

"Why can't we stay here at night?" Mimi asked.

"It's for your safety."

"But it's very safe here. It's safer here than in Beijing."

"Something might happen," the man said. "And if anything happens, it's our responsibility."

The officers were friendly but adamant, and that evening we left the village. The next time we came out, the same thing happened. Our house rental was handled by a local man named Wei Ziqi, who finally explained the reason. One of the neighbors called the police every time we arrived in Sancha.

"Do you remember the first time you came here?" Wei Ziqi said. "You looked at two houses: this one, and a house that belongs to another man. He's the one who calls the police."

"Why does he do that?"

"Because you're not renting from him," Wei Ziqi said. "He's angry about that."

Most men in our part of the village were related, and the whistle-blower shared Wei Ziqi's family name: they had the same great-great-grandfather. But they weren't close, and Wei Ziqi responded quickly when we asked what the man was like. "I'll give you an example," he said. "In the mountains you aren't allowed to cut down certain trees for firewood. This is true even if they're dead, which doesn't make sense. So people do it anyway, but sometimes that man will call the police to report it. That's the kind of person he is. He likes to cause trouble."

It was the first time I'd heard a character sketch that involves firewood, but who doesn't know a man like that? Certainly our first impressions had made us wary. He was in his late forties, and he had a handsome face, but his gaze was unsettling. There was something calculated about it—he had none of the open curiosity of the other villagers. He spent most of his time alone, although sometimes I heard him speaking gruffly to his wife. She had a haunted, nervous air; whenever I encountered her on the village pathways she smiled uncomfortably and stammered so fast that I couldn't understand. Other villagers told me that she was mentally ill, and some of them believed that she had been possessed by a spirit. One evening, when I was spending the night alone in my house, I heard a noise and went outside to investigate. At the edge of the threshing platform, something rustled in the shadows; I shone a flashlight and saw that it was the woman. She muttered incoherently and scurried away into the darkness. Nobody else had ever responded like that—if they came to stare, they simply stared. For much of that night I lay awake, listening to the wind in the trees, but I never saw her near my home again.

We could have rented her husband's house, which might have seemed like the simplest solution. The place was terrible, with a dirt floor and smoke-stained walls; the rent was low and we could have paid the money and left it empty. But it seemed a bad precedent, and it would only open up further dealings with the neighbor. Between ourselves, Mimi and I called him the Shitkicker: he stirred things up in the village. In this case, he had involved the police down in the valley, and over the next year we did everything possible to win their trust. We stopped frequently at the police station, and periodically we gave gifts—mooncakes at the Mid-Autumn Festival, fruit and cigarettes at the Spring Festival. Mimi's parents, who live in Beijing, drove out and took the chief of police and other officials out to an expensive lunch. I talked to a lawyer friend, who gave me a Beijing newspaper article about how foreigners can reside in the countryside, so long as they register with the authorities. I gave the story to one of the police officers, and eventually we worked out a system where the cops allowed us to stay as long as we alerted them before every visit. In the end, that was all it took—a reassurance that rules were being followed. Chinese police can be brutal, but usually they're as pragmatic as everybody else in the country. Quite often their primary goal is to be absolved of any responsibility whatsoever. For months the Shitkicker kept calling, but finally the cops told him to cut it out.

In the beginning, everything I learned about the village came from Wei Ziqi. He handled the rent for our house, although it didn't belong to him; the owner was his nephew, the young man who had moved with his wife to the city. Wei Ziqi was one of the few people of that generation who had stayed in Sancha—almost everybody else in their twenties and thirties was gone. All of them had grown up in rural poverty, but by adulthood they could see the ways in which the reforms were changing the cities, and departure was usually an easy choice. Wei Ziqi told me that as a child he was so poor that he often ate elm bark—villagers mixed it with corn and made noodles.

In 1987, after finishing the tenth grade, Wei Ziqi followed most of his classmates and left Sancha. He found a factory job on the outskirts of Beijing, where he worked on the assembly line, turning out electrical capacitors for televisions. After a year he switched to another plant that manufactured cardboard boxes. But he never liked factory work, and he didn't see a future to the jobs. "It was the same thing every day," he told me once. "If you're in a factory, you're always on the same place in the assembly line, and nothing changes." Wei Ziqi was naturally intelligent, but his formal education was limited, and there are few options for a rural man with such a background. If he had been a woman, he might have actually found better opportunities—smart Chinese women with little education often become accountants or secretaries, and from these positions they can rise in the factory world. But uneducated men have fewer alternatives to the assembly line; usually they work on construction crews or they become security guards. Eventually, Wei Ziqi found a job as a guard at another factory, but after a couple of years he decided the work was leading him nowhere.

Probably he was also limited by his physical appearance. In the Chinese work world, looks matter greatly, especially for jobs with little educational requirement. It's common for job listings to request applicants to be of a certain height: security guards at good companies often have to be at least five foot eight inches tall. Wei Ziqi stands less than five and a half feet, and he has the rough complexion of a farmer. He's barrel-chested, with squat, powerful legs; his hands are scarred from fieldwork. He looks like somebody who belongs in Sancha, and finally that's where he returned. In 1996, after nine years of city work, he came back to the village, where he acquired the rights to farmland that had been left behind by other migrants. He tended nearly two hundred walnut and chestnut trees, and his apricot groves were scattered among the high peaks. He lived with his wife and son, and he also cared for his oldest brother, who was mentally disabled. Their income was modest: less than two thousand dollars a year for four people. The arrival of Mimi and me didn't represent a windfall, because our rent money went to the nephew in the city.

Nearly all of Wei Ziqi's peers were gone. The local school that he once attended had been shut down, and of his eleven former classmates, only three still lived in the village. His able-bodied siblings—two older brothers, two older sisters—had all left. His path was unusual, but he refused to see it as a retreat; in his mind, the village wasn't doomed. He was convinced that someday there would be an advantage to staying behind, and he dreamed of doing something other than farming. Every time he visited relatives who had moved to Huairou, the nearest city, he kept an eye out for business ideas.

Such possibilities can be found everywhere in a small city like Huairou, where many entrepreneurs have originally come from the countryside. On the streets people pass out pamphlets for direct-marketing schemes, and buildings are plastered with ads for training courses, door-to-door products, and get-rich-quick scams. Even television offers ideas. Whenever Wei Ziqi visited Huairou, he stayed with relatives who had cable, and he liked watching China Central Television Channel 7. Some programs cater to viewers who are making the transition from farming to business, and they often feature successful rural entrepreneurs. One evening in Huairou, Wei Ziqi happened to watch a Channel 7 program about leeches. The host interviewed farmers in Hebei Province who raised leeches to be sold to manufacturers of traditional Chinese medicine used to treat numbness and paralysis. Some of these leech entrepreneurs supposedly earned nearly three thousand dollars a year, and after the show was over, Wei Ziqi called the television station for more information.

In 2002, that became his first attempt at business. He visited three successful leech farmers in the Huairou region, and then he raised investment money from his nephew and a neighbor. Together the three men collected five hundred and fifty dollars. Wei Ziqi used some of the cash to build a small cement pool beside his house, and then he traveled alone to Tangxian County. The journey represented the farthest he had ever been from Sancha: four hours by bus. Tangxian is home to a major leech farm, and Wei Ziqi visited the place and picked up two thousand young leeches for two hundred fifty dollars. He stocked them in a pair of water-filled barrels for the long bus ride home.

That month, whenever I visited the village, Wei Ziqi was busy with leech maintenance. He fiddled with the cement pool; he stirred the waters; he inspected the tiny creatures. They were so small they looked like the squiggles of a calligrapher's brush, and in the beginning they swarmed across the pool's surface. Every day, Wei Ziqi fed them the fresh blood of chickens, sheep, and pigs. He told me that he planned to eventually sell them to a medicine factory in Anguo County. But after two weeks the squiggles in Wei Ziqi's pool began to diminish. He wasn't sure why: maybe the temperature was too cold, or perhaps the pool was too deep. But soon all the creatures had died, and the investment money was gone; and that was the end of Wei Ziqi's career as a leech farmer.

The leeches were followed by Amway. The company was becoming popular in China, especially in smaller cities, and somebody in Huairou gave Wei Ziqi some pamphlets. For a spell he thought seriously about it, but then he decided that the village was too small for direct marketing. Briefly he became interested in a Chinese company that called itself Worldnet. Wei Ziqi picked up a flyer in the city, and he showed me a copy and asked what I thought. I told him the truth: it looked like a classic pyramid scheme.

Increasingly, though, he talked about tourism. He knew that Beijing car owners didn't spend much time in the countryside, but occasionally they visited tourist sections of the Great Wall, like Badaling and Mutianyu. He believed that eventually, as the drivers fanned out and began to explore, they'd find their way to more remote places like Sancha. In his opinion, the village needed to develop some sort of identity, so in his spare time he took notes on possibilities. He collected these writings in an exercise book that he called his *Xiaoxi*, or "Information." The Information featured key data, like altitude and range of temperatures, and it listed local landmarks: Dragon's Head Mountain, Eagle-beak Cliff. Wei Ziqi sketched simple maps of the Great Wall and local trails. I rarely met Chinese who were so intent on tracking their surroundings, especially in the countryside; the only other time I'd met a mapmaker was near the Shanxi border, where the old man named Chen researched the local Great Wall. But Wei Ziqi was interested in business, not history. He filled one page with potential names for a guesthouse:

1. *Farmyard Leisure Garden*
2. *Mountain Peace and Happiness Village*
3. *Sancha Farmyard Paradise*
4. *Sweet Waterhead Farmyard Villa*
5. *Great Nature Mountain Farmyard Villa*
6. *Sancha Plant Garden*
7. *Sancha Great Nature Farmyard Leisure Paradise*
8. *Nature Ecological Leisure Farmyard Villa*
9. *Natural Ecological Plant Paradise*
10. *Natural Ecological Village*

The list was followed by a rough outline of a business plan:

> *If each family invests a little money we can receive the tourists in our yards, and if the big developers invest in our project then we can turn our village into a paradise where tourists can go sightseeing, appreciate the wild scenery, climb the Great Wall, enjoy peasant family meals, and pick wild mountain fruits and vegetables.*

But it seemed unlikely that Wei Ziqi would find business partners in Sancha. Nobody else was as motivated; most people with aspirations had left the village long ago. There was something lonely about his ambition, and I could tell that he was thrilled when Mimi and I began visiting from the big city. He liked the fact that we were involved in writing and photography, and his questions about the outside world had a depth that was rare in the village. Even a common subject, like the time zones in America, became more interesting when Wei Ziqi brought it up. Once he kept asking me detailed questions about the time in America, and finally I told him that if you flew directly from Beijing to Los Angeles, you would arrive earlier than your departure, because of the international date line. For a minute the man was completely silent. He sketched some vertical lines on a piece of paper, and drew another trail intersecting them; he studied the thing hard until his face lit up. After that, I often heard him explaining the Beijing to L.A. flight to other villagers. None of them seemed to understand—they simply nodded, a dazed look in their eyes.

Wei Ziqi was also the most literate person in Sancha. In 1998, after returning to the village, he'd taken a correspondence course in law, and he had a collection of more than thirty books, mostly legal guides to the Reform era: *Economic Law, International Law, A Survey of the Chinese Constitution, Compilation of Laws and Regulations in Common Use.* These were new books, but they reflected an old tradition in rural China. Even as far back as the seventeenth century, printed books could be found in villages, where literate peasants often kept guides that showed them how to write up simple legal agreements. When Mimi and I first arranged to rent the Sancha house, Wei Ziqi consulted a book called *Modern Economic Contracts.* It was a cheap paperback with a cover photo that featured the EU flag superimposed atop the Hong Kong skyline. Using the book as a guide, Wei Ziqi produced a handwritten agreement with eleven clauses, all of which were written in formal language: "Party A offers Party B private rooms which are located at Shuiquan Valley of Sancha Village of Bohai Township of Huairou County (the rooms include a kitchen)." The contract noted that our agreement was "based on the mutual benefit principle." Clause number six specified that we could not use the house to "store contraband inflammable objects or explosives."

FEW PEOPLE IN THE village had traveled as much as Wei Ziqi. It was hard to go anywhere; there wasn't any bus service to Sancha, and the mountain roads are too steep for bicycling. If locals needed to go to the city, they hiked down to Dongtai, three miles away, where minibuses stopped. From there it was forty-five minutes to Huairou, and then another hour to Beijing. But some villagers had never even seen the capital. A couple of local women still had bound feet—members of that unfortunate last generation who had had their feet broken as children. Once, Mimi and I stopped by to visit with one of the bound-foot women. She was eighty-two years old, and she lay on her *kang* with her shoes off. She wore thin nylon socks and her deformed feet were visible, toes clenched tight against the soles like angry little fists. She said that in eight decades she had never been to Beijing. I asked her if she'd like to go, and she nodded.

"But I can't," she said. "You know why? Because I get carsick!"

Recently she had taken motion sickness pills and made the journey to Huairou, to visit family. That was her first trip to a settlement of any size, and I asked her what she thought. "Not bad," the woman said, and left it at that. She had grown up in a village across one of the mountain passes, a long day's walk from Sancha. When I asked what Sancha had been like in the old days, she spoke bluntly. "There's nothing interesting about this place," she said. "Living in these mountains, at the bottom of a deep gorge—what can possibly happen here?" The only topic of conversation that interested the woman involved her children and their shortcomings. They had left Sancha for the city, and they rarely returned; young people are like that nowadays! They're all so selfish! Nobody cares about old people! These complaints seemed to make the woman happy—stretched out on the *kang*, resting her crumpled feet, her face became peaceful as she decried the thoughtlessness of the young.

People in Sancha sometimes still traveled long distances by foot or donkey, especially if they headed north. The village name means "Three Forks," because the main settlement is located at the junction of a trio of valleys that fan northward. Each valley contains a footpath that leads to a high pass: one trail to the village of Chashikou, another to Haizikou, the third to the Huanghua Zhen road. All of these routes cross an old section of wall made of dry fieldstone. This part of the ancient Chinese defense network wasn't built with brick and mortar, and the date of construction is unknown; texts from the late Ming dynasty simply refer to it as *lao changcheng*, "the old Great Wall." A couple of miles north of the fortified passes, in the valleys of Haizikou and Chashikou, there is yet another stone barrier. This region was heavily fortified—the distance between these three parallel lines of Great Wall is only five miles. Sancha lies in the middle, with one Great Wall to the south, and two more to the north.

Wei Ziqi had relatives in Chashikou, beyond the second barrier, and sometimes he set off in the morning and hiked across the pass. If he had to carry a lot, he saddled up a donkey. In the afternoons, when I was finished writing for the day, I went for long hikes along these routes. They were rocky trails, winding through the orchards, and they passed the ruins of remote settlements that had been abandoned. Along the path to Haizikou, there was a place where people had been gone for more than a decade, and the stone foundations of their homes had already been overgrown by young walnut trees. Grindstones lay in the weeds beside the trail—the last relics of the labor that once shaped this terrain.

There was still one man living on the route that led toward the Huanghua Zhen pass. Of all the trails, that was the least traveled, and the pass could be hard to find during summer months, when the brush came up. Until the 1990s, this valley was home to two small communities of houses. They were named after the families that lived there: one settlement is known as the Land of the Mas, and the other is the Land of the Lis. By the time I moved to Sancha, the Land of the Lis was completely abandoned—a half dozen buildings stood empty, their paper windows torn and flapping in the breeze. But an elderly man named Ma Yufa remained in the other enclave. Local officials had offered him a room in a retirement home down in the valley, but Ma refused to go. He still farmed, despite his age. He told the officials that whenever he became too old to work, he would simply lie down on his *kang* and wait for death.

One morning I hiked up the trail and saw Ma Yufa watering his donkey. It was February, and the man was bundled against the cold; he wore padded army pants, a military jacket covered with patches, and old cloth shoes that had been sewed repeatedly. The torn army clothes gave him the look of a deserter—one of those soldiers who's been hiding in a jungle for decades, unaware that the war has ended. But his face was strikingly handsome, weathered like a slab of local walnut, and he had thick black eyebrows. He told me that he was in his seventies, and I asked which year he'd been born.

"*Sha shei zhidao?*" he said with a snort. "Who knows that?"

He invited me into his home for a cup of tea, and we passed through the ruins of the Land of the Mas. He pointed out two sets of stone foundations that had been overgrown with brush. "Those people were named Ma, and the other ones over there were called Zhao," he said. "They left ten years ago." We trudged past another ruined home. "The people there were also called Ma. That was my uncle." Ma Yufa's brother's house was still standing, although the occupant had moved to Huai-rou. A hand-carved coffin leaned near the entrance. "Whenever he dies, he'll be buried in that," Ma Yufa said.

Ma Yufa lived in a two-room house with mud walls, and he had no telephone or refrigerator. He told me that every day, at each meal, he ate corn porridge and flour cakes. "You need to eat meat when you're young, but not when you're old," he said. Across the pass it's nearly four miles of mountain walking to Haizikou, the nearest place with a shop, and the man and his donkey had last made the trip in December, two months earlier. He didn't expect to return until April. There wasn't much he needed: a few times a year, he bought corn and flour, and he sold his walnuts in the autumn. Other than those short journeys he had no contact with anybody. His annual income was less than two hundred dollars. Technically he was a Beijing resident—as with so many Chinese cities, the capital's administrative boundaries stretch deep into the countryside. Until I met Ma Yufa, I had never imagined how isolated a human being could be in a city of thirteen million.

We sat on his *kang*, sipping tea, and he talked about the past. He remembered the Communist victory of 1949, but he said it hadn't changed his life much. "We were so poor it didn't matter," he said. He hadn't spent a single day in school, and he couldn't read. He had never married. "Nobody would want to marry somebody who lives in a place like this," he said. He had a radio and a television with a cheap satellite dish, but he must not have been watching the news. When I asked who was the top official in China, he paused to think.

"Hu Yaobang is the nation's leader," he finally said. In fact Hu Yao-bang had never led China, although in 1981 he rose to become Party Chairman of the Chinese Communist Party. He was purged in 1987, and two years later his death inspired the initial student protests on Tiananmen Square. Those events may have shaken the world, but they were meaningless in the Land of the Mas.

One thing Ma Yufa seemed completely aware of was time. The room was decorated with three calendars, and two of them had tear-off sheets, marked to the correct page. He didn't throw away the used days; he stacked the little squares of paper neatly in a pan. He had an alarm clock with a second hand that ticked loudly. The longer I sat on the *kang*, the more the ticking of the clock unsettled me, until finally I thanked him for the tea and excused myself. Outside, the hills were silent—I felt relieved to see the bigness of the sky.

AT HOME, FROM THE desk beside my window, I could look across the valley and see the Great Wall climbing the western mountains. That was my retreat—I went there whenever I wanted to escape the city and do some writing. I liked the sounds of the village, which was so quiet that every noise seemed clear and distinct. Wind rustled the leaves of the big walnut tree outside my house, and occasionally a donkey brayed. Three times a day, at morning, noon, and early evening, the village propaganda speakers crackled to life. They broadcast local announcements, county news, and national events, all of it jumbled together, the Party's words distorted by the echoes of the deep valley. Whenever a peddler's truck appeared, I heard the villagers chattering as they gathered around the makeshift market at the end of the road. Apart from that, there were few voices, and I rarely heard the noise of children playing.

There was only one child in the upper part of the village. My house was surrounded by fifteen other buildings, but nearly all families with young children had moved away. Only Wei Ziqi and his wife Cao Chunmei were raising a young child, a boy named Wei Jia. He was the smallest five-year-old I had ever known—he weighed thirty pounds, and his mother fretted about his health, because he was a finicky eater. But he had a wiry strength that I rarely saw among city children in China. Since the age of four, Wei Jia had roamed unsupervised around the village, and he knew his way along the mountain paths. His sense of balance was remarkable, and he could roughhouse endlessly; it was impossible to wear him out. He almost never cried. It was as if the toughness and dexterity of a nine-year-old had been squeezed into a three-year-old's body, and I could never resist chasing the kid down and tossing him into the air. He called me *mogui*—"monster"—and at one point his parents reminded him to use the proper term of respect for an adult. That was how I came to be known as Mogui Shushu: "Uncle Monster."

Wei Jia often came to my house, and if I was writing I told him to play quietly and leave Uncle Monster alone. As the only child in the village, he was accustomed to entertaining himself, and sometimes I worked for an hour and forgot that he was still there. He had no toys to speak of, so he improvised with whatever happened to be lying around: a rusty rake, a broken plate. Once he spent a morning on my threshing platform, using an old cart and an empty beer bottle to pretend that he was driving a peddler's truck. When Mimi or I took friends to the village, they sometimes gave toys to Wei Jia as gifts. "That's a waste," his father said once. "He's only going to break it." And that was true—the boy was so unaccustomed to real toys that he invariably destroyed them. If he got a toy, he might try stepping on it, or he'd twist some moving part until it snapped. After it was ruined, he didn't seem at all bothered: for Wei Jia, a toy was a nondurable resource. If you were fortunate enough to get one, you should enjoy it as quickly as possible.

The boy's face was a perfect oval. He had black hair cropped close, and long thin eyes that sparked when he laughed. His ears were wonderful—that's often the most endearing feature of small Chinese boys, whose ears stick straight out, giving them a perpetually startled expression. Neither of Wei Jia's parents was particularly good-looking, but the boy was handsome. Sometimes, if I wanted to annoy Mimi, I'd praise him.

"Wei Jia is so good-looking," I'd say.

"He's ugly," his mother would answer immediately.

"He's so smart."

"He's stupid," she said. "Not one bit smart."

"Cut it out," Mimi would say, in English, but I'd continue: "What a nice child."

"He's a bad boy."

In the countryside, traditional parents avoid flattery, and the mother's responses were automatic—it was like knocking her knee with a rubber hammer. She didn't want to spoil the child, but there was also the Chinese superstition that pride attracts misfortune. The only praise I ever heard the parents give Wei Jia was a single adjective: *laoshi*. The dictionary defines it as "honest," but the term is difficult to translate. It also means obedient, as well as having a certain sense of propriety that is characteristic of people in the countryside. "Wei Jia is *laoshi*," his parents would say, and that was the closest they came to pride.

In the fall of 2002, the boy was scheduled to start kindergarten. He would attend a school twenty miles away, in the village where his mother had grown up, and he would return home only on the weekends. In rural China, because of poor transportation, it's common for small children to board at school. The afternoon before Wei Jia started, Mimi and I drove up from Beijing, so we could take him the next day. In the evening we ate dinner with the family. "Are you excited?" I asked.

Wei Jia was eating rice and he didn't look up from his bowl.

"Answer your Uncle Monster," his mother said sternly. Usually the boy was talkative, babbling so fast that nobody could understand. But tonight he was silent—he sat there staring at his bowl. It occurred to me that I had never seen him leave the village before.

"That's OK," I said. "He doesn't have to answer."

We finished dinner and the parents prepared Wei Jia's new school clothes and backpack. He went to bed in silence. All evening he had refused to say a single word about starting school.

THE BOY WAS OF the sixth generation of Weis known to have lived in Sancha. In the upper part of the village, nearly all male residents share that family name, and the Weis are all related in one way or another. The women have all sorts of names—Cao, Li, Zhao, Han, Yuan—and most grew up in other villages around Beijing. In rural China, that's the traditional pattern: men inherit their family's land, and women marry in from the outside.

Nobody is certain how the village was first settled. In the past, most residents were illiterate, and there are few historical documents in Sancha. The oldest known words are located a thousand feet above the village, where an inscribed stone tablet leans against a section of Great Wall. Of the three lines of wall near Sancha, this is by far the most impressive, and it's the only local stretch that was built of brick and quarried stone. Originally many sections of brick fortifications contained inscribed tablets, but most have been looted or broken; nowadays fewer than twenty are known to still exist on the wall in the Beijing area. The tablet above Sancha has survived by virtue of remoteness—from the village it takes more than two hours of hard hiking to reach that spot. The inscription notes that in AD 1615, a crew of 2,400 soldiers built a section of Great Wall that is exactly fifty-eight *zhang* and five *cun* long. The tablet reflects the precision of Ming bureaucratic records: the *cun* is a unit of measurement shorter than an inch. All told, the length of this 1615 construction project was 638 feet, and it required a full three months of labor. The soldiers came from the eastern province of Shandong.

Some villagers believe themselves to be the descendants of these soldiers. Others tell a different story: during the early Qing dynasty, there was a failed plot to assassinate an emperor, and a band of wanted men fled to the mountains. They settled at a fork in three valleys, founding the village that eventually became Sancha. Yet another tale involves an empress named Yan. Desiring to see the countryside, Empress Yan was borne north from the Forbidden City on a sedan chair. Upon reaching the mountains, she was so pleased by the journey that she granted the land to her bearers. In her honor they adopted the same family name, and to this day the lower village is home to a large number of Yans.

All of these tales sound suspiciously familiar—they have an awful lot in common with the historical soap operas that villagers like watching on television. Such shows feature imperial courts and elaborate plots, and nowadays this is how many rural Chinese learn history. It seems natural that the people in Sancha would apply such tales to their own village, although I doubt that in fact the place was settled by failed assassins or sedan-chair bearers. It's also unlikely that the builders of the Great Wall founded Sancha. During the Ming dynasty, soldiers typically returned to their homes after construction projects.

Wei Ziqi has another theory about his family origins that sounds more reasonable. He's heard that his ancestors arrived in the late nineteenth century, having fled a famine on the loess plateau, in Shanxi Province. But he has no idea if this is true, and he has never seen the Wei *jiapu*, the traditional genealogy kept by Chinese families. Some of these documents go back hundreds of years, and many people hid them during the Cultural Revolution, when political campaigns targeted such relics of the feudal past. In Sancha, the Wei *jiapu* survived that turmoil, but during the Reform years it suffered a different fate: the document fell into the hands of the Shitkicker.

"He won't let anybody see it," Wei Ziqi said. "We don't even know where he keeps it. He has it hidden somewhere."

I asked what the man planned to do with the genealogy.

"Nothing," Wei Ziqi said. "It doesn't do him any good. He just wants to keep other people from seeing it."

Wei Ziqi's personal family history is limited to a half dozen tattered land contracts that are signed by his ancestors. But none of these documents is still legally binding, and to him they're just curiosities. He rarely talks about his ancestors or his parents, and like other villagers he doesn't care much about history. He told me that when he was a boy, nobody in Sancha showed the least interest in the Ming-dynasty ruins. Locals didn't even call it the Great Wall—back then, they referred to it as *bianqiang*, or "border walls," a term that was commonly used during the Ming. Along with other children, Wei Ziqi played in the remnants of kilns that had been used to fire bricks for the wall. Sometimes children found intact bricks or other relics, but eventually the village expanded and people built their homes atop the kilns. In the 1970s, Sancha residents demolished a massive fortified gate that stood along the main road to the village. They used the huge blocks of stone for house foundations and road construction. Nowadays, there are some regrets about the destruction, because villagers believe the gate might have attracted tourists.

Like everybody in urban China, they now call it Changcheng, the Great Wall, and occasionally they hike up and wander around the ruins. If they find anything interesting they take it back home, and over the years Wei Ziqi has collected two Ming-dynasty signal cannons. They are simple tubes of carved stone, open at one end; each is about the size of a large flowerpot. There's a notched hole in the bottom for lighting a fuse. In the old days soldiers packed them with gunpowder, ignited the fuse, and conveyed messages with the sound. When I moved to the village, Wei Ziqi never seemed particularly interested in the four-hundred-year-old artifacts, which he kept on a dusty shelf. Once he asked me casually if I'd like to bring a cannon back to America. As far as he was concerned, there was no reason to explore history for its own sake—his instinct was always to look ahead. He liked the study of law because it's practical, and that was also true of his Information. He drew maps of the Great Wall because he figured there must be some way to make money from tourism.

The only time the village commemorates the past is during the annual grave-sweeping holiday of Qing Ming. The festival's name means the Day of Clear Brightness, and it's celebrated across China during the first week of April. In the southwestern province of Sichuan, where I lived for two years, Qing Ming is a family celebration—entire clans hike up to their ancestral tombs, where they burn offerings and enjoy long, rowdy picnics. In Sancha, though, only the men participate. They leave before dawn, carrying shovels on their shoulders, and they trudge up the steep hillside behind the village. The land levels out to a strip of cornfields, and behind the crops is the Sancha cemetery. It consists of simple dirt mounds, three feet tall and unmarked. They are arranged in neat rows, and each row represents a different generation. There are four lines—a hundred years of Weis buried on this mountainside.

The first year I went to Sancha for Qing Ming, the apricot trees were in full bloom, sweeping white across the hills like a spring snowstorm. By 6:30 a.m., all the men were there: Wei Ziqi, the Shitkicker, the Party Secretary's husband, the cousins who lived down in the valley. Mimi came along; because she was an outsider, the usual rule about women didn't apply. There were no children—Wei Jia was too small to participate. Some people had arrived from out of town, including an old man named Wei Minghe, who had moved to Huairou years ago. He shoveled dirt onto his parents' grave, and then he poured a bottle of grain alcohol in front of the mound. "The pile represents a house," he explained. "We have a tradition here that you have to come before sunrise. If you pour dirt on the grave before the sun comes up, it means that in the afterlife they get a house with a tiled roof. If you don't make it in time, they get a grass roof."

Each man began by tending the tomb of his most immediate relatives: parents, grandparents, uncles. Sometimes they left special gifts, like small bottles of alcohol or packs of cigarettes that had been enjoyed by the departed. Then they worked their way down the generations, carefully weeding the mounds and shoveling dirt, and as they moved back in time they became less certain of identities. Wei Ziqi thought that one mound belonged to his great-grandfather, but he wasn't sure—it might have been another uncle. On the last rows, the work became communal: everybody pitched in for every mound, and nobody knew who was buried where. The final pile of dirt was isolated in its own row. I asked Wei Ziqi who it belonged to.

"Lao Zu," he said. "The Ancestor." There was no other name for the original settler, whose details had been lost with the *jiapu*.

In the afternoon, Mimi and I gave Wei Minghe a ride home. The old man said that nowadays he rarely returned to Sancha; apart from the occasional holiday, there wasn't much reason to go back. He lived in a suburb of Huairou, where a row of brick houses had been laid out beside the road to Beijing. When peasants move to cities, they often end up in neighborhoods like this: dozens of identical buildings, cheaply built and poorly planned, lined up with all the imagination of a factory floor. But I remembered what Wei Minghe had said about shoveling dirt before dawn—tile roofs versus grass roofs. The ancestors are abstract, but today's choices are tangible, and the old man had made his decision. One thing he said about Huairou was that now he finally had good heat.

ON THE FIRST DAY of school, Wei Jia wore new khaki trousers and a red T-shirt. The clothes looked stiff and foreign—all summer the boy had played around the village wearing nothing but a dirty tank top and a pair of underpants. For school, I had given him a Mickey Mouse backpack, and his mother had put a new pencil box in one of the pockets. Inside the box was a single pencil, freshly sharpened.

The boy still wasn't saying much, and he walked in silence to the road. Mimi had borrowed her parents' Volkswagen Santana for the weekend, and all of us climbed into the car. I sat in front with Wei Jia on my lap; his parents took the backseat. Between them sat the Idiot.

Once, I asked Cao Chunmei what the Idiot's real name is, but she didn't know. He is Wei Ziqi's oldest brother, born in 1948—the year before the Communists came to power, when the civil war still raged across northern China. Those were difficult times, and poverty probably caused the Idiot's disability. Most likely it was a lack of iodine: if a pregnant woman doesn't consume enough, she runs the risk of bearing a mentally disabled child. Nowadays the government ensures that iodized salt is widely distributed in the countryside, and such birth defects have become rare. But there is still an older generation of disabled people, a reminder of China's recent poverty, and I often encountered them on my drive across China. Many villages have one or two residents with mental disabilities, and locals typically call them Shazi: "Idiot."

In Sancha, the Idiot lived with the Weis, who made sure that he was clothed and fed. They gave him simple chores: he swept the floor, shelled walnuts, and searched for kindling along mountain trails. But he couldn't participate in the harvest, and he couldn't cook for himself. He was deaf and dumb. Whenever he wanted to communicate, he contorted his face with such passion that it seemed as if the power of speech had fled precisely at that moment and he was just beginning to grapple with its loss. But in fact he had never spoken. The villagers ignored his contorted face, and they didn't address him by any of the usual terms for an adult: "uncle," or "big brother," or "little brother." To them, he was simply Shazi, the Idiot, and although he was well cared for, he was never treated like a full-fledged person. Wei Jia was the only villager who took an interest—he was too young to understand that his uncle was disabled. Sometimes the child played with the Idiot, and the man's face lit up with joy. Mimi and I often talked with him, engaging him with eye contact, but the villagers were quick to tell us it was pointless. "He doesn't understand anything you say," Wei Ziqi always told me.

On the first day of school I was surprised to see the Idiot accompanying us, and I asked Wei Ziqi if anything was wrong. "It's nothing," he said. "We just have a little problem to take care of at the government office."

We drove out of the village, and Wei Jia leaned forward with both hands on the dashboard. The boy was obsessed with automobiles—he seldom saw cars, and the experience of riding in one was a rare treat. It was anything but passive: at every turn, I felt Wei Jia edging toward the windshield, trying to see what was around the bend. He lurched forward on hills; he leaned back at stops. He should have been in the backseat—I knew it was wrong to keep a child on my lap like that. But nobody in rural China uses child seats, and it would have broken Wei Jia's heart to be relegated to the back. And so I held him tightly, and Mimi drove carefully, and the six of us descended into the valley of the Huaisha River.

The walnut harvest had begun, and the roads were busy with farmers on their way to the fields. We passed dozens of men who carried thin sticks, ten feet long and perfectly straight. Some of them rode bicycles to their orchards, poles balanced across the handlebars like knights at the joust. They used the sticks to knock walnuts off the trees, and the road was full of discarded husks. They crunched beneath our tires—another drive-through harvest.

In the valley we began to see packs of children on foot, dressed in new clothes and making their way down the road. "See, they have backpacks, too," Cao Chunmei said to Wei Jia. "They're going to school just like you."

We passed a farmer carrying insecticide in a plastic box on his back. "He's going to school with his backpack, too," I said.

"That's not a backpack," Wei Jia said quickly. It was the first time he'd spoken since we left the village; his arms were stiff against the dash. For an instant we caught a whiff of insecticide, the heavy sweet smell filling the car, and then it was gone.

AS WE APPROACHED BOHAI Township, Wei Ziqi asked Mimi to stop at the government office. She was pulling into the driveway when he finally explained why the Idiot had come along.

"The government is supposed to pay a monthly fee to help us take care of him," Wei Ziqi said. "That's the law. I've asked the Party Secretary in Sancha about it, but she hasn't helped. So the only thing to do is to come here ourselves. I'll ask them to pay the fee now, and if they don't, then I'll leave the Idiot until they're willing to pay it. It's their responsibility."

"You're going to leave him at the government office?" Mimi asked.

"Yes," Wei Ziqi said. "It's the only way to get their attention."

Mimi asked how much the monthly fee should be.

"Fifty yuan at the very least," Wei Ziqi said. It was the equivalent of about six dollars.

Before we could respond, Wei Ziqi had already helped his brother out of the car. He led him through the front courtyard, which was decorated by a massive sculpture. It consisted of a shiny steel ball surrounded by a twisted rod; the shapes were vaguely abstract, like so much of the public art in China. Around Sancha, all local townships have erected sculptures in such a style, accompanied by slogans intended to inspire images of modernity and prosperity. The Bohai Township slogan is "The Star of the Century." Wei Ziqi led his brother past the twisted sculpture and through the open gate. The Idiot's face was blank—he'd been silent ever since entering the car.

Wei Jia kept his hands impatiently on the dash while we waited. Five minutes later, the boy's father returned. He was alone. We kept driving.

THE CROPS SHIFTED AS we descended into the Beijing plain. There was more corn here, as well as wheat, and the harvest had started earlier; walnut trees were already stripped bare. Roadside villages became bigger, with real traffic: buses and cars and minivans. There were shops, too. Suddenly words appeared everywhere—in these larger villages, the government had covered brick walls with family planning slogans. "Daughters Are Also Descendants," proclaimed one sign. "Planned Birth Benefits the Country." Usually I found the slogans oppressive, but here they were almost reassuring. Nobody had bothered to paint them in Sancha—that was the clearest indication that the village was dying.

In fact, if any young people had stayed in Sancha, they wouldn't necessarily have been limited to a single child. A couple who initially gives birth to a girl is allowed to have another baby, with a maximum of two children. Sancha is granted that right because of its remoteness, and because of the traditional desire to have a boy who can help with farming. But if you descend to the Beijing plain, a journey of less than ten miles, the rules change, and families are restricted to one child regardless of gender.

The Chinese planned birth policy is heavily localized, depending on geography and ethnicity. It requires an enormous bureaucracy, and in the countryside I often saw evidence of enforcement. During my drive across the north, in Gansu Province, I once saw a new Iveco van with the words painted across the side: "Planned Birth Services Vehicle." It was equipped with police lights, propaganda speakers, and a gas-powered generator; the back doors opened to reveal a sink and two hospital-style beds. I talked to the driver, who told me that they took the van into rural areas, where they performed surgeries. When I asked about the most common procedures, he matter-of-factly jotted two terms in my notebook: "abortion" and "tying tubes." In that region, family size depends largely on race: Han Chinese are limited to one child; urban Mongolian residents can have two; and rural Mongolians are allowed to have three.

In Sancha, people can have two children if the first is a girl, and there are other exceptions as well. Because the Weis care for the Idiot, they can legally have another child, but Wei Ziqi refused; he believed that raising two children would be too expensive. Chinese with aspirations often feel that way, especially in the cities, where the government has been effective in convincing people that they're better off with only one kid. Urban Chinese rarely complain about the rules, and they tend to be scornful of those in the countryside who try to have more children. But one unintended result of the policy is a marked gender disparity. Accurate statistics are hard to come by, because some rural people avoid registering their children, but the most reliable figures indicate that there are 118 boys born for every 100 girls. Even the government acknowledges that it's a problem—the National Population and Family Planning Commission has reported that there will be thirty million more men of marriageable age than women by the year 2020. That's the same year that Wei Jia will turn twenty-three.

It's illegal for a Chinese doctor to tell a pregnant woman the gender of her child, but bribes are common. Once, I accompanied the Weis to a doctor's appointment in Huairou, where the hospital room contained an ultrasound machine. Printed atop the equipment was a large sign in both Chinese and English. The foreign words had been miswritten so they ran together, but the meaning was clear:

BOYORGIRL

LETITBE

WE PARKED AT THE back gate of the Xingying Elementary School. A teacher greeted us and led us inside; Wei Jia's face was expressionless. He walked into the classroom, stopped dead beside the blackboard, and announced loudly, "This place is no good!"

The boy's parents tried to grab him but he squirmed free and ran out the door. He was crying now, rushing back toward the car. "I'm going home!" he yelled. "I want to go home! I don't want to be here!"

His mother followed, while the rest of us lingered in the classroom. I had to admit that Wei Jia had a point—these were by far the worst conditions I had ever seen in a school in the Beijing region. There was a gaping hole in the ceiling, and the classroom was filthy; metal bars covered the windows. The blackboard was chipped and scarred. On the walls, the only decorations consisted of a half-dozen Styrofoam cutouts of animals. They had been so hastily made that the figures were barely recognizable: a warped elephant, a twisted monkey, a clumsy-looking mouse.

The other children had already arrived, and they sat quietly behind tiny desks, playing with Lego-like blocks. There were twenty total, only three of whom were girls. One was a strikingly pretty five-year-old with pigtails, and another had her hair cut short like a boy. The third girl was undersized, with enormous black eyes, and the teacher told us immediately that she was a *ruozhi*. It's another term for somebody who is disabled: literally it means "weak wit." The girl looked up when the teacher said it—obviously she was accustomed to people uttering this word in her presence.

Outside, Wei Jia stood in the dust beside the car. He was crying harder now, and he struggled against anybody who tried to lead him back to the classroom. First his mother spoke to him, and then his father. Usually Wei Ziqi was strict with his son, but he seemed to sympathize with this particular fear. "Everybody goes to school," Wei Ziqi said gently. "I went to school, and so did your mother. Aunt Mimi went to school, and so did Uncle Monster."

The fact that Uncle Monster was educated didn't soothe the boy in the least. In the schoolyard, the daily flag-raising began: loudspeakers crackled, the national anthem played, and children marched out wearing the red kerchiefs of the Communist Party Young Pioneers. Wei Jia's face was creased with panic; he had never seen so many children together in one place. By now he was mute—he simply lunged at the car whenever somebody tried to pull him away.

It took nearly forty-five minutes to calm the boy. Finally his father carried him into the classroom; his mother seated him behind a desk. Other kids turned to stare—the girl known as the *ruozhi* spun around in her chair, eyes blazing. Wei Jia's chest was heaving; his cheeks shone with tears. After ten minutes, he made another attempt for the door, but this time they caught him. He cried again, a final hard burst, and then he calmed down, exhausted. Lines of resignation crept across his forehead, like the furrows of an old man's brow.

We left as quietly as we could. I asked Wei Ziqi where the bathroom was, and he told me to use the schoolyard fence on the way out. I could hear children's voices—talking, laughing, reciting lessons—while I pissed in the weeds. On the way home the car seemed empty without the boy and the Idiot.

THAT DAY THE IDIOT escaped twice from the government office. The first time, the cadres caught him just outside the gate. The second time, he made it into Bohai Township, and it took a while for them to track him down.

The officials telephoned Wei Ziqi and told him to pick up his brother; Wei Ziqi demanded the subsidy. Neither side would budge, and finally, late in the day, the cadres put the Idiot in a car and drove into the mountains. They dropped him off two miles outside of Sancha. The

Idiot had never been alone so far from home, but he found his way back—some instinct must have told him to walk uphill.

I learned all of this later from Wei Ziqi. He said his brother had been exhausted and frightened, but otherwise he was fine; nobody in the government had mistreated him. Wei Ziqi seemed satisfied with this chain of events: in his view, he had shown the cadres that he was serious. They had finally agreed to submit the request to the county government, a higher level of authority, and Wei Ziqi believed he had a good chance of receiving the subsidy. As far as he was concerned, this had been the best course of action. Officials are often inclined to ignore responsibility, and sometimes you have to act aggressively in order to push them.

I felt guilty about the incident, although I had no idea what I should have done differently. And I hadn't fully understood the situation while it was unfolding. I often felt like that in China; the place had a way of making me feel slow-witted. Sometimes I benefited from this stupidity, especially as a writer. Over the years I had learned to be patient, and probably I was more open-minded than I had ever been in America. But my reactions could be slow and sometimes a situation developed before I could respond. In any case, life is complicated in China, and often there isn't a good solution regardless of how quick you are. The people have a common expression for that: *Mei banfa*, they often say. Nothing can be done.

I had always liked the challenge of living in China, and there was something about the foreigner's solitude that appealed to me. The villagers accepted this—they understood that I was different, and that I spent a great deal of time alone, and they didn't judge me for that. They were curious only in the broadest sense: people often asked me what time it was in America, and they were always interested in how much something had cost. They asked detailed questions about the things I eat and don't eat. But they never inquired about my writing or my personal life, which was one reason I felt so comfortable in Sancha. Often the villagers referred to Mimi as my *laopo*, or wife, and I didn't bother to correct them. In fact we had dated briefly before finding the country home, but we rented the place as friends. Over time, each of us dated other people, and we continued to share the house; sometimes we brought new partners to Sancha. The villagers couldn't have cared less—that was the distance between their world and ours.

A week after the incident with the Idiot, I went to Sancha for a few days. It was as if the man had been waiting for me: he stood at the top of the road, where he greeted me with a huge grin, pointing at my parked car. I had never seen him so animated; he kept grunting and gesturing toward the vehicle. I realized that he was telling the story of our drive into the valley. "I know," I said. "I remember." I wanted to apologize; I wished I could let him know that I hadn't understood that situation until it was too late—*Mei banfa*. But there was no way to communicate my regret, and the Idiot continued his wild gestures. He seemed thrilled to see me again.

WEI JIA'S FIRST HOLIDAY was in October, for National Day. All Chinese schools had a week off, and the boy returned to the village. His teacher reported that he was still unaccustomed to the classroom; in her words, he had "a wild-eyed look." Wei Jia had always had a penchant for roughhousing, and initially his parents weren't concerned when they noticed a pattern of bruises across his back.

In the village, the corn harvest had just come in, and Wei Ziqi had gathered six hundred pounds of the crop. He stacked the corn alongside their house, and Wei Jia spent a morning climbing and sliding down the bright yellow pile. Afterward his mother noticed more bruises across the boy's legs—angry smudges of purple that covered every few inches of skin. Wei Jia said he felt fine, but his face looked pale. Mimi and I had driven out to the village in her family's car, and now I offered to take Wei Ziqi and the boy to the hospital in Huairou.

It was the afternoon of the holiday, the fifty-third anniversary of the founding of Communist China. The roads were empty all the way to Huairou, and we parked at the city's main hospital. Inside, a nurse wrote a prescription, and we went to the blood clinic for a test. The place had the feel of a speakeasy: patients shoved their arms through a hole in the wall, where an unseen technician waited with a needle. At first Wei Jia resisted but his father spoke sternly: "Be *laoshi*!" The boy wrinkled his face but didn't cry. Afterward the nurse gave us a computer printout and told us that his *xuexiaoban* count was low. I didn't understand the technical term, and I hadn't brought my dictionary; but I could see from the woman's face that it was serious.

"His count is only seventeen thousand," she said. "It should be more than a hundred and fifty thousand." She recommended that we go immediately to the Children's Hospital in downtown Beijing for further tests.

Wei Jia had been born at a hospital in the capital, and this was his first time back to the city. Usually the boy was excited to be in a car, chattering questions about everything along the road, but today he was quiet. The moment we entered the Children's Hospital, I knew that it was a mistake to come here. Kids were screaming; parents chased down stubborn charges; the staff looked harried. Wei Ziqi seemed overwhelmed: he entered the place and halted right in the doorway. A city man bumped him from behind, cursing under his breath ("Out of the way!") as he hurried past. Wei Ziqi wore army pants and a military-green Public Security vest, and here in the city it was as if the camouflage actually worked. People jostled him, and jabbed with elbows, and brushed him aside. When he asked hospital employees for help, they just waved him away. He might as well have been invisible—that's what happens when you wear peasant clothes into the city.

Finally I picked up Wei Jia and marched to an information booth. The attendant snapped to attention and answered all of my questions; it made all the difference in the world when she saw a foreigner instead of a peasant. The woman told me where to go for the blood test, and we paid a fee of a few dollars and joined a line of waiting patients. A sign hung on the wall of the blood clinic:

WITH YOUR COOPERATION AND OUR EXPERIENCE
WE WILL TAKE GOOD CARE OF YOUR PRECIOUS

The line already contained more than twenty Preciouses. Each was accompanied by at least two adults; some kids were surrounded by both parents and two full sets of grandparents. In urban China, young children possess a freakish gravity—the smaller the kid, the closer the adults hover, like massive planets trapped in orbit around some dense little sun. But such proximity does nothing for discipline, and the waiting room rang with shouts and screams. Preciouses chased each other around the room, darting in and out of line; at the front they screamed bloody murder when it was time to get pricked. We had been there for less than five minutes when one Precious vomited straight onto the floor. Another girl broke free of her orbiting adults and slipped into the testing area, where she fiddled with a rack of tubes. "Stop that!" shouted a nurse, slapping the girl's hand.

Wei Jia was by far the worst-dressed kid in the room. He wore a filthy green sweatshirt, and there were holes in the toes of his cloth shoes; his neck was streaked with dirt. But he was calm—I was grateful for that. When he finally reached the front of the line, his face twisted, and his father spoke again—"Be *laoshi*!"—and then the blood test was over.

It wasn't until later that I realized only a fool goes to the Children's Hospital on a holiday. The doctor on duty just hoped to evacuate the place—he glanced at Wei Jia's test results, scribbled a prescription onto a piece of paper, and told us the boy should rest. We picked up the medicine: a bottle of Vitamin C pills. On the way back, I decided to take the new Badaling Expressway, and both father and son became alert. "This is a highway," Wei Ziqi explained to the boy. "Look how big it is—that's so people can drive faster here." The boy fell asleep, but his father woke him up in the heart of the Jundu Mountains so he could see his first tunnel. By the time we reached Sancha, it was dark, but Cao Chunmei and Mimi were waiting at the end of the road, flashlights in hand. Mimi told me that ever since we had left, the mother had worried incessantly about *baixuebing*, "white blood cell disease." Wei Ziqi reassured her, repeating the doctor's words, and they put the boy to bed. But that night I couldn't sleep. I found myself thinking about the same thing—"white blood cell disease" is the Chinese term for leukemia.

⊙   ⊙   ⊙

MY OWN CHILDHOOD HAD included more than its share of medical problems. As a boy, I'd been hospitalized for asthma and pneumonia, and I was injury-prone—the kind of kid whose parents were always getting phone calls about broken bones and bad injuries. Part of the problem was size: I was always one of the smallest children in my class. In 1974, when I was five years old, I weighed only thirty-five pounds— not much bigger than Wei Jia. My nursery school teacher recommended that I repeat the year, to give me time to grow.

Wei Ziqi and I are almost exactly the same age: I was born two weeks ahead of him, in June of 1969. Once, we discussed our educational experiences, comparing the years that we had entered various grades, and after a while he looked shrewdly at me. "Did you flunk?" he said.

In all my years of American education, I had always been a year older than my classmates, but nobody ever asked me that question. Back in 1974, my parents referred to it as "being held back," and they always stressed that I was undersized rather than stupid. But there is no such euphemism in the language of the Chinese countryside.

"Yes," I said to Wei Ziqi. "I flunked nursery school."

"I figured you must have flunked a year," he said with a grin. He told me that he'd failed as well—he'd repeated fifth grade, mostly because he was also undersized.

By the time I was an adolescent, my health was good, but I never shook a lingering fear of hospitals. Taking Wei Jia into Beijing had been a kind of torture—it reminded me how I'd often felt as a child. The morning after his blood test, I left the village and returned home to downtown Beijing, where I finally had a chance to look up *xuexiaoban* in a dictionary. The term means "platelet," and I went online, searching for childhood diseases with bruising and low platelet counts. Over and over, the same thing kept coming up: leukemia. In a panic, I sent e-mails to three doctor friends in the United States, copying the printouts from Wei Jia's blood tests. The messages went out late at night, my time; by early morning all the doctors had already responded: one from

San Francisco, one from Missouri, one from New Jersey. Each believed that leukemia seemed unlikely, although they recommended a biopsy. Independently, they all guessed that it was a condition known as ITP—immune thrombocytopenic purpura. ITP is a disease with unknown causes, and it often strikes children. Usually, if the patient rests and eats well, the situation resolves itself within two months. Rarely is it chronic, but Wei Jia's platelet count was so dangerously low that his blood might not clot; in particular, there was a risk of bleeding in the brain. "I'd give him steroids or immune globulin," one doctor wrote. My friend Eileen Kavanagh, who was finishing medical school in New Jersey, responded, "The thing that bothers me the most is that they didn't put him in the hospital to figure all of this out."

I telephoned Sancha and Cao Chunmei answered. "He's fine," she said. "He just had a nosebleed, but it wasn't serious."

"You can't let him do anything rough," I said. "Don't let him play or run around. Just keep him in bed while we figure out what to do. This is serious—make sure he stays quiet."

I called Mimi and we considered the options. There was no transport in the village, apart from motorcycles. Mimi had her family car, but we had no idea where to take him; I wasn't going to return to the Children's Hospital. While we were talking, my cell phone rang.

"Now his nose won't stop bleeding," Cao Chunmei said. She put her husband on the line. "It's OK as long as he's lying down," Wei Ziqi said. "But if he sits up it starts bleeding again."

"He should be in the hospital," I said. "The doctor made a mistake. Just keep him lying down and I'll be there as soon as I can."

I ran to Mimi's apartment to get the car keys; she was already telephoning people, searching for a different hospital. I started the Santana and headed north, cursing the Beijing traffic. If I was lucky I'd make it there in less than two hours.

CAO CHUNMEI GREW UP on the opposite side of the brick-and-stone Great Wall. Her home village is located down in the valley, where conditions are better than in Sancha, and her family wasn't as poor as

Wei Ziqi's. But life was simple during her childhood, and she paid for school supplies with eggs—money was rarely used in those days. Every weekend, along with her brother and sister, she hiked the five miles to her grandmother's house. Their route took them across the high pass at Jiankou, one of the most spectacularly steep sections of the Great Wall. The impressive brick fortifications were completed around the turn of the seventeenth century, near the end of the Ming dynasty, but none of that history mattered to Cao Chunmei as a girl. From her perspective, the Great Wall simply defined the two worlds of her childhood. It was the barrier between school and family, weekdays and weekends, and countless times she crossed the threshold of crumbling bricks.

After finishing the eighth grade, Cao Chunmei left school and began working at a nearby garment factory where her older sister already had a job. The plant produced military clothes: standard-issue shirts and jackets, the kind of gear that's also worn by peasants. On the assembly line, Cao Chunmei started by making collars; then she moved to cuffs, finally to button-sewing. She lived at home with her parents. By bicycle it was only a half hour ride, and her family was prosperous enough to allow her to keep her earnings. Later she recalled these years as some of the happiest of her life.

On the assembly line, Cao Chunmei worked with a young woman from Sancha. One day, the woman asked if Cao Chunmei had a boyfriend, and she answered yes. But the woman didn't seem to listen. "You should meet my uncle," she said. She told Cao Chunmei that the uncle was only a little older than her, and he wasn't married.

"I decided to do it," Cao Chunmei remembered, years later. "I thought my boyfriend at the time was too young, and he was from a place very close to my hometown. I'm not sure why I felt that way, but for some reason I didn't want to marry somebody close to home."

The coworker, it turned out, was the daughter of the Shitkicker. The man and Wei Ziqi are distant cousins—they share the same great-great-grandfather—and the daughter arranged a meeting between Cao Chunmei and Wei Ziqi. In the countryside, evaluations of potential partners tend to be swift and brutal, and the passage of time does not necessarily soften them with gauzy nostalgia. More than a decade after they met, Cao Chunmei still recalled her exact impressions. "I thought he was very short and very black," she said. "His skin was so dark! But when he spoke, I thought he was funny. He had a good sense of humor. He didn't talk in the way that most people do; he was more interesting, and he said things that might not have been appropriate. I thought he seemed fun."

Eight months later, on New Year's Day of 1993, they were married. They held the wedding at a restaurant in the small town of Miaocheng. Nearly fifteen years after Cao Chunmei's wedding, she could not recall the name of the restaurant, the dishes that were served, or the guest list—the sort of details that, for an American woman, would be etched across memory for all time. But Cao Chunmei could still note every financial detail in perfect order. The banquet cost six hundred and ninety yuan—around eighty-five dollars. Gifts were cash, as is traditional at Chinese weddings, and the most the couple received from a single guest was twelve dollars. The wedding resulted in a net profit of one hundred and sixty dollars. When Cao Chunmei talked about the event, she recited these numbers like an accountant.

For two years the young couple lived in Huairou, where Cao Chunmei worked as a cook. But she never felt comfortable in the city. "Too many people," she told me once. "It makes me nervous. In the village, if you want to go somewhere, it's easier to get around. And it's quiet and peaceful. If you're done with your work, you can relax in peace, or you can go for a walk."

Wei Ziqi held a similar opinion of city life, and after Cao Chunmei became pregnant they moved back across the Great Wall to Sancha. They lived with Wei Ziqi's parents, whose house still had dirt floors and walls made of mud mixed with sorghum stalks. The conditions were far worse than what Cao Chunmei was accustomed to, but this didn't particularly bother her. She liked the quietness of the village, and initially she was happy to live in a place that seemed poor but peaceful.

Over time, though, her feelings about Sancha changed. In 1997, she gave birth to Wei Jia, and then both her in-laws died within the span of a year. Cao Chunmei became friends with other village women, most of whom had also married in from the outside, and she began to hear stories. At first they were hard to believe—the kind of tales that were told in whispers. She learned that one local woman had been involved in a decades-long affair with a relative of her husband. They even had a child together, although everybody pretended that it was the husband's son. Another woman had borne three children to three different men. She had done it through migration—often this is the best way to avoid the planned-birth policy. Periodically the Sancha woman found work in a new city, where she invariably found a new partner and had a baby. Her legal husband remained in the village, where he conducted an ongoing affair with a neighbor's wife. It was another open secret: whenever the neighbor went to work in the fields, the other man crept over to his house.

"There's a lot of this sort of thing in Sancha," Cao Chunmei told me, after we'd known each other for a long time. She said there were a number of village affairs, and even some rumors of incest. "It has something to do with the local environment," she said. "Somehow it became more accepted because this place is so remote. This sort of thing doesn't happen so often in my village. But in my village there are more than two hundred families, and here there are so few.

"When I first came here," she continued, "I thought that everything was fine, that it was a normal place. But then in my second year I began to learn about all the affairs and the wrong things that people did. Wei Ziqi never talked to me about these things. Many people here are from his family, so he can't speak openly about it." She told me that sometimes an affair leads to violence, and inevitably the woman is the target. "Sometimes the man will beat his wife," she said. "But there's never a fight between the two men involved."

In her first decade at Sancha, Cao Chunmei never visited the Great Wall above the village. For her, the ruins belong strictly to childhood, when she used to hike to her grandmother's house, and she sees no point in making the two-hour trek in her new home. She is a heavy-set woman with a round face, and her hair is white—it started to turn when she was only a teenager. Nowadays she dyes it black, but the roots still show pale. Her left eye is blue, her right eye brown. She has a quick, gentle smile, and she always seems happiest with Wei Jia; but there is a distinct sadness behind the woman's mismatched eyes. She's seen the peacefulness of the countryside dissolve like a mirage, and she knows there's nothing easy about raising the last child in a village.

I PARKED AT THE top of the dead-end road. Inside the Weis' house, the boy lay on the *kang*. His face was pale and flecks of blood had dried dark around his nose. He didn't say anything when I touched his forehead.

"It's a lot of trouble for you to come out here," Cao Chunmei said.

"It's no problem," I said. I pressed the boy's brow—he was on fire. His eyes looked frightened but still he didn't speak.

"Will you eat some lunch?" Cao Chunmei asked politely.

"I already ate," I said. "I think we should go now."

They decided that Cao Chunmei would stay behind until Wei Jia was settled in the hospital. She had prepared a change of clothes and a roll of toilet paper in the Mickey Mouse backpack. Wei Ziqi carried his son down the hill and into the backseat of the car. The boy lay with his head in his father's lap.

The road from the village is steeply switchbacked, and I drove slowly, so the car wouldn't bounce. After ten minutes Wei Jia said that he felt sick, and I pulled over. He made gagging noises and twin trails of blood trickled down from his nostrils. Wei Ziqi dabbed at them with the toilet paper; in the sunlight the boy looked even paler. After a minute we set off again.

Autumn is the best season in northern China, and it was a beautiful day, the sky clear and bright. The peasants had come to the final crop of the year, the soybeans, and rows of men with short-handled scythes stood bent in the fields, heads bowed like penitent monks. People threshed the haylike stalks all along the road. We had nearly an hour of rough mountain driving before the Badaling Expressway, and I tried to keep calm by focusing on the details of the countryside. We climbed out of the Huaisha River valley, across the tunneled pass, and then we descended to Nine-Crossings River. The waterway colors caught my eye—the orange-painted rails of the bridge, the dark pools of stagnant water, the white-barked poplars along the banks. At Black Mountain Stockade we had to stop again; this time the boy vomited. His nose was bleeding steadily. His father tore off fresh pieces of paper and shoved them inside to stop the flow.

The road climbed again, winding steeply through walnut orchards, and then we reached the last pass of the day. From there it's all downhill to the valley where the Ming emperors are buried. Their tombs are scattered across the plain, each laid out to face the south, and the gold-tiled roofs shined bright in the October sunshine. We drove by the grave of Xuande, the fifth Ming ruler. According to legend he killed three Mongols with his own bow. Next we passed the tomb of his grandfather, Yongle, the great ruler who established the capital in Beijing in 1421. Just beyond that grave, Wei Ziqi asked me to stop again.

Wei Jia murmured that he had to go to the bathroom. His father took down the boy's pants and he produced a sickly stream of diarrhea. He was completely white now and there was no expression in his eyes. We were less than ten minutes from the highway.

"I think we should keep moving," I said.

"Give him a minute," Wei Ziqi said.

I had pulled over in a ditch beside an apple orchard that had been recently harvested. On the road, a steady line of tour buses roared past on their way to the Ming tombs. I wondered if any tourists caught a glimpse of the scene: the parked car with its flashing lights; the father in the ditch, cradling his son. The harvested orchard, fruit picked clean, branches bare in the stark autumn light.

MIMI HAD ARRANGED A spot for Wei Jia in the children's ward of the Peking University Health Center Number Three, where the blood specialists were supposed to be good. We registered the boy, and after he was in bed he seemed to recover some of his color. But now he was so frightened that he struggled against anybody in a white coat; when they tried to take a blood test, he bit one nurse and took a swing at another. His father and I pinned him to the bed while they performed the test. Afterward he calmed down, and a nurse said that he would be kept under close observation to see if his platelet count improved. She asked who would stay with the boy tonight.

"I will," Wei Ziqi said.

"You can't!" the woman said sharply. "Only female comrades are allowed to spend the night in the hospital."

"His mother will come tomorrow," Wei Ziqi said. "Can't I stay with him for one night?"

"Absolutely not! Only female comrades allowed!"

"Look, they live two hours away," Mimi said. "I'm sorry, but the only family he has here is his father."

"The father cannot stay here! Female comrades only! You can stay if you wish, but not the father!"

The nurse was a heavyset woman in her fifties, and she had planted herself solidly in front of Wei Jia's bed. She kept repeating that phrase— *Female comrades only!* The more she said it, the stranger it sounded; almost nobody used those old Communist terms anymore. The boy began to cry again, his face panicked. "I don't want to stay here alone!" he said. "I don't want to stay here alone!"

"Don't worry, you're not going to stay here alone," Mimi said, and I turned to the nurse: "Can we talk about this outside?"

I didn't want to get angry, because Chinese hospitals have a reputation for mistreating people from the countryside. As calmly as possible, I explained the situation, and Mimi begged the nurse to make an exception. But she was adamant—people in Chinese bureaucracies often behave this way, especially those who are middle-aged. They were educated during the chaotic years of the Cultural Revolution, and many of them have spent their entire adult lives in the work-unit system of Communist China. They essentially missed out on the Reform years, and they lack the flexibility and pragmatism that have become so common among younger Chinese. In the hospital the nurse refused to budge, and finally I decided to drive back to the village and pick up Cao Chunmei.

"You better be back here by ten o'clock!" the nurse said. "If she comes after ten, we won't let her in. We lock the doors at night. Those are the rules!"

I called Cao Chunmei and asked her to find a motorcycle ride down into the valley, so we could save time. But half an hour later she called back: only one neighbor had a motorbike, and tonight he was already too drunk to drive. It was dark by the time I reached the dead-end road. Cao Chunmei waited with a bag she had packed for the hospital. It contained several bottles of local spring water—most villagers believe that Sancha water is healthier than anything you can buy in the city.

"It's a lot of trouble for you," she said, hurrying into the car.

"It's not a problem," I said. "Do you have everything you need?"

"I'm fine," she said. "Have you eaten yet?"

"I already ate," I said. In truth I hadn't had a meal since morning, but there was something reassuring about the polite exchange. In rural China, no matter how stressful a situation becomes, you can always count on certain conversations, and Cao Chunmei's words made me feel calmer. Driving fast through the mountains, I watched the shadowy landmarks slip past for the fourth time since dawn: the Huaisha River valley, the Nine-Crossings River, the Black Mountain Stockade. The roofs of the Ming tombs shone ghostlike in the darkness. The expressway was empty; we made it to the hospital with half an hour to spare. Wei Jia was already fast asleep, and the boy didn't stir when I told his parents good night.

FOR MOST OF THAT week Wei Jia ran a fever. On the fifth day, it reached one hundred and four degrees, and his platelet count dipped beneath fifteen thousand. If it went much lower, there was a serious risk of bleeding in the brain.

Mimi and I visited daily, and every night I wrote my doctor friends in the United States. They told me that a combination of rest and good diet often stabilizes a child with ITP, but we still weren't certain of the diagnosis. In the States, a patient in his condition would be given a blood transfusion, but the Chinese doctors hadn't recommended it yet. And I had advised the parents that such measures should be a last resort. The blood supply in China isn't safe; donors are in short supply and the system relies primarily on people who are paid for giving blood. At the time of Wei Jia's illness, experts estimated that more than one million Chinese had been infected with H.I.V. The epidemic was particularly severe in Henan Province, just south of Beijing, because of unsanitary donor practices. The big cities had problems, too—I knew a Chinese-American journalist who had recently visited one Beijing donor center and was immediately offered a fake ID so she could sell her blood. Even better-run clinics usually limited their blood analysis to antibody tests, which are cheaper and less reliable than the molecular diagnostics used in developed countries.

On the seventh day Wei Jia began to bleed from his gums. That morning the doctors gave him a bone-marrow test for leukemia, and finally they decided that he needed a transfusion. Wei Ziqi telephoned me and asked to borrow nearly a thousand dollars. In China, there is no national health insurance, and city residents usually rely on their work units for coverage. Most farmers are completely on their own, which is one reason they tend to be so careful with their savings—a rural person has to be prepared to pay cash for a medical emergency. And hospitals tend to mistreat peasants as a result. Doctors are wary of getting stuck with an unpaid bill, so they always demand money up front. It wasn't until 2009 that the central government began to take steps toward establishing some form of universal health care, although it's still unclear how comprehensive such coverage will be.

At the time of Wei Jia's illness, only private insurance would cover a family in the countryside. Unlike most farmers, the Weis had purchased a policy for their son. It had been offered when he entered kindergarten, and the Weis had been smart enough to buy it; now the majority of his treatment would be covered. But the hospital wouldn't wait for reimbursement: they demanded cash now. In such situations, families usually raise money from relatives, which might take days to organize.

Mimi was preparing to leave for a work trip to Europe, so I went alone to the hospital. Wei Jia slept fitfully; his mother told me the doctors had drugged him. Dried blood had caked around his mouth—his gums were still oozing. Accompanied by Wei Ziqi, I introduced myself to the physician on duty. Her name was Dr. Zhao, and she sat in an office with another physician and three nurses. I asked if the transfusion was critical.

"Who is this?" she said sharply to Wei Ziqi. "Why is he here? Why is he asking questions?"

"He's a writer," Wei Ziqi said proudly.

"I'm a friend, as I just explained," I said quickly. "I was the one who brought the boy to the hospital. I have some simple questions about what we should do."

"This isn't his affair!" Dr. Zhao said to Wei Ziqi. "You're the parent, and you have responsibility. He has nothing to do with it."

"I care about the child," I said. "I've been trying to help them since he got sick. I just want us to make the right decision."

"The decision has already been made!" With that, the woman turned her back on me. For a moment I stood in silence. In China, I was accustomed to people being more patient with me; in general they're inclined to grant a sort of exaggerated respect to any foreigner who speaks the language. Usually this deference makes life easier, and like any long-term foreign resident I learned to play it to my advantage. But I had no illusions about what it really meant. At the root of that respect is insecurity: deep down, many Chinese, especially educated people, are slightly ashamed of the way their country might appear to an outsider. Dr. Zhao didn't see me as a person who cared for a sick child; in her eyes I was simply a foreigner who distrusted her competence.

And she was clearly annoyed by Wei Ziqi's faith in my judgment. Together we brought out the city woman's worst instincts, from both sides of the spectrum: she responded to the peasant with arrogance and the foreigner with insecurity. I turned to the other women in the room. "Who can I talk to about this?" I said, but they ignored me. I repeated the question: silence. One of the nurses whispered a joke that I couldn't hear; the others laughed. I felt my face turn red, and that was when my patience ended—I wasn't going to listen to their laughter while the child suffered next door.

"It's very simple," I said. "I'm paying for this. Before I pay the money, I have to know why he needs the transfusion now. If you don't talk to me, I won't pay it."

Dr. Zhao turned to me, her face tight with anger. "He needs immune globulin," she said. "If he doesn't get it, there's a risk that he'll have brain damage. Already he's bleeding inside his mouth. We know what to do, and you don't understand anything about it."

"I'm trying to understand as much as I can," I said. "If you speak slowly, it helps. I'm only asking questions because I care about the boy."

"If you care, then let us give him the transfusion!"

"I've talked with other doctors who say that maybe a transfusion isn't necessary," I said. "They said that usually they would wait for the biopsy results."

"How long will that be?" the woman said loudly. "We don't even know. It could be a week. We can't wait that long!"

"Why hasn't he been tested to see if he has a virus that's causing his fever?"

"We know that his platelet level is low! That's our primary concern!"

"Have you done a test for hepatitis?"

"He doesn't have hepatitis!"

"Have you tested for it? I was told that it's a possibility."

"There's no need to test for it! Hepatitis isn't a concern!"

"If you give him gamma globulin, is there a risk that the blood might carry some disease?"

"Of course there's a risk!" Dr. Zhao spat out the words. "It could have H.I.V. or hepatitis or something else!"

"Don't they test the blood?"

"You can't test it completely."

"I think you can," I said.

"Believe me, you can't!"

It disgusted me to hear a doctor say such nonsense, but I tried another approach: "Where does the blood come from?"

"How am I supposed to know?" The woman was shouting now, and I backed out of the room with Wei Ziqi. I told him that the blood supply was my main concern, and he nodded calmly. Using my cell phone, I called an American I knew who worked for a medical company in Beijing. She told me that her organization followed international testing standards for blood, and she checked to see if it was possible to arrange a sale of gamma globulin. A moment later she called back.

"They can deliver it to you," she said. "It costs three hundred and seventy-eight dollars per unit. I think that one unit should be enough for a five-year-old, if he's not too big."

"He's very small," I said.

"That should be fine," she said. "They'll deliver it, but you have to get the hospital there to accept it."

Technically it's illegal for such an organization to sell blood, but that's how many things work in China. I took a deep breath and returned to the doctor's room. "If I buy clean blood, can we use that?" I said.

"There's no guaranteed clean blood in Beijing," the doctor said.

"There is," I said, and then I told her the name of the organization. "They have clean blood."

"No, they don't," she said. "There's no way to test for all of these things."

"I'm certain they can test for H.I.V. and hepatitis," I said.

"It's impossible," the doctor said. "There's no test."

"Forget about the test," I said. "That isn't important right now. What I want to know is, if I get blood from them and have it delivered here, will you give it to the child?"

"That's impossible! They won't sell you blood!"

"I've already talked to them," I said. "They've agreed to sell it."

"We won't accept it," she said. "It's against hospital policy. What kind of question is this? Why do you even think of doing something like this? Who do you think you are?"

"You won't tell me where your blood comes from, and you won't tell me whether it's safe," I said. "So I'm trying to find a source that's safe. This is the only reason I'm asking."

"There's no safe blood in Beijing," she said. "You have no option other than using what we have. There's a risk, but the risk is higher if he doesn't get the gamma globulin. You need to make this decision right now!"

I was shaking with anger by the time I left the room. I called the American woman and explained the situation; she said that there was one more thing we could do. "I know some Chinese doctors who used to work at your hospital," she said. "I'll ask them to check on the blood supply. They'll know where the blood comes from, and we can see if the donor center is reliable or not. I'll call you back."

I waited in Wei Jia's hospital room with the parents. Throughout the past week, they had remained perfectly calm: no tears, no panicking, no raised voices. Life in the countryside had toughened them, and it had also taught them the meaning of *Mei banfa*: Nothing can be done. During my arguments with the doctor, Wei Ziqi had stood quietly in the background. He made it clear that he deferred to my judgment; he had great faith in my unseen American medical friends, and he shared none of the insecurities of the educated Chinese. For him it was simply logical: he didn't know anything about these issues, and he had no way of gaining information, and so he trusted the foreigner with his son's health. My own reaction was different—I was also badly out of my element, but the seriousness of the situation made me want to control it. In truth all I could do was try to get information, hoping to make the right decision, and now it was a matter of waiting for a phone call.

Wei Jia's hospital room was shared by two other boys. One was a twelve-year-old suffering from inflammation of the cardiac muscle, and the other was an eight-year-old with kidney problems. The room's walls had been painted light pink and the only decoration was a Mickey Mouse clock. A clothesline hung across one wall, used by the mothers who had been living with their sons.

The eight-year-old came from Jilin Province, in the northeast, and his parents had brought him to Beijing for medical care. This was his second extended stay in the hospital, and since June the doctors had treated him with massive amounts of hormones. Over the past three months his body weight had increased by 50 percent. Everything about the child looked swollen: he had a big belly, sausage-link legs, and a face as round as a mooncake. He was constantly eating, and his mother was constantly talking about his eating. The Chinese love to talk about food and in particular there's nothing better than talking about food and children. Over the past week the mothers had become friends—most

Chinese are naturally so social that if you throw them together they talk endlessly, even in the most stressful situation. I sat there listening, my phone in hand.

"He didn't get fat until he started the hormones," said the boy's mother. "Now he eats all the time, but he won't eat fruit."

"Wei Jia won't eat fruit, either," Cao Chunmei said. She sat on the bed beside her sleeping son.

"Fruit, eggs, milk—he won't eat anything that's good for him," said the kidney mother.

"Neither will Wei Jia."

"They should give him hormones, too," the woman said. "He's too small."

The twelve-year-old wore headphones and listened to a CD player. He had the gangly look of an adolescent and for the past week he had been living in this room, surrounded by the parents and their constant conversation. He had his music turned up loud. His grandmother was also there, a sixty-eight-year-old woman from the countryside of Hebei. Of all the adults, she was the most talkative, and now she offered advice to Cao Chunmei.

"The first thing you need to take care of is the boy's health," the old woman said. "If somebody is healthy, he can always work and earn a living. The second most important thing is education. When I was young, I had no schooling—I still can't read! When I was a little girl, I remember one of my aunts saying to my father, 'Why should you pay for her to be educated? She'll just marry into another family eventually. That means you're paying for the education of somebody else's family. Why would you do that?' So they didn't send me to school. That's why I say that education is so important."

"I'm hungry," said the fat child.

Wei Ziqi laughed. "He's hungry again!"

"He's always hungry," Cao Chunmei said admiringly. "That's why he's so fat."

"You just ate!" the fat boy's mother said.

"I'm hungry! I'm hungry!" The boy's voice rose as if he were going to cry. He cried all the time—he had the whining air of a city kid who knows how to get what he wants. The mother opened a wooden cabinet next to the bed and took out a hospital tray of half-eaten pork and rice. The boy set to it eagerly. Wei Jia was still sleeping. My cell phone rang.

"It's pretty good news," the American woman said to me. She had discovered that our hospital used the same blood bank as her company; the only difference was that our hospital didn't test as thoroughly. "I talked with doctors here," she said. "They haven't ever come up with a positive for H.I.V. That blood bank has been safe so far."

I thanked her and hung up. On impulse, I called Ted Scott, my doctor friend in San Francisco, and a cheerful voice picked up: "Hi! This is Ted, sorry I can't come to the phone right now . . ." I had no idea what time it was; later he told me that he was working the swing shift at the ER. I stared at my phone, trying to think of somebody else I could talk to. I wanted to hear that we had done everything possible, that it would all turn out fine. But there was nobody else: *Mei banfa.* Finally I looked up at Wei Ziqi.

"I think it's OK," I said.

We went downstairs to the hospital's payment division. Clerks sat behind windows like tellers at a bank, and cash was everywhere: packed into drawers, strewn across tables, spinning in counting machines. In China the largest bill is only one hundred yuan, the equivalent of about twelve dollars, and any major purchase requires a huge stack of cash. I had brought eight thousand yuan—a sheaf as thick as a novel in manuscript. I pulled the money out of my bag and handed it over to a clerk, who tossed it into a machine without a word.

Upstairs, after I gave the receipt to the nurse, the doctors began to prepare for the transfusion. I knew the medical people didn't want me around, so I told Wei Ziqi and Cao Chunmei I'd come back tomorrow. Wei Jia had woken up; the boy looked pale but he gave me a smile. I promised that once he got better we'd go to the zoo. I caught a cab home, took a shower, and had dinner alone. In the evening the numbness lifted and all at once, sitting in my empty apartment, I felt so helpless I could hardly breathe.

◎　◎　◎

AFTER THE TRANSFUSION, WEI Jia's fever broke. Within two days his platelet count returned to normal, and it held steady for the rest of the week. The bone-marrow test showed no leukemia. The doctors decided that the condition was in fact ITP, and the worst threat had passed.

At the end of that week a group of relatives came to visit. There were four men: Wei Jia's maternal grandfather, his great-uncle, another uncle, and a distant relative named Li Ziwen. All but one of the men had arrived directly from the countryside, and they wore peasant clothes of military green and dark blue. The great-uncle was seventy-one years old and he told me that he hadn't been to Beijing for almost three decades. Li Ziwen was the only city resident—he had grown up in Haizikou, across the pass from Sancha, but as a young man he had joined the military. After a decade of service he had accepted a government-assigned job in the capital, and now he had risen to become a low-ranking official. He wore black leather loafers with the Playboy logo and a sweater that said "Wolsey" on the breast. He had lost the leanness of the countryside—a soft cadre belly spilled over his belt.

The men entered the hospital room and gathered around the bed. Wei Jia sat cross-legged; he had been reading a picture book. Cao Jifu, the grandfather, put his hand on the boy's back and spoke softly to him. The sudden attention made Wei Jia shy and he bowed his head. The sheets had not been changed for more than a week and they were covered with red-brown stains from all the blood tests.

After a few minutes somebody mentioned lunch. Li Ziwen, the city dweller, reached into his pocket and pulled out a wad of bills: all hundreds. He dropped the money onto the bed.

"Use this for the child," he said.

Wei Ziqi tried to give the money back, but Li refused. For a minute, the two men argued gently, and finally Wei Ziqi nodded his head in thanks. Then the uncle stepped forward and placed another stack of bills on the bed, followed by the grandfather. The great-uncle went last. He was poorer than the others and his stack included some tens and twenties. The money lay in four bright piles on the bloodstained sheets. There was an awkward silence, and then Cao Chunmei pushed the cash out of sight, beneath the boy's pillow. Somebody mentioned lunch again.

Cao Chunmei stayed with Wei Jia while the men went to a restaurant across the street. We hired a private room, where after another brief argument the grandfather was given the seat of honor, facing the door. Wei Ziqi studied the menu for a good five minutes before ordering. When the waitress brought a bottle of 120-proof grain alcohol, he examined the seal. "Can you guarantee this bottle isn't counterfeit?" he said.

The waitress seemed surprised. "I'm pretty sure," she said. "But I guess I can't say for certain."

Li Ziwen took the bottle and ran his finger along the cap. "I don't know," he said. "There's a lot of fake *baijiu* nowadays. The fake stuff is bad for your health."

So is the real stuff, I thought to myself. Wei Ziqi sent the bottle back, and the next one as well. Finally the waitress returned with Red Star Erguotou. "We can guarantee this one," she said.

Wei Ziqi poured the Erguotou into shot glasses. The food began to appear, dish by dish, and each arrival inspired a fresh round of commentary. At a well-organized Chinese banquet there are no lulls in conversation: as long as you have food, you have something to talk about.

"The fish-flavored pork is better than the one we had the other night," Wei Ziqi said. "But the iron-plate beef at this place isn't as good."

"It's a little salty."

"These beans are OK. Just OK, though."

The waitress brought a dish of dried beef. Wei Ziqi tried it and said, "This doesn't taste right."

One by one, the men tasted the beef and complained.

"No, it's not good."

"It's too old, I think."

"If you eat that you'll get sick."

Wei Ziqi called the waitress into the room. "This dish is bad," he said. "You should take it back."

The woman removed the dish. The next time she entered the room, Wei Ziqi complained that they had failed to put the duck's head into our soup. "You should do that as a matter of course," he said sternly. Here in the restaurant—inspecting the bottles, judging the food, making quick decisions—he seemed completely different from the man who had stood in the background during the arguments about his son's blood transfusion. But it was simply rural logic: Wei Ziqi didn't know anything about platelets and biopsies, whereas food was his trade, so here at the restaurant he was the expert. And perhaps he wanted the others to see him in control.

The men drank steadily and the grandfather's face was the first to turn red from the alcohol. He stood up and gave me a formal toast, using my Chinese name: "Ho Wei, we appreciate all of your help with Wei Jia."

Everybody held up his glass, and we drained them. "Ho Wei has a lot of friends in America who are doctors," Wei Ziqi said. "They gave us a lot of help, too."

Somebody asked about the boy's platelet count, and Wei Ziqi said that it had improved since the transfusion. He described our drive into Beijing, when Wei Jia was bleeding and we had stopped repeatedly on the mountain roads. After the story was finished, the other men continued discussing the boy's health, and Wei Ziqi turned to me. "You know," he said quietly, "I was frightened during that drive."

I told him that I'd been scared, too.

All of the men had turned red and now the toasts came faster. Li Ziwen, the city resident, exchanged shots with the grandfather. "This is the second time we've drunk together," the grandfather said.

Li Ziwen laughed. "The first time was when Wei Jia was born," he said. "Back then I was in the military, and they gave me two days' vacation."

"We drank a lot that day!" the grandfather said. He raised his glass, and Li Ziwen joined him, and together they drank to the memory of the boy's birth.

II
———

WINTER IS THE QUIETEST SEASON IN SANCHA. THERE ARE no crops, and almost no work in the orchards, apart from occasional pruning and grafting. The men gather firewood, and sometimes they follow game trails into the mountains, where they set loop snares in hopes of catching a badger or a feral pig. Mostly, though, people stay indoors. Snowfall is rare, because of the dryness, but the temperature is usually below freezing. At home the *kang* is the only source of heat. Much of daily life takes place atop those large brick beds, and if you walk into a home at nine in the morning there's a good chance that people will still be huddled under the covers. They eat less—in winter they have two daily meals instead of three. They sleep nine or ten hours a night, and they often doze away the afternoon. Mornings are silent. On a cold day in the village, the place is so still that it seems as if the residents are in hibernation.

After Wei Jia returned from the hospital, in November of 2002, he stayed home from kindergarten. For two months he hardly left the house, and his parents gave him a course of steroids that had been prescribed by the doctors. There was a brief period during which the boy whined and cried easily—he had learned this behavior from his roommate in the hospital, the pudgy city child. Whenever Wei Jia cried, his parents mocked him relentlessly. "You look like a monkey," his father would say, laughing at the kid's tears. "Cry, monkey, cry!" His mother joined in the fun, and soon the child abandoned that routine. Over the winter he gained nine pounds. His father taught him how to write some simple Chinese characters, and together they listened to English-language tapes.

Winter became one of my favorite times to visit the countryside. Without the summer brush, trails were clear, and sometimes I hiked for hours along the Great Wall. The mountains were peaceful and there was a sleepy openness to the village; at night the peasants often gathered in somebody's house to drink *baijiu* and play cards. One evening that winter, Wei Ziqi and I had dinner with his nephew Wei Quanyou, and the men began to talk about automobiles. Wei Ziqi hoped to get a license someday—that was a plan he often mentioned.

"Ho Wei is a good driver," Wei Ziqi said.

"I'm average," I said.

"No, you're not. How long have you been driving?"

"Since I was sixteen. Many Americans start when they're sixteen."

"Almost twenty years!"

"Not quite."

"You should have seen what it was like when Wei Jia was sick," Wei Ziqi said, and he told the story of our drive into Beijing. Wei Quanyou listened attentively, although I was certain that he had already heard the tale. The story had become a familiar one in the village, where there is a tradition of helping neighbors with medical problems. If somebody in Sancha goes to the hospital, other villagers stop by the home with cash donations—in a nation without rural health insurance, this is how the villagers protect each other against medical expenses. Recovery always means that the grateful family hosts a banquet. Wei Jia's illness represented the first time that Mimi and I were truly involved in village life—we responded in ways that were recognizable to locals, and now they greeted us more warmly than in the past. And the experiences of the last year had made me feel differently about Sancha. In the beginning I had seen the village as an escape, a place where I could hike and write in peace; but now I went there for different reasons. In China it was the closest I ever came to home.

That evening, Wei Quanyou had invited me to dinner, as a way of showing gratitude. He was a tiny man, not much taller than five feet, and he had the sweetest smile in the village. He never said much—at dinners he always seemed to be listening to other people's stories. He lived in a rough-built house whose walls had been covered with old newspapers, and the only decoration was a cheap paper map of China. Across the map, various cities had been numbered by hand from one to thirty-four. The numbers began with Beijing and ended with Macau; in between they ran through Shanghai, Tianjin, Xi'an, Lhasa, Ürümqi—the whole range of the country.

"Are these places you've traveled to?" I asked, after we had started eating.

"Of course not!" Wei Quanyou said. "The farthest I've been is Beijing."

"So why did you write the numbers?"

"Those are the cities on the China Central Television weather forecast," he said. He explained: every night on CCTV, the forecast appears in the same order, with Beijing first, then Shanghai, and then all the rest, with Macau last. Wei Quanyou had memorized the order and marked it on his map.

For a moment I was confused. "Is there a special reason you did that?"

"No reason." He laughed as if to say, What else are you going to do in Sancha during January?

For Wei Ziqi, though, that was the first year the winter routines began to change. Six months earlier, in the summer of 2002, the government had paved the dirt road to the upper village, and then motorists began to find their way to the empty lot at the top of the hill. The capital's car boom was gaining momentum—that year, Beijing residents purchased more than a quarter million new vehicles, the largest increase in the city's history. More drivers were exploring the countryside, and during the summer Wei Ziqi and Cao Chunmei started serving simple meals in their home. They charged two and a half dollars a head, and business was good.

In the winter Wei Ziqi decided to expand into a real restaurant and guesthouse. While the rest of the village hibernated, he worked hard: he paved the threshing platform in front of his house, and he built a new kitchen. He made frequent trips to Huairou in order to buy cement and other supplies. He began carrying a cell phone that could be used in Huairou; there was still no reception in the village. In the past, he'd always dressed the same regardless of where he was going, but now he was careful to avoid peasant clothes on trips to town—he'd learned that from our visits to the hospital. He bought a set of nonmilitary clothes, as well as a pair of city shoes: black leather loafers that cost four dollars. The brand name was Yidali—"Italy"—and he kept the box displayed prominently in his house. In the village he still wore camouflaged sneakers, like everybody else, but he slipped on the Italy whenever it was time to go to Huairou.

Huairou lies halfway between Sancha and Beijing, and this midpoint is social as well as geographic. It's hard to define exactly how the place feels: not quite a city, not quite a village. Fifteen years ago it was much closer to the village end of the spectrum. In 1995, when the Chinese government hosted the United Nations' Fourth World Women's Conference, they decided that they didn't want Hillary Clinton and five thousand other politically oriented foreign women descending on the capital. So they sent them to Huairou instead—a type of banishment. At that time, most buildings were of the type that had already become outdated in the capital: squat, blocky structures of three or four stories, covered in white tile and blue glass. Streets were wide; cars were few. Huairou was a city of exile—there was no good reason to go there from Beijing.

But over time it became something different to those who arrive from the opposite direction. Huairou is situated at the northern edge of the Beijing Plain, where roads fan out into the mountains, and the city is a natural first destination for people who leave villages. Beijing is often too big and disorienting, but Huairou is manageable for a person from the countryside. In the decade after the Women's Conference, it grew rapidly, and today the downtown population is nearly one hundred thousand. Neither city nor village, it's actually both: a city of villagers. Few residents are more than a generation removed from farmwork, and local businesses depend heavily on people moving back and forth between the countryside.

Like so many new towns in China, Huairou has the feel of a training ground. It's a city of gawkers and loiterers; people often appear to be lost. They stare at seven-story buildings; they gaze into shop windows; they wander into traffic—a Huairou driver learns to be attentive. On sunny days, crowds mill around the former site of the Women's Conference, which is now flanked by a KFC and a McDonald's. These fast-food restaurants are always packed, and the same is true for the single department store in town, which is called Da Shijie: The Big World. The Big World is five stories tall and stocked with virtually everything a Huairou shopper could want—appliances, clothes, toys, books. Peasants go there to ride the escalators. They stand poised before the moving metal, waiting for the perfect moment to take the leap; after a successful mount they clutch the rubber railings like a gymnast gripping the parallel bars. At the end of the line they hop to safety. They have a tendency to stop dead after dismount, as if waiting for a judge's score. Within the department store, there's a lot of good-natured jostling: people bump each other at the end of backed-up escalators, and they plow through crowded shop aisles, and they step on the heels of folks who are rubbernecking the central atrium. The decorating scheme of the Big World is simple in theme but complicated in execution. The theme is: things that shine and things that make noise. There are mirrors and glass railings and columns of polished steel; there are beeping lights and blaring loudspeakers; there are more reflective surfaces here than on a disco ball. It's hard to imagine any place more different from a quiet mountain village, and people from the countryside love the Big World—they stagger up the escalators and blink happily in the glaring lights. That's the trick of Huairou: it's a city of transformation, where people change as quick as a peasant with a pair of Italy loafers.

Wei Ziqi had relatives in the city, an older brother as well as various cousins from Sancha, and they introduced him to hardware shops where he could stock up for his renovations. During the early months of 2003, he found businesspeople he could trust. These were new types of relationships—in the village, it was rare to have any sort of link that was strictly economic. Urban Chinese describe such associations as *guanxi*, "connections," and a businessman learns to *la guanxi*. Literally the verb means "to pull, to drag, to haul," and the description is apt: *guanxi* takes work. Wei Ziqi invited contacts to restaurants; he drank shots of *baijiu*; he handed out cigarettes. He began to smoke himself. Previously he had abstained, because he believed the habit to be unhealthy and a waste of money. But for a Chinese male doing business, sharing smokes is a crucial part of pulling *guanxi*, and whenever Wei Ziqi went to Huairou he carried packs of Red Plum Blossom cigarettes.

At the end of winter, after paving his threshing platform and building a new kitchen, Wei Ziqi constructed a fishpond. The old leech pool still stood nearby, a relic of his first attempt at business, but the new pond was four times as big. He planned to stock it with rainbow trout. For advertising he found a discarded truck hood that was dented beyond recognition. He painted the metal blue, added the name of his restaurant in big red characters, and propped the sign against some rocks at the end of the Sancha road. At a printer's shop in Huairou he had business cards made up. For his restaurant, he had considered all sorts of grand titles—Sancha Farmyard Paradise, Sweet Waterhead Farmyard Villa, Sancha Great Nature Farmyard Leisure Paradise. But in the end he settled on something simpler: "An Outpost on the Great Wall." Even as he learned to pull *guanxi* city-style, he knew instinctively that his best selling point was old-fashioned rural simplicity. The business cards listed all the humble activities that a visitor could enjoy in Sancha:

> *Climb Mountains, Climb the Great Wall, Admire Wildflowers,*
> *Drink Springwater,*
> *Eat Wood-fired Meals, Sleep on a Heated Kang, Eat from the*
> *Five Grains,*
> *Learn from Observation of the Simple and the Plain,*
> *Return to the Simple Nature of the Past*

THE COUNTRYSIDE IS ONE of the few places that make urban Chinese feel nostalgic. In cities, the rush to modernity is headlong, and most old neighborhoods and landmarks have been razed. Residents have little time to think about the past, and history usually feels either irrelevant, like the ancient dynasties and the Great Wall, or extremely painful, like the campaigns of the Cultural Revolution. But there's a distance with rural life that makes people more comfortable. They've left it behind—most urban Chinese have some distant family history in the countryside, but it's not something they have to think about every day. As middle-class people become more prosperous, buying cars and having enough money for tourism, they realize how pleasant it is to go back to the countryside periodically. For a city person, it's one aspect of the past that feels easy to control—they can drive there, spend a night, and then return to the modern world.

But in truth there's no other part of China that is so trapped by history, at least when it comes to policies. In Sancha, people rarely talk about the past, but their relationship to the farmland is still fundamentally troubled in ways that it has been for more than a century. Some villagers, like Wei Ziqi, still have a few scattered documents that track this history. He's lost access to the family genealogy, but he keeps a collection of tattered land contracts that were passed down through the generations. During the Cultural Revolution, Wei Ziqi's father hid these papers inside the ceiling of the family home. Wei Ziqi himself is less careful—he folds them up, wraps them in a dirty red cloth, and leaves them at the bottom of a drawer.

The oldest document dates to the Qing dynasty, in the thirteenth year of the reign of the Guangxu Emperor. That was 1887, and the handwritten contract describes the leasing of a piece of land to a man named Yu Manjiang. No money changes hands—the agreed annual payment is only one *dou* of grain every year, a total of about two and a half gallons. Farming must have gone badly for Yu Manjiang, because the next contract shows that he pawned his land "due to lack of money." This agreement is from 1906, and it marks the first known legal appearance of a Wei ancestor: Wei Yongliang, the great-grandfather of Wei Ziqi. He agrees to pay 150 *diao* for the use of the land. Four years later, he buys it outright, for a total of 356 *diao*.

A *diao* is a string of copper coins, and the amounts documented on the Wei family contracts are tiny. Sometimes land is leased or pawned, which was common in those days. In imperial China, big landowners tended to dominate villages, and in Sancha the wealthiest family was named Yan. Poorer residents leased fields from the Yans, and even a family that was able to buy its own land often struggled to support itself. A couple of the Wei contracts describe how fields are divided between siblings; one document specifies that two sons will split the funeral costs when their father dies. In every case these agreements are written out by proxies, often poorly, and the farmers who sign them are clearly illiterate.

The Qing dynasty collapsed in 1912, giving way to the Republic of China, but little changed in the countryside. During the war decades of the 1930s and 1940s, conditions became particularly bad in the north, and this is reflected by the Wei contracts. Of all the agreements, the worst written is from 1946, and it's signed by Wei Mingyue, the Shitkicker's father. Because of financial problems, he agrees to pawn a plot of land to a cousin in exchange for thirteen gallons of corn. The contract states: "Next year, when the early-spring grains arrive, pay back the price and the land will be returned." The cousin who takes the land is Wei Youtan, the grandfather of Wei Ziqi. In the village, tensions between neighbors often have deep roots, although many details have been lost in the haze of the unwritten past. Wei Ziqi can't read the classical Chinese of the contracts, and he didn't know about the pawned land until I told him. When I asked about relations with the Shitkicker, he simply remarked, "It's complicated." In any case, the old contracts reflect degrees of poverty. Wei Ziqi's grandfather had enough grain to take land from the Shitkicker's father, but it wasn't enough to support a healthy family. Two years after that 1946 contract, the Idiot was born, the victim of a disability that was endemic in regions with poor diet.

By then the Communists had already risen to power in northern China. They made their base in Shaanxi Province, in the rugged hills of the loess plateau, and their core support consisted of poor peasants. One of Mao Zedong's main goals was to grant land ownership to the people who actually farmed, ending the system of landlord domination. As the Communists gained control of the country, they instituted this reform with remarkable speed. It helped that they had no scruples about violence: during the 1940s and 1950s, thousands of landlords were killed in cold blood. Fields were given to tenant farmers, and an additional fifty million families, mostly poor, suddenly received title. Most had never held any sort of legal ownership; many couldn't even sign their names.

In the Wei family contracts, this landmark historical change appears in a document from September of 1949, one month before the official founding of the People's Republic. The contract is beautifully illustrated: the borders are decorated with fat red ears of corn, and the bottom features pictures of farmers planting and harvesting under a healthy sun. At the top is an unsmiling portrait of Mao Zedong. The text explains that five members of the Wei family have the right to seven plots of land. The plots are listed, and in terms of acreage they are minuscule: 0.20 acres, 0.12 acres, 0.05 acres, 0.05 acres, 0.02 acres, 0.02 acres, and 0.025 acres. In total it's less than half an acre for an extended family, but it's more than the Weis ever possessed in the past. One plot formerly belonged to the Shitkicker's father—apparently he hadn't been able to redeem the pawned land—but there's no mention of who formerly owned the other fields. Wei Ziqi told me that they once belonged to members of the Yan family, the big local landlords, although he didn't know what became of them. "They were struggled against," he said, vaguely, and left it at that. His father never told him many stories about the past.

Across rural China, this initial stage of Communist land reform had an immediate effect. The new sense of ownership made farmers more likely to work hard, and in the early 1950s the nation's rural productivity increased, along with living standards. But these improvements turned out to be short-lived, because Mao became obsessed with deepening the revolution. During the second half of the 1950s, he commanded that rural land be reorganized once more, this time into village communes. Farmers lost their new titles, as well as their right to individual profit. Everything was to be shared in common—the fields, the labor, the harvest—and the outcome was disastrous. During the Great Leap Forward, from 1958 to 1961, Mao instructed farmers to contribute to industrial development; communes were expected to meet steel production quotas. They ended up melting down farm implements and cooking tools, and in many places the people stopped raising crops. A famine swept across rural China, and tens of millions starved to death.

Wei Ziqi's father never told any stories about this period, either. Like most people in the countryside, he refused to linger on unhappy memories, and the family collection of contracts essentially ends at the commune period. There's nothing to mark the beginning of collectivization, and there's no document from 1961, when the Great Leap Forward was finally abandoned. After that, the Chinese commune system remained in place, and if the Weis were given contracts, they didn't keep them. Only one document survives: an undated labor card that most likely was used in the late 1960s. The card notes how many workdays were contributed to the commune by "the wife of Wei Mingyuan" during the month of July. The woman isn't even named—such details are irrelevant in a male-dominated world of group labor. And the commune system never functioned well; without the possibility of personal gain, farmers lacked motivation, and rural poverty was still endemic in the 1970s. Those were the years of Wei Ziqi's childhood, when he often ate noodles made of elm bark.

After Deng Xiaoping came to power in 1978, he and other reformers wanted to grant some type of landownership to individuals. But this issue was extremely sensitive: privatizing land in Communist China, especially in the countryside, would be tantamount to admitting that the revolution had failed. Instead, officials developed something called the "Household Responsibility System." Farmers contracted land from the village commune, agreeing to pay a certain amount annually in either cash or harvest quotas, and they were allowed to keep any surplus. It was a variation on the pre-Communist tenant system, except that now the nation essentially served as the landlord.

The policy was adopted nationwide, and it became the next best thing to private ownership. Individual motivation returned to the fields, and from 1979 to 1984, the average net income for rural people increased by 11 percent. City dwellers actually lagged during this period, at least in relative terms—the average urban income increased by only 8.7 percent. But the nation still had a dual economy—rules were different for urban and rural regions. In the mid-1980s, government policies began to favor urban development, because leaders wanted to build the export economy. They improved city infrastructure, and they built special economic zones in places like Shenzhen. Most important, in the

1990s they reformed laws about the use of urban land. In Chinese cities, all land still technically belonged to the government, but private individuals were given the right to buy and sell dwellings. They couldn't own the land, but they could own the building or apartment atop the land; they were free to sell it, or lease it, or apply for a mortgage. This change had an immediate effect—it helped spur the growth of the new middle class. Nowadays in Chinese cities, a person's most valuable possession is typically his apartment.

None of these reforms apply to rural residents. In the countryside, an individual can't buy or sell his farmland, and he can't mortgage it. He can't use his house as collateral on a loan. The best he can do is a long-term lease on his land, which is still owned by the village collective. And a farmer has no bargaining power if a developer comes to town—an individual can't oppose a land sale or negotiate for a higher price. The law gives cities and townships the right to acquire any suburban land that's in the "public interest," a term that's never been defined, and the result is that urban places expand at will. When cities buy farmland, they pay set rates that are kept artificially low. Such transactions are handled by the village governments, which are supposed to reimburse any farmer who loses his land, but corruption often siphons off funds. Beginning in the 1990s, as urban areas grew rapidly, such land grabs became more common—by one estimate, during the period from 1990 to 2002, sixty-six million farmers lost their land. And the rural system turned into a particularly unfair combination of the old and the new, the communist and the capitalist. Profits are individual, but risk is communal: local cadres benefit from land sales while villagers are stuck with the ramifications. A half century after the revolution, rural land reform has accomplished exactly the opposite of its original intentions.

Over time, the government has taken some steps to improve the rural situation. They've sponsored road-building campaigns, and they stopped demanding harvest quotas and agricultural taxes. But the land law remains a fundamental problem, along with the sheer number of people. In 2005, according to a government survey, the agricultural population was still over eight hundred million, and the average rural household consisted of 4.55 people who tended less than an acre of land. This plot, tiny in Western eyes, is adequate to feed a Chinese family and even provide a surplus to sell. With all the migration, land should be consolidated, but migrants have a tendency to cling to farming rights after they've left the village. There isn't any alternative—after all, they can't sell. They usually lend the plots to relatives or neighbors, who farm with less enthusiasm than if they actually owned the fields. When I moved to Sancha, my house still belonged to the young couple who were now in Huairou. They couldn't legally sell the building; the best we could do was a long-term lease, and this agreement had no legal status. It came down to *guanxi*—as long as I had good relations with the Weis, I could trust the contract, but it would never hold up in court. From my perspective, it seemed unfair, but it was even worse for the village. I wasn't inclined to improve the property, and the young couple would never get the capital from a sale.

In a place like Sancha, real local power is held by the members of the Communist Party. When I came to the village, there were seventeen members, and these cadres made all important decisions. They settled land disputes, handled public funds, and selected the Party Secretary, the highest local official. They controlled Party membership: nobody else could join without their approval. They held meetings on all sorts of subjects—after Mimi and I first moved to Sancha, the local Party members gathered to discuss our presence. I learned about this afterward, when I was told that they were divided on the question of whether we should be allowed to stay. I knew who led the opposition: one of the Party members was the Shitkicker.

But the person with the most clout was the Party Secretary, who was named Liu Xiuying. She was one of the few women who grew up in the village and eventually settled there, instead of marrying out. In the 1970s, after finishing middle school, she left Sancha to continue her education, a rare opportunity at that time; eventually she was trained as a "barefoot doctor." During the Cultural Revolution, rural health care depended heavily on such people, who served in places too poor and remote to receive regular medical services. Liu Xiuying was assigned back to Sancha, where she married and also farmed. In 1998, she was elected Party Secretary, and three years later she won a second term. There were fewer than a half dozen female Party secretaries in the whole county, and she was the only one in the twenty-three villages that are under the jurisdiction of Bohai Township.

In the abstract, Liu Xiuying's status was highly unusual, but it was far less surprising in person. She was powerfully built, with broad shoulders and thick callused hands, and she moved with a distinct physical confidence. Chinese women rarely have such a presence—in the city it would be unimaginable. Young urban women are called *xiaojie*, or "miss," and nowadays most *xiaojie* cultivate a distinct physical helplessness. They are great arm-flailers and foot-stampers; they wear impractical clothes and they stagger around on stiletto heels. Everything is designed to attract attention, and in the entire animal kingdom there's no more striking vision than a *xiaojie* running to catch a cab. It's like the mating dance of a peacock: plumage everywhere, a stunning profligacy of flash and color, so much movement combined with so little obvious purpose.

But the Sancha Party Secretary belongs to a completely different world. When she moves, things get done, and they get done fast. She performs the same farm labor as local men, and she works with them on village road construction crews. During breaks, if they drink *baijiu* and play cards, she does the same. She is in her late forties, with black hair cropped short; her handsome face ends abruptly in a square jaw. She is not a tall woman but she holds her head high. She has a gruff, booming voice—from my house I heard it every time she answered her phone. Whenever I came to the village, she greeted me in a way that was both friendly and blunt: "Hey! You just get here?" But I knew that she was ambivalent about my presence, or at least that was her stance during the Communist Party meeting about foreigners in Sancha. She was shrewder than the Shitkicker, who played his hand immediately: he wanted us out, which meant that he was left with nothing when we were finally allowed to stay. In contrast, the Party Secretary avoided expressing a clear opinion—in China that often means you're waiting to see how things turn out. After our first year in Sancha, as a gesture of goodwill, Mimi and I donated one hundred dollars' worth of cement to the village, specifying that it could be used to make any necessary repairs to the new Sancha road. The Party Secretary took the gift and paved a perfect sidewalk to her house, and now she could ride her motorcycle all the way to the front door.

Wei Ziqi's relationship with the woman—their *guanxi*, in the village sense—was deeply uncertain. Her husband was a Wei: he shared the same great-great-grandfather as both Wei Ziqi and the Shitkicker. Wei Ziqi respected the woman's ability, and he told me that she was especially skilled at dealing with officials from higher levels. Most villagers appreciated that quality—they believed the Party Secretary had been instrumental in getting government funding for the new paved road. But I sensed some wariness in Wei Ziqi, and over time I recognized it as the caution of a potential rival. Without question they were the two most capable individuals in the village.

Wei Ziqi was not a member of the Communist Party. When I first came to know him, he told me that he had no interest in such affairs, and he was much younger than the village leaders—most were middle-aged or older. After Wei Jia's illness, Wei Ziqi visited a Huairou fortune-teller, who read his palm and gave a warning: avoid politics at all costs. But in a village as small as Sancha, an apolitical position is precarious, especially for somebody starting a new business. There are countless ways in which local leaders can make things difficult for an entrepreneur, especially if he hopes to get a bank loan. Because Chinese farmers can't use their land as collateral, they need village backing for any loan application.

Wei Ziqi never directly challenged the Party Secretary until the day he dropped off the Idiot at the township government. The subsidy was the woman's responsibility, and she had ignored Wei Ziqi's repeated requests for help with the matter. By going straight to the township government, he had circumvented her authority, exposing her to higher officials. In 2003, the subsidy began to arrive: six dollars every month. At Spring Festival, the government delivered a jug of cooking oil, a fifty-pound sack of flour, and a huge bag of rice as a way of showing support to the disabled man and his family.

After we had taken the Idiot into the valley, I initially believed that Wei Ziqi simply cared about the money. As time passed, though, I realized that he had also made a political statement: he proved that he could get things done without the support of local cadres. When I asked him about the Party Secretary's reaction, he said that she had been mad, but there was nothing she could do, because the law was in Wei Ziqi's favor. And he seemed pleased at the woman's anger. "Lots of people in the village have been in situations like that," he said. "But I went ahead and did something. Other people wouldn't have had the guts to do that. She wasn't happy, but now she knows what I'm capable of doing."

THERE WERE MANY THINGS in the village that Wei Ziqi couldn't control, and it was also true that he didn't know his potential customers. He had little contact with the urban middle class in Beijing; all of his plans were essentially guesswork. But the man's timing couldn't have been better. He happened to expand his fledgling business in the spring of 2003, which turned out to be the Year of the Car: the most significant period in China's auto boom.

The boom came from all directions, as if every factor had been coordinated with precise timing: infrastructure projects, manufacturing strategies, consumer decisions, even mystery viruses. Beginning in 2003, the government embarked on a major two-year construction campaign in the countryside, paving 119,000 miles of rural roads. During that two-year span, the People's Republic built more country roads of asphalt and cement than it had during the previous half century. Meanwhile, urban consumer patterns were changing, sometimes for unexpected reasons. In the spring of 2003, panic over the SARS virus swept across the nation, and for weeks the residents of major cities avoided crowds and public transport. Subways and buses were empty; taxis became suspect. In the end, the risk of the disease turned out to have been greatly exaggerated, but it had a lingering effect on the mindset of the middle class. People were newly inspired to learn to drive—in 2003, nearly half a million Beijing residents acquired their driver's licenses, an average of over 1,300 people every day.

At the same time, the market for cars was changing. By 2003, Toyota, Nissan, and Hyundai had started production in China, and these Asian companies made an immediate impact. Meanwhile, Chinese automakers were becoming formidable competitors. In June of 2003, Chery, the company where I witnessed a test-drive, unveiled a new subcompact called the QQ. It was even smaller than a Mini Cooper—the QQ was less than twelve feet long, and it had a 0.8-liter engine. It looked almost exactly like the Chevy Spark, a vehicle that General Motors planned to unveil in China later that year. In fact, the cars were so similar that even the doors could be swapped. In China, it's common for companies to knock off foreign products, but this was a new twist: Chery had found a way to produce something exactly like the Spark before the original even made it to market. There was speculation that Chery had somehow acquired the blueprints, probably through industrial espionage, but nobody was ever able to prove anything. (A lawsuit by GM was eventually settled out of court.) In the end, the price was all that mattered. A new QQ sold for around six thousand dollars, 25 percent less than the GM car, and for most consumers it was an easy choice. That year, Chery doubled the number of units sold from 2002. Along with other small manufacturers, they revolutionized the market, and automakers were forced to drop prices. Beginning in April of 2003, over a period of twelve months, the average price for which cars were sold to dealers dropped by 8.8 percent. In 2003, China's passenger-car sales leaped by 80 percent. In Beijing alone, 339,344 new automobiles hit the road.

Inevitably, some of them found their way to the top of the dead-end road. Weekends in Sancha became busy with visitors, and city investors began to notice. One Beijing businessman paved the lower reaches of the old footpath to Huanghua Zhen, and he opened a restaurant and guesthouse near the Sancha reservoir. It was the first real restaurant in the village: they had a dozen tables, an outdoor grill, and a big pond stocked with rainbow trout. The surroundings were stunning—high rock walls, the placid water of the reservoir—and Beijing people loved it; you could see the stress vanish from their faces the moment they cruised into the village. If they had continued on foot past the reservoir for another half hour, they would have arrived at the home of Ma Yufa, the hermit of Sancha, still living alone with his ticking clock. But there were rumors that investors wanted to develop that area, too. For years the village had been dying, isolated from Beijing, but now the tentacles of city life had begun to creep into the high valleys.

Wei Ziqi and Cao Chunmei kept busy all summer. The new restaurant in the lower village didn't affect them much, because there were always nostalgic city customers who preferred a traditional rural meal, served in a real peasant home. At least that's what they said—they probably would have felt differently if they were served a bowl of elm-bark noodles. In fact they usually ate rainbow trout that originally came from Swiss stock. In recent years the foreign breed was introduced to the big fish farms down in the valley, and it became the standard meal for weekend visitors: practically every rural family that opened a restaurant had a sign that said "Rainbow Trout." The new Chinese cuisine is full of such transplants and fabrications. In Beijing, the upper classes enjoy going to restaurants that serve "authentic" dishes from various parts of the country: there are Yunnan restaurants, Hakka restaurants, and Guizhou restaurants; and if you take these dishes back to their supposed regions of origin, the natives will be puzzled. The capital's Sichuanese restaurants serve meals that I never ate in two years of living in Sichuan. But it's natural in a country where living standards have risen so fast: the market demands new traditions, even ones of rural simplicity. As a child Wei Ziqi never saw a rainbow trout, and the fish is as local as a cuckoo clock.

Trucks carried live trout into the hills, where they were delivered to small entrepreneurs like Wei Ziqi. He built his own holding pool, cement-lined and fed with springwater, and the trout did infinitely better than the leeches of old. Usually he grilled the fish for a price of roughly four dollars. In the new kitchen, Cao Chunmei worked over a massive wok, preparing dishes: scrambled eggs with tomato, fried pork and peppers, wheat pancakes. She was an excellent cook, and the customers often returned.

In 2003, from farming and business, the family earned over 3,800 dollars. The income represented a 50 percent increase over the previous year, and it seemed that business should only improve; by midsummer they were already having repeat customers. But Cao Chunmei looked exhausted and Wei Ziqi seemed troubled. In the beginning, he lit up

Red Plum Blossoms sporadically, whenever he met a new contact or greeted a guest, but now he chain-smoked to relieve stress. At night he often stayed up late drinking *baijiu*. Sometimes it seemed as if all the tension that the city folk discarded on their weekend trips went straight to the man's heart. "Too much pressure," he often said, when I asked him what was wrong. "It makes me nervous all the time."

I told him to be happy—for years he had dreamed of having his own business, and now it was off to a great start. But he worried endlessly about money. He had borrowed from family: the equivalent of over sixteen hundred American dollars from his relatives, and another thousand from Cao Chunmei's older sister. I had agreed to pay several years' rent in advance, for long-term security on my house, but that wasn't technically his money. The house belonged to his nephew, so that was the equivalent of another family loan: nearly twenty-five hundred dollars. He had already spent all of the money on the renovations, and he prepared to apply for a bank loan, in order to build a guesthouse for next year.

In China, there isn't a tradition of credit for private individuals, and debt makes people uncomfortable. Credit cards are still rare, and so are bank loans. In 2003, the vast majority of those new car owners paid cash: fewer than one in five used a loan. Most Chinese save for years before making a major purchase, and if they have to raise capital they depend on family. It results in yet another type of *guanxi*, and Wei Ziqi was juggling them all: the political issues of the village, the new territory of Huairou business, the complexities of family loans. A year earlier, when his son's life was in danger, Wei Ziqi had seemed completely calm. But he had been prepared for that experience: in Sancha, where everybody grew up poor, they know what it means to struggle with sickness and death. Success is the hard part—as an entrepreneur, Wei Ziqi stepped into uncharted territory.

WEI JIA TURNED SIX years old that summer. For his birthday, his parents served him a special meal of instant noodles topped with a fried egg. The noodles were a rare treat, because the boy almost never ate packaged foods. Periodically his parents took him to Beijing for follow-up blood tests, and they all came back normal. He was bigger now, and he had started to develop a barrel chest like his father. Sometimes he was given chores around the house, such as sweeping the threshing platform. Around this time he learned to ignore the Idiot like everybody else. As a small boy, Wei Jia had sometimes played with the disabled man, and engaged him by making faces and gestures, but soon he recognized that there was something wrong with him. And now the Idiot was finally alone—once the last child in the village grew up, there was nobody left who perceived the man as normal.

At the end of summer Wei Jia's parents prepared him for school. He had missed nearly all of kindergarten, and in fact last year's school had been condemned, because conditions were so bad. This year Wei Jia would attend first grade in Shayu, a village about six miles away, where he would board in the dormitory with other children. During the final weeks of summer, the boy's parents trained him to sleep alone. Like most rural families, they usually spent nights together on the *kang*, but now they forced Wei Jia to occupy a bed in a side room. For the first few nights he complained and slept poorly, but by the end of the month he was used to it.

The week before Wei Jia was to start school, I rented a Jetta and drove to the village. I offered to take Wei Jia and Cao Chunmei down to the valley for registration, and she said it would take place on either Sunday or Monday. "They still haven't made the announcement," she explained, referring to Sancha's daily propaganda broadcasts.

"There aren't any other first-graders in the village, are there?" I asked.

"No," she said. "He's the only one."

"If there's only one kid, are you sure they're going to announce it?"

"They'll announce it," she said.

I wondered if perhaps it might be worth a phone call, but this is the way of the countryside: wait for the information to come to you. Sure enough, at precisely noon on Friday the speakers crackled to life. A shrill woman's voice rang out across the valley, echoing off the cliff walls, resounding among the high peaks, alerting all relevant parties:

ATTENTION!
ALL FIRST-GRADERS MUST REPORT
TO SHAYU ELEMENTARY SCHOOL AT 8:00 A.M.
ON SUNDAY MORNING!

ATTENTION!
ALL FIRST-GRADERS MUST REPORT
TO SHAYU ELEMENTARY SCHOOL AT 8:00 A.M.
ON SUNDAY MORNING!

ATTENTION!
ALL FIRST-GRADERS MUST . . .

Early Sunday morning, all first-graders in the village reported to duty, and every single one of them sat on Cao Chunmei's lap in the front of my Jetta. Wei Ziqi remained in Sancha, because he expected guests that afternoon. Wei Jia had taken a bath the night before, and he picked out clean clothes for himself. He wore blue trousers and a matching shirt with a cartoon cat that said, in English, "Ready-Witted." He still had the Mickey Mouse backpack from kindergarten.

"Do you remember what happened last year?" Cao Chunmei said.

"Yes," Wei Jia said.

"Are you going to cry again?"

"No."

"You can't cry this year," she warned him. "You're a first-grader now. If you cry, I'll smack you."

Wei Jia grinned; this particular conversation had been recurring for days. He leaned forward as we cruised into the valley. The walnut season had returned, and we passed dozens of men armed with their long sticks. It was a beautiful morning—clear and warm, the sun about to rise above the eastern ridgeline. All along the road there were children in clean clothes, carrying new backpacks, heading toward Shayu. Our first stop was the dormitory, where Wei Jia checked in. He was assigned to room number four, bed number two. Eight bunks in all: rough metal frames with thin mattresses atop wooden boards. Windows were barred. The moment I saw these military-style quarters, my heart sank, but the boy seemed unperturbed. He liked the fact that he had been assigned a metal locker with a key.

We still hadn't seen his classmates, because the children were gathering in the schoolyard for registration. The three of us walked in that direction, and when we reached the school gate, Cao Chunmei stopped. "Now, you're not going to be surprised to see so many children, are you?"

"No," said Wei Jia.

"It's not like last year, is it?"

"No."

Inside the schoolyard, a teacher named Yang was arranging the first-graders into lines: one for boys, one for girls. The children were quiet—they listened intently as the teacher gave instructions. Slowly she moved through the line, greeting each child individually, and at the end she came to Wei Jia. "Good morning, what's your name?" Teacher Yang said.

"Wei Jia," he said, and then he spoke in English: "Good morning, teacher!"

"That's very good!" she said in Chinese. "Who taught you that?"

"My Uncle Monster," he replied.

"Who?"

"My Uncle Monster!" The boy's face was so serious that Teacher Yang couldn't help laughing. And that was where we left him, standing in line in the schoolyard, the smallest child among all the first-graders.

DURING THE FIRST SIX weeks of school, Wei Jia distinguished himself by an early interest in English, an unruffled demeanor, and a complete refusal to sit still. In a Chinese classroom, the group is the foundation for every endeavor, and each child always knows his place within that organization. Some positions are formally assigned to kids: the Homework Monitor collects assignments, the Politeness Monitor reports on bad behavior, the Class Monitor helps the teacher organize fellow students. In dormitories, each room includes a Room Monitor and a Vice Room Monitor, who make sure that daily cleaning is carried out. Peer discipline is crucial—children who misbehave are often asked to stand before the class, where other students help the teacher criticize the guilty party. At the beginning none of this seemed to faze Wei Jia. Having missed kindergarten, he had no concept of school routines; he talked out of turn and he played with pencils at his desk. He lost school assignments and he forgot homework. He wandered the classroom during lessons. One morning, the entire student body gathered outside to listen to a speech by the principal, and as usual the children were instructed to stand at attention—knees locked, heads up, arms stiff at their sides. All kids obeyed except for one: Wei Jia, who became bored by the speech and finally knelt down to play with pebbles in the dirt.

These infractions, along with a host of others, were described at the first parent-teacher conference. In Chinese schools, such meetings are communal: all of the parents attend at once, and all of them listen as the teacher summarizes each student's performance. The good students are praised, the bad students are criticized, and the listening parents are socialized in much the same way as the children: by the power of the group. There is no greater loss of face than hearing in public that your child does poorly at school. And the bad ones always receive the most attention. At the first Shayu parent-teacher conference, certain children emerged as prominent subjects of public discussion. Zhang Yan was a bully. Wang Wei cracked jokes. Li Xiaomei was a dormitory bed-wetter. ("She doesn't do it at home!" the girl's mother said, at one of the many subsequent conferences that harped on the poor child.) And Wei Jia— he was the fidgeter, the classroom-wanderer, the kid who played with pebbles in the principal's presence. The boy's father was forced to listen to all of these infractions in excruciating detail, and then he made his way back to Sancha.

That evening I had dinner with the family. Wei Ziqi was quiet throughout the meal, eating quickly and avoiding eye contact. He had a sharp temper, and his outbursts were usually preceded by silence— that heavy dead air before a storm. Nobody knew this weather pattern better than Wei Jia, but now he did his best to feign ignorance. After dinner he sat on the *kang*, looking at a picture book. His father stared at him for a good five minutes, and I could see the boy tracking him out of the corner of his eye. Finally Wei Ziqi spoke.

"What do you think you're doing?"

"Reading a book," Wei Jia said.

"Where's your homework?"

"In my bag."

"Get it out, now."

On the whole, six-year-old boys are not naturally cut out for the demands of boarding school, and Wei Jia was especially disorganized. Often I picked him up on Friday afternoons, on my way to the village, and I always reminded him to make sure he brought the books he needed. But every Friday evening, back in Sancha, it was a complete mystery what would emerge from within the bowels of the Mickey Mouse backpack. Wei Jia opened the bag like a magician: anything could come out, and the trick was that even the boy had no idea. Tonight he conjured up four textbooks, a few pencils, and a dozen crumpled papers. His father snatched one of the pages.

"What's this? This is your homework! How are you going to do your homework if it's torn up like this?"

Wei Jia stared down at the *kang*.

"Where's your math book?"

Hopefully, the boy looked inside the Mickey Mouse backpack, but it was empty—no more magic tonight.

"Where's your math book?"

"I forgot it," Wei Jia said softly.

"How are you going to do your homework if you don't have the book?" Wei Ziqi's voice became sharp. "You know what Teacher Yang said today? She said that you always forget your homework. And you don't pay attention in class! What's going to happen to you if you don't study well?"

The boy glanced over at the picture book, but his father snatched it away. "And she said that you weren't paying attention during the principal's speech! Every other child stood there, but you had to kneel down. What's wrong with you? Look at me!"

But the child refused to make eye contact. His mouth held stubborn until Wei Ziqi reached over and cuffed him sharply on the side of the head; all at once the boy collapsed into tears. "You need to listen to

Teacher Yang!" Wei Ziqi shouted. "She says you walk around the classroom whenever you feel like it. You can't do that! And she says you don't eat all of your dinner in the dormitory."

Cao Chunmei spoke up: "You know what will happen if you don't eat well? You'll get sick again. Do you want to go back to the hospital?"

Suddenly Wei Ziqi reached over and pulled the boy's trousers up to his knees, revealing his bare legs. "What if you get those bruises again?" Wei Ziqi shouted. "What are we going to do if that happens?"

Cao Chunmei rushed over to examine the boy. "You need to eat well or you'll get sick! You don't want to get sick again!"

The parents' voices grew shrill, almost panicked. But there was a sudden tenderness to their touch; together they inspected the child's legs, looking for bruises. It was as if all the unspoken fears from last year's crisis had returned, and they gathered close on the *kang*. The boy wept—he threw back his head and wailed.

THE FEARS OF CAO Chunmei ran deeper than those of her husband. Wei Ziqi's approach to life was essentially pragmatic, and tangible threats tended to occupy his attention: the burden of loans, the politics of the village, his son's health and education. He felt the pressures of his new business, but he had faith in the outcome of hard work. And he watched his customers carefully—he picked up cues from the city folk. He dressed neatly whenever he went to Huairou, but he still wore peasant clothes at home. He recognized that this is what customers expect: nobody goes to the countryside because they want to see a peasant aping an urbanite. Wei Ziqi became skilled at playing both roles, shifting between the demands of Sancha and Huairou.

For Cao Chunmei, though, contact with the outside world was far more jarring. She was essentially stuck in Sancha, working in the kitchen. It wasn't her responsibility to gather funding or supplies, and thus she never had the opportunity to enter Huairou or Beijing on her own terms. Instead, city people came to her, and these interactions sometimes left her feeling ashamed. Once a customer from Beijing wandered into the kitchen, curious to see how countryside people cook, and the city woman blurted out, "Your hands are so black!" She didn't mean any harm, but afterward Cao Chunmei felt bad. She started scrubbing her hands frequently when customers were around. She dressed better, too—she bought a new silk shirt with sequins that she often wore on weekends.

Her changes were different from Wei Ziqi's. His shifts were more calculated; he wore new clothes and smoked cigarettes not strictly out of shame, but rather because it helped him do business. At some level, he was comfortable with being from the countryside—after all, that was the appeal of his restaurant. But Cao Chunmei had never felt entirely at home in Sancha, and now she realized that even a successful business wouldn't expand her world beyond the village.

For years she had been searching for some more meaningful connection with the outside. Young people in Sancha often felt that way; it was hard to live in a place where neighbors and friends had departed. Back in the mid-1990s, the village hit a low point: the population was dropping fast, and the people who remained had a tendency to gossip about the affairs and scandals of their neighbors. But something changed when a few villagers began to practice the breathing exercises and simple calisthenics known as Falun Gong. At that time, Falun Gong had the appeal of feeling both new and old: it was invented by a contemporary, a man in the northeast named Li Hongzhi, and he drew on familiar traditions of Daoism, Buddhism, and tai chi. Falun Gong was hard to define—in some ways it felt like a religion or a philosophy, but it was also a basic exercise routine. All of these elements combined to create something enormously popular, and this was especially true in the economically troubled parts of northern China. In Sancha, practitioners liked having a new structure to their lives, and soon others began to join them. By the late 1990s it seemed that most villagers met every morning in the lot at the top of the dead-end road. Cao Chunmei and Wei Ziqi became part of the faithful, and years later she described that period fondly. "It was good for our health," she told me. "Wei Ziqi didn't drink or smoke in those days, because Falun Gong says you shouldn't do that. And he wasn't so angry then. It seemed that people in the village were happy; we all spent time together in the mornings."

Falun Gong's range of influences appealed to average people, but the lack of definition was a political liability. In China, the Communist Party allows only five official religions: Buddhism, Daoism, Islam, Catholicism, and Protestantism. All faiths are monitored by government agencies, and there's no tolerance for independent leadership; for example, Chinese Catholics aren't allowed to recognize the pope. From this perspective, Li Hongzhi represented a problem, especially after he emigrated to the United States. And as Falun Gong became more popular, it attracted critics as well as adherents. Chinese journalists sometimes attacked the practice in print, claiming that it was nothing more than superstition. In April of 1999, a critical article inspired more than ten thousand believers to assemble in downtown Beijing. They peacefully surrounded the central government compound, hoping to receive some sort of recognition. Sure enough, they got noticed—this represented the biggest protest in the capital since the Tiananmen Square student demonstrations of 1989. Within months the Party banned Falun Gong, and soon the organizers of the protest were being sent to labor camps for reeducation.

Nobody in Sancha had attended the Beijing protest, but the village quickly felt the crackdown. Local Party members, some of whom had been avid practitioners, held meetings to criticize Falun Gong, and the morning rituals in the empty lot came to an abrupt end. In China, the coordination of such nationwide campaigns is a strength of the Communist Party. As a source of new ideas, the Party might be bankrupt, but it's still incredibly well organized and coordinated. And the Party understands the significance of local power in a nation that's mostly rural. A command can be given in Beijing and immediately reach countless settlements, and there are essentially no rural residents who live beyond the reach of village politics. When I visited Ma Yufa, the hermit of Sancha, he had no idea who was the leader of China. But he answered immediately when I asked about the village Party Secretary. He knew her name, and her husband's name; he told me exactly how the man was related to the Wei family. In Chinese villages, those are the politics that matter, and after 1999 they were turned against Falun Gong.

Across China, the crackdown was often brutal. According to human rights groups, hundreds of believers died in custody, usually when local police used excessive force in order to gain a conversion or a promise to stop practicing. Thousands more were sent to labor camps. But practitioners originally numbered in the tens of millions, and most of these people simply decided not to participate anymore. In Sancha I knew of only one villager who was reluctant to give up his new faith, and he changed his mind after spending a week in a Huairou jail. Even when it comes to religion, the Chinese can be pragmatic—they might possess the desire to believe, but few will cling to a doomed faith once the government applies serious pressure. And the religious impulse often has more to do with a search for community than anything else. In China, rapid change has left many people with a hollow feeling: they no longer believe in the Communist ideology of old, and the forces of migration and urbanization have radically transformed society. The new pursuit of wealth can seem empty and exhausting; many people wish for a more meaningful connection with others. Some of them turn to religion not necessarily because they desire a personal relationship with God, but because they want to share something with neighbors and friends. This is one reason why the crackdown on Falun Gong was largely successful— after the community was broken, most people saw no reason to believe in that particular faith. A half century of Communism had taught them patience; they knew that something else would eventually appear.

By 2003, when the Wei family business began to succeed, it had been nearly four years since Cao Chunmei abandoned Falun Gong. During that time she had stayed alert to new ideas, especially after the business began to bring more visitors to Sancha. One weekend, she heard a group of tourists from Beijing talking about Buddhism. They were middle-class, the type of city people who often scorn peasants, but Cao Chunmei noticed a difference with this group. They treated her with respect, and they talked in a way that appealed to her. "In their conversation, they often referred to the Buddha," she told me later. "They talked about all sorts of situations, and they were interested in how a person should respond to each. Every time something complicated came up, they were able to refer to the Buddha. I thought there was something good about it. They had ideas about how a person should live."

Shyly, Cao Chunmei worked up the courage to ask one woman a question. "I asked her what effect Buddhism had on her life," Cao Chunmei remembered. "I asked her if it had helped her solve any special problems. She said that wasn't the only reason she believed in Buddhism—it wasn't because of some specific need she had. It didn't solve problems quickly like that. But it helped her understand the right way to act in many different situations, and that was more important."

Cao Chunmei knew exactly what the woman meant—she often felt a desire that ran deeper than the mundane details of daily life. It was the first time she had ever felt a connection to her city customers, and a couple of weeks later the Beijing woman returned to Sancha. This time she brought two books: *The Book of Third-Generation Karma* and *The Book of Ksitigarbha and Bodhisattva*. Cao Chunmei studied the texts, and she noticed that they helped her feel calmer. After a while she built a shrine in the family's main room. She placed a table against the wall, covered it with yellow silk, and erected two large plastic statues. One was Guanyin, the Goddess of Mercy, and the other was Caishen, the God of Wealth. In the mornings Cao Chunmei burned incense before the statues, and she made offerings, always in odd numbers: three oranges, five apples, three glasses of *baijiu*. Such shrines are common in southern China, especially among people doing business, but they're rare in Beijing homes. The first time I noticed the statues I asked Cao Chunmei who had arranged them.

"I did," she said proudly. "They came from a shop in Huairou."

And then—I had been in China too long; the question was all but automatic—I asked how much the statues had cost. Cao Chunmei's tone was friendly but she set me straight.

"We don't say that we 'bought' something like this," she said. "We say that we 'invited' the statues to come here. I invited them here because I thought they would help our household."

IN SANCHA, 2004 BECAME the Year of Construction. Modern Chinese time works like that—the traditional calendar follows its path through the zodiac, from monkey to rooster to dog; but for most people it's the details of development that matter most. The Year of the Horse—2002—is memorable in Sancha because that's when the road was paved. The Year of the Ram was the Year of the New Car. The Year of the Monkey was the Year of Construction. And unlike the age-old patterns of the zodiac, there was no mystery about the modern parade of Road to Car to Construction. The new road allowed new cars to bring new people to Sancha, and they brought new money that could be used for construction. New sounds, too—all year the village rang with the pounding of hammers and the hum of drills and saws.

Like many economic changes in Sancha, the work was pioneered by Wei Ziqi. First he refinished the interior of his home, and then he built a small guesthouse. He designed it himself, a low cement building with a half dozen rooms, and he organized all the construction. For labor he hired his neighbors and close relatives at a rate of three dollars per day, which was standard for any Sancha building project, public or private. In Chinese villages, locals typically provide such labor, which is why the government's road-building campaign of 2003 and 2004 was so important. It improved transport in the countryside, but it also gave underemployed farmers something to do.

In the Sancha region, the government even commissioned a modern version of the Great Wall. County officials had noticed how the Beijing car boom was bringing more people to northern villages, where one of the main attractions was the Ming relic. Recognizing an opportunity for subtle branding, the cadres decreed that all settlements must decorate their roads with structures that resembled the top of the Great Wall. These fake walls were built of red brick, covered in cement, and painted gray. They had crenellations etched with lines that resembled seventeenth-century stonework. From a defensive point of view, the barriers were of questionable value—they were only two and a half feet tall, and if a Mongol had been moving south on a moonless night, at a high rate of speed, maybe his horse would have stubbed a hoof on the new Great Wall. But this structure had been designed with the automobile in mind. The new walls often ran on both sides of the road, giving motorists the impression that they were driving atop the Great Wall. It finally fulfilled one of the dreams of the 1920s, when the

Shenbao newspaper had suggested that converting the Great Wall into a highway "would make it easier to do business."

Certainly it was an effective way to put money into peasants' pockets. Everybody who built the walls earned the standard wage of three dollars per day, and in Sancha the villagers were happy to have the work. They built the new Great Wall, and they worked on Wei Ziqi's home and guesthouse; and they made repairs to the paved road. The day wages added up, and soon other villagers started to make improvements to their homes. The empty lot at the dead-end road became a depot for construction materials—every time I drove out to the village, I parked amid piles of sand and brick. For a while I mourned the lost tranquility. It seemed like ages since my first year in the village, when the road was still dirt and I could sit at my desk and hear nothing but the wind in the walnut trees. That had been 2001: the last year of silence.

But I had lived in China long enough to accept that nothing stays the same, and finally I did what everybody else was doing: I remodeled. Mimi and I had always believed that our house should remain at the local standard, but by 2004 that standard was changing. We hired a crew of local workers, who made the same interior renovations that they had just finished in the home of Wei Ziqi. He had undertaken the most extensive improvements in the village: new ceilings of plaster, linoleum floors with the pattern of wood grain, and clean white walls covered with paint instead of old copies of the *People's Daily*. Once the Party Secretary saw the results, she immediately commissioned the same thing for her own house—she wasn't about to fall behind Wei Ziqi. Over time, most locals followed suit, and the work crews moved throughout the village. In the same steady way that they had built the new Great Wall, crenellation after crenellation, they gave every house the same marks of modernity: plaster ceilings, linoleum floors, painted walls.

That was also the year Wei Ziqi joined the Communist Party and acquired a driver's license. In the past, Wei Ziqi had never spoken about becoming a Party member, and the Huairou fortune-teller had specifically warned him to avoid getting involved in political matters. In China, even basic membership is complicated—it's not like the United States, where a political party will accept anybody. The Communists require a formal application, followed by meetings and interviews; local members have the authority to reject anybody they deem inadequate. And membership is rare: across China, only seventy million people, or roughly 5 percent of the population, are card-carrying Communists.

In 2004, Sancha was home to seventeen members of the Party. The majority were older than fifty, and none was under the age of thirty. It was rare for a motivated young person to apply—most people of that description had left the village entirely. As a result, Sancha's local leadership was conservative, and a few members had been slow to accept even the most basic elements of the new economy. Some could barely read. There were only three women, each of whom had some family link to the organization. The Party Secretary's mother had been the first woman in the village to join, before the Revolution was even finished, and she had encouraged her daughter to become involved in politics. The third female member was married to a local official. None of the Sancha Party members was engaged in business on a significant scale. When Wei Ziqi applied, he represented something entirely different: the village's youngest prospective member, and the first to have succeeded as an entrepreneur.

He rarely spoke in detail about his motivations. In China, people tend to be closemouthed about such matters; you can be friends with a person for years and never have a conversation about what he does in the Party. Wei Ziqi's application took six months, and during that time he was evaluated repeatedly at village meetings. Sometimes he gave self-criticisms—a common routine in China. I asked him what he talked about in such situations.

"I say that I'm not enthusiastic enough about physical labor," he said.

"What does that mean?"

"If there's some work in the village, and everybody is supposed to contribute, then sometimes I'm slow to participate. That's how I criticize myself."

Whenever I asked him why he applied, his answer was the same. "I want to help the country," he said. "And I want to help the village. This is the best way to do it." He left it at that—he never referred to personal benefits. But I knew that he was trying to solidify *guanxi* in the village, where his rise in status had made him vulnerable. In 2004 his income became the highest in Sancha, but his business plans were ambitious; he took out a loan of nearly three thousand dollars from the Agricultural Bank of China. Like all rural loans to individual farmers, it had to be approved by the village, and I suspected that Wei Ziqi's pending Party status might have helped. In the end, there was little resistance to his application to join the Party, and only three members opposed it. The Shitkicker led this small clique, but Wei Ziqi easily gained the required majority. On July 1 of 2004, the eighty-third anniversary of the founding of the Chinese Communist Party, Wei Ziqi officially became a member.

It took another five months for him to get the driver's license. He waited until the end of the harvest and the fall tourist season, and then he signed up for a driving course in Shunyi, a small city not far from Huairou. Tuition was costly—nearly five hundred American dollars—and this indoctrination was just as mysterious as the Communist Party membership. For one thing, Shunyi-trained drivers were expected to begin every maneuver in the second gear. The coach was adamant on this point, and I asked Wei Ziqi why it was so important.

"It's harder in second gear," he said. "The coach says it will make us better with the clutch if we drive in second."

One day not long after he received his license, I rented a Jetta and drove out to the village. About an hour after I arrived, Wei Ziqi stopped by and asked me to move the car, because somebody needed to mix cement in the lot at the end of the road. Nowadays there was always activity out there, because of the construction boom; it seemed that every time I visited, I had to move the car. In the past I never would have imagined that parking in Sancha would become a problem.

That morning, I was writing at my desk, and Wei Ziqi offered to move the Jetta for me. I had let him drive a few times in the past, but only under close observation; he still wasn't capable of driving alone, despite having spent fifty-eight hours learning how to start a truck in second gear. This time, though, I figured it was harmless—my car needed to be moved only a few feet. I gave him the keys and went back to work.

Half an hour later Wei Ziqi returned. He stood in the doorway for a while without saying anything. Finally I asked if everything was all right.

"There's a problem with the car," he said slowly. He was smiling, but it was a tight Chinese grin of embarrassment. Whenever I saw that expression I felt my pulse quicken.

"What kind of problem?" I said.

"I think you should come see it."

In the lot, a couple of villagers had gathered around the car; they were grinning, too. The front bumper had been knocked completely off. It lay on the road, leaving the Jetta's grille gaping, like a child who's lost three teeth and can't stop smiling. Why did everybody look so goddamn happy?

"I forgot about the front end," Wei Ziqi said.

"What do you mean?"

"I'm not used to driving something with a front end," he explained. "During my course, we only drove Liberation trucks. They're flat in front."

I had parked parallel to the fake Great Wall that bordered the village lot. Wei Ziqi had backed up and turned the wheel sharply, not realizing that the front end would swing in the opposite direction, toward the barrier. Last year, when the villagers built the tiny Great Wall, I thought it looked ridiculous, but now I realized that from a defensive point of view it served exactly one purpose. The crenellations were at the perfect height to tear the bumper off a Volkswagen Jetta. Kneeling in the lot, I inspected the metal—it was hopelessly bent.

"What do you think the rental company is going to say?" Wei Ziqi asked me.

"I have no idea," I said. "I've never done something like this before."

I was still renting from Mr. Wang at Capital Motors. In the past I had never reached the bottom of his patience, although I certainly plumbed the depths. I had broken virtually every company rule: I took Jettas onto dirt roads; I drove Jeeps onto dried-up creekbeds; I did unspeakable things to Santanas. I returned cars with dented doors and damaged tires, and I blew out a starter in Inner Mongolia. After signing contracts agreeing to keep a vehicle within the Beijing city limits, I had driven all the way to the Tibetan plateau. Every time I shattered another regulation, Mr. Wang smiled and told me, "*Mei wenti!*"—No problem! "You're an old customer," he always said happily, and his pride in our *guanxi* was so touching that it made me feel guilty. I couldn't imagine a worse renter.

Now I had to return a car without a front bumper. Wei Ziqi offered repeatedly to pay for it, but I told him not to worry; I should have known better than to let him drive in the first place. For the next two days the car sat in the village lot, bumperless, while I steeled myself for the journey back to the city. When it came time to leave, Wei Ziqi used some old wire to reattach the bumper so it hung off the front end. I went slow on the expressway, hoping that the thing wouldn't fly off. Back in Beijing, when Mr. Wang saw the car, his eyes widened.

"*Waah!*" he said. "How did you do that?"

"I didn't," I said. "I let somebody else drive. I'm sorry, I shouldn't have done that." I began to describe Wei Ziqi's lack of experience with cars that had front ends, and Mr. Wang looked confused; the more I expanded on this topic, the blanker his expression became. I realized that if I continued with all the relevant details—the Liberation trucks, the Shunyi driving school regulations about starting in second gear, the Jetta-sized Great Wall in Sancha village—Mr. Wang's head would probably explode. At last I abandoned the story and offered to pay for the bumper.

"*Mei wenti!*" Mr. Wang said, smiling. "No problem! We have insurance! You just need to write an accident report. Do you have your chop?"

In China, the chop is an official stamp, registered to a company. My formal registration was in the name of the *New Yorker* magazine's Beijing office, although in fact this operation consisted of nothing more than me and a pile of paperwork. I almost never used the chop, and I told Mr. Wang that it was at home.

"*Mei wenti!*" he said. "Just bring it next time." In the rental car office, he opened a drawer and pulled out a stack of papers. Each was blank except for a red stamp. Mr. Wang rifled through the pile, selected one, and laid it in front of me. The chop read: "U.S.-China Tractor Association."

"What's this?" I said.

"It doesn't matter," he said. "They had an accident, but they didn't have their chop, so they used somebody else's. Then they brought this page to replace it. Now you can write your report on their page, and next time bring a piece of paper with your chop, so the next person can use it. Understand?"

I didn't—he had to explain this arrangement three times. Finally it dawned on me that the wrecked bumper, which hadn't been my fault, and in a sense had not been Wei Ziqi's fault either, because of the unexpected front end, would now be blamed on the U.S.-China Tractor Association. "But you shouldn't say it happened in the countryside," Mr. Wang instructed. "That's too complicated. Just say you had an accident in our parking lot."

I followed his advice—the report left out everything about the countryside and the Liberation trucks and the fake Great Wall. Instead it said that, driving on behalf of the U.S.-China Tractor Association, I had wrecked the Jetta's bumper in the parking lot of Capital Motors. I signed my Chinese name across the tractor chop. Mr. Wang beamed and lit another cigarette, and that was where I left him, sitting beneath the company sign:

CUSTOMER SATISFACTION RATING: 90%
EFFICIENCY RATING: 97%
APPROPRIATE SERVICE DICTION RATING: 98%
SERVICE ATTITUDE RATING: 99%

AFTER FOUR YEARS, SANCHA felt as familiar as any place I had known during adulthood. Much of my last decade had been spent traveling; it was a nomad's life, and for the most part I enjoyed it. But in Sancha I came to know something different. I had routines—I knew what to expect from every season, every day. At dawn I awoke with the propaganda speakers, and then I wrote through the morning; at night

I had dinner with the Weis. When the weather was hot, I swam in the reservoirs near the hermit's home, and in winter I went for long hikes across the passes. I came to know the trails well, and on foot I visited neighboring towns: Huanghua, Haizikou, Chashikou, Sihai, Guojiawan. They were sleepy, tiny villages, but all of them had started to change; even the quietest place had a new restaurant or guesthouse. And I noticed that the trails became harder to follow with each passing year. In the old days they had been used frequently by farmers and peddlers with their donkeys, but now buses and cars went to most of these towns. In another decade many footpaths would be gone.

The longer I stayed in Sancha, the more I appreciated the rhythm of the countryside, the way that life moved through the cycles of the seasons. Nowadays in rural China the overall trajectory is usually one of decline—that's what I witnessed during my drive across the north. In the dying villages I glimpsed how local life was disappearing, but in Sancha I watched something different. Progress had arrived: each year led to some new major change, and always there was the sense of time rushing ahead. But the regularity of the seasons helped me keep my bearings. I liked being in Sancha at certain times—I liked the weeks in April when the apricot trees bloomed, and I liked the rush of the September harvest. I liked the calm steady days of winter. I liked to drive out for the Spring Festival, when the villagers stayed up past midnight and set off fireworks from their threshing platforms. I learned to be conscious of village time, and I made sure to be there for certain holidays and seasons.

In April of 2005, on the morning of Qing Ming, Wei Ziqi and I woke up at 5:30 and hiked up the mountain behind his house. He carried his basket and shovel; he wore camouflage farming gear. Down in the valley the apricot trees had just begun to bloom and the buds glowed like stars in the morning half-light. As we climbed higher, where mountain temperatures were cooler, the buds diminished. By the time we reached the cemetery they had disappeared entirely.

That year only seven villagers tended the tombs. The men worked steadily, piling dirt atop the grave mounds, and they chatted idly about who lay beneath.

"That's my grandfather's."

"That's not your grandfather's!"

"I think it is."

"*Xiashuo!* That's nonsense! That's your father's older brother."

They rarely mentioned names; every individual was simply a relation. There were no details, either—no specific memories attached to these mounds. As the morning light began to shine behind the eastern mountains I noticed a patch of burned earth where somebody must have made an offering a few days earlier. This time of year, the propaganda speakers always announced that the government had banned such burnings, but the villagers ignored the rules.

One grave had already been decorated before we arrived. Fresh dirt was piled high, and three white paper wreaths stood in front, marked with the character *dian*, 奠: "Offering to the dead." Dozens of white pendants had been pinned to a nearby poplar tree. Atop the mound was a candle, decorated with the words "Eternally Young." Sancha graves rarely had such elaborate memorials, and it meant that the occupant had died recently. I asked Wei Ziqi who was buried there.

"Wei Minghe," he said. "He was the man who used to live in the suburbs of Huairou. He used to come back every year at Qing Ming. You gave him a ride home a few years ago."

I remembered: the friendly old man, pouring *baijiu* atop the grave of his parents. That year he had told me about the good heat he enjoyed in his new city home. I asked Wei Ziqi when the old man had passed away.

"Last year. I don't remember which month."

Another man spoke up: "This is the first time we're marking his grave."

"Last year he poured dirt on other people's graves," somebody else said. "This year we pour dirt on his."

I picked up a shovel and added to the pile. Wei Ziqi took a stack of grave money and ignited it; the flame quickly devoured the banknotes. After he finished, somebody lit a Red Plum Blossom cigarette and stuck it in Wei Minghe's grave. The cigarette stood straight upright like a stick of incense. The men stepped back and looked at the mound.

"Actually he didn't smoke Red Plum Blossom."

"No, he didn't. Too expensive. In the old days he smoked Black Chrysanthemum."

"You can't even buy those anymore. They were popular in the 1980s."

That was the first detail anybody had attached to the dead and the group stood in silence for a moment. Finally Wei Ziqi spoke up. "*Hao*," he said. "Let's go."

Before leaving the field, one of the men turned around. "That cigarette will be fine, right?"

"It's not a problem."

A tiny wisp of smoke drifted upward into the sky. Together we followed the switchbacked trails, descending to the valley, where the apricot buds were scattered across the orchards. Entering the village we heard the propaganda speakers announce the annual ban on grave-burning. It was 6:30 in the morning; the men dropped off their baskets and shovels and returned to work in the fields. For the next two months the mountains were alive with spring labor.

THAT YEAR I HAD promised Wei Jia that after his exams were finished, and summer vacation began, I would take him on a trip to the city. When the day arrived, and I picked him up in the village, he wore shorts and a T-shirt. He carried nothing—no duffel bag, no backpack. He didn't have a change of clothes, or a toothbrush, or one *jiao* of Chinese currency. His mother was preparing a meal for some guests, and I asked her if the boy needed anything for his trip.

"No," she said. "He's only going for three days."

American parents fill minivans whenever a child travels five blocks, but things are different in the Chinese countryside. I asked Cao Chunmei if there was anything the boy shouldn't eat.

"Don't give him cold drinks," she said. "And don't let him eat ice cream. He'll ask you for it, but don't give it to him."

According to traditional Chinese medical beliefs, it's bad to put anything cold in your stomach.

"Is it OK if he watches me eat ice cream?" I asked.

"That's fine," Cao Chunmei said, smiling.

When we arrived in Beijing, I gave Wei Jia a tour of my apartment. He was impressed by all the books.

"Did you write all of these?" the boy said.

There were more than a hundred on the shelves. "No," I said. "Those books were written by other people."

"All of them?"

"All of them."

"What about those?" He pointed to a stack of magazines on a table. "Did you write those?"

"No."

Wei Jia looked vaguely disappointed, as he did whenever we had some version of this conversation. In the village he often stopped by my house, and if I was reading a book he always asked the same thing: "Did you write that?" I had explained to him repeatedly that I had written only one book, and now I was working on the second, but he never quite understood. How could it take so long? And what's the point of being a writer if you don't sit around reading your own books?

The boy was the easiest guest I ever hosted. He never complained, and one advantage of a child without possessions is that he has nothing to lose. Every detail of the city impressed him, even the miserable parts—a packed subway train was an adventure, and he enjoyed getting stuck in traffic, because it allowed him to stare at cars. After I took him for a boat ride on Houhai, a small lake near my apartment, he asked if the ocean is any bigger. He absolutely loved taxis. From his perspective, it was a miracle of city life: if you wave your hand, pretty much any red car will stop immediately. By the second day I learned to watch him, because he liked to call cabs on his own. We'd be on foot, a block from my apartment, and his little arm would pop up; I'd have to tell the poor driver that in fact we weren't going anywhere. People had no idea what we were doing together. Sometimes a taxi driver asked delicately what our relation was, and Wei Jia always answered matter-of-factly that I was his uncle. We went to Shijingshan, the amusement park outside Beijing, where we spent the day with two friends named Frances and Alice.

Frances is Chinese, the wife of a good friend of mine, and Alice is the daughter of another American friend. The child speaks Chinese and is about the same age as Wei Jia; she's blond and has skin as fair as porcelain. All afternoon we drew stares—nobody knew what to make of this mongrel family. People must have assumed that's what happens when a Chinese and an American have kids: sometimes you get one that's really white, and sometimes you get one that looks a lot like a peasant.

The single disappointment was pizza. For some reason, *pizza* was one of the first words covered in Wei Jia's English class at school. His first-grade textbook featured a lesson that described children going to eat pizza with a monkey named Mocky. Why pizza? Why a monkey? Why the name Mocky? But these weren't questions that concerned Wei Jia, and all year he had talked about trying pizza. In Beijing, we met Mimi at Pizza Hut, and the boy finally got his wish—and then he discovered another new word: *cheese*. In the Chinese countryside nobody eats that stuff; the boy wrinkled his face and spat it out. He scraped it off and ate the crust. Over the years, the Beijing visits became our summer ritual, and we rode endless cabs and revisited the amusement park. But we never ate pizza again—as far as Wei Jia was concerned, that was monkey food.

WEI JIA'S INITIAL EXPERIENCES with education could hardly have been less auspicious. He missed almost all of kindergarten because of illness, and the following year his first parent-teacher conference turned into an inquisition. The other targets of that meeting all continued to struggle: Li Xiaomei, the bed-wetter, flunked first grade, and the bully named Zhang Yan met his Waterloo the following year, when he was required to repeat the second grade. But Wei Jia sailed on—in fact, he did much better than that. Never again was his father shamed at a conference, and by the end of first grade the boy had the highest math scores in his class. In virtually all subjects he was near the top.

Every semester he brought home his report card, which began with a twenty-item list entitled "Elementary School Rules of Daily Behavior." The first rule was, "Be interested in national events, respect the national flag, respect the national emblem, know how to sing the national anthem." Rule two: "Cherish the honor of the group and be a responsible member of the group." Rule three involved good posture. It wasn't until five that a regulation touched briefly on academics, and then rule six instructed students to "diligently perform your eye exercises." Rule ten echoed Polonius: "If you borrow something, return it, and if you damage something, offer to pay compensation." Pupils were reminded to trim their nails and bathe regularly. Spitting was banned. No playing with fire. No playing on public roads or railways. Stay away from wharves and docks. Avoid electric shocks. Don't drown. Respect the elderly. On public buses, give your seat to pregnant women. Do your part to protect cultural relics. Cherish the fruits of physical labor. Stay away from "feudal and superstitious activities." Don't be noisy. No dangerous games. In the entire list, only one item was directly academic. The word *bu*—"do not"—was used twenty-eight times.

The report cards were over thirty pages long, and evaluations ranged from academics to physical fitness to behavior. One page was entitled "Psychological Health." (In second grade, Wei Jia was analyzed to be optimistic, in control of himself, and "capable of adapting to the environment.") Most grades were given by the teacher, but parents and peers also contributed evaluations. Even Wei Jia was asked to self-evaluate. One part of the report featured unfinished faces where children drew mouths—smiley, straight, or frowning—depending on how they judged their own performance. By second grade, Wei Jia had figured out this part of the routine, and he gave himself straight smileys for "has an orderly life and takes care of himself" and "is capable of using common tools." He drew a tensely straight mouth on "participates in labor for the collective welfare." And on number five—"cherishes the fruits of physical labor"—he drew a big fat frown.

Body measurements were taken each term and compared to the national average. The reports listed the boy's height, weight, chest circumference, eyesight, hearing, and lung capacity. (Fourteen hundred milliliters in fourth grade.) When Wei Jia brought home a report card, his father sometimes got out a tape measure to double-check the stats. Invariably the boy was subpar on everything physical. (A fourth-grade male should have a lung capacity of 2,123 milliliters, according to the report card.)

The terror of this document would have been unmitigated if it weren't for a final section in which the instructor contributed a personalized evaluation. In second grade Teacher Liu wrote: "Everybody loves you. Your thinking is very nimble and the teacher and the other students all admire you. But only if cleverness is combined with hard work will you have improvement and an even higher score. You shouldn't wait for others to press you. You have to take the initiative and study diligently, let's go!"

That's the saving grace of Chinese education—people sincerely care, and their faith in learning runs deep. Despite low pay, teachers tend to be dedicated, and parents try to do their part, regardless of their own background. In the history of Sancha, only three students had ever made it to college, and neither of Wei Jia's parents went past the tenth grade. But they recognized that their son might have a chance in a rapidly changing society, and they pushed him to work hard. This mentality is common all across China, where Confucian temples might be long gone but the traditional value of education still remains. Even the poorest people have faith in books—I almost never met a parent without educational aspirations for his child. It's different from the United States, where people without much schooling have trouble encouraging their children, and some communities become essentially disengaged from formal learning.

But if the strength of Chinese schooling consists of good intentions, the weakness lies in the details. I was amazed at the stuff Wei Jia learned—the most incredible collection of unrelated facts and desystemized knowledge that had ever been crammed into a child with a lung capacity of 1,400 milliliters. A surprising amount of it came from overseas. He had one textbook called *The Primary School Olympic Reader*, which focused on the Games that Beijing would host in 2008. Here in the Chinese countryside, in the shadow of the Great Wall, children studied pictures of naked Greeks wrestling and learned about a Frenchman named Gu Bai Dan who had reintroduced the Olympics to Europe in 1896. Another text was called *Environmental and Sustainable Development*.

It must have been the product of some well-intentioned foreign NGO; the book taught the theory of "the 5 R's"—Reduce, Re-evaluate, Reuse, Recycle, Rescue wildlife—which made no sense in translation. Fifth-graders had an entire textbook devoted to learning how to use Microsoft FrontPage XP. One Friday, I picked up Wei Jia from school, and he told me they had just studied Google. "It was started by a brother and a sister in America," he said. "They started the company together and became rich." That was the rural Chinese spin on Google—it might not be accurate, but at least it endorsed family values. That same weekend I heard Wei Jia reciting the opening verses of the *Dao De Jing*:

> Dao ke dao, fei chang dao,
> Ming ke ming, fei chang ming. . . .
> The Way that can be told of is not an Unvarying Way;
> The names that can be named are not unvarying names. . . .

Ever since the nineteenth century, Chinese educators have struggled to find some balance between old and new, native and foreign, and the battle is still being fought in schools like Wei Jia's. They've found ways to include new subject matter, but they haven't yet reformed the basic learning strategies and classroom structures. Everything still revolves around memorization and repetition, the old cornerstones of Chinese education. Some of this tradition comes from the difficult script, which can be learned only if children copy characters again and again. In Wei Jia's school, students diligently practiced their calligraphy, and they applied the same learning strategy to other subjects. It worked beautifully for math—those textbooks were far more advanced than the equivalent in an American school.

But other subjects were taught without attention to analysis or creativity. When I heard Wei Jia reciting verses from the *Dao De Jing*, I asked him what they meant, and he didn't have the faintest idea. In writing class, he wasn't encouraged to tell stories or express opinions; instead he copied set phrases and idioms that are part of the Chinese literary tradition. On weekends, he sat for hours on the *kang*, writing the phrases over and over: "long and thin-thin," "thick and soft-soft," "sweet and silky-silky." When he finally began to work on longer compositions, a typical assignment was: "Write an essay about your lamp." (One evening I watched Wei Jia struggle with that topic. He wrote: "My lamp is very bright"—and then he stared at the blank page for half an hour.) In geography he never drew a map. Rarely was any subject personalized or contextualized; the world devolved into statistics and numbers and facts. One weekend in third grade, Wei Jia came home after a lesson about the giant carved Buddha statue in the city of Leshan. He knew all the details: Leshan is in Sichuan, the statue is exactly seventy-one meters tall, four children can sit on the big toe. I asked Wei Jia where Sichuan is located.

"Is it in China?" he asked.

"Yes," I said. "Sichuan is a province. Do you know what a province is?"

He had no idea. I asked him what country Lhasa is in.

"The United States."

"Where is San Francisco?"

"China."

His geography text included few maps, and every one was the same: a basic diagram of China. Nothing about provinces or cities, no sections about foreign countries. History lessons were narrowly aimed at proving the greatness of the Communist Party, and the revolutionaries of the past were so exalted that they seemed immortal. When I asked Wei Jia who led today's country, he answered, "Chairman Mao." In second grade he joined the Party's Young Pioneers, like everybody else. The class did everything together, and the emphasis was always on their collective identity. No divisions were made with regard to ability level; there wasn't such a thing as a reading group or a math group. If a child excelled, he learned to wait; if he lagged, he dealt with shame. Poor performances were public, and anybody who misbehaved was forced to stand in front of the class, where other kids helped the teacher point out shortcomings. Report cards always included a negative comment from some randomly selected peer.

In second grade, Wei Jia brought home a report card with a criticism from a boy named Zhao. He had written, "Wei Jia, I hope that you can improve your handwriting." I asked Wei Jia who he had judged, and he cocked his head, thinking.

"*Wang le*," he said finally. "I can't remember."

"Do you remember what you wrote?"

"I can't remember."

"Do you remember if you criticized his behavior or his school-work?"

"I don't know."

He was so deluged with negative remarks that they spilled off his back like water off a duck. None of it seemed to bother him, and like any Chinese child he became skilled at the self-criticism. He knew the right language, the correct tone, the proper pose: head down, voice soft. Certain targets were easy—the standard self-criticism is to say that you don't work hard enough. Each semester, in the self-evaluation section of the report card, Wei Jia drew a frown across the face of physical labor.

In third grade the teacher named him Politeness Monitor. The class was full of little cadres in training: there was also a Class Monitor, a Homework Monitor, and a Hygiene Monitor. I asked Wei Jia about his responsibilities as Politeness Monitor.

"If somebody bullies somebody else, or starts a fight, or insults people, or says bad words, then I deduct points and tell the teachers."

"How many points?"

"Five or ten."

"What are some of the bad things that people say?"

"Fuck you, fuck your mother, stupid cunt," Wei Jia said matter-of-factly. "Things like that."

"What's the most points you've deducted at one time?"

"I don't know."

"Who gets in trouble the most?"

"I don't know."

He clearly wasn't interested in talking about this subject, but I tried again. "Is it Wang Wei?" I asked, naming a child who Wei Jia often talked about.

"Maybe. I don't know."

"Do you remember the last person you penalized?"

"No."

For a Politeness Monitor, these responses seemed awfully terse and uncommunicative, but who was I to judge? I was one of the few people who wasn't asked to criticize Wei Jia on a regular basis. In any case, a foreigner often feels most foreign while witnessing the early education of another culture. It's truly the foundation—everything begins in places like Shayu Elementary School. The classroom reflects the way people behave in the streets, the way village governments function, even the way the Communist Party structures its power. Sometimes it depressed me, but I had to admit that the education was extremely functional. Wei Jia wasn't necessarily learning the skills that I valued, but there was no question that he was being prepared for Chinese society.

It was also true that he enjoyed school. He was comfortable with his classmates, and he excelled in his studies; he almost never complained. He liked his stark dorm room—bars on the window, eight mattresses on steel frames, a rusty radiator that stayed rock-cold until November 15. (Heat, like everything else at school, followed a strict timetable.) A child can adapt to anything, and there's always a spark of the individual, even amid the most intense collectivization. Wei Jia's Young Pioneer scarf never looked quite right; he knotted it at an odd angle and the edges were frayed and torn. His favorite subject was English—he seemed to like the fact that he had studied it earlier than the other children and could pronounce words better. He said that when he grew up he wanted to be either a professional driver or a computer technician.

On Friday afternoons I often picked him up from school and drove him back to Sancha. In the upper village there was never any traffic, and usually I let him sit on my lap and steer the car through the switchbacks. On Monday mornings he guided us back down the hill. I never noticed much difference in his demeanor; he was just as happy to return to school as he was to leave every weekend. One Friday, when I stopped in the dorm to pick him up, he asked if I wanted to see something. He glanced around, made sure nobody was looking, and lifted the corner of his mattress. There were treasures hidden beneath: a trading card of the cartoon character Ultraman, a toy gun made from elaborately folded paper. A creased photograph featured Wei Jia in a red martial-arts costume, standing at attention, on a day when he had been chosen to represent the school at the visit of a Japanese dignitary to the Great Wall. After we studied these treasures, and Wei Jia told me their stories, he glanced around and replaced the mattress. That was his secret—it remained safe every weekend, hidden in the dormitory, while he followed the long winding road back to the village.

III

WEI ZIQI'S BUSINESS LED HIM TO JOIN THE PARTY, AND the Party in turn led him to more business. Cadres from out of town occasionally came to the restaurant, especially if they had reason to go somewhere off the beaten track. For a while, a group of corrupt officials from Shunyi visited regularly in order to play high-stakes mah-jongg. Sancha was remote enough for them to gamble without drawing attention, and they knew that Wei Ziqi was politically reliable. Sometimes Wei Jia was enlisted to serve beer to guests, and for a while I wondered if he'd grow up like an errand-boy in a mafia movie: overhearing conversations, learning the ropes, plotting his own rise to Party Secretary. But the high-stakes mah-jongg games suddenly ended, probably because of some crackdown on corruption, and the Shunyi cadres stopped coming out.

In 2005, the government launched a development campaign to "Build New Countryside." China's national leadership had changed hands—in 2002, Hu Jintao became General Secretary of the Party, replacing Jiang Zemin. Jiang had always been known for favoring the cities, but Hu began to put more emphasis on rural development. Every morning in Sancha, the propaganda speakers blared reports about initiatives and campaigns, and then funds started to trickle into town. That year, the local county used some of the money to support rural businesses that catered to the new car tourists. Wei Ziqi found a way to profit from this campaign; he applied for and received a cash grant to remodel his kitchen. It was another perk of Party membership—he often figured out how to capitalize on government programs.

For the remodeling, he hired a crew of three villagers. In Sancha, anybody who hires laborers also serves them dinner, and one evening I joined the remodeling crew. A worker asked if there was anything I don't eat.

"He doesn't eat eggs," Wei Ziqi said, before I could respond. "He won't eat intestines or any other organs. He doesn't like meat on the bone. He doesn't like bean paste. He likes fish and he likes vegetables."

Villagers spend a great deal of time talking about food, and over the years the family had studied every quirk in my diet. Tonight the men discussed the evening's dishes, and then the conversation shifted abruptly to international events.

"Look how small Japan is," one man said. "How many Beijings would fit inside Japan?"

I told him that I had no idea.

"Well, I'm sure it's not very many," he said. "Japan is such a small country, but they controlled a lot of China during the war. Look how small it is compared to Manchuria!"

"The Japanese are originally Chinese," another man said. He was the tallest in the group, and he spoke forcefully, stabbing the air with his chopsticks as if carving out space in the conversation. "Qin Shihuang sent soldiers across the ocean," he continued. "He was searching for ways to live longer. That's how they discovered Japan—they didn't come back and they settled the place. So you can say that the Japanese are originally Chinese."

I mentioned that in the northern islands there are people called the Ainu who are racially different from the Japanese. "Some archaeologists believe that they were the original inhabitants," I said. The man held his chopsticks still for a moment, as if processing this information. Then he said, "Qin Shihuang sent soldiers across the ocean. He was searching for ways to live longer. That's how they discovered Japan. So you can say that the Japanese were originally Chinese."

Point taken—I decided to abandon the Ainu. The man brandished his chopsticks and slashed another hole in the conversation. "The Koreans were originally Chinese, too," he said.

"Korea was part of our country during the Qing dynasty," somebody else said.

"So was Mongolia."

"So was Vietnam. They were originally Chinese, too."

"The Japanese also controlled Korea during the war."

"Such a small country!"

When Sancha men are at leisure, their talk moves in unexpected spurts, like a hawk that hovers motionless until it catches some invisible air current. Usually the villagers discuss mundane matters—food, weather, prices—but at any time the subject matter can shoot into the stratosphere. The villagers span oceans and continents; they soar from ancient dynasty to ancient dynasty. They like to talk about China's former greatness, especially in contrast to today's nation, and they have a fondness for sweeping discourses. Foreign subjects tend to produce staggering generalizations. These remarks aren't mean-spirited; the men are curious about the world, and they like to draw connections between China and the outside. But it can be confusing as hell to follow such talk as it zings back and forth across the table. A man might begin with a statement that deserves at least half a minute of amplification—"There is no doubt that the greatest period in Chinese history was the Tang dynasty"—but one breath later he'll describe a TV show about prostitutes in Africa.

With the remodeling crew, all at once we landed on the Korean peninsula.

"North Korea is still a socialist country," somebody said.

"They've been divided for fifty years."

"North Korea is even poorer than China!"

Wei Ziqi turned to me: "Have you ever been to North Korea?"

In 1999, I had spent some time on the northern border with China, and I told a story from my trip. That year, North Korea was suffering a famine, and refugees had been fleeing across the river. In the Chinese border town of Tumen I was walking along the banks when I came upon what appeared to be a child. I approached him from the back, assuming that he was ten or eleven years old; but then I glanced at his face. It was ageless: he could have been thirty; he could have been fifty.

It was as if an old man's head had been attached to a child's body, and I stopped in my tracks, realizing that the person was a victim of the famine.

The moment I finished the tale everybody at the table burst out laughing.

"I told you North Korea is even poorer than China!"

"He was as small as a child!"

"He had an old man's head!"

"Imagine somebody like that trying to work! He wouldn't last one day!"

There was never any way of knowing what would happen when you tossed something into a village conversation. The men drank *baijiu*, and after a while Wei Ziqi got out the Johnnie Walker. I had given it to him years ago, after picking it up at an airport shop. There were two small bottles in a gift box with a clear plastic cover. Usually Wei Ziqi kept it in a place of honor at the front cabinet, but now he showed it to the men at the table.

"How much was this?" he asked me.

"I can't remember exactly," I said.

"It was more than two hundred yuan, right?"

"Probably more than three hundred."

The tall man with the chopsticks was impressed. "So expensive! You could buy ten bottles of Erguotou."

The men passed around the Johnnie Walker. After everybody had taken a good long look, Wei Ziqi returned the box to the cabinet. Originally I had felt a pang of guilt about the gift, because I knew he had a tendency to drink too much. But over time I realized that he would never open something so valuable; it was far more enjoyable to show it off.

Periodically the Communist Party distributed presents to every member in the village. Often these were decorative items, usually connected to some anniversary or series of meetings. As a new member, Wei Ziqi displayed the Party gifts prominently, because they were a sign of status in the village. For August 1, the anniversary of the founding of the People's Liberation Army, the Party gave all Sancha members a framed portrait of a tank gilded in gold. At New Year's they handed out a calendar that celebrated major infrastructure projects. In Chinese government offices, it's common to see such pictures, which often feature bridges or highways or cloverleaf exchanges. Usually the scenes are airbrushed to a brightness that's almost lurid—development porn.

On Wei Ziqi's infrastructure calendar, photos were accompanied by numbered inscriptions that described the responsibilities of a Party member. The page for November said:

> *The Duty of a Party Member (Number Seven): Integrate closely*
> *with the masses, propagate the Party's positions to the masses,*
> *consult with the masses, promptly communicate the masses' ideas*
> *and requests to the Party, defend the benefits of the masses.*

The most impressive gift that the Communist Party ever gave Sancha members was the "Computerized Digital Information Calendar." Its plastic frame included digital readouts of the temperature, time, and date, both in the Western and traditional lunar calendars, and all of this surrounded a three-foot-wide framed photograph of an unnamed foreign city. The city in the picture was hard to identify: it consisted of an undistinguished cluster of midsize skyscrapers, all of them touched up to appear artificially bright. Railroad bridges stood in the foreground, where the photo editor missed some rust. The scene had the slightly decrepit and anonymous look of any sprawling city in the American Midwest, but I couldn't recognize it.

Wei Ziqi hung the portrait in a place of honor behind the dinner table, where customers often sat. Cao Chunmei's Buddhist shrine was nearby. The first time I saw the photograph, I asked Wei Ziqi what the city was.

"I don't know," he said. "It's some foreign place."

At first I thought it might be Cleveland or Detroit. Finally a friend from the States happened to visit, and he recognized it as Denver, Colorado: a pinup in the Chinese world of development porn.

In 2005, the same year that every Party member in Sancha received the Mile-High skyline, they attended a series of meetings under the title of "Preserving the Progressiveness." It was another local echo of national change—in Communist China, whenever a new leader takes office, he sponsors a slogan-filled study campaign as a way of consolidating power. "Preserving the Progressiveness" was Hu Jintao's first attempt at theory, and the precise meaning of the catchphrase was characteristically vague. It was intended to resemble a grassroots operation, although of course all directives and study materials came straight from the top. And clearly the Party was concerned about its rural base; they had already started to increase funding in the countryside. Ouyang Song, a vice minister in charge of the study campaign, told reporters that so many migrants had left villages that there was now a shortage of young candidates for membership.

In Sancha, Wei Ziqi and the others dutifully attended the meetings, where they studied the Party constitution and historic speeches by Mao and Deng. All of these documents were read aloud, a mind-numbing ritual—the Party constitution is 17,000 words long. Because Wei Ziqi was one of the youngest and most literate members, he was often assigned the task of reading. One afternoon during the heart of the campaign, I drove to the village and found him drinking *baijiu* alone. He appeared unhappy, and he was clutching the left side of his face, which looked swollen. I asked if something was wrong.

"I hurt my tooth," he said.

"How did that happen?"

"Opening a beer bottle," he said. In rural China, where people often can't be bothered to use a bottle opener, dental injuries are a common side effect of alcohol. Sometimes I wondered if that might be the next campaign: Build New Countryside, Preserve the Progressiveness, Stop Opening Bottles with Your Teeth.

I asked Wei Ziqi if he planned to see a dentist, and he shook his head. He generally avoided any sort of medical attention, regardless of what sort of misadventure occurred in the village. One year he was bitten by a badger. Armed with only a stick, and acting more or less out of boredom, Wei Ziqi trapped the badger in a hole; it took a nasty bite out of his finger before he could beat it to death. "Badgers don't carry rabies," he said, when I suggested seeing a doctor in Huairou. I looked it up online and confirmed that this theory was wrong, but he didn't care.

He treated the badger bite with the same medicine as the injured tooth: repeated shots of Erguotou.

After the attack of the beer bottle, we sat together at the table while he applied *baijiu* therapy. He told me that all morning the tooth pain had been doubly annoying because of the Party campaign. Today's meeting had lasted five hours, and they had reached the stage of self-criticisms. I asked him what failing he had targeted.

"Labor. I said that when the village had been repairing the road, I didn't contribute enough physical work."

"What did the others say about you?"

"The same thing," he said. "They criticized me for not offering to do enough work."

"What did the Party Secretary criticize herself for?"

"Bad temper," Wei Ziqi said.

Any tensions between the Party Secretary and Wei Ziqi had been set aside temporarily. He had done well since joining the Party—during summer he had been chosen to spend a week studying at the Huairou District Chinese Communist Party School. In China, such centers serve to train cadres, and the study session was a sign that Wei Ziqi was being groomed for a possible political position. At the school he reviewed local policies, and he returned to the village with a stack of Party books. One volume was entitled *A Textbook for Urbanizing the Countryside*. The book featured the usual spread of enticing photographs, mostly featuring road infrastructure around Huairou: broad downtown intersections, the recently finished road to Changping, the expressway that would soon connect with Beijing. The first chapter was entitled "Increased Urbanization is the Natural Choice for Huairou's Economic and Social Development." It read, "To have an upstairs and a downstairs, electric lights and telephones—these were the desires of people in the 1950s, and they reflected their concept of a modern life. Nowadays if we examine these longings, they seem superficial and naive." Another chapter described the Party's challenges in a semirural region like Huairou:

> With hundreds and thousands of years of feudal peasant habits, there is a pronounced trend toward small peasant thinking, in the

way that people live, in their customs, in their cultural level. All traditions of the countryside have been deeply branded into the people, and this creates a conflict with the desire to urbanize and improve.

One of the Party's goals in rural regions was to give people some contact with the outside. Each summer the Sancha members were taken on a free vacation, and in 2005 they traveled to the beach resort of Beidaihe. It was the first time Wei Ziqi had ever seen the ocean, and he talked about the experience for weeks. Increasingly he spent time in Huairou, both for business and for the Party. His clothing continued to change—he upgraded his city shoes, and he bought a new pair of blue jeans and a black jacket made of artificial leather. He carried different cigarette brands for town and country. In the village he smoked Red Plum Blossom, the white packs, which cost less than forty cents. But in Huairou, where it was important not to look like a peasant, he made sure to carry the more expensive red or yellow packs. Sometimes a wealthy person stayed at the guesthouse and left a box of high-end smokes, which Wei Ziqi hoarded for crucial business situations.

For a Chinese male, nothing captures the texture of *guanxi* better than cigarettes. They're a kind of semaphore—in a world where much is left unsaid, every gesture with a cigarette means something. You offer a smoke at certain moments, and you receive them at others; the give-and-take establishes a level of communication. And sometimes the absence of an exchange marks boundaries. A city person has little to say to a peasant and naturally he will not accept his cigarettes. Even between two businessmen, one person might refuse a smoke as a way of establishing superiority, especially if he carries a better brand. All told there are more than four hundred different types of Chinese cigarettes, each with a distinct identity and meaning. Around Beijing, peasants smoke Red Plum Blossom whites. Red Pagoda Mountain can be found in the pockets of average city folk. Middle-class entrepreneurs like Zhongnanhai Lights. Businessmen with a flair for the foreign sport State Express 555. A nouveau riche tosses out Chunghwa like it's rice. Pandas are the rarest beast of all. That was Deng Xiaoping's favorite brand, and government quotas make them hard to find; a single pack costs more than twelve dollars. If you carry Panda, you're probably just being pretentious.

Most men don't worry that cigarettes are bad for their health. In the southern city of Wenzhou, I once met a businessman in his thirties who described smoking as a career move. When I asked if he wanted to quit, the man looked at me like I was crazy. "No way!" he said. "I know it's not good for you, but I'm young so I don't feel any effect. And it's important for business. If you're trying to pull *guanxi* with somebody, you have to take him out to dinner, and you need to smoke and drink with him."

The Chinese government operates under similar logic. All tobacco companies are state-owned, and the industry provides significant revenue; it also directly employs more than half a million people. From the government's perspective, smoking is important to stability, both economic and social. Some cigarettes are even subsidized—the cheapest brands cost as little as thirty cents a pack, because officials fear that farmers will become unhappy if they can't afford to smoke. And the issue of health is essentially separate. In 2000, the Chinese Center for Disease Control and Prevention commissioned a study that showed that the health-related costs of smoking outweigh the revenue benefits. But that's not the key calculus: all that matters is who pays what. Until now, there has been no nationwide health insurance, so the government has collected its cigarette profits without paying for the damage. Each year, over one million Chinese people die from smoking-related illness, and that figure is expected to double by the year 2025. Now that the government is trying to establish some form of universal health coverage, perhaps their attitude toward the tobacco industry will change, but for the time being it remains a source of revenue.

Wei Ziqi put away more than a pack a day. He knew it was bad for him, and on several occasions he tried to quit. But the status was far more addictive than the nicotine. Once he told a story about a recent trip to the city. "I had dinner with a number of people I know in Huairou," he said. "Some of them were government officials, and some were Party members from other villages. I had a pack of Chunghwa cigarettes that had been given to me by a customer. That made me feel good, to have cigarettes like that. There was one man at the table who had Red Pagoda Mountain, and another had State Express 555. But I was the one with the most expensive brand.

"They were all important people," he continued, smiling at the memory. "You could say that each one had some possible use to me. I'm thinking about installing a solar water heater for the guesthouse, and there's a government program that pays for things like that in the countryside. One of the men at the dinner deals with that program. So it might be possible for me to install it for free."

AT HARVEST TIME THE old routines always return. The Party doesn't hold rural meetings during that season, and farmers like Wei Ziqi put aside their Huairou trips; everything is aimed at bringing in the crops. By far the most important task is gathering walnuts, which ripen so quickly that villagers have to work in groups. That's the only local harvest whose labor is still communal—a band of eight or nine will work together, starting with one person's trees and then moving on to the next. The profits stay with each individual owner, but the labor is shared and so are the meals. Each evening, the group eats in the home of the owner of that day's trees. Over the course of two weeks, they move steadily through the village, by day and by night—orchard to orchard, home to home.

In September of 2005, I joined Wei Ziqi's crew on the first day they harvested his trees. There were nine other people, mostly close relatives; they had already been working together for a week. We started at seven-thirty in the morning, and by nine o'clock it was already hot. The mid-September sunshine was still strong, filtering through the leaves of the orchard, covering the ground with a quilt of mottled shadows. The trees grew on terraced tracts, bordered by walls of stone, and already a scattering of fresh walnuts had fallen to the forest floor.

There is only one tool for this kind of work: a thin lilac stick, ten feet long and tapered at the end. For smaller trees, a person can stand on the ground and use the pole to reach most branches. The harvest always begins this way: the crew circles a tree, eyes trained upward, beating the branches like children at a piñata party. When somebody makes good contact, the stick emits a loud *thwack*, and three or four walnuts thud to the ground. There are leaves as well—bits of branches that catch the sunlight as they flutter down. With everybody working, the calmness of the forest is shattered all at once, and there's a beauty to the shifting sound and light: the whistling sticks, the fresh leaves floating through the air, the walnuts thudding heavily into the dirt. After it's over the trees seem to sigh—branches hum softly, still vibrating with the memory of the assault.

Bigger trees grow as tall as fifty feet, and harvesters have to climb onto the limbs. For Wei Ziqi, it's easy: he wedges his fingers into the crevices of the bark and pulls himself up. Amid the branches he can move without relying on his hands. He wears soft-soled military sneakers, the kind he avoids for Huairou trips, and he curls the toes around limbs for balance. He edges out onto thicker branches, step by step, carrying his pole in both hands. If there's a convenient limb at his back, he leans against it, but often he relies on nothing but balance. There's no ladder, no ropes, no harness—no safety equipment of any kind. But high in the trees he moves easily, and his build is perfect for such work: short-limbed and efficiently muscled, with the right combination of strength and balance.

On the day of the harvest, I watched Wei Ziqi climb into the branches of the first big tree, and then he lowered himself to the ground. I asked if he had ever fallen, and he shook his head.

"Does anybody ever fall?"

"Almost never," he said. "A couple of years ago one of the neighbors fell and broke his shoulder."

We continued to the next tree, and once more he reached the top in a flash. I realized that in the past I had so often seen him out of his element—in the Beijing hospitals, in the shops of Huairou, in the driver's seat of an unfamiliar car. Over the years I had witnessed his transition from farming to business, country to city; but I had rarely seen him work in the orchards. Here in the trees he was completely at home.

The Sancha harvest is overwhelmingly male. The only woman who climbs the trees is the Party Secretary; she's strong enough to handle even the most demanding labor. Other wives do lighter work, like collecting walnuts on the ground and shelling the harvested crop. In the evenings, they cook meals for the work crews. This agricultural divide has shaped local culture, which is extremely male-dominated, even by rural Chinese standards. Apart from the anomaly of the Party Secretary, men wield the most power, and some local traditions, like grave-sweeping, are restricted to males only. In the southwest, where I once lived, the gender divide never seems quite so broad. But in those regions the main crop is rice, which requires a great deal of work but little strength, and women spend as much time in the paddies as men do.

Our harvest-day group of ten included only two women. They stayed on the ground, along with me and Cao Chunmei's father, who had come from out of town to help. Each of us had some excuse to avoid climbing—gender or age or foreignness—and it was our job to collect the walnuts that fell from the high branches. They rolled down rocky slopes, and into bushes, and through thick weeds. Soon my arms began to itch, and my back ached; my hands turned black from the walnuts. Everybody else chatted idly, as if this were a social occasion. They talked about food and money, and they discussed the price of walnuts. Villagers usually sold to buyers who traveled around the countryside during autumn, and in past years the prices remained stable throughout a season. But nowadays rates changed rapidly—sometimes as much as 10 percent in the span of a single day. It was all because of the new roads: buyers could more easily reach the villages, and more people did this kind of business; their competition led to price wars. Villagers had to decide the best time to sell, and this was a common line of conversation while we chased walnuts through the undergrowth.

When they weren't talking about food or prices, or the price of food, they ate. Sometimes a walnut shattered on its way down, and the harvesters finished it off. They ate an amazing amount—the sounds of chewing were as common as the rustle of branches. When Cao Chunmei's father offered me one, I politely refused. The last thing I wanted on a hot day of hard labor was a fresh walnut.

"Ho Wei doesn't like walnuts," he said.

"Why doesn't he like walnuts?"

"Foreigners eat different things."

Forty feet high in the tree, Wei Ziqi was invisible, but his voice recited a familiar litany: "He doesn't like eggs, either. He won't eat meat on the bone. He doesn't like bean paste . . ."

The feel of the walnuts—the cool rough texture and the fresh scent on my hands—brought back childhood memories. The trees had been common in my Missouri hometown, where most people saw the crop as a nuisance; walnuts clogged up lawnmowers and rolled into streets. Kids liked to throw them at cars. One year my mother heard about a business in the nearby town of Booneville that bought walnuts in bulk. For a week, my sisters and I composed a small but determined peasant work crew, ringing doorbells to ask for permission to fill garbage bags with the harvest. We packed them into the family's AMC Hornet and drove to Booneville, where a man emptied the walnuts into an automatic desheller and grinder. The black pulp that came out was so condensed that it fit into a single supermarket-sized bag. The man placed it on a scale, consulted a fee book, and wrote a check for one dollar and seventy cents. For months the Hornet stank of walnuts, and it wasn't for many years that I understood why my mother couldn't help laughing when the man handed us the check.

In the Sancha orchards I told the story to Wei Ziqi. He was impressed that Americans leave walnuts to rot in the street—he picked up a big one and remarked that it was worth one *jiao*, or one and a quarter American cents. That year the walnut market was good, and it was getting better— every couple of days the dealers raised their prices.

After night fell, all of us ate dinner in the Weis' home. Cao Chunmei had spent the afternoon cooking: potatoes and tofu and pork, fresh-picked beans and fried corn cakes. She barbecued trout from the family pond. But she didn't sit down to eat with the men: Sancha meals are often segregated. Even the two women who had labored alongside me were relegated to a smaller table in the back room.

The men gathered around the main table, where they argued briefly about the place of honor. Finally Cao Chunmei's father agreed to accept—at fifty-eight he was the oldest harvester. He was seated at the table's head, directly below the Denver skyline. The digital readout on the portrait said that it was twenty degrees Celsius.

One harvester was named Wei Congfa. He is Wei Ziqi's cousin, and he's slightly deaf. The man had never seen the Denver photograph before, and now he looked at it quizzically. "Is that the temperature in that city?" he asked.

"It's the temperature in this room," somebody explained.

But Wei Congfa couldn't hear. "It's the temperature where?"

"IT'S—THE—TEMPERATURE—IN—THIS—ROOM!"

"Here in the house?"

"IN—THIS—ROOM!"

"So what's that city for?"

I sat next to Yan Kejun, a man in his thirties who lived in the lower part of Sancha. He was one of the brightest people in the village, the kind of man who liked watching the news, and he always had questions about America. For the past month he had been focused on the news of Hurricane Katrina. A couple of days earlier, at another harvest dinner, we had a conversation about the events in New Orleans.

"You know," he said, "when something like that happens in America, it actually matters. The population is so low that you have to worry about losing a few hundred or even a thousand people."

He took a sip of *baijiu*. "This might sound ugly," he said, "but in China we could lose one hundred million people and it wouldn't matter. It would probably be good for the country."

In other parts of the world, people had been shocked that such a thing could happen in the United States. But in rural China, a man could watch and conclude: Maybe that would be a good thing if it happened here. I tried to think of a response, but before I could say anything, Yan changed the subject, and the conversation, like so many village discussions, soared off to new ground.

Beneath the Denver skyline the men exchanged shots of *baijiu*. Cao Chunmei's father was the first to turn red; the toasts came faster and by the end of the evening everybody was drunk. At 7:30 the next morning they returned to the orchards. I drove back to Beijing, where my legs were sore for days from all the squatting and chasing after walnuts. For most of a week my hands stayed black. All told, on that hot day in September, in eleven hours of labor, ten of us had harvested three thousand six hundred pounds of walnuts. They sold for four hundred American dollars.

DURING THE YEARS THAT I lived in Sancha, feral pigs became common. Locals called them "wild boars," but most likely they were the descendants of domesticated animals that had escaped. If a pig begins to live by foraging, it changes shape: the shoulders broaden, long hair covers the body, and tusks poke from the corners of the mouth. In the past, such animals would have been hunted down quickly, because peasants spent more time in the highlands. But nowadays so many people had migrated, and those who stayed behind had new routines. Farmers used their spare time to work construction or do business, and increasingly their attention turned to the cities; the land around them grew more wild. In Sancha the highest crop terraces had been abandoned, and this was where the feral pigs proliferated. Sometimes they ventured down to the valley and ravaged a farmer's corn.

During winter a few residents set snares, and in February Wei Ziqi captured a hundred-pounder. He had set the trap near the Haizikou pass, and it was simple—a loop of wire attached to a tree. But the animal stepped right into it, and the wire held firm. She was still struggling fiercely when Wei Ziqi and a neighbor checked the trap. They found a nearby tree, cut off two branches, and pummeled the animal to death. A day later, Wei Jia and I hiked up to look at the site. The undergrowth had been thrashed flat by the struggling beast, whose gore marked the trail. Drops of blood ran all the way to the village, a full two miles, tracing the route where the men had carried their prize.

For weeks the family ate boar every evening. The meat was leaner than pork, dark and rich and pungent; Cao Chunmei stir-fried strips with onions. But she made sure she had nothing to do with the killing or the butchering. It was bad karma, she told me—she left that part of the routine to Wei Ziqi. If he was plagued by any karmic worries, he overcame them heroically. While butchering the feral pig, he discovered that the animal was pregnant, so he cut out the fetus and put it in a jar of *baijiu*. Surrounded by the clear fluid it looked like a child's plastic toy—a tiny white pig. The first time I saw the thing, I was so shocked I couldn't take my eyes off it. Finally I said, "Why did you do that?"

"It's for medicine," Wei Ziqi said. The Chinese often make medicinal *baijiu*, filling a bottle of alcohol with herbs and even reptiles; snakes are particularly popular. But I had never seen a *baijiu* mammal, and Wei Ziqi couldn't explain the specific health benefits of this drink. "It's good for the qi," he said vaguely—*qi* means "energy." But I noticed that he never touched the stuff, and neither did anybody else. It was the first time I saw an animal product that was too gruesome for the villagers.

The jar was displayed in the main room of the family home. This space had been expanded during the last remodeling, and since then the Weis had accumulated more possessions. The decor represented a study in contradictions: the pig fetus floated a few feet away from the Buddhist shrine; the Denver skyline faced a People's Liberation Army tank. There were two bottles of Johnnie Walker, along with the two Ming-dynasty signal cannons that Wei Ziqi had foraged from the Great Wall. A calendar was dedicated to Huairou infrastructure. Sometimes, when we sat down for dinner at the family table, I looked around and thought: How could anybody hope to make sense of this world?

The family's changes seemed especially hard on Cao Chunmei. In the beginning, the pressure of loans and investment weighed on Wei Ziqi, but now business had been stable for two years. He took pride in his rising status—there was a new confidence to the way he moved around the village. But in Sancha a woman rarely occupies that role, and for Cao Chunmei, more customers only meant more work. On busy weekends she rarely left the kitchen; most mornings she woke up to a stack of dirty dishes from the previous night's guests. She gained little pleasure from the new income, and her contact with outsiders was fleeting. The most important thing they had taught her was religion, but even Buddhism provided uncertain solace. She hated the killing of fish and animals at the restaurant—in the past it hadn't bothered her, but the more she read about Buddhism, the more she disliked the butchering. If

Wei Ziqi was around, he handled this work, but there were times when he was in Huairou on business.

Cao Chunmei told me that she prayed for forgiveness during her morning offerings at the shrine. In the family, she was the only member who didn't undergo Party-monitored criticisms, and unlike the others she couldn't take the easy way out, saying that she didn't work hard enough. Her self-criticisms were sincere: she felt incredible guilt about the meals she served. "If I have to kill a fish or a chicken, I pray for them," she said. "They're innocent; they had a good life, but I killed them. So I pray for their souls to be released from purgatory. If I don't pray for them to be released, then I'm afraid that their souls will come back to punish me."

She also worried about other spirits around the home. These are old countryside beliefs, older than the recent resurgence of Buddhism, older than the brief fascination with Falun Gong, older than even the Communist revolution. Villagers speak of snake spirits, fox spirits, rabbit spirits, and weasel spirits; any of these animals can inhabit a home and turn it good or bad. Certain individuals have the gift of understanding this world, and the villagers call them *mingbairen*: clairvoyants. In the old days, a famous clairvoyant lived in Sancha, and people often traveled to see him. If a visitor arrived, the clairvoyant held his wrist, felt his pulse, and spoke in detail about the animal spirits that affected him. Back then, the clairvoyant lived near the Shitkicker's childhood home, and the boy used to pour tea at the great man's rituals. But it all ended during the Cultural Revolution, when the Communists intensified their suppression of religion. Eventually, the clairvoyant passed away, and the village was left without a seer.

But religion, like some traditions, began to recover during the Reform years. The crackdown on Falun Gong was an anomaly, and it occurred because the government perceived the organization as a political threat. For the most part, the Communists allowed individuals to seek out faiths, and during the late 1990s and early 2000s the religious climate became more vibrant. Quietly the clairvoyants began to reappear, even in Sancha. Some villagers believed the Shitkicker had such powers—they had rubbed off during his boyhood contact with the local seer. Occasionally a person went to the Shitkicker for analysis, but Cao Chunmei preferred to go elsewhere. She knew a clairvoyant in Huairou who was famous for his gift, and early in 2006 she visited him. He told her that a fox spirit was active in her home, and he advised her to erect a shrine. And so a new ring of incense appeared in the main room, joining the two Buddhist statues, the feral pig fetus, the Johnnie Walker, the infrastructure calendar, the Ming-dynasty cannons, and the photograph of Denver.

A fox spirit can bring unhappiness to a family, and it was true that Cao Chunmei and Wei Ziqi fought more often nowadays. They shared the responsibilities of the business, but it wasn't a partnership; there was no doubt that the man made key decisions and gained the most benefit. And the deeper he moved into the routines of Party and business, the less interested he was in his home. If they didn't have customers, he stayed away for days, visiting friends in Huairou; at night he sometimes came home dead drunk. For Cao Chunmei, the simplest solution was to try to ignore the problems. "I don't manage him," she said. "I don't know what he does. It's not my business."

She often adopted a pose of distance, even renunciation. On the surface it seemed Buddhist—she was removed from the world—but beneath the calmness ran an undercurrent of frustration. And there was more than a touch of passive-aggression. When Wei Jia misbehaved, she emphasized her powerlessness. "He won't listen to me," she said. "There's nothing I can do about him." If I asked about village politics, she waved her hand. "I don't know anything about that," she said. "It's not my affair." Once, when Wei Jia and I were reviewing some of his school materials, I asked Cao Chunmei who is the president of China. "Jiang Zemin?" she said, naming the politician who had been out of power for years. "I don't know that stuff." It might have been true—rural people have a remarkable ability to ignore national affairs—but the Sancha propaganda speakers had been barking about Hu Jintao three times a day since 2002. I suspected she was emphasizing her approach to life, her effort to distance herself from things she couldn't control. For her, religion was partly a retreat. Even as the village became obsessed with materialism and modern progress, there were people like

Cao Chunmei who moved in the other direction, toward older traditional beliefs.

But such reactions are never simple, and there was another part of Cao Chunmei that longed to be more active. No matter how much she disliked her husband's new routines, she envied the freedom and the entrepreneurial status. Once she came up with an idea for her own business. She was an excellent cook, and she made corn noodles that she thought would appeal to middle-class people in the city. She described them as "organic"—that word was gaining currency in Beijing, where Western ideas about food had already changed the high-end restaurant scene. Cao Chunmei prepared some samples and traveled to the city, where she visited restaurants and tried to sell them on the notion of organic corn noodles. But despite all her authenticity, she lacked the male Chinese business tools: the packs of Chunghwa, the shots of *baijiu*. In the end, nobody ordered a regular supply, and she abandoned the idea.

Periodically she tried to change her appearance. She dyed her hair and bought new clothes, and she dieted. One month she lost twenty pounds with astonishing speed, because of a dietary supplement that she'd picked up in Huairou. When Chinese women want to lose weight, they often stop eating and rely on such drugs, which are essentially amphetamines. Cao Chunmei took the medicine during a particularly busy month, and whenever I talked to her in the kitchen she seemed dazed. Later she regained the weight almost as fast as she had lost it.

The family's living standard had risen rapidly, but one effect was perverse: as they made more money, each member became noticeably less healthy. By far the biggest change occurred in Wei Jia, especially after 2005, when the village experienced the Year of Cable Television. In the past, villagers had access to only seven television channels; now they received more than fifty for a price of less than twenty dollars a year. The Weis bought a new twenty-nine-inch set, which was always on; during weekends, whenever the boy finished his homework, he sat on the *kang* and watched cartoons. At vacation time he did little else. City guests had a tendency to bring packaged snacks on their trips to the countryside, and they often gave the leftovers to the family before driving back to Beijing. Soon junk food composed a good part of Wei Jia's diet. Whenever he pleased, he helped himself to the stash of chips and instant noodles; at meals he was rarely hungry. "He likes anything that comes in a package," his mother complained. "He'll always prefer that to whatever I cook. I can't get him to eat anything else."

There was no concept of discipline with regard to consumption. In the recent past the village had been so poor that people ate whenever they could, and a parent's main responsibility was to feed a child as much as possible. Fifteen years ago, it would have been unimaginable that any mother would deliberately withhold something from her son, but all of that had changed so fast that people couldn't adjust. I tried to explain to Cao Chunmei and Wei Ziqi that this is a common problem in America, where a careful parent has to limit television and snacks. And given the boy's history of health problems, it was particularly important to monitor his diet. But the village mindset ran too deep: a child eating was always a good thing, and there was no point in having a new television if you didn't use it.

During vacations the boy changed almost before my eyes. At school he couldn't get snacks, and the cafeteria food wasn't so fattening, but at home he watched cartoons and ate chips. Soon he had a belly; his cheeks grew round and his legs got flabby. By the time he was nine years old, he was overweight. Sometimes I forced him out to the empty lot to play soccer, but he got winded after five minutes. In the past, he'd always impressed me as incredibly tough—once, as a seven-year-old, he tagged along on a five-hour hike to the Great Wall without a word of complaint. But now if I tried to take him on a walk, he gasped for air and stopped for long rests. The child I remembered as wiry and quick had suddenly grown soft and domesticated—he was moving in the opposite direction of the feral pigs. "He doesn't look like a peasant anymore," his mother once told me. She said it proudly: from her perspective it was good that Wei Jia had started to resemble a city kid.

Wei Ziqi was the only family member who didn't gain weight. He still did a great deal of physical labor, especially during the spring and fall, but he drank too much and his smoking was incessant. Every now and then he tried to quit cigarettes, turning to the kind of quack medicines that are popular in China. One year in Beijing he bought something with the English title: "EXXCig: The Cocktail Treatment." It was expensive—over thirty-five dollars—and the package featured an American stop sign and photographs of happy foreigners who had supposedly used the product. The list of ingredients included Vitamin C, CQ10 auxiliary enzyme, and something called "bull sulpher acid." The advertisement promised to "Keep Smoke Feeling," which was exactly what happened: within two weeks Wei Ziqi was back on the packs of Red Plum Blossom.

Periodically he appeared in Beijing on some mysterious errand. There was never any advance warning for these trips; he didn't call ahead to see if I'd be free. Instead, my telephone would ring and Wei Ziqi would announce that he was standing at an intersection a block away from my apartment. He seemed to envision the capital as another village, only bigger: he didn't understand that people from other parts of the city rarely drop in on friends without a phone call ahead of time. In any case, he preferred not to talk about his city plans in advance. Even as he became successful, and learned the businessman's game, he didn't brag about future projects. In that sense he remained a peasant: he was careful with his words.

In December of 2005, he called one morning and said that he was waiting at the corner of Jiaodaokou intersection. I met him outside, where I recognized his city clothes: blue jeans and a brand-new black parka. His best leather shoes had been shined; his hair was neatly combed. He carried a fake leather bag, the kind that Chinese male entrepreneurs always tote around the city. The only difference between him and countless others was alertness. Whenever Wei Ziqi came to Beijing, he was extremely watchful, in part because he feared getting cheated.

On that day he had arrived to join the Great Wall Society of China. He had never mentioned it in the past, but now he explained that last year a Chinese hiker had stayed in the guesthouse before going up to the Great Wall. "He was a member of the Society," Wei Ziqi said. "He told me I should join, too. It doesn't cost very much." Guesthouse conversations often had a deep impact on Wei Ziqi. He listened carefully to his city customers, and he kept their business cards in a special box in the family room, not far from the Denver skyline. Today he had written the man's name onto a sheet of paper, along with the address of the Great Wall Society.

I walked with him to the Society's offices, which weren't far from my apartment. The application process was simple: Wei Ziqi paid his five dollars in dues, and he gave two passport-sized photos to the office secretary. The only hitch occurred in the application section entitled "Résumé."

"Is it OK if I don't fill this out?" Wei Ziqi said.

The office secretary explained that every member of the Great Wall Society needs a résumé. Wei Ziqi studied the page for a minute. Finally he wrote:

> *1969–1976   Born and became a child in the village*
> *1976–1988   Studied at school*
> *1989–1991   Worked as a security guard*
> *1991–Present Worked as a peasant in the village*

He was too modest to mention his business. The secretary looked through the forms to make sure everything had been filled out. She paused at one section entitled "Political Status."

"You're a Party member, huh?" she said.

"Yes," Wei Ziqi said shyly. "Is that good?"

"Of course it's good," the secretary said, laughing. "In school I was only a Communist Youth League member!" She pasted his photograph onto an ID card, applied a red ink chop, and then it was final: Wei Ziqi was a member of the Great Wall Society of China.

Afterward I took him to lunch at a Sichuanese restaurant. I noticed he was carrying a new Party gift: a stainless steel thermos embossed with the words "Commemorating the Bohai Township Party Members Advanced Education Activity." The thermos marked another twenty-day study session; Wei Ziqi said that they had been recently reviewing speeches by Jiang Zemin and Hu Jintao. He filled me in on other village news: he planned to build a bigger fishpond, and he hoped to remodel some of the guesthouse rooms. Down in the lower village, a city investor had recently acquired another tract of land, and there were plans to build a small road into the hills. Near the end of the meal Wei Ziqi suddenly remarked, "Some people say that I might become the Party Secretary someday."

He had never mentioned this before. I asked when it might happen.

"Not soon," he said. "Whenever the current Party Secretary retires."

"When will that be?"

"It depends on a few things," he said. "The main question is whether she receives another term." He was silent for a moment. "This isn't something I talk about," he continued. "I don't talk about becoming the Party Secretary. Other villagers are the ones who talk about it."

I asked if the Party members would be free after they finished the current meetings at the end of the month.

"No. There will be more meetings."

"About what?"

"About our own affairs. Self-criticisms."

"When does that start?"

"Next month."

I asked if he already knew what he was going to criticize about himself.

"I don't know," he said. "I haven't thought about it yet."

OVER THE YEARS I learned that every act of Wei Ziqi's served a purpose. It was a quality I associated with the countryside, where people are efficient with everything, even their words. At leisure they might engage in long conversations about faraway lands and distant events, but they are close-lipped when it comes to personal affairs. And quite often they are single-minded. Wei Ziqi might spend months on a secret plan, preparing in silence, and then all at once he would take action. And he always followed up on a serious endeavor. I wasn't surprised when one day in the village he asked if I'd drive him and the Idiot down to the valley, to visit the Shayu police station.

"Afterward we're going to take him back home, right?" I asked.

"Yes," Wei Ziqi said. "He just needs a government identity card. That's the only reason we're going."

It had been nearly four years since Mimi and I had last driven the Idiot down into the valley. During that period the man's life had changed dramatically, like everything else in the village, and I often wondered how he interpreted these shifting routines. He had been given his own room at the end of the guesthouse—because the family was wealthier, with more space, they were able to segregate him. In the past, on winter evenings, the Idiot sat on the *kang* with everybody else; now he stayed in his own room. On weekends, when the family hosted customers, they often dressed the Idiot in new clothes, to make a better impression. One day, when Wei Ziqi and Cao Chunmei both had to leave in order to take care of business responsibilities, the Idiot panicked and ran down the village road. In the past he had never been left alone and the sudden solitude unnerved him. They found him at the signpost for Tianhua Cave, a couple of miles from Sancha. Apart from that brief flight, the man hadn't left the village since our adventure of 2002.

Today I found him waiting silently beside Wei Ziqi in the parking lot. I opened the back door to my rented Jetta, and the Idiot calmly entered. On the drive down he pressed his face close to the window, watching the scenery as we descended into the valley. Wei Ziqi explained that he still lacked an official identity card, which was necessary if the family continued with the government support program. Ever since the first incident, the Party Secretary had made sure that the Weis received their monthly payments. Each year at the Spring Festival holiday, they were given an extra twelve dollars, along with a jug of cooking oil and a bag of rice or flour.

At the Shayu police station, a young woman led the Idiot to a stool in front of a white backdrop. He sat on his hands like a nervous child, tucking his legs behind the stool. He looked worried while the woman fiddled with a digital camera. The machine flashed and hummed, and the moment after the picture was taken, the Idiot finally relaxed into a toothless grin.

In another room a policeman prepared an official note for Wei Ziqi. "He's a *longya*, right?" the man asked. The word means "deaf-mute."

"That's right."

The officer wrote quickly onto police stationery; he handed the paper to Wei Ziqi. "Give this to the Party Secretary," he said. "She'll give it to the township. He should get his ID card in about a month."

The Idiot watched intently on the drive back, as if savoring the journey. The next time I appeared in the village, he greeted me warmly, pointing to the Jetta in the parking lot. But I never saw him enter an automobile again. Now that he was officially registered, there was no need for him to go anywhere. Those two journeys, the ones I had witnessed, represented the farthest he had ever traveled in his life.

Exactly a month later the Idiot received a twenty-one-inch Hisense brand color television. It was part of a new government program for the disabled, and now I realized why it had been so important to register that afternoon, although Wei Ziqi hadn't mentioned the TV. The family already had a bigger set, so they gave the government television to one of Wei Ziqi's relatives. The Idiot never watched TV anyway; he couldn't hear the programs and in the evenings he sat alone in his room. The family didn't accept money for the set, but I was sure that somehow, someday, it would be repaid through the complicated world of village *guanxi*. That's also the way of the countryside: no wasted gestures.

The Idiot's new ID card listed his birth date and given name, and for the first time I saw who he really was. He was born on December 11, 1948, and his name is Wei Zonglou. On the ID, Wei Zonglou looks very old and very worried. He's hunched forward, and his eyes appear almost sad; if only the picture had been taken a moment later, it would have captured his gentle smile. That character *zong* was also given to all three of the man's brothers—it's the mark of their generation. The word means "ancestor."

IN SANCHA, 2006 BECAME the Year of Garbage. For half a decade, everything had led to this point: there were new roads and new cars and new construction; the villagers acquired cable television and cell phone coverage. But the clearest evidence of their prosperity was trash. When I first moved to Sancha, people simply threw their garbage down the hillside into the creek that ran dry most of the year. In those days there wasn't much waste; villagers reused almost everything and they rarely ate packaged food. But all of that changed with business and tourism. Instant-noodle containers and cookie wrappers accumulated, and soon the creekbed was choked with Styrofoam and plastic. One year Mimi sponsored a cleanup, but it wasn't until 2006 that the county government finally instituted regular garbage truck service. That same year, peddlers started appearing in flatbed trucks to buy anything recyclable: bottles, cans, newspapers. In the past it would have been unimaginable—driving all the way to Sancha to buy garbage!

Inevitably some city folk had started to settle there. In Beijing it was becoming popular for middle- and upper-class people to find second homes in the countryside, and sometimes a village turned over completely to outsiders. Down in the valley, not far from Sancha, one section of a place called Tiekuangyu was purchased wholesale by city folk. Within months local life was finished: the natives moved out, the houses were demolished, and new mansions of concrete and glass rose above the orchards. In Sancha, villagers hustled to sell long-term contracts on any empty residence. They weren't allowed to build new structures without government approval, and soon all the abandoned houses in town had been snapped up. Even the Shitkicker arranged a deal with a man from Beijing. After they made an agreement, the Shitkicker began an ambitious remodeling of his home. When the work was half finished, and new walls of brick had risen fifteen feet high, he abruptly raised the price. There was no legal foundation for any of this, because individual villagers can't sell their property; any long-term rental agreement depends entirely on goodwill and faith. Contracts are common but they're worthless, and there was nothing the Beijing resident could do but pay the extra cash or walk away from the deal. To everybody's surprise, he walked. And that was when the Shitkicker realized that he was completely out of money.

After that, the building's frame stood untouched. If he could have finished construction, perhaps he would have found another renter, but like anybody in the countryside he had few ways to raise capital. In the old days he might have pawned land—this is what his own father did in 1946, when he was broke and turned his fields over to Wei Ziqi's grandfather. But the Shitkicker didn't have this option, and he couldn't apply directly for a bank loan. He needed approval from the village, which denied his application. The Party Secretary was responsible for this rejection: for years there had been bad blood between her and the Shitkicker. They were both Party members and distant relatives by marriage, but they didn't get along, and in the end the man had no recourse for a loan. Along with his wife, he was forced to live in the dirt-floored shack that he had once tried to rent to Mimi and me. The place was so small that most belongings had to be piled up outside, covered in plastic. They were the only villagers whose living conditions had deteriorated since the car boom began. At twilight I often saw him wandering around the abandoned construction site, muttering to himself. Nowadays he greeted me politely; his hatred wasn't directed at me anymore. He had more important enemies to think about.

There were rumors about the Party Secretary. In the past, most villagers had spoken of her respectfully; the woman was clearly competent and in particular she was skilled at acquiring government funding for projects. But the sudden influx of private investment seemed to have changed people's opinions. Recently there had been three major land deals made by Beijing businessmen, who planned to develop some of the village areas for tourism. Two projects were located in high valleys that didn't have any residents, and the details of the transactions had never been made public. Nobody knew the price that had been paid, or who the investors were, or how they planned to develop the valleys.

In China such lack of transparency is common, especially in the countryside. If the Party Secretary had profited from these deals, she was smart enough not to show the money. Her house was the nicest in the upper village, but it wasn't extravagant, and nothing about her appearance changed. Whenever I saw her, she greeted me with the same friendly gruffness as always: "Hey! You just get here?" But some villagers believed that she had stashed money in a Huairou bank account, and her son had recently purchased a new apartment in the city. Soon, people began to talk about something else: the upcoming village elections.

In Chinese villages, two political offices matter most: the Party Secretary and the Village Chief. The Village Chief is elected directly by all residents, through secret ballot, and candidates are not necessarily members of the Communist Party. But only members can become Party Secretary, which is the highest position. In Sancha, Liu Xiuying had begun her political career as Village Chief. She first won that position in 1993, and five years later she was elected Party Secretary. Since then she had held both offices simultaneously, a situation that has become increasingly common in rural China. The government encourages it, so bureaucracy will be streamlined, but it also serves to consolidate power.

In Sancha there had never been a serious challenge to the Party Secretary's authority. But by 2006 the situation had changed, and the difference was money. In 2001, when I moved to Sancha, the per capita income was around two hundred and fifty dollars; in the span of five years it had risen to over eight hundred. In 2003, the day wage for a laborer was three dollars; now it was six. The village had acquired a good road, a cell phone tower, cable television—it even had garbage to sell. All of this could have represented a success for the Party Secretary, because the village had prospered under her leadership; but the frame of reference mattered more than anything else. Instead of comparing their situation to the past, people in Sancha had started to think about the outside. They saw city people moving in, and they knew that real-estate deals were being struck, and all at once they feared missing out on profits.

For an alternative they naturally turned to the most successful local businessman. In the evenings, after it grew dark, the Shitkicker often visited the Weis' home. If I was there, the man would greet me with a curt nod, and then he would take a seat away from the table. He never participated in our conversation. He simply waited for me to leave—his arrival was a cue that I should go home. When I asked Wei Ziqi why the Shitkicker had started coming around, he shrugged off the question. "It's not a big deal," Wei Ziqi said, and left it at that.

It took me a while to realize that this is how a village political campaign begins. After weeks of visits, Wei Ziqi finally brought up the subject. He told me there would be an election in the beginning of 2007, and some people in Sancha wanted him to run for Party Secretary.

"Are you going to do that?" I asked.

"No," he said. "It's too much trouble." But something about his tone seemed less than absolute. I asked who was encouraging him, and he mentioned the Shitkicker's name.

"But didn't he oppose you when you first tried to join the Party?"

"Yes," Wei Ziqi said. "That's true."

"So why does he want you to become Party Secretary now?"

"It's complicated."

I asked if he trusted the man, and Wei Ziqi grinned.

"He has his own objectives," he said. "Everybody has his own objectives."

The Shitkicker's motivation was as obvious as the unfinished walls of his house. And it was just as clear why Wei Ziqi represented a logical candidate. He had learned to negotiate the worlds of both the Party and Huairou, and nobody else's status had risen so rapidly. In 2003, the Wei family business earned thirty-five hundred American dollars; in 2006 they made more than eight thousand. Once, when I asked him about the business income, he qualified his success with a telling remark. "It's the highest *known* income in Sancha," he said. "There might be other people with more money, but it's not open. As far as farming and business go, I make the most money."

In June of 2006, as the local political campaign gained momentum, the Party members traveled to Chengde on their annual junket. The city lies to the northeast, and during the Qing dynasty it was the summer retreat of the Manchu rulers. Emperors went there to hunt; the court stocked game parks with deer and boar. Now the parks are open to tourism, and people can wander through the palaces and temples that once served the Manchus. The Sancha contingent visited all the sites, and in the evenings they shared *baijiu* banquets at the hotel. Upon his return Wei Ziqi showed me photographs, which looked like the ones from previous trips. In every picture the Sancha Communist Party members stand in a long row and stare at the camera. They wear casual clothes but nobody smiles. It's hard to tell that they are vacationers, and their relationship is also unclear: they could be coworkers or neighbors or even extended family. There is, however, a striking combination of intimacy and distance to their pose. These people aren't necessarily close friends, and their union may not be by choice; perhaps they even dislike each other. But it's clear from the photographs that they spend a great deal of time together.

ONE MORNING IN AUGUST, Wei Ziqi telephoned to announce that he was standing at an intersection near my apartment. As usual, the call took me by surprise, although this time I guessed the reason for the trip to Beijing. For half a year he had been thinking about buying a car.

Nobody else in the upper village owned one. In recent years motorcycles had become more common, and a couple of locals had the kind of three-wheeled mini-trucks that are used for freight in the countryside. One man purchased a used Lada sedan—but as Wei Ziqi said, that didn't really count. The old Russian-made car was in such bad shape that it could hardly be driven, and the owner got rid of it almost immediately. As far as the village was concerned, the parking lot at the end of the road was still waiting for the first locally owned automobile.

Ever since acquiring his driver's license, Wei Ziqi had been saving money. He stocked *guanxi* as well—whenever he went to Huairou, he asked friends if they knew of any good secondhand vehicles. But the biggest stroke of luck came when a used-car salesman from Beijing happened to stay at the guesthouse. Wei Ziqi filed away the man's business card, and a few months later, after he had saved enough, he called the number. The salesman told him to meet just after noon at the Beijing Old Car Transaction Market.

Wei Ziqi and I took a taxi to the market. The moment the cabbie heard the address, he perked up. "You buying a car?" he said. "How much you want to spend?"

Wei Ziqi said shyly that he hoped to keep the price under fifteen thousand yuan, which was around two thousand dollars.

"You should get a Xiali," the cabbie said. "They save gas and they're easy to repair. If you're getting an old one, this is a really good time to buy. A lot of the old Xialis aren't registered legally, so the police check them more often. People are afraid of getting hassled, so they're less likely to buy them. That's why the prices are good right now."

That's a Chinese market fluctuation: police problems go up, prices go down. And the Xiali is a classic Beijing car, with a distinct owner stereotype: lower-income, chain-smoking, tough-talking. Until the year 2000, the most popular Xialis were modeled after a Korean car with the inauspicious name of the Daihatsu Charade. They were boxy, ugly vehicles, but they were durable, and our cabbie told us he had bought an illegal Xiali three years ago for fourteen thousand yuan. "I drove it for a year as a cab and then sold it for eleven thousand," he said. "I never got fined!" As we cruised along the Fourth Ring Road, he pointed out old Xialis ("That's a '98!"). He advised us to avoid a Citroën at all costs ("Wastes gas!"). Jilis and Suzukis were better ("Saves gas!"). The man laughed when Wei Ziqi asked if a Xiali is safer than the tiny "breadbox" vans that are common in the countryside. "Of course!" he said. "You get in a wreck going sixty kilometers per hour in a breadbox, and everybody inside is going to die! Guaranteed!"

While waiting for Wei Ziqi's contact to arrive, we wandered around the Beijing Old Car Transaction Market. It's located on the city's southern outskirts, where dusty lots sprawl amid cheap apartment blocks. This is Beijing's biggest used-car exchange—on any given day, as many as twenty thousand vehicles are offered for sale. Some permanent dealerships stock high-end models, but most sellers are individuals who pay twenty-five cents an hour for the right to park their cars in the dirt lot. They scrawl makeshift ads on strips of cardboard: "2003 model, one owner. All registrations legal." Paperwork is a prominent selling point— often that's the first thing people mention, because buyers worry about passing inspection. Owners give the age of a car in months, the way people do with babies. "December, 1998," one woman with a red Xiali said to Wei Ziqi. "That's basically the same as a 1999!" To the Chinese, usage matters more than model, which is why they track the months.

On the day we visited, it was hot and dusty, and apparently nobody had thought of washing their cars. Virtually every vehicle was caked with dirt, and there seemed to be a competition for the most hideous seat covers. Owners had to stay near their cars, in case customers walked by, and people dealt with the boredom by playing cards and Chinese chess. Sometimes an owner was sprawled in the backseat, sleeping. Almost nobody openly named a price; if you asked, they invariably responded, "How much do you want to pay?" A major selling point was the inclusion of a spare and a tire jack. Another common sales pitch was *san xiang*: "Three compartments." Owners called it out proudly—"Three compartments! Three compartments!"—and I asked Wei Ziqi about the meaning. "It means the car has front doors, back doors, and a trunk," he explained.

"But that's obvious. Why do they have to say it?"

At last it dawned on me that nobody in the market had the faintest idea what he was doing. How many people in China had experience buying or selling a car? They were all flying blind, and Wei Ziqi did his best to go with the flow. He looked at a few Xialis, but he was too intimidated to ask the price. When we passed a Citroën, he brightened and said, "Wastes gas!" He looked immensely relieved when his contact finally arrived.

The man's name was Yuan Shaochun, and he wore a white tank top, khaki shorts, leather loafers, and black socks pulled up to his kneecaps. He carried a fake leather money bag in one hand and a dirty white towel in the other. He gasped in the midsummer heat—he had a fat belly and short bowlegs that seemed on the verge of collapse. He used the towel to mop sweat off his neck. The moment the man arrived, Wei Ziqi whipped out his Red Plum Blossoms—red pack, city use only—and offered Mr. Yuan a smoke. The man shook his head disdainfully, wiped his neck, and took out a pack of Zhongnanhai Lights. He didn't offer one to Wei Ziqi. When he saw me standing there, he cocked his thumb: "Who's the foreigner?"

Mr. Yuan became more friendly when he learned that I had written books. He told me he had *guanxi* with a publishing company, and perhaps all of us could get together and work something out. "Maybe they can translate your books into Chinese," he said. He scratched a number in my notebook and told me to call if I ever wanted a hookup with the Ningxia People's Press. Ningxia is the Muslim province in the far west; years ago that was where I got the City Special stuck in sand. Mr. Yuan also ran a cigarette and *baijiu* shop in the southeastern outskirts of Beijing. As a sideline he had been dealing cars on and off for a decade. He drove a Citroën. ("Wastes gas!") In the back of the car he had an aluminum Louisville Slugger, color red, Model FP29. I had never seen a real softball bat in Beijing; the handle was taped and everything. I asked the man if he played. "*Fang shen*," he grunted. "That's for protection."

At the moment he had nothing to sell. He was there to help Wei Ziqi find a car, and he led us around the lot, brandishing his sweat rag and complaining about the budget. "You're not going to find anything for fifteen thousand," he said. "If you want something from the year 2000 or later, it's going to be twenty thousand at least." Periodically he stopped to criticize a parked car. "That one was definitely in an accident," he said, after inspecting a green Xiali. "The owner's lying about that."

Wei Ziqi paused at a white Xiali sedan. It was a decommissioned cab; the taxi sign was still stuck to the roof. According to Beijing law, any Xiali that had been used as a taxi could stay on the road for only six years. The city instituted these rules for reasons of safety and pollution, but they were also a boon to the auto industry.

The man with the white Xiali told Wei Ziqi that the cab was five years old. "You can drive it for one more year in Beijing," he said. "After that you can still use it in the suburbs."

"Has this car ever had an accident?" Wei Ziqi asked. He had picked up on that question from watching Mr. Yuan.

"It's a taxi!" the salesman retorted. "If you want a car that's never had an accident, don't look at taxis!" He shook his head and continued. "Almost all the Xiali cabs are red," he said. "There are so few white ones that they don't get checked as much. Cops are always pulling over the red Xialis and checking the papers. You won't get noticed in a car like this."

But Mr. Yuan advised against the Invisible Xiali. He had a better option: a friend in the suburbs who specialized in vehicles from bankrupt work units. If a work unit registers an automobile, it can remain in use for fifteen years, regardless of how bad the condition happens to be. The trick is to find a car that's outlived its company; fortunately, countless state-owned firms have gone belly-up during the Reform years. Later that week we embarked on a mission to find the Bankrupt Xiali.

◉   ◉   ◉

THE FIRST SIGN OF an imminent deal was when Mr. Yuan began accepting Wei Ziqi's cigarettes. At the auto market he hadn't touched a Red Plum Blossom; now he took them graciously. That was also a pretty good indication that he had some stake in the sale. His shop—the Magnificent Cigarette and Liquor Emporium—was located directly across the street from the car dealer, who ran a repair garage. We were fifteen miles southwest of downtown Beijing, in a place called Fangshan. It's home to one of the capital's largest cement plants, and white dust covered everything in the neighborhood, as fine and light as a cold-snap snow.

The dealer had parked the car in front of his garage. The red Xiali dated to October of 1998; the plates were fully legal. Technically the vehicle still belonged to a tourism firm called the Beijing Shanqili Guest Services Company, but that organization had gone bankrupt and now existed only in paperwork that fit neatly inside the glove compartment. The car was unwashed. Like everything else, it was sprinkled with cement dust; the dealer used a dirty rag to wipe off the windshield. The first thing he showed Wei Ziqi was the trunk: a spare and a jack, no extra charge! "It's never had an accident," the dealer said. But there was a scar across the hood and dimpled dents covered the lower body like smallpox. The dealer said we could do a test-drive, and he handed the keys to Wei Ziqi, who looked at me.

I knew he had no business driving. The last time I'd allowed him to operate a vehicle unattended, he destroyed the bumper of my rented Jetta, but something about today's situation made me reluctant to take the keys. Mostly it was *mianzi*, or face—this was an important moment for Wei Ziqi, the first automobile in his life, the fledgling businessman dealing with established entrepreneurs. Every foreigner who lives in China learns about the cultural importance of *mianzi*, and the fear of losing it; but sometimes the outsider overcompensates. In fact Wei Ziqi had an intense awareness of his own limitations, like many rural Chinese. He was a proud man but he wasn't stupid, and now he wanted me to drive. But I misinterpreted his glance, and I failed to take the keys.

With a nervous expression, Wei Ziqi settled into the driver's seat. He asked the dealer which gear was reverse—not a good sign—and then he turned the ignition. The rest of us stood nearby, watching. He popped the emergency brake, put it into gear, slammed the gas to the floor, and opened the clutch. He didn't want to stall the thing but he had no idea it would move so fast. The engine roared and the tires spun; it sped backward through a huge puddle of dirty water, spraying a cement-colored arc of crap across the lot; and then the car headed directly toward a telephone pole. By this point Wei Ziqi wasn't even attempting to look where he was going. He had his head down, studying the floor, searching desperately for the foot brake. At the last possible moment he found it—the car stopped less than three feet from the pole. My heart pounded in my chest; my *mianzi* must have been white. Once my voice returned, I said, "OK, I'll drive."

I went for a test run with Wei Ziqi in the passenger's seat. I wasn't sure how to evaluate this vehicle, or where to set expectations—it was, after all, a Chinese version of a South Korean subcompact called the Charade. The last time I had been involved in the purchase of a used automobile, I was a high school student in Missouri, where I bought a 1974 Dodge Dart for seven hundred bucks. In many ways the Xiali reminded me of that Dart. There was very little power and the brakes were soft. The body looked like hell. But the engine sounded decent—no pings, no knocks. There was even a spare tire and jack. After driving with Wei Ziqi for a few miles, I said the same thing my father had said about the Dart back in 1986: "I think it's OK."

At the garage Wei Ziqi handed out a round of Red Plum Blossoms. The cigarettes put the dealer in a magnanimous mood, and he said he'd throw in the sweat-stained bamboo seat covers for free. "Usually I'd sell this car for sixteen thousand yuan," the man said. "But I'll sell it for fifteen because you're a friend of Yuan's."

"Could you go cheaper?" Wei Ziqi said. "Maybe two hundred yuan cheaper?"

The man agreed: twenty-five dollars less. "Is there anything else you'd look at?" Wei Ziqi said to me.

"What's the mileage?" I asked.

"You can check," the dealer said with a shrug. I poked my head inside: 14,255 kilometers. The odometer only had five digits, and there was no telling how many times it had rolled over: the total could have been 14,255 kilometers or 114,255 kilometers or 1,014,255 kilometers. There was no repair history, no mechanic's approval. We knew nothing about how the Xiali had been used, or what role it had played in the demise of the Beijing Shanqili Guest Services Company. The dealer wouldn't even write out a contract. "My calligraphy is bad," he said. "Let Mr. Yuan write it."

He gave Mr. Yuan a preprinted form with the heading "Contract." Mr. Yuan began filling out blanks—buyer, seller, date—and stopped. "My calligraphy is bad, too," he said. Finally Wei Ziqi wrote the whole thing. The dealer convinced him to leave out the price. ("It's simpler that way.") The dealer also refused to sign his name. ("You can write it for me. My calligraphy's really bad!") Wei Ziqi hesitated but eventually signed both names. After it was over, and the cash had changed hands, the dealer handed out Red Gold Dragons, as a way of marking the end of the transaction.

I drove the Xiali back to the city. We had to stop at the gas station down the street, because the owner had made sure the car's tank was dry as a bone when it left his hands. I asked Wei Ziqi why the dealer had been so reluctant to sign the contract.

"I don't know," Wei Ziqi said. "It seemed a little strange."

"What will you do if there's a problem?"

"I'll talk to Mr. Yuan," he said.

Another friend helped him drive from Beijing back to Sancha. Later that afternoon I rented a Jetta and headed out to the village. When I arrived, Wei Ziqi was in the village lot, wiping down the Xiali. He had parked beneath the only shade tree, and the pockmarked hood was so clean it almost shone. Wei Ziqi was beaming, too—it was the happiest he'd looked in a long time. When I saw Cao Chunmei, I asked her what she thought of the Xiali. She shook her head and said, "What a terrible car!"

❖   ❖   ❖

FROM THE BEGINNING CAO Chunmei had opposed the purchase. She said they didn't need a car, and it was too expensive; the family still had loans at the bank and with relatives. But the real reason for Cao Chunmei's opposition was that an automobile represented freedom. "He already does whatever he wants," she told me. "He goes into Huairou, he goes drinking with his friends. If he has a car, then it'll be even easier for him to do that." She reacted in a similar way to the village rumors that Wei Ziqi should run for Party Secretary. "I don't want him to become Party Secretary," Cao Chunmei told me bluntly. "I think it'll turn into a big hassle. I see how busy the current Party Secretary is. If Wei Ziqi gets busier dealing with the village affairs, then he won't have time to take care of things around here."

Despite Cao Chunmei's distaste for local politics, she had decided that she wanted to join the Party herself. In some ways it was surprising—her Buddhist beliefs seemed incompatible with the Communists, who had always scorned religion. But Cao Chunmei's interests in the Party weren't philosophical, or even political: she simply wanted to be part of a group, and she wanted to go places. "They get to take a good trip every summer," she said. "They get gifts and things like that. It just seems like it would be interesting to join." For Cao Chunmei, success had become profoundly isolating; she was responsible for much of the business's drudge work, and even the solace of Buddhism was something she experienced alone. It was the opposite of Wei Ziqi, whose every step led to more *guanxi*, more power within the village, more contact with the outside world.

He also demanded more authority in the family. When Cao Chunmei began to talk about joining the Party, Wei Ziqi flatly refused. "There's no need," he told her, and left it at that. He rarely felt the urge to explain his decisions to his wife, and he kept his plans to himself. Whenever I asked Cao Chunmei about the village's political rumors, she claimed that she didn't know any more than I did. "Wei Ziqi won't tell me anything," she said. "He'll do what he wants. I don't control him." That was her typical response to conflicts: *Wo bu guan*. I don't control it. Her dream of Party membership, like the plan to start her own business, was abandoned quietly.

LATER THAT YEAR, AFTER Wei Ziqi had become more comfortable with the car, he drove to Huairou and acquired a new name for his son. Like virtually all of Wei Ziqi's projects, it wasn't mentioned until it was finished. One Friday afternoon he picked up Wei Jia from school and informed the boy that from now on he would be known as Wei Xiaosong.

In China it isn't unusual for a name to be changed, especially if the person is a child or a young adult. Wei Ziqi had done this himself: originally he had been called Wei Zongguo. It's the kind of patriotic name that was common in the countryside for babies born during the Cultural Revolution—*guo* means "nation." In 1993, when Wei Ziqi was living in the city, he changed the name as part of his early attempt to become something other than a peasant. Back then, he read a book called *Name and Life*, which explained that a person called "ziqi" is likely to enjoy a career that's "stable and developed."

Sometimes a child's name change occurs for more serious reasons. Parents believe that an inauspicious name brings bad fortune, and a child who is chronically ill might benefit from a new title. When I taught in Sichuan, one of my colleagues had a daughter who suffered from childhood cancer, and after years of treatment the parents finally gave her a new name. Around the same time, they were granted permission to have another baby by the local Planned Birth authorities, who sometimes make an exception if the couple's first kid has serious medical problems. The sick daughter was school-age—old enough to understand exactly what it means when your name is changed and your mother becomes pregnant. Later that year the poor girl died, and I always thought it was awful that she spent her last months with an unfamiliar name. It seemed terrible to leave the world as somebody else.

Wei Jia's given name is simple: the character *jia* means "good." But it requires fourteen strokes of the pen, an unlucky number in China, and the boy's health had never been strong. He no longer suffered from blood problems, but he often complained of stomachaches and he had a tendency to catch colds. In the early years I blamed it on boarding at school; dormitory conditions were poor and he didn't like the cafeteria meals. But recently junk food and inactivity had become bigger threats. The parents were strict about his studies; during weekends they made sure that he stayed on the *kang*, doing his homework. Their respect for education was admirable, but the boy never got any exercise, and certain traditional ideas about health were counterproductive. Given Wei Jia's chronic colds, I recommended that he eat oranges, but his mother believed that a person should avoid too much fruit during winter—it's bad for the qi, she said. Like most people in China, Wei Jia rarely drank water. The Chinese have countless obscure beliefs about which times of day are bad for fluids, and the end result is that most people simply don't drink much. Once, Cao Chunmei and I took Wei Jia to Huairou for a routine checkup, and the doctor couldn't run the urine test—the boy was so dehydrated that he had blood in his sample. But I couldn't convince the parents to make sure he drank more, ate vegetables and fruits, and got more exercise. It was typical that the father responded to the boy's health problems by changing his name. Sometimes they seemed to grasp instinctively at the worst of both worlds: the worst modern habits, the worst traditional beliefs.

The longer I lived in China, the more I worried about how people responded to rapid change. This wasn't an issue of modernization, at least not in the absolute sense; I never opposed progress. I understood why people were eager to escape poverty, and I had a deep respect for their willingness to work and adapt. But there were costs when this process happened so fast. Often the problems were subtle—this was hard to recognize as an outsider. In the West, newspaper stories about China tended to focus on the dramatic and the political, and they emphasized the risk of instability, especially the localized protests that often occurred in the countryside. But from what I saw, the nation's greatest turmoil was more personal and internal. Many people were searching; they longed for some kind of religious or philosophical truth, and they wanted a meaningful connection with others. They had trouble applying past experiences to current challenges. Parents and children occupied different worlds, and marriages were complicated—rarely did I know a Chinese couple who seemed happy together. It was all but impossible for people to keep their bearings in a country that changed so fast.

Wei Jia's new name had been selected by computer. This detail was important to Wei Ziqi—he told me that computerized name analysis was becoming more common in the cities. A man in Huairou special- ized in the service, which he usually performed for a fee of fifty yuan, or about six dollars. But he waived it for Wei Ziqi, because they had friends and *guanxi* in common. He gave Wei Ziqi a one-page computer print- out with extensive analysis of the new name and its future prospects. As Wei Xiaosong, the boy could expect to enjoy good fortune and longev- ity, as well as wealth and honor. His personality would be self-restrained and generous. The machine spat out character traits that ran down the page like listings on a stock ticker: "Strong affections. Moderate. Chaste. Graceful."

The computer also examined the boy's birth date and concluded that of the five traditional elements, water was the one most lacking. I didn't need a machine to tell me that—pretty much everybody I knew in China was dehydrated. In any case, the computerized solution was to give the boy the character *Song*, which is the name of a river near Shanghai. *Xiao* means "little." That was his new name: Little Song River.

Cao Chunmei's response was to wash her hands of the whole affair. "*Wo bu guan*," she said. "I don't control that. I don't much like the name, but it's not my business. It's Wei Ziqi's business."

We had dinner together on the weekend of the name change. It was Sunday night, and Wei Ziqi had driven down to the valley with another Party member for some mysterious meeting. It had something to do with the upcoming elections—often they met away from the village to avoid drawing attention. Wei Jia had finished his homework, and in the afternoon he read a book about dinosaurs. He was a fourth-grader now, and his reading was good; he still excelled at school. But every time somebody mentioned the new name he became very quiet. I had to ask about it several times before he answered.

"*Bu hao*," he finally said. "It's no good."

I asked Wei Jia why the name was no good, and he answered in a voice so low it was almost a whisper.

"*Bu hao ting*," he said. "It sounds bad."

And that was all he said—he refused to expand on the topic. At dinner we ate fish and dumplings, and I could tell that Cao Chunmei was distracted. After the meal she made a phone call; she must have been trying to reach Wei Ziqi's cell phone, but somebody else picked up. She listened for a moment and then cut in impatiently. "He's drunk, isn't he?" she said. "Is he coming back tonight? He has to go to Huairou tomorrow morning. Tell him to call me!"

She brooded at the table for most of an hour. Wei Jia seemed oblivious—he was in good spirits, and after dinner we played a game with his chess pieces. He had a bad cough; for a week now he had been struggling with another cold. Finally the phone rang. Cao Chunmei went to the next room to answer it, but I could hear her words.

"You need to come home tonight," she said sharply. She told him there was a village meeting tomorrow morning at seven o'clock. "Do you understand? You have to come back tonight!"

If Wei Jia heard anything, he gave no indication. We read a couple of his books, and then I told him I'd be back in the morning, to take him to school. On the way out of the house I was surprised to find that Wei Ziqi had returned. He was in the front room, leaning against a table; all the lights were off. When I flicked a switch I realized that the man was so drunk he could hardly stand.

"Are you OK?" I said. But he couldn't speak either. He slumped against the table, eyes unfocused. Cao Chunmei had followed me into the room. I asked her how he had gotten home.

"Somebody drove his car back," she said.

"Will he be all right?"

"It's fine," she said.

The next morning it was still dark when I picked up Wei Jia. His parents were asleep on the *kang*, and the boy got ready for school in the family dining room. The place was a mess; a bag of sunflower seeds had been scattered across the floor. I asked him what had happened.

"Dad was drunk," he said matter-of-factly. "He was trying to pour some water and he spilled it and then he got mad and knocked those seeds everywhere."

Wei Jia had already dressed in his school uniform and now he packed his bag.

"Is he like that often?" I asked.

"Yes," he said. The boy was still focused on his school bag. He didn't look up and I changed the subject.

"Do you have your red scarf?"

"Yes," he said. The scarf is the symbol of the Young Pioneers, worn by all schoolchildren.

"Then put it on," I said.

He tied the knot around his neck. As usual Wei Jia's scarf was ragged; it had a big rip in the side and greasy stains covered the front. Most Young Pioneers are well scrubbed but occasionally you see one with the look of a frontline soldier. Down in the valley we stopped for breakfast. Wei Jia had a racking cough but he ate his wonton soup eagerly, hunched over the bowl in the cold of the roadside restaurant.

FOR THE NEXT MONTH the new name hung over Wei Jia's head. His father told him he had no choice, and they needed to make the change now; in another year and a half he would enter middle school. They would register him as Wei Xiaosong, and he might as well get accustomed to it now. Once he started using the name, it would feel more natural.

The boy never gave any reasons for his reluctance. He didn't explain why he liked the old name, or what it was about the new one that bothered him; he didn't ask for a third option. He didn't get angry and he didn't cry to his mother, as he sometimes had during past conflicts. In fact he hardly said anything at all. When the topic came up, his only response was, "*Bu hao*"—No good. He muttered the words to himself, and over time the refrain acquired an odd combination of impotence and power. His father couldn't penetrate *Bu hao*; soon he became frustrated. It reminded me of Bartleby—"I would prefer not to." But I also recognized both parents in that simple phrase. His mother washed her hands of things she couldn't control: *Bu hao*. His father was determined to change his world at all costs: *Bu hao*. As for Wei Xiaosong, the computer promised good fortune and longevity, and wealth and honor, and self-restraint and generosity; but in the end it was all *bu hao*. The boy simply refused to accept the name. After a few weeks his father gave up and never mentioned the change again. He had always been Wei Jia, the last child in the upper village, the first child to grow up in a businessman's home; and now he would be Wei Jia forever.

THAT WINTER THE IDIOT didn't receive his Spring Festival holiday bonus from the government. He was given the usual sack of rice, along with the jug of cooking oil, but the twelve dollars were missing. The amount was too small for the family to bother with a complaint, and they knew exactly what it meant. The Party Secretary was sending a message: she still had power in the village, and she wasn't happy about the election rumors.

By now the talk was everywhere, and even Cao Chunmei couldn't hide her interest. "People are discussing it all the time," she told me. "They don't want the Party Secretary and the Vice Party Secretary to be in office anymore. Lots of people curse them—behind their backs, of course. In the past people were satisfied with the Party Secretary, but now they don't feel that way anymore. Her ideas are different. As time goes by, her thinking is, 'I've been in power for some time, so I deserve some benefits.' It's bureaucratism."

I often heard villagers use that phrase—*guanliao zhuyi*, or "bureaucratism." "It means she doesn't listen to other people's ideas," Cao Chunmei said. It's an old Cultural Revolution term: during the Maoist campaigns, rural people sometimes used the phrase to justify attacks on local cadres. In those days, revolutionary politics were all that mattered, but now the Sancha villagers used the same accusation in a new context—they were worried about capitalist profiteering. They complained about recent land deals, whose details remained mysterious but were now starting to show their effects. A new restaurant was being constructed between the two sections of the village, where it would become the largest building in town. And two new roads were being built in the high valleys. Nobody had proven any corruption, but for many villagers the secrecy of these deals was evidence enough. In any case, the sudden influx of outside investment suggested that eventually most profits from tourism would leave the village.

People began to talk, but there still wasn't anything like a grassroots campaign. In rural China, significant political disruptions often begin on the peripheries of authority. Trouble can start within the Party itself: a member becomes personally aggrieved, or a lower-level official gets angry about something. Such people have traction—they know the rules, and they know how to stir things up. And they're accustomed to a degree of authority, as opposed to the average farmer, who might grumble but do nothing.

In Sancha, the trouble began with the Shitkicker. Many villagers distrusted him, but he had an undeniable power, and it came in different forms. He had links to the past—some people believed he was a clairvoyant—and he was also a Party member. He understood how local elections operated, and he recognized the ability of Wei Ziqi. And he was patient: at first, for a period of days, he visited the Wei family home, talking idly and never mentioning the campaign. After a number of casual conversations, he made a more open proposal. Accompanied by another Party member from the lower village, the Shitkicker told Wei Ziqi that he should run. "They said my abilities were better than hers," Wei Ziqi told me, after the meeting. "They talked about my speaking ability, and my ability to take care of things outside of the village, and my thinking. It has a lot to do with my doing business—they see that as a reflection of my abilities."

Despite the praise, Wei Ziqi remained noncommittal, which was the expected form. But soon the men began to review a list of local Party members, evaluating who would be likely to support which candidate. All told, there were now twenty-three members in the village, and the most powerful loyalties were those of blood. They were split down the middle: five people were closely related to Wei Ziqi, and five were closely related to the Party Secretary. Among the other members, some were good friends of Wei Ziqi, and others seemed likely to want change; the men tried to calculate how many would fall into his camp. They began to interview people face to face, in secrecy. At this stage of the process, Wei Ziqi never participated; he needed to be able to step away if support was thin. The Shitkicker served as his lieutenant, and for weeks he moved discreetly around the village, conducting the dirty work of hushed discussions and late-night meetings.

Soon the Party Secretary mobilized a lieutenant of her own. One evening, the Vice Party Secretary came to the Wei family home, greeted Wei Ziqi politely, and sat down to talk. The men had never been close, but this visit wasn't a surprise, and the Vice Party Secretary quickly came to the point. "You'll be a good candidate someday, but it's better if you wait," he said. "You're young, you're doing well—wait until next time. Be patient."

Wei Ziqi smiled and said something to the effect that his words made sense. But by this point it was too late—the Shitkicker had already finished the canvassing, and he believed the numbers were promising. By his calculation, ten Party members could be counted on to support Wei Ziqi, and ten belonged to the Party Secretary. That left only three who were undecided.

THERE WERE NO ISSUES in the campaign. Nobody talked about specific plans for the village, or changes that needed to be made; there was no platform or philosophy. Only a fool would have made public promises. The goal was to be as vague as possible, and each candidate avoided speaking directly about the election. Family mattered more than anything else: people marshaled their close relatives and tried to recruit more distant cousins. A great deal of energy was spent on analyzing motivations, trying to figure out who was likely to support whom. Politics had been distilled to its purest essence—an exercise in village *guanxi*.

Everything took place out of sight, among the local elite. Now it seemed that every night the Shitkicker came to the Weis' home, and often there were other visitors, men who gave terse greetings and then waited for me to leave. The only people who talked openly were the ones who weren't involved. Cao Chunmei and the other women discussed the election all the time; they loved to speculate on the outcome and the strategies. They said the Party Secretary was nervous, and whenever I saw the woman I sensed some tension in her face. But she still greeted me gruffly: "Hey! You just get here?"

In the final stages the campaign proceeded to formal dinners. The Shitkicker hosted a banquet at a good restaurant in Huairou, where ten Party members showed up. These men had all promised to vote for Wei Ziqi, and the meal was intended to confirm their support. But when I asked Wei Ziqi about the banquet, he told me that nobody had said one word about the election. The men enjoyed the meal, drank their *baijiu*, smoked their cigarettes, and then at the end the Shitkicker asked a question. "Has there been any change?" he said. One by one, the men responded no, and that was the end of the banquet in Huairou.

Three days later the Party Secretary invited Wei Ziqi and the four youngest Party members to a restaurant down in the valley. Since the start of the campaign, there had been little contact between the woman and Wei Ziqi, and after the dinner I asked what they talked about.

"Not about the election," he said.

"So what was the conversation about?"

"I don't know, just normal things," he said. "I don't remember very well. It wasn't so comfortable."

If it represented a last-ditch attempt to convince Wei Ziqi to withdraw, it was as indirect as every other aspect of the campaign. In the final days, there were rumors that the Party Secretary had offered money to some voters, but nobody could substantiate it, and such talk came mostly from nonmembers. Eventually the political rumors must have moved beyond the village, because at last, three days before the election, officials from the township government made a visit.

THERE WERE TWO CADRES. The higher-ranked official worked at the township's Communist Party Committee, and he was accompanied by another cadre who served beneath him. In China, a township has authority over local villages, and it's rare for officials from this level to appear in a place like Sancha. Usually villagers travel to the township for meetings—that's the typical movement along the chain of power. But something about the current political campaign was important enough to bring the men to Sancha, where they called a meeting of all Party members.

The Committee cadre began with a speech. He talked about the upcoming election, and he emphasized the importance of following correct procedures. He told the Party members to guard diligently against the sale of votes—he emphasized this point several times. After that, the man's words became vague. He didn't mention the recent land sales in the village, or the lack of financial openness; he avoided all specific local issues. He seemed to ramble, talking about development and infrastructure improvements.

"He talked for a long time," Wei Ziqi said after the meeting. "The basic meaning was that we should stay with the same Party secretary. It's hard to describe, because he said a lot of things and most of it wasn't very direct. But the meaning was obvious. Basically he was saying that our current leader has done a lot of good things for us. Then he started asking questions about things that have improved in the village. He said, 'You have a new road, don't you? You just received streetlights, didn't you?' Finally at the end he said, 'You can see that this leader has ability.'"

The cadre never mentioned Wei Ziqi's name or the surreptitious campaign. After he was finished, he called upon each individual member to comment openly on the Party Secretary's performance. One by one, people stood up and followed the cadre's cue, praising the Party Secretary. They mentioned the new road, the cell phone tower, the streetlights, the garbage collection. Only a handful of members said anything negative. The Shitkicker was the most outspoken—he complained about the land deals and the mystery of village finances.

Finally the township cadre called on Wei Ziqi. Wei Ziqi stood up and spoke one sentence. "*Gande bucuo*," he said. "She's done a fine job." And then he sat back down again.

◉   ◉   ◉

AFTER THAT THERE WERE no surprises. Three days later, they held the vote, with every member listing his top candidates, and the Party Secretary's name appeared on fifteen ballots. Wei Ziqi received ten nominations. Standard protocol called for voting to go to a second round, with choices limited to the top five names, and Wei Ziqi came in fourth. The Party Secretary won, and the Vice Party Secretary took second, which meant that both positions were retained. Third place became the village's Party Committee Member. Wei Ziqi was left with nothing—he failed to pick up even a low-ranking office.

He learned that one of his supposed adherents, a farmer who lived in the lower village and claimed to admire Wei Ziqi, had in fact served as a spy in the campaign. The farmer had pretended to back Wei Ziqi, attending all the dinners and late-night meetings; and meanwhile at every step he secretly briefed the Party Secretary. With this knowledge the woman was able to track the campaign, finding ways to convince key voters. As for how she managed to convince them, nobody could say for certain. Wei Ziqi refused to speculate—he was tired of the politics.

He had realized it was hopeless the moment the township cadre gave his speech. "*Mei banfa*," Wei Ziqi said. "There was nothing I could do." In his opinion the man's words represented the turning point, even more so than the actions of the spy. And the speech was the reason that Wei Ziqi said so little when asked to comment about the Party Secretary's performance. That was his final calculation of the campaign—at the last moment, after all the secrecy and planning, he hedged his bets.

FOR A SPELL WEI Ziqi drank heavily. He claimed the loss didn't matter, and he often said that he had campaigned only because he had been recruited to do so; but in truth the defeat left him depressed. He often remembered the fortune-teller's warning: Avoid politics at all costs. But Wei Ziqi hadn't listened, and now he paid for his pride; he swore that never again would he challenge local authority. The only way he would run for office was if the Party Secretary retired and approved Wei

Ziqi as her successor. "If she supports me, then I'll do it," he said. "If she doesn't, then I don't have a chance."

Their relations were strained on a personal level, but Wei Ziqi believed she wouldn't seek revenge. He said she still feared his abilities, and she remembered what had happened when Wei Ziqi dropped off the Idiot at the township government. In Wei Ziqi's opinion, the memory of that action was critical to his security in the village. "If somebody goes to a higher authority like that, it causes a problem for her," he said. "Others don't do this because they don't really understand the policies and the law. I understand because I studied the law."

In 2007, the Communist Party started a national campaign called "Develop Modern Agriculture." They hoped to introduce new technology and management strategies to the countryside, and they also wanted to give rural cadres a glimpse of city life. In Sancha, that year's annual Party junket took the members to Dalian, a major city on the northeastern coast near the Korean peninsula. For Wei Ziqi, and nearly everybody else in the delegation, it was the first time they had ever flown in an airplane. The Air China flight was delayed by five hours and it was after midnight when they finally departed.

For half a week the Sancha Party members toured Dalian. Every night they ate seafood, the local specialty, and during the days they were taken to see various tourist sites and examples of modern infrastructure. Dalian is one of the most prosperous places in northern China, and it's also one of the best planned, with elevated highways that ease congestion. The Sancha cadres rode on the highways, and they visited Dalian's new development zone. Pfizer, Toshiba, and Mitsubishi had already set up operations in the industrial park, and Intel had recently announced that it planned to build a Dalian factory dedicated to making semiconductors.

But the cadres seemed most deeply impressed by a variety show that featured Thai transvestites. In recent years, the Chinese government had loosened restrictions on international travel, and Thailand had become a popular destination for middle- and upper-class people. Whenever Chinese tour groups went to Bangkok, they made sure to schedule an evening at a transvestite show. As more and more people went abroad, the shows became increasingly famous, until finally the folks in Dalian decided to import some Thai transvestites of their own.

After Wei Ziqi returned from the northeast, he couldn't stop talking about the variety show. "You've been to Thailand," he said. "About the *renyao*—is that true?"

I said I was pretty certain they're actually men.

"That's not what I mean," he said. "We were told they take children when they're really small, maybe four or five years old, and then they train them to be transvestites. They said they spend years and years on this training. Is that true?"

"I doubt it," I said. "I think they probably do this as adults. It shouldn't take that long to become a transvestite."

"That's what I thought," Wei Ziqi said. He seemed happy that I had confirmed his analysis. "All the other Party members believed it," he said, "but I didn't."

IN 2007, CAO CHUNMEI decided that she wanted a driver's license. Now that they had a car, she thought it made sense; she could pick up groceries down in the valley. But Wei Ziqi wouldn't spend money on another driving course. "It's not necessary," he told her. "We already have one license." For a while, Cao Chunmei tried to change his mind, but he was too stubborn, and eventually she gave up on the idea of driving.

In the spring she began to experience panic attacks. Periodically her heart raced and her mind filled with dread; sometimes she was struck almost helpless. Finally she saw a doctor of traditional Chinese medicine, and she also went to Huairou to visit the clairvoyant. The man took her right wrist, felt her pulse, and informed her that new spirits had entered the home. Now she needed to appease a snake spirit, a rabbit spirit, and a fox spirit. Rabbit spirits are particularly jumpy; they often cause marital problems. Cao Chunmei prayed diligently at her shrines, and she did everything she could to avoid the slaughter of fish and chickens, and by summer she felt calmer again.

Wei Ziqi seemed to recover when the customers reappeared. He cut down on his drinking, and he focused once again on expanding his business; he renovated the patio and built a new pond for the Swiss trout. To determine the most auspicious location for the pond, he called in a clairvoyant from down in the valley. Wei Ziqi had never been religious, and he ignored his wife's shrines in the living room, but he obeyed the clairvoyant's instructions. That was one thing Wei Ziqi had learned— never again would he ignore a fortune-teller's warning.

As for Wei Jia, he picked up his own lessons about politics. In school, fifth grade is the first year that Chinese children campaign for class-room cadre positions, as opposed to being appointed by the teacher. Wei Jia had been successful as Politeness Monitor; he was well liked by other kids and the instructors trusted him. They encouraged him to run for office, but he flatly refused. "It's too much hassle," he told me. "Let somebody else do that stuff." His favorite subjects were English and computers. He never talked much about what he wanted to be when he grew up, but he said that someday, after he left the village, he'd live in downtown Beijing, near the lake of Houhai.

In autumn the Party Secretary's mother died. It happened at the end of harvest, and the villagers gathered in the dead woman's home to pay their respects. She had been an important person: the first Sancha woman to join the Party, and the inspiration for her daughter's rise. The funeral lasted three days. On the first day, I happened to walk past while the Party Secretary was mourning. She wore funeral white, and she had fallen onto her knees before the coffin. She was keening—her high-pitched wails echoed off the stony walls of the valley. In the past I had only seen her brusqueness, the sense of control that she carried around the village, and I had never entirely trusted her. But the sight of the funeral made me feel something different, and I realized that part of me was relieved that Wei Ziqi had lost the election. Cao Chunmei was right: he already had enough to worry about. In the countryside there are many ways to be humbled, and a man is lucky if a brush with politics turns out to be his worst moment.

The Shitkicker's new house remained empty. The unfinished brick walls still dominated the upper village, and piles of cement lay abandoned along the walk. He never found a buyer, and he never made another attempt at a local coup. But in other respects his status grew. Half a century after pouring tea for the local clairvoyant, he seemed to draw more of the old man's power. The Shitkicker was gaining clarity—he could see the unseen; he could speak the unspoken. He felt the wrists and he described the visions, the spirits of snakes and rabbits and foxes, and soon more villagers sought wisdom in the shadow of the empty house.

BOOK III

THE FACTORY

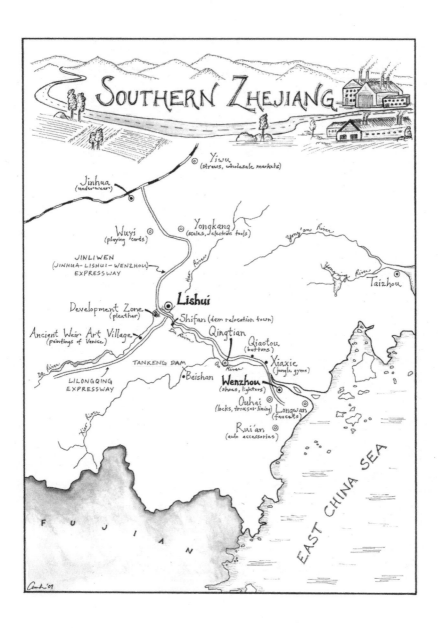

SOUTHERN ZHEJIANG

Yiwu
(straws, wholesale markets)

Jinhua
(underwear)

Wuyi
(playing cards)

Yongkang
(scales, electric tools)

Yong'an River

Yongning River

Taizhou

JINLIWEN
(JINHUA–LISHUI–WENZHOU)
EXPRESSWAY

Ou River

Lishui

Development Zone
(pleather)

Shifan (dam relocation town)

Qingtian

Ancient Weir Art Village
(paintings of Venice)

Qiaotou
(buttons)

Ou River

Da River

TANKENG DAM

Xiaxie
(jungle gyms)

Da River

LILONGQING
EXPRESSWAY

•Beishan

Wenzhou
(shoes, lighters)

Xiao River

Ouhai
(locks, trouser lining)

Longwan
(faucets)

Rui'an
(auto accessories)

EAST CHINA SEA

F U J I A N

Comb '09

I

—

IN THE CITY OF WENZHOU THEY RENTED OUT CARS WITH an empty tank. The first time I went there and picked up a Volkswagen Santana, in July of 2005, that was my welcome: I paid my deposit, put the key in the ignition, and the low-fuel warning light flashed on. There was barely enough in the tank to make it to a gas station. In the past, when I'd rented from Beijing's Capital Motors, I complained about inconsistent fuel levels, but the folks at the Wenzhou Prosperous Automobile Rental Company had solved that problem in their own entrepreneurial way. If I returned the Santana with so much as a gallon left in the tank, it would be siphoned out and sold.

Before that year, I had never rented a car in the south, and I hadn't spent much time driving in Chinese cities. Almost all of my journeys had been in the countryside of the north, where I became accustomed to rural rhythms: the busy mornings of spring planting, the road-threshing of autumn. In winter I spent quiet days in villages where most young people were already gone. But there had never been any mystery about where they were going, or how they were getting there. They followed the new roads south, and each year there were more migrants, more ways to leave. In 2003, the central government embarked on a major two-year road-building campaign in the countryside, and after that was finished they turned their attention to the cities. These places were being transformed by the auto boom: in the four years since I acquired my driver's license, the number of passenger vehicles in China had more than doubled. In January of 2005, officials announced plans to construct another thirty thousand miles of high-speed expressways. Eventually this network would connect every city with a population of over two hundred thousand people, stretching all the way from the factory towns of the eastern coast to the far western border with Kyrgyzstan. China may have come late to the world of high-speed transport—the nation's first expressway wasn't completed until 1988—but by 2020 they intended to have more highway miles than the United States.

When the government announced the expansion, they specifically mentioned the States as a source of inspiration. Zhang Chunxian, the Minister of Communications, hosted a press conference in Beijing, and he responded to one question with a story about Condoleezza Rice. Recently she had visited China, where apparently she told an official that they should follow the example of America in the 1950s and build more roads. "She said when she was young, she took a lot of trips with her family across America," Zhang explained. "This was how she became interested in the country's highways, and she said those trips helped her love the United States. By building expressways, we can boost the auto industry, but that's only a small part of it. What's important is the implication for national development and the improvement in people's lives."

In the southeast, one of the new routes was the Jinliwen Expressway. The road would begin in Wenzhou, not far from the coast, and it would run west and north for 145 miles, connecting the cities of Lishui and Jinhua. Much of the route paralleled the outdated National Highway 330, and on my first trip I drove the Santana along the old two-lane road, past miles of construction. Some parts of the new expressway were mostly finished; other sections were still in the early stages, with rows of cement pylons running along the banks of the Ou River. There were workers everywhere—total investment was over 1.5 billion dollars, and it was a priority project, which in China means that construction continues day and night. Driving along the old road, looking out the window, I saw workers hauling rebar, and mixing cement, and scurrying nimbly across webbed scaffolding. Sometimes a half dozen men knelt in a line, using hand tools to smooth a stretch of fresh-laid roadway. They worked patiently, moving backward step by step, and their steady progress represented the first traffic of the Jinliwen Expressway. At night the glow of welding torches could be seen from miles away, an intimation of the headlights that would someday sweep across this road.

I had come to southern Zhejiang Province in search of a city. Years ago, my first long driving trip had followed relics of the past, the stretches of the Great Wall that went through dying villages; and I had found a home in Sancha because I wanted some link to the countryside of today. But here in Zhejiang I was thinking about the future. In southern China, nothing changes the landscape faster than a new expressway: farmland disappears, and factories sprout up, and entrepreneurs and migrants pour into town. I was curious about this early rush—I wanted to know what life is like for the pioneering factory owners and workers. But first I had to find a city, and the Jinliwen Expressway would be my guide. The new highway was scheduled to open by the end of 2005, and after that these places would boom.

There had already been several generations of road building along this route. It's rugged countryside, following the banks of the Ou River, where most hillsides are too steep for crop terracing. Much of this region was inaccessible until the original version of Highway 330 was completed in 1934, during China's first wave of modern road construction. Back then they had also looked to the example of the United States, and American engineers oversaw much of the early work across the country. Those packed-dirt roads were typically suited for speeds of only thirty miles per hour, and many of them were damaged or destroyed during the war. In southern Zhejiang, Highway 330 was finally paved in the late 1970s, and it wasn't improved significantly until 1987.

Even then, when the Reform period was still in the early stages, the new road had an immediate effect. It transformed villages along its path, especially in the regions close to Wenzhou, where people traditionally raised rice and fish. With access to the new Highway 330, they left farming behind, and over time they came to make the most unexpected things. Driving northwest from Wenzhou, I sometimes could see the products from the road. In Xiaxie, a village ten miles outside of the city, I passed endless rows of playground equipment. It was stored in bulk everywhere beside the street: piles of swing sets, big stacks of red plastic slides, long lines of blue and yellow monkey bars. There wasn't a child in sight, and most buildings had the industrial squareness of factories. I pulled over to chat with locals, who told me that making playground equipment had become the local specialty. Xiaxie was part of Qiaoxia Township, which was currently home to 270 individual manufacturers, all of them producing some version of the same thing. Half of China's domestic market for playground equipment was supplied by this single town.

Another ten miles down Highway 330, past another bend in the river, the town of Qiaotou had erected a statue of a button. It was a huge disk of silver, ten feet wide and topped by wings that spun whenever the wind came up. Qiaotou's population was only 64,000, but the town had 380 factories that manufactured more than 70 percent of the buttons for clothes made in China. In honor of this status, the village elders erected the statue in the center of town, right in front of a new building called "Button City." Button City was four stories tall, and the ground-floor market was dedicated entirely to Qiaotou's distinctive product. Clothes manufacturers arrived to buy in bulk, and sellers organized their wares by size and style. Former peasants hawked buttons out of grain sacks— big twenty-five-pound bags, still labeled "Rice" and "Flour," now filled with nothing but buttons.

On the day I drove through, many dealers were women with small children, and the kids sat on the cement floor. Whenever they began to cry, somebody tossed them another handful of buttons to play with. I could only imagine how much of Button City was being processed by tiny intestines on a daily basis, and it occurred to me that with a little organization, these kids could be shipped out to Xiaxie every morning to play on the jungle gyms. But there was no overlap between the towns, and moving from one to the other, at least in the economic sense, was almost as absolute as crossing an international border. People told me that even the local dialects were essentially unintelligible.

This part of Zhejiang is famous for difficult dialects, and it's also full of one-product towns. Locals tend to specialize in some simple object, in part because they have little formal training and it's easiest to manufacture something that doesn't require much technology and investment. Whenever Highway 330 led me to a place of decent size, I pulled over and asked a bystander, "What do people make here?" Usually they could answer the question in a sentence; sometimes they didn't need to say a word. In the town of Wuyi, a man responded by reaching into his pocket and pulling out a handful of playing cards. I subsequently learned that Wuyi manufactures one billion decks a year: half of China's domestic market. Fifty miles away, Yiwu makes one quarter of the world's plastic drinking straws. A place called Yongkang produces 95 percent of Chinese scales. In another part of Zhejiang, Songxia turns out 350 million umbrellas every year. Fenshui specializes in pens; Shangguan manufactures table tennis paddles. Datang produces one-third of the socks on earth. Forty percent of the world's neckties are made in a place called Shengzhou.

Between factory towns I drove through countryside of remarkable beauty. Sometimes the Ou River narrowed, bordered by big cliffs of stone, and the valley deepened into a gorge. Highway 330 follows the river upstream, into the provincial highlands, and with every mile the mountains become more impressive. Unlike northern China, these areas receive heavy rainfall and there's a lushness to the landscape. And after a couple of days I began to enjoy the journey's contrasts: the stunning scenery and the odd products, the way the landscape expanded to vistas of rivers and mountains, and then suddenly narrowed into a town that made something tiny: cards, pens, straws.

In the evenings I usually stayed at the International Hotel. Many factory towns had a guesthouse with that name, to serve the foreign buyers and managers who occasionally passed through. In the lobby they displayed flyers from local companies; sometimes, if there was a factory that made something more elaborate than a button or a straw, they featured a high-end model in the room. In the city of Yongkang, famous for scales and electrical tools, my room contained something called the Human Body Ingredient Test Device. It looked like a scale covered with electrodes; wires ran in all directions and a sign in English had been posted atop the thing: "WARNING: Prohibited for pregnant woman and the man with heart getting up abundantly." I decided to take a pass on the Human Body Ingredient Test Device. Beside my bed stood another local product called the Light-Wave Health Room. It was the size of a closet, made of wood, and the door was studded with electric switches—the thing looked like an outhouse from the future. Instructions read in English:

PLEASE DON'T USE THE APPLIANCE
IF YOU HAVE THESE SITUATIONS.

1. *The one with the bleeding wound and fester inflammation.*
2. *The one with serious eyes inflammation (if not serious, please cover some wet cloth and cotton balls on the eyes).*
3. *The one is burned seriously within 4 months.*
4. *Prohibited for the advances man, pregnant woman, baby.*
5. *Prohibited for the one with serious sick, dangerous patient.*
6. *Some people have the temperature taboo, please use it under the direction of doctor.*
7. *Don't put pets into appliance.*
8. *Prohibited for the drunk man.*

In the city of Lishui I finally found what I was looking for. It was located seventy-five miles from Wenzhou, where Highway 330 was in bad shape. The drive from the coast usually took at least three hours, and accidents often caused delays; it was too remote for businessmen, at least until the new expressway was completed. The surrounding mountains were the highest I'd seen thus far, with green peaks rising a thousand feet above the city. Lishui lay at the intersection of the Da and the Hao rivers, and people still farmed within a mile of downtown—fruit orchards were everywhere in the suburbs. When I asked what Lishui manufactured, people laughed and said, "Tangerines." One local entrepreneur told me earnestly, "This is the Tibet of Zhejiang." Here in bustling southeastern China, within a few hours' drive of the coast, it was an oxymoron—like calling a place the Alaska of New Jersey. But there was no doubt that Lishui was isolated by Zhejiang standards. When I first visited, it had the lowest per capita urban income of any city in the province, and industry was so young that Lishui had yet to settle on a local product. From an economic standpoint, it was still a blank slate: a place without buttons or playing cards or jungle gyms.

But already changes had begun. South of town, where the new expressway would soon have an exit, the government was building the Lishui Economic Development Zone. Until recently this region had all been agricultural, as timeless as any farmland in China—a quiet place where peasants followed the regular cycles of seasons and months, planting and harvest. But now the fields were being replaced with a sprawling industrial park, and the government hoped to attract investors from the coast. Once the new road was finished, the three-hour journey from Wenzhou would be reduced to little more than sixty minutes. In the future, that was the kind of time that would matter to Lishui: the hours and minutes of a businessman's schedule.

ON MY NEXT JOURNEY to Lishui, three months later, I noticed a man in new clothes standing beside a half-built factory in the development zone. His outfit caught my eye: stiff black jeans, black sweater, thin-soled leather shoes with a square front. The shoes identified him as a Wenzhou native: the city is famous for its shoe factories and often local bosses adopt the export fashions. That year, a European-style loafer with squared toes was everywhere in Wenzhou, and the moment I saw the shoes I knew the man was not from Lishui.

It was also unusual to see somebody so clean in the development zone. Roads were still dirt, and most buildings were covered with scaffolding; very few factories had started producing. Virtually everybody outside was a construction worker dressed in a grimy military uniform, carrying a sledgehammer or saw. But this man's clothes were spotless and he held nothing but a black fake-leather money bag. His white Buick Sail was parked nearby. He looked nervous; he chain-smoked State Express 555 cigarettes. But he answered in a friendly way when I asked why he was in the development zone.

"I'm waiting for my partner," he said. "We're opening a business here."

He introduced himself as Gao Xiaomeng, and he was thirty-three years old. His partner was his uncle, a man named Wang Aiguo who was also from the coast. Boss Gao said they were involved in the manufacturing of "clothing accessories"; he didn't go into detail about what they produced. This afternoon they were supposed to design their new factory, but Boss Wang was late. He was stuck on Highway 330—a common occurrence on the narrow road, where accidents sometimes backed up traffic for an hour. Until the new expressway was finished, and the four lanes opened for traffic, nobody would be able to predict how long it took to drive from Wenzhou.

Every five minutes Boss Gao checked his cell phone. Every fifteen minutes he lit another cigarette. We stood in the shade of the half-built factory, chatting idly; we exchanged business cards and discussed the Lishui weather. By the time Boss Wang finally showed up, Boss Gao introduced me as a friend. In the development zone it was easy to meet people; everybody was an outsider and nobody knew what to expect from this place. It felt wide open—most structures were empty shells, and the half-built roads were bordered by blank billboards still waiting for sponsors. The silver surfaces reflected the sky, advertising nothing but late October sunlight.

AT 2:30 IN THE afternoon, after Boss Wang had finally arrived, the men started designing the factory. The two bosses were joined by a contractor and his assistant, both of whom were natives of Lishui. There was no architect, no draftsman; nobody had brought a ruler or plumb line. The only tools carried by the men were disposable lighters, and Boss Gao's first act was to distribute a round of State Express 555 cigarettes. After everybody lit up, he rummaged in his bag for a crumpled piece of scrap paper. He smoothed it atop the surface of a cheap folding table, and then he began to draw.

Apart from the table, the room was empty: white walls, bare floors, untouched pillars. Naked lightbulbs dangled on cords from the ceiling like unripe fruit. The plumbing had been installed, but the water was still off; the front door had no lock. On the blank page, Boss Gao sketched the room's walls in the shape of a rectangle, and then he added two lines in the southeastern corner. They represented walls to be constructed: someday that space would enclose a machine room. Boss Gao turned to the contractor. They spoke Mandarin—in Zhejiang, local dialects are so difficult that businessmen use the national language whenever they go to another town.

"What's the standard width for a door?" Boss Gao asked.

"Usually about one and a half meters."

"I want it wider. Can you do two and a half?"

"That won't work. If you want to use standard doors, make it one and a half."

Boss Gao returned to the paper, sketching fast, and four more rooms took shape: a chemist's laboratory, a storage closet, two additional spaces for machines. Boss Wang leaned over to study the diagram. "We don't need this room," he said to his nephew.

"Don't you want two more for the machines?"

"One is enough. Put them all together."

Boss Wang took the pen, scratched out a line, and the planned room disappeared. The older man was more conscious of money, and he knew that every new wall only meant higher costs. He had been in business for twenty years, and many of the best opportunities had passed him by, but his nephew still had the nervous eagerness of youth. Boss Gao's previous endeavor had been a moderate success, and he dressed the part, with a sort of understated coolness. He was proud of his Buick Sail—when we first met, he made sure to tell me that he drove an American car. In fact the Sail is based on the platform of the Opel Corsa, which gives it the distinction of being an Opel-engineered car built by Chinese workers under the brand of a troubled American automaker. But such details didn't matter to Boss Gao, who had already come a long way from peasant roots. His father had been a rice farmer and local schoolteacher, and Boss Gao was the first member of his family to succeed in business.

At 2:57 the bosses finished designing the ground level. They moved to the second floor, where Boss Gao reached once more into his quiver of State Express 555s. He handed out the cigarettes and then flipped over the sheet of paper.

"This is too small for an office."

"Put the wall here instead. That's big enough."

"Can you put a wall in here?"

"It'll be too dark if you do it like that."

"This room isn't for workers anyway."

"*Budui!* That doesn't look right."

The two bosses conferred and the uncle scribbled out another wall. In twenty-three minutes they designed an office, a hallway, and three living quarters for factory managers. They moved to the top floor. Two bathrooms, a kitchen, nine dormitory rooms for workers: fourteen minutes. All told, they had mapped out a 21,000-square-foot factory, from bottom to top, in one hour and four minutes. Boss Gao handed the scrap of paper to the Lishui contractor. The man asked when they wanted the estimate.

"How about this afternoon?" Boss Gao said.

The contractor looked at his watch. It was 3:48 p.m.

"I can't do it that fast!"

"Well, then tell me early in the morning."

They went outside to discuss building materials. The contractor showed them two kinds of cinder blocks: one sold for 18.6 American cents; the other was 19.8 cents. Boss Wang chose the cheaper blocks. When it came to plaster, he said, "We just don't want that kind that rubs off on your clothes when you brush against it." The contractor asked if they needed a detailed estimate, with square footage itemized and calculated, but Boss Wang didn't have time for that. "Just give us the price," he said. The last thing they discussed was doors. The new factory would require fifteen total, and for some reason this particular item concerned Boss Wang.

"Don't buy those cheap five-dollar doors that look terrible," he said sternly. "We want the ten-dollar doors. And don't try to make money by getting cheaper materials. That's not the way you make money. I'll tell you how to do it—do a good job now and then we'll hire you again. That's how we make money in Wenzhou. If you do it right, you'll get more business. Do you understand?"

◉ ◉ ◉

ALL ACROSS CHINA THE people of Wenzhou are famous for their entrepreneurial skill. In a nation where millions have made the transition from countryside to city, from farming to business, the natives of southern Zhejiang are the prototypical peasant-entrepreneurs. Back in the 1980s, when China's private economy took its first tentative steps, the Wenzhou people responded so quickly that the central government began to praise the "Wenzhou model" of rural development. As a business strategy it couldn't have been simpler: low investment, low-quality products, low profit margins. Low education, too—even today, after two decades of a booming economy, nearly 80 percent of all Wenzhou entrepreneurs have fewer than nine years of formal schooling. But somehow it works, and the city has come to dominate certain industries. Today, roughly a quarter of the shoes sold in China come from Wenzhou. The city produces an estimated 70 percent of the world's cigarette lighters. Over 90 percent of the Wenzhou economy is private—unlike other parts of the nation, state-owned industries have played little role in local development.

Over time, Wenzhou entrepreneurs have spread out across the south. Often they follow new roads, which was part of the plan for the Jinliwen Expressway: it was designed to transport factory goods to the coast, but it would also allow businessmen to travel into the interior. This had already happened along other routes, like Highway 330. Wenzhou businessmen often came to a village, started a few factories, and then locals picked up on the idea. Many of the one-product towns began in this manner, and it had contributed to the overall success of Zhejiang Province. Despite having been relatively poor in the 1970s, Zhejiang now has the highest per capita urban and rural incomes of any province.

The Wenzhou people themselves love to talk about the mystery of their success. In general, the Chinese are highly attuned to regional differences, and they're quick to bring up the shortcomings of some other part of the country. Beijing natives ridicule the low class of the Henanese; people in Shenzhen disparage migrants from Hunan and Sichuan;

lots of folks have something bad to say about women from Shanghai. But Wenzhou has an unusual taste for self-analysis. At the airport bookstore, an entire section is devoted to volumes about Wenzhou business: *The Collected Secrets of How Wenzhou People Make Money*, *The Feared Wenzhou People*, *The Wenzhou Code*, *Actually You Don't Understand the Wenzhou People*. These books are popular with visitors, but it's also common for natives to read up on themselves. Once I saw Boss Gao studying a book called *The Jews of the East: The Commercial Stories of Fifty Wenzhou Entrepreneurs*. He asked me if I knew any Jews in America, and I said yes.

"Are they good at business?" Boss Gao said.

I said that some of them did business, and some of them did other things.

"It says here that Jews in Europe are famous for doing business," he said.

"I guess that's true historically," I said. "But it doesn't mean that all Jews do business nowadays."

"This book says that the Jews are the Wenzhou people of Europe," said Boss Gao.

It took me a minute to wrap my head around that one. But eventually I learned what to expect in conversations about Wenzhou development. Entrepreneurs often asked the same question: "Why do you think that we Wenzhou people are so good at business?" It pleased them if I said, "The environment." This response agreed with the Wenzhou books, which generally propagate theories of environmental determinism. The region possesses little arable soil, and during imperial times there were poor transport links to the interior, because of the rugged landscape. With few options, Wenzhou natives turned to the sea, and they had already developed a strong trading culture by the end of the Ming dynasty, in the seventeenth century. They also built a tradition of migration, and pockets of Wenzhou émigrés gained footholds in port cities around the world. These networks survived the isolation of the Mao years, and so did the Wenzhou business instinct. Once the Communists allowed them to leave farms and start factories, the local economy took off.

The environmental theory makes sense, but there's also an element of self-determinism. People in southern Zhejiang believe in their business acumen, and they take pride in their ability to cut margins and develop trade networks. They have faith in themselves, and they have faith in business—there's no shame in being a cold-blooded entrepreneur. A few years ago, a Wenzhou newspaper called *Fortune Weekly* ran a special Valentine's Day supplement that included a survey of local male millionaires. The newspaper asked the men where they liked to have romantic Valentine's Day dinners, and it listed the gifts they purchased for their wives and girlfriends. One question called upon respondents to recall "the time in your life when you felt the deepest emotion." The two most common responses were "When I started my business" and "When I got divorced." Another question asked: "If forced to choose between your business and your family, which would it be?" Of the respondents, 60 percent chose business, and 20 percent chose family. The other 20 percent couldn't make up their minds.

BY MY THIRD TRIP to Zhejiang, I learned how to return a rental car with an empty tank. The first couple of times I miscalculated, bringing back the Santana with plenty of gas, which obviously pleased the men who ran the Wenzhou Prosperous Automobile Rental Company. The trick was to never fill the thing up: I added gas in five- and ten-dollar increments, and at the end of a journey I timed it so the low-fuel light flashed just before I made it back to Wenzhou Prosperous. And it was obvious that so long as I paid my thirty dollars per day, I could do whatever I pleased to a Wenzhou car. There weren't any rules about where I could drive, and the company never checked for damage; they couldn't have cared less about dents and scratches. In this part of China, it was hopeless—the rental cars were already riddled with marks.

I had never been any place in the country where driving was so dangerous. Part of the problem was infrastructure, which often had a slapdash quality. Wenzhou never benefited from the kind of central planning that shaped other key cities like Shenzhen and Shanghai, and here in Zhejiang the local governments usually had to figure out things on their own. Roads were undersized and in poor repair; traffic control was a disaster. And the Wenzhou business instinct made things worse, because people were in a rush and they liked to take risks.

There was nothing more terrifying than a drive through the city's coastal suburbs. Fifteen years ago, this region was all farmland, but it boomed so fast that old village boundaries disappeared. Now you judged transitions by advertisements on the side of the road, which featured local products. Once, I toured this region, heading south past the airport. First I cruised through a neighborhood where virtually every billboard displayed hinges, and then I began to see signs for electric plugs and adaptors. Soon they were replaced by plastic light switches; next came fluorescent bulbs. Everywhere I passed warehouses and factory buildings, but the road itself remained of rural dimensions: two lanes, no shoulder, badly pitted. Periodically a minor accident caused a traffic jam, and drivers leaned on their horns while staring at advertisements for hinges or light switches. In a place called Longwan I reached faucets—this area was home to nearly seven hundred factories that made water spouts. Automobile axles were next, then metal punch presses.

At last I came to the district of Rui'an, which according to the local government was home to exactly 1,208 manufacturers of automobile engine accessories, brakes, and steering systems. I passed pieces of vehicles in all the roadside shops: dozens of wheels in one window, rows of brake pads in the next, and then a block of stores that featured nothing but car ignitions. In the middle of town I came upon a fatal accident that had occurred just moments earlier. A young woman had been driving a scooter, and she must have been moving at a high rate of speed when she struck a car. The larger vehicle was badly dented and the scooter was smashed beyond recognition. Traffic had slowed to a crawl, and I had no choice but to drive directly past the accident site. A crowd had already gathered, pointing and chattering excitedly; nobody had bothered to cover the body. The woman hadn't worn a helmet and she had struck the ground headfirst: legs bent backward, arms splayed out, face pressed flat down. When I drove past, before I could look away, I caught an image of her brains poured onto the pavement. It was late afternoon and the light was sharp; blood pooled bright around tangled hair.

A block further, the pedestrian crowd thinned out and traffic returned to normal. Motor scooters zipped along; cars jockeyed for position; horns sang out in the streets. Billboards advertised more pieces of automobiles: hubcaps, pedals, spark plugs. Wipers and windshields, seats and steering wheels. Tires, tires, tires. My hands were still shaking when I pulled over for the evening at Rui'an's International Hotel. The parking lot was packed with rows of black cars: Audis and Buicks and Volkswagens. Buyers and sellers, businessmen and cadres—and out on the bustling evening streets, where the neon shop signs came to life, nobody would have guessed that there was one less driver in the city.

WHEN I RETURNED TO the Lishui factory in January of 2006, the bosses were testing the machinery. It had been only three months since my last visit, but during that time the place had been transformed. The contractor's work was finished; the dividing walls had been erected and the ten-dollar doors were all in place. Three big punch press machines stood in the main room. Crates and boxes had been piled everywhere, full of equipment waiting to be assembled. There were workers, too— Boss Gao, the younger of the two entrepreneurs, was accompanied by three technicians who had been hired to get the factory running. On my last trip, the bosses had spoken vaguely of their products as "clothing accessories," and now I asked one of the technicians for more detail.

The man's name was Tian Hongguo, and originally he had come from Sichuan Province. He was in his late thirties, an advanced age in the factory world; everybody called him "Old Tian." He was tiny, weighing just over one hundred pounds, and he had an elflike face: pointed chin, big ears, wide mouth. He grinned at my question.

"We're going to make two things," he said, and he took samples out of a box. One was a ring so small that it wouldn't fit around my little finger. The other was a larger band of steel, razor-thin and covered with plastic at both ends. It was bent in the shape of a wide-open U, and Old Tian handed me a couple, in different sizes. One was just large enough for a billiard ball to pass through. The other was about the size of a softball. I asked Old Tian what they were for.

"It's for women's clothing," he said.

He held the band to his breast so that the tips faced up, like a smile. Suddenly it dawned on me—these were support structures for brassieres.

"It helps women dress more beautifully," Old Tian said. "We have different sizes, too. Some are small and some are big. Some are *really* big." He gestured with his hands, forming the shape of an object roughly the size of a basketball. I couldn't imagine he was still talking about bras, so I figured those wires must have a different function.

"The ones that are that big," I asked, "what are they used for?"

"For Russians," Old Tian said.

FOR THE PAST DECADE Boss Gao had manufactured obscure pieces of clothing. He had grown up in the marshlands south of Wenzhou, in the region known as Ouhai, where his father grew rice and taught in the local middle school. Boss Gao attended two years of trade school, studying machinery, and in the mid-1990s he opened a small workshop with his family. They manufactured lining for trousers—the cheap white fabric that's attached to the beltline. Like so many Wenzhou products, it required very little in the way of labor or technology. Initially the Gaos invested less than four thousand American dollars, and the family represented the entire work force: Boss Gao, his parents, and his two sisters. They sold to local clothing factories, and their profit margin in the early years was roughly 50 percent. They made enough money to expand, buying new machinery and hiring a half dozen workers.

In the beginning there were only five or six other workshops in the region that made the same product. But soon others in town noticed the Gao family's success, and new factories began to spring up. By 2003, their neighborhood had become home to twenty different producers of nonwoven fabric, and profit margins had plummeted to 15 percent. That year, Boss Gao gave up on trouser lining. He was still making money, but he didn't want to ride the industry all the way to the bottom.

"It was a lot easier to do business in the 1990s," he told me once. "There weren't so many people starting factories back then." He often spoke fondly about that time; for Boss Gao, who was all of thirty-three years old, the 1990s were the good old days, when competition wasn't so intense. "Back then it was the product that mattered," he said wistfully. "It used to be that you'd try to find a product that nobody else was making. But now everything is already being made by somebody in China. No matter what you make, you're going to have competition. So now it's not the product that counts. It's the volume."

After abandoning trouser lining, Boss Gao partnered with his uncle, who produced underwire for brassieres. It's another product with a low cost of entry: all it requires is an electric metal-punch machine, which bends the steel, cuts the pieces, and cranks out nearly a hundred wires per minute. Demand is steady, which is the only good thing about underwire. "As long as there are women, you'll have customers," Boss Gao once said philosophically. "It's like sanitary napkins." But nobody gets rich from the wires, and Boss Gao and Boss Wang began to look for a new product. Their goal was to find something that required significant investment in technical machinery, which was one way to weed out the copycats.

Together the bosses searched far and wide—well, at any rate they thoroughly explored the brassiere. From the Wenzhou perspective, the product represents a vast world unto itself, since the final assembly of each bra consists of twelve separate components. The bosses started their search at the bottom, with the underwire, and then they worked their way up the bra, weighing the possibilities of each separate component. They thought about thread; they looked at lace; they considered the clasp. When they reached the top, where tiny 0- and 8-shaped rings adjust the straps, they found what they were looking for.

To a consumer, a bra ring seems simple to the point of invisibility. It consists of thin steel coated with nylon, and it weighs only half a gram; the average bra contains four such rings. They connect to nylon straps, and hardly any woman in America or Europe gives the objects a second thought. But in fact the rings are the most technically complicated component of the garment. In order to coat a steel ring evenly with high-gloss nylon, a manufacturer must have an assembly line with three distinct stages, each of which heats the ring to over five hundred degrees Celsius. All of it must be computer-controlled: the temperature, the oscillating mechanism of the powder mixer, the speed of each conveyor belt. Such machinery can't be cobbled together from spare parts, and it's not cheap: Boss Gao and Boss Wang purchased their assembly line for sixty-five thousand dollars. In the past, neither entrepreneur had spent even a tenth as much on a piece of equipment, and all of their plans depended on this assembly line working smoothly.

The Machine sat on the ground floor, in the first room that Boss Gao had designed. It was a squat, sullen-looking thing: the exterior had been painted seasick-green and the two main assembly lines stretched fifty feet long. They were arranged one on top of the other, double-decker fashion. The conveyor belts were made of polished steel and they gleamed mirror-bright beneath bare lightbulbs. The whole thing weighed six tons, because the belts were propped up by unbelievably thick pillars of steel. These supports easily could have hoisted a house—there's no logical reason why the manufacture of tiny bra rings requires such thick pillars. But steel, like cement, is one of the basic construction materials that tend to be overused in urban China. It's an economy of scale: in such a massive country, at a time of incredible growth, companies turn out raw materials so fast that the prices are relatively cheap. Foreign architects often comment on the staggering amounts of cement and steel that go into a typical Chinese building project.

I visited the factory on the day they first tested the Machine. A technician named Luo Shouyun hit a switch, and gas burners ignited blue flames; the conveyor belts lurched forward. A digital console tracked the temperature. The room itself was cold—outside it wasn't much above freezing, and the bosses, like most people in Zhejiang, didn't heat their factory. But soon the digital numbers began to rise as the gas flames warmed the Machine. It hit ninety degrees Celsius, then 150. Within fifteen minutes the temperature had broken 400. The number topped out at 474, and then it suddenly plummeted. The Machine needed to sustain a level of at least 500 degrees before production could begin.

"Maybe it's because it's colder here than in Guangdong," Luo Shouyun said. In the far south of China, he had spent most of a decade working on bra rings, and everybody called him Luo Shifu: Master Luo. He had been poached from a competing factory, and he was the only one in the room who truly understood how the Machine worked. Now he put on a pair of fireproof gloves and tried to open the door to one of the heating elements. But the metal had been welded so poorly that the joints melted away in the heat, and the handle came off in Master Luo's hand. He cursed and dropped the red-hot metal, which lay on the cold cement floor, hissing like an angry snake.

"*Mei shir,*" Boss Gao said. "No problem. Don't worry about that."

He lit another State Express 555 and gave one to Master Luo. Cigarette clenched between his teeth, Master Luo tinkered with the control panel, which was covered with two dozen switches. He decided to run an initial batch of rings through the assembly line, to see how they came out. At the end of the line he measured them with a digital caliper. They were 1.7 millimeters in width—far too fat for a bra ring, whose ideal thickness ranges from 1.2 to 1.3 millimeters. The nylon wasn't melting evenly; the Machine was running too cold. Now the temperature of the assembly line wouldn't even break 400. "Is it the weather?" Boss Gao said.

"In Guangdong during winter it was usually seventeen or eighteen degrees in the factory," Master Luo said. He tinkered with the Machine's gas valves, using a wrench. "Today it's about six degrees," he said. "Maybe that's the difference."

"Or it could be a problem with the gas," Boss Gao said.

A half dozen natural gas canisters stood in the next room. They were four feet tall and made of metal, with rubber hoses that ran to the Machine. The men checked the connections: everything looked fine. Somebody theorized that a little movement might help. First they shook the gas canisters gently, rocking the huge tubes back and forth, but the Machine's temperature console didn't budge. They began to push harder. The men were still smoking and cigarettes dangled from their mouths while they clanged the metal tubes against the cement floor. Quietly, I edged toward the doorway, hoping to duck out if something blew.

"Maybe we need to heat them up," Boss Gao said. "I'll boil some water." He turned on a stove in the main room and began to heat some kettles. Old Tian retrieved a stepladder and pushed it next to the gas canisters. After the water came to a boil, Boss Gao poured it into a bucket, hoisted the thing onto his shoulder, and climbed the ladder. He still had a State Express 555 cigarette clamped in his mouth. That was my final vision of Boss Gao—at that point I decided it was no longer necessary to rely on eyesight to document these proceedings. From the next room I listened to what came next.

First a great sizzling sound, like meat hitting a hot grill; then a series of splashes; finally silence. I poked my head back inside the doorway. Steam had filled the room, and the newly baptized canisters glistened under bare lightbulbs. Master Luo checked the Machine's temperature: no change. By the end of the evening, they had been fiddling with the assembly line for nearly four hours without any progress. They theorized that the natural gas might be low quality; Boss Gao said he'd try a different supplier. But that sounded like wishful thinking, and everybody seemed reluctant to confront the most likely reason—that there was some flaw in their brand-new Machine.

THE MACHINE'S ANCESTORS HAD originally come from Europe. In Chinese factories, there's always a genealogy to the equipment, and usually it can be traced to the outside world. Back in the 1980s, the bra ring industry was dominated by French and German manufacturers, but then production shifted to Taiwan, where labor was cheap. A number of Taiwanese factories imported the European machinery, and by the early 1990s the island supplied most of the world's market for rings. In the middle of that decade, a Taiwanese-invested company called Daming decided to move production to China. This shift would become increasingly common for all industries over the next decade, until finally most of Taiwan's labor-intensive plants relocated to the mainland.

Daming set up shop in Xiamen, one of China's "special economic zones," designed to attract foreign investment. The boss—for the sake of the story, it's simplest to call him the First Boss—imported a European-made Machine. In the early years that Machine essentially minted money. Labor costs were even cheaper than in Taiwan, and there wasn't any local competition, because the sophisticated production process made it difficult for knockoff artists. Over time, First Boss came to rely heavily on a worker named Liu Hongwei, a migrant from rural Sichuan province. Liu had little formal education, but he was extremely intelligent, and over time he became an expert in the maintenance of the Machine.

Liu Hongwei also had the gift of remarkable memory. At Daming, in secret, he somehow created a detailed blueprint of the Machine. None of Liu's coworkers ever saw him measuring or sketching the assembly line, and later they theorized that he must have memorized it section by section, studying the thing by day and then drawing it at night. After Liu finished his blueprints, he took them to the city of Shantou, another special economic zone in southern China. He met with Second Boss, who ran a company called Shangang Keji. In 1998, Second Boss hired Liu Hongwei and took the blueprints to a custom-tooling plant, which built another Machine. Initially the thing didn't work—nobody's memory is perfect, after all—but a couple months of adjustments solved the problems. Shangang Keji began producing bra rings, and soon Second Boss was rich, too.

It didn't take long for Third Boss to enter the picture. He was also based in Shantou, where he started a company called Jinde, and he poached Liu Hongwei. Together they used the blueprints once more, custom building another Machine. By now the price of bra rings had already dropped significantly, but the margins were still good, and Third Boss did well, too. Nevertheless, he was furious when he heard that Liu Hongwei had secretly begun negotiations with Fourth Boss.

I first heard this story from Master Luo, who had worked alongside Liu Hongwei in the city of Shantou. Back then people said that Liu had received approximately twenty thousand American dollars for the sales of his blueprints, but nobody knew for certain. Master Luo did know, however, the exact amount of the bounty that was placed on the man's head by Third Boss: one hundred thousand yuan, or more than twelve thousand dollars. "He just wanted information," Master Luo explained. "He said he would pay that money to anybody who could tell him where Liu Hongwei had gone. He was really angry about what he had done."

I asked what Third Boss planned to do if he found the man.

"You know how business is in the south," Master Luo said, grinning. "It would be like killing a dog."

But as far as profits went, it was already too late. Once the Machine became available on the open market, anybody with sixty-five thousand American dollars could buy one. Over the past few years, Fourth Boss had been joined by Fifth Boss, and Sixth Boss, and Seventh Boss, and on and on. By the time the Lishui company got started, there were already twenty major factories in China involved in the business, and the bulk price of a bra ring had plummeted by 60 percent. Nowadays the profit margin often comes down to transport, which is why Boss Gao and Boss Wang chose to make the product in Lishui. No other major bra ring manufacturer was located in this part of Zhejiang, and with the new expressway they would have an advantage in supplying the province's brassiere factories.

Master Luo often talked about Liu Hongwei, referring to him as "the worker who tricked three bosses." The story had the ring of myth, a laborer's legend, and finally, out of curiosity, I flew to Shantou to try to confirm it. First Boss, Second Boss, and Third Boss all refused to talk—they clearly did not wish to revisit this incident. But I met with others who had worked with Liu Hongwei, and all of them told the same basic story, although certain details changed with every narrator. Some people believed that Liu wasn't his real name; others thought he lied about his home region. A couple of coworkers described him as a master forger, although one factory manager, who had seen Liu's government-issued ID card with his own eyes, swore that it was authentic.

Eventually, I was even shown the plans for the stolen Machine. They were held in the city of Guangzhou, at the Qingsui Machinery Manufacture Company, which had custom-made the equipment according to Liu's specifications. "His schooling wasn't really very good, so it was hard to get the assembly line to work," the manager at Qingsui told me. "It took us two months to make all the adjustments." The manager was friendly and open, and I sensed that he showed me the blueprints because he hoped to sell me a Machine, even though I told him repeatedly I was a writer. His most recent deal had been with Boss Gao and Boss Wang.

At the Lishui factory, where the first test of the equipment ended in failure, Master Luo eventually realized that the Machine still had a major design problem. He spent two weeks taking the thing apart and replacing key sections. He adjusted the gas burners closer to the conveyor belt, and he tinkered with the design of the oscillator. He jury-rigged some sections of the Machine with plywood and string, and he never bothered to reattach the handle that had melted off. By the time they started production, the Machine was already bruised and battered—there was a big gash where the handle used to be, and the adjusted burners had left black scorch marks across the steel. Master Luo told me the support pillars were needlessly thick because Liu Hongwei hadn't paid so much attention to that part of the design. "The blueprints still aren't very good," he said.

Master Luo believed that Liu Hongwei was a false name, and he described his former coworker in many of the same terms I heard from others. People said Liu Hongwei was tall and thin, with the dark-skinned appearance of a peasant. He was poorly educated. He supposedly had a wife and child, although nobody had ever met them. And despite the impressive bounty offered by Third Boss, the twelve thousand dollars were never claimed, because Liu successfully disappeared without a trace. He was *jiaohua*, tricky—that's the word most closely associated with Liu Hongwei. I heard it again and again, in all the places where bra rings are made, in Lishui and Shantou and Guangzhou; everywhere people shook their heads and said Liu was *jiaohua*. Nobody had the slightest idea where the man had gone.

BY THE TIME THE Machine was working, in January of 2006, the Jinliwen Expressway had opened. It consisted of two lanes in each direction, and shoulders were broad; the median had been meticulously landscaped with bushes that blocked the headlights of oncoming vehicles. All along the road, at an interval of every thousand meters, stood a free emergency phone—a detail that would have seemed extravagant in the United States, and one that's hardly necessary in China, where cell phone coverage is excellent. Along the Ou River, mountains are so steep that in many places the highway crews had to blast straight through the cliffs. From Wenzhou to Lishui, there were twenty-nine new tunnels, the longest of which stretched for over two miles. The only detail still lacking involved maps. On government-published atlases, the express-way's route hadn't been marked out yet, but Chinese maps always lag behind construction. Sometimes it seems as if people can build things faster than they can draw them.

For a driver in China there is no greater pleasure than a new high-way. The first few times I took the Jinliwen Expressway, traffic was light, because many local ramps had yet to open. It was possible to drive the seventy-five miles from Wenzhou to Lishui, but you couldn't exit or enter along the way, and often I cruised for dozens of miles without seeing another vehicle. Some sections of the highway were elevated, passing right above factory towns like Qiaotou. The new road stood so close to the warehouses that I could see local life: workers enter-ing buildings, trucks picking up goods, cement mixers starting new construction projects. But nobody was entering the expressway, which was still off-limits to these places. It felt like flying—glimpses from the window as I cruised overhead.

All along the highway, billboards touted cement brands: Golden Garden Cement, Red Lion Cement, Capital of the Immortals Cement. Those were the first advertisements, and the highway was also marked by information signs, which were the same shade of green as in the United States. Many Zhejiang road signs had even been translated into English. In Wenzhou, the exit read "Shoe Center of China." The express-way's lanes had been labeled "Slow Lane" and "Quickly Lane." "Dirve Carefully"—that mangled notice was everywhere. Another commanded "Do Not Get Tired." Periodically a strange couplet appeared on a sign beside the road:

PLEASE NOT TRY TIRED DRIVING
KEEP OFF THE TRAFFIC ACCIDENT

At Lishui, the exit led straight to the city's Economic Development Zone. After the peacefulness of the new expressway, it was a shock to enter the half-built industrial park, where most roads had yet to be paved. Earthmovers and bulldozers worked around the clock, and rugged farmland surrounded the zone on all sides, a reminder of how this place had looked until recently. The scale of the construction project was impressive—nearly six square miles. The director of the economic zone, a man named Wang Lijiong, told me that in order to prepare for the factories they had leveled exactly one hundred and eight mountains and hills.

Chinese officials have a way with statistics—they rattle off overwhelming numbers in the most casual fashion. One of Director Wang's government colleagues, a man named Yang Xiaohong, told me that from 2000 to 2005, Lishui's urban population had grown from 160,000 to 250,000, because of all the migrants who came to work construction and factory jobs. With the new development zone, he expected the population to double to half a million in the next fifteen years. He also said the Lishui government had invested $8.8 billion in infrastructure from 2000 to 2005. During those five years, according to Yang, the city's infrastructure investment was five times the amount spent during the previous half century.

Every time I met an official, I scrambled to write down the numbers, and then in the evening I'd look at my notebook and wonder if they could possibly be true. But Director Wang Lijiong's remark about moving one hundred and eight mountains made me stop scribbling. I asked the man to explain what he meant.

"Pretend that this is a mountain," he said, pointing at a spot on the table between us. He moved his finger a few inches over. "This is another mountain. Between them there's a valley. So we take the tops off the two mountains, and we fill in the valley. We lower the high parts and raise the low parts, and we make it as flat as possible."

He ran his hand along the table—perfectly flat. He continued: "There's a saying here in Lishui. 'For every nine acres of mountains, there's half an acre of water and half an acre of farmland.' With such a small percentage of good land, we had no choice but to move the mountains."

Director Wang was in his late forties, and he dressed casually, in jeans and sweaters. He wore wire-rimmed glasses and a gold Omega watch. He was a member of the Communist Party. In his pocket, he carried a laser pointer, and during our discussions he occasionally used it to illuminate some detail on the map of Lishui that hung on his office wall. It was a map of the future—the drawing featured all the roads in the development zone that had yet to be built. Director Wang was friendly and easygoing, and he answered my questions with a directness that surprised me. He also returned my phone calls—I had never known a Chinese official who did that. Most of them are wary and secretive; they see no reason to talk to a foreign reporter. But Director Wang was different, and once I asked him about his background.

"My experiences are very complicated," he began. He explained that during the Cultural Revolution he had been sent down to the countryside, like many city youths, and afterward he was assigned to a job in a dynamite factory. Then he joined the People's Liberation Army and trained as a tank driver. For five years he drove tanks, after which he left the military and was appointed to a banking job. Ten years of banking were followed by a cadre position in a development zone. After that, he moved from town to town, rising steadily through the bureaucracy, until at last he had been chosen to lead Lishui's new industrial park. He had very little formal education, but his son was a graduate student in international finance at the University of Auckland. The fact that in two generations this family had gone from driving tanks to studying foreign economics was not particularly stunning. Many men of Director Wang's age possess illogical résumés, full of disjointed transitions and unexpected career jumps. But when they tell these stories, it's the trajectory that matters, not the specific steps themselves. Dynamite to tanks to banks to development zones—who can argue that this isn't progress?

Director Wang still drew lessons from his days in the military. "In a tank, you go directly at your goal," he said. "You can't worry about whether the road is good or bad, or if something happens along the way. You have to be focused; you need the spirit of persistence. I'm that way here at the development zone. I don't get discouraged by problems."

He explained that his tank-driving years had inspired the slogan for the Lishui Economic Development Zone: "Each person does the work of two people, and two days' work is done in a single day." For Director Wang, the biggest threat was time. Development zones had already been functioning for twenty years in other parts of China, and new ones constantly cropped up. Their basic strategy was the same everywhere: prepare infrastructure, sell land-use rights at cut rates to factory owners, and grant tax breaks for initial years of production. If a city came late to this strategy and hoped to distinguish itself, there weren't many options. Occasionally the local government discovered some major industry that was ripe for exploitation—this happened in Wuhu, the city in Anhui Province that decided to produce Chery cars. But such opportunities were increasingly rare, and nowadays it was far more likely that a latecomer ended up making products that other places hoped to avoid.

By 2006, Lishui had already become home to more than a dozen major plants producing synthetic leather. If cement and steel are the characteristic elements of Chinese cities, overused in construction projects, synthetic leather plays a similar role for consumers. Foreigners living in China call the stuff "pleather"—shorthand for "plastic leather"—and it's amazing how many permutations can be found in daily life. Virtually every Chinese entrepreneur carries a pleather money bag, and the cooler ones wear pleather jackets. Women dress in pleather skirts; men have pleather loafers. I've visited apartments in which every piece of furniture is covered in pleather. The stuff is so plentiful that it seems like a natural resource—sometimes I imagined they were mining it straight out of the ground in some forgotten part of Shanxi Province.

In fact a lot of it comes from the Wenzhou region. Pleather factories first developed in the coastal suburbs, near the airport, and the industry's effects are one of the first things that a visitor notices upon arrival: the air is a dirty brown and a sickly sweet smell lingers over the airport. The pleather industry is notorious for a solvent called DMF, or dimethylformamide, which is used in production. In the United States, studies have shown that people who work with DMF often suffer from watery eyes, dry throat, and coughing. They lose their sense of smell and they become intolerant of alcohol. Long-term exposure to DMF causes liver damage, and studies suggest that female workers have increased risk of stillbirths. In laboratory tests with animals, DMF has been proven to cause birth defects.

In Wenzhou, the pleather factories developed early in the city's boom, before officials were concerned about pollution or health problems. But in recent years the city government has become determined to rid itself of the industry, preventing expansions and making it harder for current factories to renew permits. When I first started visiting southern Zhejiang, quite a few of the Wenzhou pleather plants were in the process of relocating to Lishui's new development zone. In the global marketplace, it represents a natural path for an ugly industry. Americans certainly don't want to make pleather, and even Wenzhou people have grown wary of the stuff, so now it finds its way to Lishui.

When I asked Director Wang about the industry, he responded carefully, claiming that Lishui would regulate it better. "They've never controlled the DMF tightly around Wenzhou," he said. "Those factories were started early, and back then there weren't good standards. We have rules about this now. The government's Environmental Protection Agency came here this year and did a long inspection, more than a month total. They said we're on the forefront of this industry." Director Wang told me that Lishui was limiting the number of pleather factories to twenty-six, because they didn't want this to become their dominant product. As a strategy, it seemed risky—invite a group of known polluters to your city in an attempt to jump-start the economy. But there weren't many options for such a remote place, and Lishui was willing to take whatever it could get. If there were mountains in the way, they had no choice but to move them.

When I first began visiting Lishui, they were still demolishing a hill not far from the bra ring factory, and one day I drove to the site. Dozens of men clambered over the hillside, and the air was full of dust from all the vehicles: thirty dump trucks, eleven Caterpillar excavators, four big hydraulic drills on wheels. A foreman told me that they had been working here for more than a year, and already on this site they had lopped off 1.2 million cubic meters of dirt and stone. They accomplished this by packing the ground with dynamite, blowing everything to hell, and then carting off the rubble. For a year they had done this repeatedly, day after day, and thus far they had reduced the mountain's elevation by about one hundred feet.

While we were talking, another worker wandered over. He wore a straw sunhat and he carried a cheap plastic shopping bag in each hand.

A slogan was printed on the bags: "Quality Number One, the Customer Comes First." The bags contained thirteen pounds of dynamite, and the man set them on the ground near my feet. He said, "Will you take my little brother to New York?"

Having lived in China for a decade, I was fairly accustomed to non sequitur conversations, but that introduction left me speechless. Anyway, I couldn't take my eyes off those bags. The man smiled and said, "I'm joking. But he really wants to go to America."

We chatted for a while, and then the man trudged up the hill; he said they were about to blow up a big boulder. That was a prelude to this morning's main event. In less than an hour they planned to ignite another 9.9 tons of dynamite that had just been packed beneath one part of the hillside. I asked who was in charge of demolition, and the foreman said it was a person named Mu Shiyou. "He's up on top of that hill," he said. What he actually meant was: He's up on top of what's left of that hill.

"Can I talk to him?" I asked.

"Sure," said the foreman.

I stood there for a while. The foreman watched the Cats crawling across the road. At last I said, "Should I just walk over there?"

"Sure," he said.

"Is it OK if I go by myself?"

"Of course!"

I set off alone toward the doomed mountain. Big trucks barreled down with loads of dirt and rock, and I skirted the road, picking my way over the rubble. After a while I saw plastic wiring coming up from holes in the ground, and I realized that this was the area that had been packed with 9.9 tons of dynamite. I began to walk faster. Was it a bad sign that nobody else was on this stretch of hillside? The foreman hadn't seemed at all concerned about my presence, but that's precisely the problem with Chinese construction sites: they're so welcoming that it makes me nervous. With half the nation being built, people have completely adapted to jackhammers and bulldozers, and construction crews rarely make a fuss about outsiders.

In Lishui, during this early stage of building, it was especially easy to wander around. Government officials and police were almost never seen in the development zone, and people assumed that if you were there, you must have a good reason. They were friendly and they were open; everybody had arrived from somewhere else. When I wandered around, I never asked permission in advance, and I visited anything that interested me. I talked my way onto the catwalk of the city's half-built bridge, two hundred feet above the Ou River, and I visited countless construction sites. Once I stopped to chat with some workers who were drilling the foundation for a new factory; they had just taken a break to drink some beer. After we talked for about fifteen minutes, they handed me a jackhammer and begged me to try it out. That was my personal contribution to the Lishui Economic Development Zone: half a foot of drilled earth, the workers laughing while I tried to make sure the damn thing didn't hit my shoes. But who was in charge of all this?

On the doomed mountain, I finally reached the top and saw the man with his plastic bags of dynamite. He introduced me to Mu Shiyou, who was organizing today's demolition. Mr. Mu was sixty years old, round-faced and balding; he had the lilting accent of the Sichuanese. He was originally from Luzhou, a town on the Yangtze River, but in recent years he had settled in Zhejiang, where there's a high demand for demolition crews. He carried government-issued identity cards that testified to his skills. They were pleather-bound, and one was embossed with gold characters that said "Zhejiang Province Demolitioner." I liked the sound of that—Mr. Mu was fully licensed to blow up Zhejiang Province. Another card was labeled "Zhejiang Province Demolition Equipment Safe Worker." "This means I've never had an accident," Mr. Mu explained.

He assured me that today's blasting wasn't at all dangerous. Before the big event, they were blowing up the smaller boulders, and periodically I heard an explosion and then a whistling sound as chunks of rock flew through the air. Every time this happened, I ducked instinctively, and Mr. Mu laughed and told me not to worry.

"I've been doing this for thirty years," he said. "I used to work on some of the nuclear sites in the west!"

That helped put things in perspective—getting hit in the head with a rock was nothing compared to a twenty-megaton blast. And it was somewhat reassuring that Mr. Mu wore a hard hat, although it would have been even better if he had offered me one, too. I followed the man as he clambered down the hillside, collecting wires from the buried dynamite. He spliced them together, taping the leads and connecting everything to a spool of white wire. He carried an electric detonator in a sack over his shoulder. The smaller blasts were finished; most dump trucks had already left the site. After a while, the foreman blew a whistle, which was the signal for the final vehicles to depart. The yellow Cat excavators crawled away, until all of them were parked in a row at the edge of the site, facing outward. They looked like big animals hunched over, their rumps turned toward the doomed hill.

The whistle blew again—this time the warning meant that everybody had to leave. The workers headed to the edge, until finally it was only Mr. Mu and me. He finished splicing the leads and began to walk away, playing out the white wire as he went. Fifty feet, one hundred feet, two hundred. The site had grown so quiet that our footsteps crunched in the dirt; I heard birds calling up above. This was the closest thing to silence that I'd experienced in Lishui's development zone—usually the place roared with trucks and machines and jackhammers.

We walked together to the line of Cats. Mr. Mu stood in the shadow of one of the vehicles, and he set the detonator atop the parked treads. The detonator had two switches labeled "Charge" and "Explode." A command crackled over Mr. Mu's radio—"Charge!"—and he flipped the first switch.

"Get out there where you can see it better!" he said. Nervously I stepped away from the Cat's shadow, looking out at the silent hillside. On the radio, a countdown began at five and ended with another command: "Explode!" Mr. Mu hit the second switch. For the briefest instant, before the mountain roared, a web of electric sparks flickered across the rocks, like lightning come to earth.

ON FEBRUARY 9 OF 2006, a week after the Chinese New Year, Boss Wang blew up two big boxes of fireworks outside the factory. In Zhejiang that's a traditional ritual for opening a business. Bigger companies hire dragon dancers to perform at the front gate, but a small entrepreneur like Boss Wang couldn't afford the troupe fees, so he limited himself to fireworks. He also paid a fortune-teller to determine the optimum date for his opening. On the lunar calendar, it was the eighth day of the first month, and eight is the luckiest number in China.

Like many Zhejiang entrepreneurs, Boss Wang was deeply superstitious. In China, religion is stronger in the south, and Christianity has become particularly popular in the regions around Wenzhou, where many people associate the foreign faith with development. But Boss Wang wasn't religious; he never spoke of Jesus or Buddha. He believed in feng shui, and he believed in fortune-tellers: he never scheduled an important business event without first having the date analyzed. Boss Wang was forty years old, and he made a much less polished figure than his partner and nephew, Boss Gao. The older man had short hair, a gentle smile, and wide-set eyes that often bore a slightly pained expression. He spoke with a stutter—his eyelids fluttered whenever he struggled with a phrase. His clothes tended to be stained with grease. "The big bosses don't mess with machines," he told me once, while repairing a metal punch press in the factory. "But I'm only a small boss, so I have to do everything I can. If a general doesn't have enough soldiers, he has to fight, too."

Boss Wang had made a career out of manufacturing odds and ends. His parents had been farmers, and in the early 1990s he first went into business by producing sections of plastic piping. After that, he made steel parts for bicycle bells, and it was the metalwork business that introduced him to bra underwire. He had never grown truly rich from any of these endeavors and he often spoke regretfully of the past. He told me that in high school he had just missed the cutoff for university admission. "It was a lot harder back then," he said. "From my generation, out of one hundred people, maybe one or two went to college." He had grown up in Longwan, one of the Wenzhou coastal regions that developed into an early factory district. "For a while they were famous for making pens, but I never made pens," Boss Wang told me. "Then they became famous for shoes, but I didn't make that either. Shoes were the best way to make money. So many of my friends went into that business, and now they're all rich. They sometimes ask me if I wished I had made shoes, too. And I have to admit that I have some regrets. A lot of those guys now have tens of millions."

Boss Wang planned to invest most of his life savings in the bra ring factory, a total of over ninety thousand dollars. In China that's a great deal of cash, and the average person would be thrilled to have such resources. But the frame of reference is all that matters, and in Longwan Boss Wang had always been surrounded by greater success. Even after coming to Lishui he found himself dwarfed by his new neighbors. Boss Wang and Boss Gao rented their factory space from Geley Electrical Company, which had been founded by a man named Ji Jinli. Ji had started out as a lowly peasant in Qiaotou, where he began to manufacture buttons like everybody else. Eventually he expanded to new products—plastic light switches and outlet covers, as well as copper wiring. He had moved to Lishui in order to take advantage of the cheap land-use prices, and his new factory consisted of three large buildings. He had so much extra space that he acted as a landlord, renting out the two-story wing to Boss Wang and Boss Gao.

In the courtyard of the Geley compound stood a cement pool and a cement stand with three flagpoles. Every day they flew the Chinese flag, a red Geley company flag, and the American Stars and Stripes. Geley's products were sold in boxes that advertised "American Geley Professional Electrical Engineering." Workers told me the business had investors from the United States, but when I asked around, I found no evidence of foreign money. Probably it was just a way of gaining prestige: people in factory towns believe that foreign-invested companies are better run. And Ji Jinli was clearly conscious of face. In Lishui he commissioned an impressive factory gate with two big cement lions, and the main entrance hall (cement steps, cement guard stand) featured a quote by the owner in his flowing calligraphy. The words had been reproduced in gold metal and blown up to such size that they covered half a wall:

THE TREMORS OF THE FUTURE
ARE HAPPENING RIGHT BEFORE YOUR EYES

This slogan was also printed atop the cardboard boxes used to ship Geley's main product line, which was marketed as "The Jane Eyre Series." The Jane Eyre Series consisted of plastic switches and electric outlet covers that began at a price of two dollars and ninety-seven cents. To some people, it might seem absurd or pretentious to name a light switch after a character in a classic Victorian novel. But such folks have probably never manufactured buttons for a living, and they most certainly did not grow up as peasants in Qiaotou.

Everything depends on perspective, and somehow Boss Wang always found himself looking up at his neighbors. Here in Lishui, he and Boss Gao had nothing to rival Geley: no cement lions, no gold calligraphy, no foreign flags, no Brontë protagonists. They hadn't even put up a sign for their factory. But at least the Machine was in working order, and three days after setting off fireworks the bosses posted a handwritten notice next to the factory door:

WORKERS WANTED

Looking for 30 female workers
and 15 male workers

Qualifications:

1. *Ages 18 to 35, middle-school education*
2. *Good health, good quality*
3. *Attentive to hygiene, willing to eat bitterness and work hard*

Boss Wang needed men to handle the big metal punch presses, which manufacture the rough rings used on the Machine's assembly line. Mostly, though, he planned to hire women. The majority of the factory's jobs were unskilled and required little strength: workers had to sort underwire, monitor assembly lines, and package finished bra rings. Like other factory managers, Boss Wang expressed a strong preference for young female workers.

"Girls have more patience and they're easier to handle," he explained. "Men are more trouble—they start fights or cause some other problem." When I asked about the ideal worker, Boss Wang said that she should be young and inexperienced. "If she's already had other jobs, then I'll just have to pay her more," he said. For the same reason he preferred a candidate to have little formal education. It was a bad sign if she dressed well or had a distinctive hairstyle. Pretty girls were a risk. "I want a person to look average," Boss Wang said. "I don't want somebody who's too complicated. I don't want somebody who thinks, 'If I feel like doing something, then I'm going to do it.' That's no good for me." One of Boss Wang's questions in job interviews was to ask about hobbies. If a candidate said "Playing cards" or "Spending time with friends," that was a negative—too frivolous. "Reading books" indicated that an applicant was lazy. Worst of all was a job candidate who said she spent free time on the Internet. "I like it if she enjoys being with her family, or caring for her mother, or something like that," Boss Wang said. "That's what a simple person from the countryside should be like. I want somebody who can eat bitterness."

IN CHINESE FACTORY TOWNS, late winter is the season of the job search. Many migrants return home for the Spring Festival holiday, when the Chinese New Year is celebrated, and afterward they board buses and trains bound for cities with development zones. It's a restless time—a month when people finally act on long-held plans to leave the village, or switch jobs, or try a new city. Even the cautious are spurred to action, and a decision made during this period often shapes the rest of the year. Occasionally, a decade later, a migrant will look back and realize that her entire career was sparked by one chance interview during a February morning long ago.

All of this was new to Lishui. Locals told me that 2006 was the first year the development zone would have a significant number of working factories, and yet somehow the news had already gone out to migrants. They poured out of the local train station, and they clogged the bus terminus; on the new expressway most traffic consisted of long-distance buses catering to job seekers. In China, where the migrant population grows by an estimated ten million every year, countless bus routes run from the provincial interior. Usually their destination is the coast, but sometimes they find their way to less established places like Lishui. That first year in the development zone, migrants dragged their bags along unfinished roads—people without jobs, newly arrived in a place without proper streets. But they knew some factories were already buzzing, and others would soon follow, and there was an advantage to arriving early.

Some migrants visited the Lishui "talent market," the local job-search center. The building was located downtown, and it featured a huge digital screen that scrolled an endless list of jobs. Young people stood in packs, necks craned upward, watching careers flash past in the terse jargon of the Chinese job listing:

BREAKING ROCKS.
MALE, GOOD HEALTH, WILLING TO EAT BITTERNESS.
40 YUAN PER DAY AND MEALS INCLUDED.

ORDINARY WORKERS NEEDED, FEMALE.
MIDDLE SCHOOL EDUCATION.
DIGNIFIED APPEARANCE, 1.55 METERS OR TALLER.

Jobs often listed height requirements, an obsession in Chinese society. This is especially true for women, whose career opportunities are sharply defined by looks:

SUPERMARKET CASHIERS NEEDED.
FEMALE, MIDDLE SCHOOL OR TRADE SCHOOL EDUCATION.
1.58 METERS OR TALLER.
SKIN FAIR AND CLEAR, GOOD APPEARANCE.

Women are also paid less—a detail that was noted openly in listings, along with regional preferences:

MALE WORKERS NEEDED FOR 35 YUAN PER DAY,
FEMALE WORKERS NEEDED FOR 25 YUAN PER DAY.

AVERAGE WORKERS NEEDED.
PEOPLE FROM JIANGXI AND SICHUAN NOT WANTED.

The listings were like telegrams—companies paid by the word, so they kept things brief. They described only the most necessary qualities, condensing human beings to whatever feature seemed most compelling to the boss. Sometimes they omitted the job description entirely, creating an odd sense of mystery. What exactly would people be doing that required only these characteristics?

FEMALE WORKERS NEEDED.
1.58 METERS TALL, GOOD APPEARANCE.
600 TO 800 PER MONTH.

WORKERS NEEDED.
EYESIGHT MUST BE 4.2 OR BETTER.
800 TO 1,200 PER MONTH.

Many factories didn't bother with the talent market. They simply posted signs on their front gates and assumed that migrants would do the legwork. During that first February in Lishui, people wandered the district in packs, and it felt like an extension of the Spring Festival holiday. Everybody was young; they wore new clothes; their voices rose in excitement as they cruised the factory strip. People from the same region tended to stick together, and often two groups met in the street to exchange information. Down the road from the bra ring factory, I joined a crowd of thirty who had gathered at the front gate of Jinchao Synthetic Leather, one of the biggest plants in the region. A factory guard checked the identification cards of potential applicants, and he turned away anybody whose ID showed a home address in Guizhou Province. Guizhou is the poorest province in China, located deep in the interior, and it's home to many ethnic minorities.

A group of young Guizhou people had just been rejected, and now they stood in the street, discussing where to go next. I asked one of them what Jinchao Synthetic Leather had against his home province. "They didn't give a reason," he said. "But lots of workers from Guizhou come to Lishui, so sometimes the factories won't accept us."

It's illegal for a Chinese company to discriminate on the basis of home province, although in practice this happens all the time. I was curious to hear Jinchao's reasons, so I followed a line of applicants inside. They made their way to the second floor, where the deputy manager conducted interviews in his office. He didn't hesitate when I asked about the restriction. "People from Guizhou like to fight," he said. "They're too much trouble in the factory. Around here a lot of the petty criminals come from Guizhou, too. So I don't want them working in the factory."

I had expected him to finesse the point, or maybe refuse to answer. But he couldn't have been more direct: he refused to hire people from Guizhou because he didn't like them. Who needs a better reason than that? He was just as straightforward with the potential workers who crowded around his desk. When one man tried to negotiate for a higher salary by complaining about the chemicals on the pleather assembly line, the manager shot back, "If you don't want to work with toxic fumes, maybe you should become a teacher." Another applicant complained that the starting wages for an unskilled worker—3.8 yuan per hour, or 47 cents—were too low. The manager said, "If you were a woman, you'd make even less. Women make only 3.4. So you should be happy with 3.8." I asked why women were paid less for the same job, which was another dumb question. "Because women aren't as strong," the manager said matter-of-factly. "There are some things that a man can do better, so we have to pay them more."

But I noticed that workers responded to this man, despite the fact that almost everything out of his mouth seemed offensive. He had an easy rapport with the returning employees, who stopped by the desk to register for the coming work year. And bolder applicants tended to be rewarded. One man wouldn't agree to the starting wage; he had already worked a similar job at another factory, and he believed that his experience was worth a higher salary. The manager flatly refused ("Go back to your old job"), but the worker wouldn't leave. He stood by the desk, making his case while the manager dealt with other applicants. Periodically they exchanged barbs ("I wouldn't have come here if I'd known you weren't fair"; "Why would I care if you came here or not?"), but neither one ever showed any anger. After a full hour, the manager finally signed him up at the higher wage. That's what it took to win his respect—patience and determination and a certain bullheadedness.

Nobody had been doing this for long. Ten years ago, most Chinese employment was government-assigned, and in those days it was rare for a Chinese person to embark on an independent job search. Since then, people have learned quickly, but the routine is still new—the blind recruit the blind. And they have no time for the polish of the American human resources department. There are no euphemisms, no indirections; nobody talks about "becoming part of the team" or "opportunities for growth" or a desire for "highly motivated, creative individuals." People say exactly what they think, and they make brutally sharp evaluations; they feel free to act on any whim or prejudice. Here in China, "human resources" has a more literal meaning: millions of people need to find work, and countless factories need them to work hard, and no subtleties of language can soften the hard calculus of supply and demand.

In Lishui, the bra ring factory was one of the local companies that was hiring for the first time, and Boss Wang and Boss Gao interviewed applicants in the second-floor office. Like everything else in the factory, the office had been designed in a rush, and the furnishings felt temporary. A dirty carpet had been tossed across the cement floor, and there was a cheap couch, a low tea table, a pair of wooden desks, and two potted plants that already appeared to be dying from neglect. Brilliantly colored bra rings had been scattered atop one of the desks. They were the only spots of brightness in the room, and whenever a job applicant asked about the factory's product, Boss Wang pushed a few rings across the desk, like a croupier in a casino. "Clothing accessories for underwear," he would say. And often that explanation was enough, especially for female applicants, who recognized the product instantly. Only men had to be told what the rings were for.

The factory offered a starting wage of three and a half yuan per hour, which was a little more than forty cents. In Lishui, that was the legal minimum. China doesn't have a nationwide standard—because of wide regional disparities in wealth, each city sets its own minimum wage. In 2006, a more developed place like Guangzhou had a minimum of 4.3 yuan per hour, but that didn't guarantee that workers earned more money. In advanced cities, low-level jobs might be harder to find, or hours might be fewer. This is a key detail for workers, who care about hours as much as they care about the starting wage. Most people want to work as much as possible—since they're away from home, there's no point in having free weekends or holidays. They're pleased to hear that a factory offers overtime hours, and the perfect job is one in which an employee can expect no vacation days apart from major national holidays, such as the Spring Festival. Sometimes an assembly-line worker told me proudly that she was clocking nearly three hundred hours per month. In that situation, Lishui's hourly minimum became a monthly wage of one hundred and twenty dollars—excellent money for an uneducated migrant.

In truth, Boss Wang didn't know how many hours he could offer, or even how many workers he needed, because it would all be determined by the demand for his product. But he told applicants what they wanted to hear: he assured them they'd have at least ten hours of labor every day, and no more than one day's vacation every month. That was the Lishui version of a boss's empty promise—he soothingly told applicants he'd work them to the bone, when in fact they might get stuck with only forty hours a week. The smarter applicants asked how long the company had been in the business, and many people inquired about the production process. Often a woman said, "Are there any fumes here?" In Lishui, that's shorthand for DMF, the solvent used in pleather factories. Word had already spread about the risks, and even uneducated newcomers had a surprisingly accurate understanding. Women who hadn't yet had children usually avoided working with pleather, because of rumors that the chemicals cause birth defects. And men only worked there if the money was good—pleather factories had to offer more than the minimum wage.

At the bra ring factory, Boss Gao's father helped with hiring, and he let me sit in his office while he interviewed workers. Most applicants were teenagers, and they stood with their heads down, mumbling answers. They fiddled nervously with the bra rings—everybody who entered the room invariably fixated on these colorful objects. But occasionally there was an applicant who stood out from the rest. During one interview, Mr. Gao asked a woman for her age, and she said, "Do you mean my real age, or the age that's on my identity card?"

"What does your identity card say?"

"It says I'm twenty-five, but that's not right. I had it changed when I first went out to work, because I was too young. That was many years ago. Now I'm really twenty-three."

Mr. Gao nodded and added her name to the list of qualified workers. It reflected how quickly time passes in a Chinese factory town: the woman had originally changed her birthdate so that she could work in her mid-teens, and now she was concerned that an advanced age of twenty-five would be held against her. After the woman left the room, I asked Mr. Gao if he worried about the kind of person who falsifies her government document. "No, that's a good sign," he said. "It just means she really wants to work. Somebody like that is probably going to be a good worker."

Initiative mattered most, regardless of how bosses imagined ideal employees. Often they made them sound like automatons—over and over, Boss Wang and others told me that they wanted applicants to be young, inexperienced, and uneducated. They didn't want distinctive hairstyles; they didn't want people with hobbies; they didn't need opinions on the work floor. But the truth was that even the most pragmatic boss was susceptible to a strong personality. By the second day, the bra ring factory had already filled its potential worker list, and Mr. Gao turned people away at the door. He told one young woman that he'd add her to the backup list, but she lingered in the office.

"Can't you put me on the regular list?" she said.

"I told you, it's full. I'll put you on the second list. If somebody decides not to work, we'll call you."

She smiled sweetly and said, "Just switch my name with somebody else's."

"I can't do that. We already have enough. We have nineteen workers for that job."

"I've already worked in a factory. I'm a good worker."

"Where did you work?"

"Guangdong."

"So young and you're already experienced!"

The woman's card identified her as Tao Yuran, born in 1988. She was only seventeen, barely old enough according to Chinese law, which requires factory workers to be at least sixteen. Tao had short-cropped hair and lively eyes; unlike many job-seekers, she looked directly at the older man when she spoke. She couldn't resist fiddling with the bra rings—nobody could—but she handled them differently from the other applicants. She picked up a few and held them tight, as if they were pieces in a game she was determined to win.

"Just change a name," she said. "Why does it matter?"

"I can't do that," Mr. Gao said.

"I would have come yesterday if I'd known."

"I'll make sure you're first on the second list," he said. He scribbled her name at the top of the paper. "See, I even wrote 'good girl' next to your name!"

But Tao refused to be patronized. She remained beside the desk, clutching the rings and pleading her case. After five minutes Mr. Gao stopped responding. He busied himself with paperwork, ignoring the woman, but she still kept pleading. "Just switch my name," she said.

Mr. Gao said nothing.

"Can't you just add it to the list?"

Silence.

"What does it matter?"

Silence.

"I'll work well. I've already worked in Guangdong."

Silence.

"None of those people will know you've changed it!"

Finally, after a full ten minutes, Mr. Gao relented. He added her name, but then he looked at the list and the Wenzhou superstition came into play. "Now it's *ershi*," he said. "Twenty. That's a bad-sounding number—

too much like *esi*, starving to death. I'll have to add another name after yours."

Tao thanked him and dropped the sweaty rings onto the desk. She was almost out the door when Mr. Gao called out a warning. "Remember, it's the boss's final decision," he said. "If the boss says twenty-one is too many, then it'll have to be nineteen."

The woman walked back to the desk, her jaw set. "Move my name up the list."

Five minutes later, after another one-sided conversation, Tao Yuran's name was squarely in the middle of the sheet. She left triumphant; the older man looked faintly exhausted. After she was gone, he turned to me and shook his head in admiration. "That girl," he said, "knows how to get things done."

In time, the bosses would learn that the young woman wasn't at all who she claimed to be. She had no experience; she had never worked in a factory; she hadn't been anywhere near Guangdong Province. She wasn't seventeen and she wasn't Tao Yuran. That was her older sister's name: she had borrowed the ID card and bluffed about everything. The girl who got things done was barely fifteen years old.

THE APPEARANCE OF WOMEN in this part of Lishui represented a new stage for the development zone. Every time I visited and drove through the future factory district, there was something new that caught my eye, some indication that progress had lurched another step forward. The bra ring factory was located on Suisong Road, and when I first drove there, in the summer of 2005, it was nothing but a dirt track. For some reason bus stop signs had already been planted—lonely metal markers with lists of destinations, most of which didn't yet exist, and none of which would be served by public transport for another year. On that initial journey virtually everybody on Suisong Road was male. Most were construction workers, but there was also an early vanguard of entrepreneurs. These pioneers settled the west side of the street, facing the half-built factories, and most of their shops were made of cheap cinder blocks. They sold construction materials, and they stocked noodles, flour, vegetables, pork: simple food that catered to low-wage laborers. The only real stores—the ones with professional signs and recognizable brands—belonged to China Mobile and China Unicom. In new factory towns, cell phone shops usually appear early, because everybody is a migrant who needs to call home.

By the time I returned in October all the bus stop markers had been stolen. Workers were laying drainage pipe beneath Suisong Road, and the western strip of shops and restaurants had grown. There was now a printing store—the first business to sell something other than food, phone cards, and construction materials. The print shop specialized in company signs and employee ID tags, and its presence was an omen that machines were about to come to life. A few factories had already posted signs in front: American Geley Professional Electrical Engineering, New Year Glass Company, Prosperous and Safe Stainless Steel Company. In January, workers finally paved Suisong Road. Dozens of men moved down the street, smoothing the surface, but they left the manholes gaping. In new factory towns, manhole covers tend to be installed late, because people steal the metal plates and sell them for scrap, like the bus stop signs.

In February I saw a woman drive the front left wheel of her Honda into an open manhole. The car was undamaged; men ran out from nearby shops and lifted the vehicle out of the hole. By the next month the covers had finally been installed. They weren't metal: a Shanghai-based company called Chunyi had created a new type of lid made of composite plastic, to foil thieves. For the first time, I could drive down Suisong Road without fear of ruining a tire, and it was also on this journey that I noticed women outnumbering men. It had happened all at once: most construction crews had moved on, and now the factory bosses hired predominately girls for the assembly lines. In the evenings, after most shifts were over, workers wandered the street in packs, many of them still dressed in their uniforms. Soon the shopping options changed: two shoe stores appeared, along with a big clothes shop whose year-round sign promised "Half Price!" There was also a medical clinic and a supermarket. A half dozen beauty parlors appeared on Suisong Road, and some of them had the red-tinged lights that suggest prostitution.

In the span of nine months the place had changed so profoundly that I could sense it with my eyes closed. At night came sounds of leisure, young people laughing and talking, and the daytime noises also took on a new character. For half a year the development zone had roared with construction: bulldozers, jackhammers, drills. This racket was fitful and erratic; a drill would whine for half a minute, and then a jackhammer would rumble, and then for a brief moment there would be silence. But the uneven syncopation ended with the factories. They had rhythm—their assembly lines hummed and sang with the regularity of a chorus. One afternoon, standing on Suisong Road, I shut my eyes and listened, picking out the song of every product. *Punch-hisss, punch-hisss, punch-hisss*—that was the pneumatic wheeze of the metal press that pounded out unfinished bra rings. *Crussshhhh, crussshhhh, crussshhhh*—the throb of a polycarbonate grinder making Jane Eyre light switches. *Whir-r-r-ring, whir-r-r-ring, whir-r-r-ring*—industrial spools wrapping copper wire for Geley Electrical Company. All of the machines sang together—*punch-hisss, punch-hisss; crussshhhh, crussshhhh; whir-r-r-ring, whir-r-r-ring*—and then I realized the other way in which these noises were different from those of construction. The factory sounds did not stop. Each was steady as a heartbeat, as reliable as breathing, and that was how the neighborhood finally came to life.

II
———

AFTER THE FIFTEEN-YEAR-OLD GIRL CAME TO WORK AT the bra ring factory, she made no attempt to hide the secret of her age. In fact, she brought her older sister to the plant, explaining that this was the person who actually owned the ID card that said "Tao Yuran." The real Tao Yuran, of course, also needed a job. With the name already on the books, and the woman standing there eager to work, the bosses could hardly do otherwise; they gave her a position on the Machine's assembly line. Meanwhile there was the issue of what to do with the fake Tao Yuran. Her name was actually Tao Yufeng, and she wouldn't be sixteen for almost a year; Chinese law forbids factories from hiring people so young. But in practice it's common, especially in cases where applicants use false IDs. What else can you do when somebody wants to work so badly? And so the bosses kept the girl, training her on the assembly line for underwire.

The next Tao to materialize was Tao Fei. He was the patriarch of the clan, and he looked the part: tall and big-boned, with the erect posture of a soldier. His hair was white and he kept it shaved close to his head. He had an angular face defined by gaunt, sunken cheeks, and he chain-smoked West Lake cigarettes. There was little about this man that could be recognized in his daughters, at least on the surface. The girls both had soft, childlike features, and they lacked their father's stately carriage. But there was a flicker of resemblance when the man smiled—a certain quickness of eye that he shared with his daughters. It was a type of native intelligence combined with sheer determination, and this sharp-eyed look was the quality that all three Taos brought to the factory.

Originally the family had farmed in Anhui Province. They came from Taihe County, the village of Taolou—literally the place name means "Manor of the Taos." Virtually everybody there was a Tao, and despite the Manored name most of them were dirt-poor. In the past, Mr. Tao and his wife farmed less than an acre and a half of corn, wheat, and soybeans. They had three children, and this line of offspring followed a classic rural progression: daughter, daughter, son. Like many peasants, Mr. Tao and his wife had evaded the planned-birth policy, paying fines after each subsequent child, until at last they were satisfied with a boy.

In recent years, as everywhere in rural China, young people had been leaving the Manor of the Taos. Often the older generation stayed at home, farming and benefiting from money remitted by their children in the factories. But Mr. Tao and his wife wanted to work, too, so they decided to migrate en masse, as a family. In Lishui they rented a room in a farmer's home for a little more than twenty dollars a month. It had mud walls, a cheap tile floor, and a total area of less than one hundred and fifty square feet. All five Taos lived there, and they also used the place to stock their goods at night. The parents were among the entrepreneurial pioneers who had settled near the bra ring factory, where they ran a small dry goods stand. It consisted of a long wooden table covered with plastic tarp and arranged with cheap products that catered to factory workers: low-end batteries, plastic razors, shampoo, and other basic toiletries. Next to the stand, Mr. Tao's wife worked a foot-powered Swan sewing machine. Her specialty was altering worker uniforms: factory girls often didn't like the baggy company garb, and they could go to the Tao family stand and pay forty American cents for a better fit. It was steady business, and the family also profited from used magazines and paperbacks. Every month, Mr. Tao visited the government-run Xinhua Bookstore in downtown Lishui, where he purchased out-of-date magazines for seventeen cents. On his stand he sold them for twenty cents. He also accepted trades—a migrant who brought two magazines received one in return. These were the margins of the Tao world, and it's a common business model for people from

Anhui Province, who are known for setting up simple stalls in Chinese factory towns.

The Taos came to Lishui after hearing about the new development zone from other villagers. Over time, more relatives appeared, and periodically a cousin or a nephew showed up in the bra ring factory. Sometimes a full third of the workforce consisted of Taos. The bosses often needed part-time labor, because they were still in the start-up phase, and there was always a Tao willing to work for a few hours. They were the Snopes of Lishui—once the family had a foothold, other members kept coming.

It had been a stroke of genius to initially send the youngest. If Mr. Tao had been the first to walk through the factory doors, he never would have been hired because of his age—bosses don't want workers in their forties and fifties. Even if Mr. Tao had been given a job, it would have put him in the awkward position of asking for a favor each time he introduced another daughter or cousin. Instead, the youngest showed up with her sister's ID, which was essentially a two-for-one; and then it was only natural that the father follow, because he was willing to work for cheap. Once he was ensconced in the factory, Mr. Tao monitored his daughters and made sure they were paid fairly. He collected their salaries every month—neither girl ever touched the money.

Yufeng, the younger daughter, had left school after seventh grade. She told me that she had never been a good student, and the fees had cost roughly one hundred dollars per year. "When I was in school, I felt like it was a burden for my family," she said. "I was happy to leave." Even if she had stayed, she only would have watched her peers vanish one by one, so she figured it was better to get an early start on her factory career. In Lishui the girl hoped to find a better job when she turned eighteen—at that point her age wouldn't be held against her, and she could work in a big plant, the kind of place that checked IDs carefully and had real uniforms. She liked the idea of a shoe factory; maybe she'd learn something about the business and start a company of her own. "If I could, I'd make a lot of money and go home and build a house," she told me. "A real house, two or three stories. My grandparents could live there." The grandparents had cared for the girl during the initial period of the family's migration, when she had been too young to accompany her parents. These elderly people were now her only link to the village. Once, I asked Yufeng what her grandparents were like, and the girl fell silent and her eyes filled with tears; and after that I didn't ask about them anymore.

At the factory she handled underwire. Her job was to take the U-shaped bands of steel, one by one, and place them between the coils of a long tight spring. Fifty-seven wires could fit on each spring, and then the wire tips were dipped into nylon powder and passed through an industrial heater. Yufeng's job was one of the few in the factory that didn't depend on the clock. It was piecework: she was paid for each wire she handled. More precisely, she was paid by the pair—after all, the wires represent brassieres. In the factory world, piecework is considered to be the lowest form of assembly-line labor, and it's often where underage workers end up.

For each pair of wires, Yufeng made the equivalent of one-twentieth of an American penny. In the beginning, when she was unaccustomed to the work, a full hour of labor earned only about a quarter. But the girl was naturally nimble, and she learned fast; soon she was able to make eighty cents an hour, nearly double Lishui's minimum wage. She wore a thimble on her left thumb, and the metal clicked each time she inserted another wire into the spring. *Clickclickclickclick*—the sounds came steady as a metronome, as fast as I could count.

One afternoon, I watched Yufeng prepare thousands of wires, all of which were size 75, B-cup. The factory went by European measurements, and often she worked ten hours straight on a single breast size. She could answer my questions without pausing or looking up: *clickclickclickclick*. She said she was glad to work with underwire instead of bra rings.

"There's no machine for this," Yufeng explained. "If you work with a machine, then the machine decides the pace. This way I'm freer. I can work whenever I want, for as long as I want." The thimble flashed: *clickclickclickclick*. The girl kept talking. "To be honest, I often have a peaceful feeling. I work alone and there's nobody to bother me. I don't think about anything in particular. If I try to think about something specific, then I don't work as fast. So I just try to keep my mind empty."

◦   ◦   ◦

IN THE EARLY MONTHS, after the factories first started producing, there weren't any formal entertainment options in the development zone. There were no theaters or bars or karaoke parlors, and the government hadn't built a public park. But the streets essentially served that purpose—traffic was light, so the roads were available to anybody who wanted to put on a makeshift show. At night, on Suisong Road, an entrepreneur usually set up a television and karaoke machine, charging ten cents per song. And often a traveling troupe came in off the expressway and offered some kind of entertainment. Low-end carnivals were common, especially those that featured games of chance, but there were also more elaborate endeavors. Once, a traditional Wu opera troupe erected a wooden stage right in the middle of Suisong Road and performed every night for a week, drawing hundreds of spectators. In the development zone, such large-scale performances are often free, because of corporate sponsors. Companies like China Mobile and China Unicom target the migrant population, which makes for a good entertainment market. The young workers are far from home, with nothing to do at night, and most are earning money for the first time in their lives.

One week the Red Star Acrobatic and Artistic Troupe came to town. They drove a battered Yukang freight truck that had been customized so the side panels folded out into a marquee, which featured color photographs of women in bikinis. The center of the marquee had been cut out to form a makeshift box office, and behind the truck they raised a canvas tent. Electric speakers blasted music into the street. A slogan had been painted around the marquee:

ACROBATIC TROUPE TOURING THE FOUR SEAS
ATTRACTING GUESTS FROM ALL OVER
WE WELCOME EVERYBODY!

They parked next to the Tongfeng Synthetic Leather Company, which is located on Suisong Road, a few blocks from the bra ring factory. Two other pleather plants are nearby: Jinyu and Huadu. The troupe chose this location carefully—they knew the pleather factories hire mostly men, and they set up their marquee with the bikini pictures in late afternoon, around the time that work shifts changed. That's the witching hour of the development zone, when streets are busy with people, and soon a crowd of fifty gathered to stare at the marquee. A member of the troupe spoke into a microphone.

"Ladies and gentlemen!" he called out. "Bosses and workers! Brothers and sisters! We welcome everybody to our acrobatics show! We know that all of you are hardworking, and you're tired at the end of the day; we welcome you to relax with our show!"

The barker was dark-skinned and rail-thin, with high cheekbones and narrow eyes. He wore a pinstriped suit with a vest, and a cheap gold-colored chain hung from his watch pocket. The clothes were baggy, and they had gotten dusty during the tent-raising, which gave the barker a certain scarecrow appearance. Despite his thinness he had big hands and muscular wrists—peasant forearms. He spoke in slow, syrupy tones, stretching out the words. "Wo-r-k-e-rs and bo-s-s-es!" he called out. "Br-o-t-h-ers and si-s-t-ers! Tonight we have a special performance . . ."

If there were any bosses in the crowd, I couldn't recognize them, and there weren't any sisters either. The bikinis on the marquee drew strictly men: they milled around in front of the sign, listening to the barker. Many of them were dressed in their work uniforms; some wore hard hats. The troupe charged five yuan for entrance—about sixty cents, a little more than an hour's wages for the average worker. Over the course of half an hour, the barker patiently coaxed them into the tent—"Wo-r-k-e-rs and bo-s-s-es!"—and all told they drew seventy customers. The audience sat on narrow benches, facing a rough stage of unpainted boards.

The show began with a middle-aged woman who sang a patriotic song about development entitled "Walking Into a New Era." After that, two girls appeared wearing bras, panties, and white bobby socks. One girl was tall and thin; the other short and fat; together they danced to electronic music. They ignored the beat and they ignored each other;

each woman seemed to dance to some private melody in her head. They did not smile and their eyes remained fixed on the boards at their feet. Periodically the barker—now he had become the MC—called into the microphone: "Shake it girls, shake it! Shake it, shake it, shake it!"

The crowd was silent, and the only signs of life were the cigarettes that glowed in the darkness. The men looked dazed—maybe that's inevitable when people breathe pleather for ten hours and then watch such an odd progression of acts. A young man came onstage and performed a halfhearted breakdance routine, and then the girls in panties and bobby socks returned. They were followed by an older man with the haggard face of a consumptive, who gave a thin-lipped smile and sang a popular song called "The Tibetan Plateau." Next, a man and a woman performed a comedy sketch that ended with the man's zipper down and the woman wielding a cleaver. After that, the MC took the stage and embarked on a long monologue. He told a story about his childhood, and how he'd grown up a lonely boy in a poor village where most adults had migrated. His mother and father left to find factory work, and over the years they lost touch, which made the boy feel guilty for depending on his grandparents. Finally he took to the road, traveling through coastal regions, searching for his parents. He visited factory towns one by one, but he never found his family; at last he was picked up by a kindly variety show troupe. At the end of the monologue, a woman appeared from the wings, carrying a fresh-cooked meal in a pot. "Mama! Mama!" the MC wailed, and then the woman stepped offstage—it was only a dream.

After the story was finished, the MC passed around a bowl, looking for donations from the audience. The men's faces remained impassive but some of them contributed small bills. They gave more freely during the shoulder act. This involved another performer standing onstage, popping his shoulder out of its socket, and writhing in pain while the cash bowl made a torturously slow circuit of the tent. The show ended when one of the dancing girls—face unsmiling, eyes fixed on the floor—slowly pulled down her panties to flash a good five seconds of frontal nudity. Finally the crowd responded: the men murmured and sat up straight and their cigarettes glowed bright. And then it was over, and the music ended, and the spectators filed outside, where the sky had turned dark and the night-shift lights shone from the windows of the Tongfeng Synthetic Leather Company.

THE RED STAR ACROBATIC and Artistic Troupe was originally from a poor village called Xiaohong in Henan Province. They were an extended family: three brothers, their father, an uncle, a distant cousin, and the wives of the younger men. They were joined by a disabled man who was a neighbor in the village; he helped with cooking and cleaning while they were on the road. At night they slept on narrow bunk beds that lined the customized truck. All of the couples had children back in the village, where they were being raised by older relatives.

The troupe was easygoing and talkative, and after the first night's show I had dinner with them beside the truck. The skinny MC was named Liu Changfu, and he had been performing for fifteen years. He had a fourth-grade education and he was blunt about his limitations. "I'm basically illiterate," he said. He had no illusions about the show, either. "It's stupid," he said. "Our level is really low; we don't even have real costumes."

The lack of quality was one reason they generally changed location every day. "After people see the show, they're probably not going to pay to see it again," Liu explained. Whenever possible, they set up near factories, because assembly-line workers represented the ideal audience: they're bored and they have low expectations. And development zones make for good campsites. Each year, the Red Star troupe followed new highways across coastal China, stopping at one factory town after another. Recently they had started in Jiangsu Province, near the city of Nanjing, and now they were working their way south. Just last week they had been kicked out of Yongkang, the town famous for making electric scales.

That was another reason they kept moving: the performance was illegal in a half dozen ways. They hadn't registered with the Cultural Affairs Bureau; their customized truck had not been approved; they didn't have a single driver's license among the eleven members. They performed a strip show, which is strictly banned in China. On this current trip they had also been kicked out of Nanjing and Hangzhou.

"Whenever we run into trouble," Liu explained, "I just say, 'Well, we're so small, what does it matter? We don't want to bother the Cultural Affairs Bureau!' Usually that works and they leave us alone."

Increasingly, though, their main problem was competition. Entertainment troupes and concerts were becoming more common in development zones, and here in Lishui, on the night they set up near the pleather factories, another opera troupe had performed down the street. Liu believed it affected sales, and the following day the Red Star troupe drove to the far southern edge of the development zone, hoping to find a better location. After half an hour they parked their truck at a place where the factory strip met the farmland. Someday soon this would be another construction site, but for the time being locals were using it as a trash dump. There were piles of garbage and swarms of flies; the air smelled foul. Above us the sky was tinged pleather-brown. But Liu was pleased with this place. "There's a village there, and another village there," he said. "And there are factories on that side." He pointed to a series of blocky buildings: a pleather plant, a chemical factory, a stainless steel company. To Liu, it all represented potential customers, and the filth was a bonus—it guaranteed that expectations would be kept to a minimum.

After they started erecting the tent, a couple of villagers wandered over. Liu's father asked one of the farmers if there had been other performances recently, and the man nodded. "Lots of them!" he said. "And there's a singing concert tonight."

Everybody froze. The father asked what kind of concert.

"A free concert," he said. "China Mobile."

Their faces fell—nothing dismayed a variety show performer more than potential competition from China Mobile. After a hurried conference, the troupe decided to send the father on a recon mission. The rest of the players continued setting up the tent, but now they also looked up at the sky, whose color had changed from pleather to something more ominous. China Mobile and rain—the only way things could get worse was if the cops showed up.

Last night they had cleared less than one hundred American dollars. Their income had been falling over the past two years, because of all the new competition, and they weren't getting as much from the lost-migrant monologue that Liu gave every night. He had first learned that routine back in the late 1990s, from another troupe. The key to the story, he explained, is sentimentality: it has to be about somebody far from home, preferably with lost parents, or abandoned children, or wives who have strayed. Since the audience is mostly male, it's important to include an unattainable female figure, which is why Liu ended his story with the dream sequence. He had two different versions of that tale: sometimes the orphan dreams of his mother, and other times he dreams of a lost wife. If it's the mother, she appears with food; if it's the wife, she carries a baby. Liu never figured out which story was more effective, so he kept both versions in his repertoire. They usually got an extra five or six dollars in the collection bowl, but a couple times in the past somebody had dropped in a hundred-yuan bill, about twelve dollars. "Maybe the story made them feel sad," Liu said. "Or maybe they thought it was funny. I don't know."

After a few minutes the father returned from his recon mission. He carried a flyer with marks of doom: the China Mobile logo and the words "Free Performance!" The company was promoting a new phone card that charged only 0.18 yuan per minute.

"We should leave," Liu Changfu said.

"It's different," his father said. "They're a singing show. We're a variety show."

The tent had already been raised; the clouds had grown darker. While they discussed the matter, a half dozen men walked over from the China Mobile show. They were in their twenties, and they had the well-groomed look of city folk. They wore white button-down shirts, and around their necks hung big China Mobile ID tags. They didn't seem angry—just curious and self-important and more than a little scornful. They faced off with the Liu men in the center of the trash-filled field.

"What's your performance?" asked one of the China Mobile men.

"Acrobatics," the father said. "All types."

The China Mobile man motioned at the marquee with its bikinis. "Where are your women?" he asked.

"They're working inside the tent. We have to finish preparing everything." In truth, the women usually remained out of sight before a show, so potential customers wouldn't realize that they weren't nearly as pretty as the pictures on the marquee.

"You know that our show is free," said China Mobile. "Nobody's going to pay to come here if they can come to ours for nothing."

"We'll be fine. Ours is different."

"You have to understand, our performance is really big," said China Mobile, tossing back his head. "The total cost of our show is five thousand yuan!"

"We have good equipment," the father said. "Our show is computerized."

As evidence he pointed at a box that contained a battered Yamaha electric organ.

"How much is your admission?" asked China Mobile.

"Five yuan."

"So cheap!"

China Mobile pointed at me. "What's the foreigner doing here? Is he performing?"

"Yes," the father said. "He's with us."

I decided to let this slide—thus far I had not spoken, and the China Mobile crew assumed that I didn't understand Chinese. And I had to admire the father's gall; he puffed out his chest and stood up to the cell phone boys. For a moment they fell silent, perhaps imagining a foreigner performing onstage with women in bikinis. But quickly they regained their swagger. "I think you'll be better off going somewhere else," China Mobile said.

"We'll stay," the father said loudly. "You draw your crowd, and we'll draw ours."

The young men shook their heads and walked away. The father's expression was proud, unyielding; he stood with his arms crossed and watched the China Mobile crew leave. The instant they were out of sight he turned to his sons.

"We have to leave right now," he said. "There's no way we're going to have any customers with those guys around."

It took them half an hour to pack up the tent and get back on the road. A few heavy drops of rain began to fall, and they headed north until they found an empty lot. But a local worker told them that a medicine company had sponsored a free concert just the night before. Next they tried a zipper factory, but the site was too cramped. Finally they settled on a promising place beside another pleather plant called Sunenew. Almost immediately after they had raised the tent, and the music began to play, a police car showed up.

It was the first time I had ever seen a patrol car in the development zone. Two cops got out, and they climbed the ramp to the box office. One of them asked Liu if the troupe had registered.

"No," Liu replied. "But we're just a small troupe. We'll only be here one night."

The cops conferred for a few minutes, and then one of them turned to Liu. "OK," he said. "But make sure you don't do anything disorderly."

After the cops were gone, Liu began his spiel: "W-o-r-k-e-rs and b-o-s-s-es!" Men in blue Sunenew factory jumpsuits gathered in front, staring at the marquee and its bikinis, and soon they began to buy tickets. The real women remained out of sight, as usual. Earlier in the day, I had asked Liu Changfu about the nudity. "It's expected for variety shows to have something like this," the skinny man explained. "Before people buy tickets, they'll ask, 'Is your performance of the more open kind?' We have to be able to say yes. It's really only a small thing, what she does at the end, but it's enough for us to say, 'Yes, our performance is open.'"

I asked if Liu's wife ever performed the final strip. She was the short fat woman who, on the night I watched the show, had performed in a bra and panties, dancing out of rhythm and staring at the floor.

"No way!" Liu said, eyes wide. "I wouldn't like that. My brother's wives don't do that either. It would be bad, you know, if a close relative had to do that. So the other woman does it every time."

In the hierarchy of the Red Star Acrobatic and Artistic Troupe, that was the lowest position: the wife of the most distant cousin. Her name was Wang, and she was twenty-three years old. She was the only member of the troupe who was pretty, with dark eyes and a gentle expression; I never heard her say much. But during one of the tent-raisings she approached me shyly. "Do you have an American dollar?" she asked.

I had one in my wallet and I showed it to her.

"I've never seen one before," she said. "How much is it worth?"

"About eight yuan."

"If I give you ten, can I have it?"

It felt like a stripper's tip—I handed over the bill and told her not to worry about it. She beamed and showed it off to the others, proud of the foreign souvenir. On the second evening, before they started the performance, I said good-bye and drove away. Liu Changfu was right: it's the kind of show you don't need to see twice. I had grown too fond of the troupe to sit through it again.

IN MARCH OF 2006, in the span of a week, the bra ring factory acquired an official logo, a Web site, business cards, and sample books. A Wenzhou designer prepared all of it for a fee of less than eight hundred dollars, and for the most part he copied the templates directly from competitors and other companies. He gave them an English name, too: the Lishui Yashun Underdress Fittings Industry Co., Ltd. On the company Web site, the designer posted a photograph of a sparkling multistory complex that had absolutely nothing to do with their facilities in Lishui. The Web site also noted that they had "many years" experience in the manufacture of bra rings, and it described the Machine with particular pride: "German import completely automatic production equipment."

The company's theme color was hot pink. On the Web site, the description of the Machine featured a hot pink border, and hot pink bubbles bounced around the home page. The sample books were the same color, and they featured photographs of sultry foreign women wearing bras and halter tops. Even the bosses' business cards had been printed in pink. They were decorated with the new company logo:

When I first saw the design, I thought that it might represent a bird in flight, or maybe a heart. Then I looked more closely and wondered if it was a pair of breasts. "I don't know what it's supposed to be," Boss Wang admitted. "It doesn't matter as long as it looks good. The designer probably took it from some other company."

The bosses had more important issues to worry about. For one thing, nobody was buying bra rings. The new company had machinery, raw materials, technicians, assembly-line workers—but not a single customer, at least for the rings. They had old buyers for the underwire, which they had produced for years, but the new product required a fresh start. Boss Gao told me this is how business works in Zhejiang. "If you don't have a product, you can't sell it," he said. "You have to produce it and then you start finding customers. That's why we had to set up all of this first."

Once the sample books were ready, the bosses began to travel around Zhejiang, meeting representatives of companies that manufacture brassieres. For *guanxi,* it's standard practice for a new factory to woo buyers with gifts; it's not enough to simply show them samples. The bra ring bosses gave out bottles of Wuliangye *baijiu* and cartons of Chunghwa cigarettes, which are the preferred brand of most Zhejiang bosses. Sometimes they handed out gift boxes with yellow croaker fish, a Wenzhou favorite. In addition to factory buyers, government officials also had their hands out. The tax bureau was particularly important—if these cadres are unhappy, they can ruin a business. "You know how China is: *toushui loushui,*" Boss Gao said. "Stolen taxes and leaked taxes." He meant that if the factory was going to follow the standard practice of under-reporting its income, they would need good relations with the cadres. "We haven't started doing this yet, but eventually we'll have to take a lot of the tax officials out to dinner," he said. I asked him if these banquets would also be used for giving gifts, but he shook his head. "You don't give a gift at dinner," he said. "Those things are separate. For the gift you stop by their home."

They had few bank loans for that reason. In China, acquiring such a loan isn't easy for a small entrepreneur, and it always requires more *guanxi.* Boss Gao told me they would need to make friends with bank officials and loan officers; everybody would expect dinners and bribes.

In order to avoid this expense, Boss Wang had invested strictly cash, and Boss Gao had only small bank loans. He saved his bribes for the more important officials. He told me that in Lishui such cadres required a gift with a value of roughly two thousand yuan—nearly three hundred dollars. In Wenzhou it would have been even more expensive, which was one reason they had located in this part of the province. "The rent is cheaper here, and it's cheaper to pull *guanxi*," Boss Gao explained.

At first, the details of *guanxi* seemed mysteriously complex, because as a foreigner I was distracted by the rituals—the banquets and the secret meetings. But over time I realized that it's actually a system, and in a place like southern Zhejiang it's highly functional. Gifts are standardized and portable, which makes them a kind of currency. A carton of Chunghwa can be received by one businessman, given to another, and then passed on to a cadre, who might in turn bestow it upon a higher-up. If only Chunghwa cigarettes could talk! There are probably boxes that have traveled from the marshes of Ouhai to the gardens of Hangzhou, spanning the whole length of Zhejiang Province, pausing for brief sojourns in Buttontown or Pleatherville. And most important, *guanxi* is convenient. Boss Gao told me that sometimes he gave officials a cash card that could be used at the local supermarket. I asked how he knew the correct amount.

"You just know," he said.

"How do you know?"

"I can't explain, but it's obvious," he said. "Around here even a schoolchild can figure it out!"

One afternoon that March, I was sitting with the bosses in their upstairs office when a trio of officials arrived from the tax bureau. The visit was completely unexpected. Boss Wang had been doing some paperwork at his desk, and Boss Gao was working on the sample books, which had just arrived. He was pasting bra rings onto the pages when the tax cadres walked in. For an instant Boss Gao froze, like a man caught playing a child's game, and then he quickly closed the book. Striking a more dignified pose, he stood up and offered the cadres a hot pink business card.

None of the officials was particularly well dressed, but they held their heads high, and one of them flashed an identification card from the Lishui State Tax Bureau. His name was Liu. He wore blue jeans and an orange T-shirt, and he had the kind of crew cut that often means trouble in China. That's the official haircut of the Chinese bully; my heart always sinks a little at the sight of a flattop. Nevertheless I handed Cadre Liu a business card of my own. He studied it for a moment and shrugged: if I wasn't connected to the factory, he had no interest in me. He turned to Boss Wang.

"We brought some of your registration papers," he said. "You need to sign them. You're supposed to have done this before you started production."

"I kn-kn-know," Boss Wang said, "we've been p-p-planning to do that. But we haven't started selling anything yet."

Boss Wang's stutter always appeared when he was nervous, and now his eyelids fluttered and his voice rose a couple of octaves. He poured cups of tea for the men, gesturing for them to sit on the pleather couch. But they remained standing. Cadre Liu wandered over to examine the door.

"This place doesn't seem very safe," he said. "Why don't you have a better lock?"

"We just moved in. We're still setting everything up."

"Somebody could come in through the window. Where do you keep the receipts?"

Boss Wang showed him a metal file box.

"You should make it more secure. There's theft around here."

The other two men made a slow circuit of the room, examining the barren furnishings. One of them studied the screen of Boss Gao's computer; another flipped through a sample book. "Is this what you make?" he said.

"Yes."

"What materials does it require?"

"Just metal and nylon coating. It's very simple."

"What are the byproducts? Anything dangerous?"

"No. Just water. And high temperature. It's not a problem."

"You know," Cadre Liu said, "it would have been better if you had contacted us earlier."

Boss Wang flushed. "I c-c-called the tax bureau but I couldn't get an answer about the registration, so I figured I'd wait. You have to understand, I don't know anybody here. We're just getting s-s-started. It's better if we meet personally, so I thought the phone wasn't convenient."

Two of the men finally settled onto the couch, but Cadre Liu still drifted. Now he stood by the window, peering out at Suisong Road. "The environment here isn't very good," he remarked.

"Everything is still new," Boss Wang said. "They haven't finished the street."

"How many workers do you have?"

"T-t-twelve or thirteen. After we have customers we'll add more."

"How many?"

"Maybe fifty to sixty."

"What about that part of the building down there?"

"That's not ours. That's being rented by another company. They're moving here from Shanghai."

"What's their product?"

"Thermoses."

Cadre Liu nodded—he probably did this everywhere, gathering intelligence on any new companies that could be shaken down. He turned again to Boss Wang. "Do you have an accountant?"

"We have a secretary who handles accounts. We don't need a real accountant yet."

"Well, you're going to need one soon."

"Once business picks up we'll hire one."

Cadre Liu took another card out of his pleather money bag. "You should call this company," he said. "My friend is the boss, and he can provide an accounting service."

There was only the slightest pause before Boss Wang responded. Then he said the right thing: "H-h-how much?"

"I think it's around six or seven hundred a month. But I'm not sure. You can call them. They're a very good company."

Boss Wang left the card sitting on his desk. For Cadre Liu, it served two purposes: a favor for a friend and an additional source of intelligence, because the accounting service would give him a line of information on the business. The best part, of course, was that the bra ring factory would pay to be monitored.

Cadre Liu produced the registration papers and Boss Wang stamped them with the company chop. At the end, the official mentioned the accountant again.

"OK," Boss Wang said. "I'll call them. I just want things to be c-c-convenient."

"We want things to be convenient, too," said Cadre Liu, smiling. He left the room; the others followed; nobody shook hands. The moment the men were gone, I realized how tense I'd felt just watching the conversation, and I sank back in my chair. But Boss Wang had already picked up the office phone. He dialed the number on the card and said, "*Wei*, I'd like to ask you to introduce an accountant to me . . ."

GUANXI IS LOGICAL ("Even a schoolchild can figure it out!"), and at the individual level it clearly works. An official receives a gift; a factory receives favorable treatment—there's no mystery to such exchanges. But it's hard to see how this system pays off for a city as a whole. In Lishui, I drove on brand-new roads past massive construction projects, and often I wondered: Who pays for all this? By Zhejiang standards, Lishui was underdeveloped; in 2006, the annual per capita GDP was only $1,460. Nowadays, with the planned economy long gone, there was relatively little money coming from the central government. Chinese cities have to raise much of their own funds, but by law they can't issue municipal bonds, like American cities. They also can't charge significant property taxes, because land is still nationalized. The tax base is weak, especially for a fledgling industrial region: in Lishui's development zone, companies received tax breaks for their initial three years of production, and after that most of them would cheat on their earnings reports anyway. It worked out well for the factories and the officials—they got favors and cash and all the Chunghwa a man could smoke—but it was impossible for the city to survive on its tax revenue.

And yet Lishui, like most Chinese cities, spent money everywhere. From 2000 to 2005, Lishui invested $8.8 billion in infrastructure, which was five times the amount for the previous half century. After that massive spending campaign, they immediately topped it: in the first half of 2006, when the bra ring factory opened, Lishui's infrastructure investment rose by another 31.7 percent, as compared to the previous year. Real estate investment increased by 57.2 percent. This was real cash, all of it parlayed into new roads and new bridges and new buildings; it wasn't just a matter of Chunghwa changing hands. But where did it all come from?

The answer lay beneath all that construction. It was land, or more precisely it was the way that land-use rights transfer from rural to urban regions. In the Chinese countryside, all land is collective, and farmers like Wei Ziqi have no right to sell their plots or homes on the open market. Instead, the village handles all deals, and even the village has little power to negotiate if a city decides to expand into their farmland. In these situations, the city can acquire the land at will, and they pay set prices that have been established by the government. After the sale is made, and the farmers have moved off the land, the city can build basic infrastructure and reclassify the region as urban. And urban land-use rights can be auctioned off at market rates, to the highest bidder. It's a type of arbitrage, buying rural land and reselling it as urban, and it can be practiced only by governments from the township level up.

The profits from such exchanges are immense. Wang Lina, an economist at the Chinese Academy of Social Sciences, told me that cities in coastal regions receive roughly half their fiscal revenue from real estate transactions. She described Chinese cities as resembling corporations, with the mayor serving as the CEO. "Their goal is to make money, obviously," she said. "But they can't only sell real estate. Investors aren't stupid—they know enough to wonder who's going to buy apartments in a city that has no industry." In order to solve this problem, local governments often build a development zone, where they sell land-use rights at cost. The cheap prices attract factories, which provide some tax revenue, but the key is that they expand the city. More bosses, more shopkeepers, more migrants—all of it means more suburbs and a better real estate market.

If a city hopes to stay solvent, it must continually expand. In order to build infrastructure, the local government takes out huge loans from state-owned banks. Wang Lijiong, the director of Lishui's development zone, told me that back in 2003 the city had borrowed over sixty million dollars in order to start blowing up the mountains and building roads. "If you want to get wool, you have to raise the sheep," he explained. But there were many parts of China where officials had gambled on investors who never arrived. When this happened, the development zone remained half-built, and the loans failed, and the whole bubble collapsed.

By 2006, the central government had realized the risks of this system, and they were trying to slow growth. They raised interest rates, and they required cities to undergo a more stringent application process for major expansions. But authority had become so decentralized that rules were hard to enforce. Wang Lina said that the Ministry of Land Resources simply didn't have enough staff to do the necessary on-site investigations. Sometimes they even relied on satellite images to try to figure out which cities were embarking on major construction projects. Budgets were a disaster, because governments could effectively decide what to report and what to hide. Wang had recently researched a town in Henan Province where the government reported a year's fiscal revenue of only two hundred million yuan, or roughly a quarter of a million dollars. But they had spent five times that amount on infrastructure projects. Wang couldn't tell where the money came from—she assumed the city had profited from real estate transactions, but there were many ways to avoid reporting such deals. The cadres, like everybody else, were involved in the *guanxi* game; major deals were accompanied by bribes and gifts, and nobody left a paper trail. And only a fool bothered to think about long-term goals. "Every five years you change the local government officials," Wang said. "So they know they have a limited opportunity. Do they worry about the next generation of leaders? They have to get it while they can."

Wang, like many scholars, believed that eventually the Chinese government will have to privatize land. With stable income from property taxes, they could end the current system of real estate speculation, but there isn't much incentive to make a change now. And the people who suffer the most are those with the least power: the farmers. Their loss of land helps subsidize China's urbanization, and they have no legal recourse—it's hard enough to overthrow a single village Party Secretary, not to mention the whole system. In any case, most peasants are so intent on migrating, or coping with the transition to private enterprise, that the last thing they worry about is changing the constitution.

In a country where everybody is on the move, the land itself is fluid, at least in the legal sense. All around a city like Lishui, farms are being converted to suburbs, and every construction site means more revenue for the government. East of downtown, one major development was happening in a place formerly known as Xiahe. Xiahe was a village on the banks of the Hao River; in the old days peasants raised rice, tangerines, and vegetables. But a few years ago the Lishui government had acquired a 16.5-acre section of the village. For the rights to this land, the city paid slightly less than one million dollars, most of which was used to compensate local farmers who had to move out. I met a Xiahe resident named Zhang Qiaoping, who had supported a family of four on a plot of land that consisted of roughly one-third of an acre. When Zhang lost his land, he was given a payment of fifteen thousand dollars.

After the city acquired the Xiahe territory, they built a network of roads and installed a sewage system, and then they sold the development rights to a private company called Yintai. Yintai planned to build an apartment complex, and Zhang Qiaoping had heard that they paid around thirty-six million dollars for the land. After talking with him, I visited Yintai's main office, where the director of development showed me documents certifying the actual price: thirty-seven million dollars. In other words, Lishui had bought land for one million and then, in the span of three years, flipped it for thirty-seven million. And much of this had been done openly—even the peasants knew the ballpark figures. When I asked Zhang Qiaoping if the deal was fair, he shrugged. "They have the right to buy it," he said. In truth, his plot of land had been worth at least two hundred thousand dollars, but he hadn't protested about his fifteen-thousand-dollar settlement. Instead, he took the cash and invested in a small shop directly across from Yintai's planned apartment complex. The project was being built day and night, and construction workers often stopped by Zhang's new shop to buy food and drinks. Knowing that he couldn't fight the system, Zhang had done what he could to profit from it.

The new apartment complex was called Jiangbin, or Riverside. It consisted of twenty-eight buildings, the tallest of which would be eleven stories. The planned centerpiece was a musical fountain larger than a football field. For this construction project, Yintai had borrowed more than twenty-eight million dollars, much of it from individuals hoping to earn high interest rates. In Zhejiang this is common—companies often raise money through private investors, because it's easier than getting bank loans. Technically, such fund-raising is illegal, but it's widely tolerated in a country where capital tends to be in short supply. At Yintai, company officials didn't believe there would be any problem paying the money back, because their timing seemed to be perfect: during the past five years, the average price of a Lishui apartment had risen sixfold. The vice chairman of the board at Yintai told me that they expected to profit nineteen million dollars total from Riverside.

The vice chairman's name was Ji Shengjun, and he was the son of Yintai's founder. Back in 1978, when the reforms began, the Jis were a poor peasant family in the town of Qiaotou. The patriarch worked for private construction crews, eventually starting his own company. He caught the early wave of the building boom, expanding his business all across Zhejiang, and now he worked with all three of his sons. Ji Shengjun was the youngest, at twenty-seven years of age. In addition to the family development company, he owned a number of businesses on the side, including a local nightclub called Masear. One evening I met him there, in the upstairs VIP room. He wore black Prada loafers, black Prada trousers, and a red and black Versace shirt. He carried a gold-plated Dupont cigarette lighter that had cost over six hundred dollars. He smoked Chunghwa cigarettes, naturally. Like everybody else in the VIP room, I was served Ji's drink of choice, which was Old Matisse Scotch sweetened with green tea and served in a wineglass. Every once in a while, after taking a drink, Ji leaned over and spat directly onto the carpet, rubbing it in with his Prada loafers. He wore no socks.

There were a half dozen people in the VIP room. The door was monitored by Ji's personal bodyguard, a well-built man in a tight T-shirt. One of the bodyguard's daily responsibilities was to carry Ji's Louis Vitton clutch purse as he cruised around Lishui. In the club, a pretty young woman sat close to Ji, her hand on his lap. When Ji told me that he was about to have a wedding, I made the mistake of referring to this woman as his fiancée, which made everybody laugh. Ji was friendly and easygoing, and whenever he smiled he showed tea-stained teeth. He had the extreme thinness that you often find in the countryside, where people are slightly malnourished—if not for the Prada clothes and the bodyguard, this man would have been indistinguishable from a peasant. And his multimillion-dollar company raised money in the peasant way, relying on *guanxi* and acquiring loans from individuals. Ji Shengjun told me offhandedly that it had cost him $1.25 million to open the nightclub. I never met his fiancée. The pretty young woman in the VIP room was sucking a lollipop. She stroked Ji's arm and cooed in his ear; from appearances it seemed romantic, but then I caught a fragment of their conversation. It was strictly business: she was pleading with Ji to help her acquire a visa so she could look for work in Portugal.

ONE JULY AFTERNOON, AT the start of a summer rainstorm, the bra ring factory received an express mail envelope. It was pleather weather—in the development zone, the initial stages of a downpour consisted of big dirty drops. The deliveryman held the envelope over his head, to guard against the filthy rain, and once he was inside the factory he wiped the package on his trousers and handed it to Master Luo. The envelope contained nothing but four nylon bra straps. Each was a different color: pink, white, brown, and light blue. There was no letter, no invoice—no explanation of any sort. The straps were a kind of semaphore, and Master Luo knew who could interpret them. "Xiao Long!" he called upstairs, to the factory dormitories. "Delivery!"

Xiao Long was the factory chemist. His full name was Long Chunming, but everybody called him Xiao Long—"Little Long." He came downstairs wearing a pair of plastic flip-flops and a blue-and-white basketball uniform. In bigger factories, workers dress in company jump-suits, but the bra ring plant was so small and informal that everybody wore whatever they pleased. Little Long's shorts and tank top were nylon knockoffs of the Puma brand, and they gave him the appearance of an athlete at game time. He studied the envelope's return address: it came from a brassiere assembly plant in a city called Dongyang.

"They ordered rings a couple of days ago, and these are the colors," he explained. It was easy to remember because the bra ring factory still had so little business. At the moment, they had only four regular buyers, all of whom were small. Boss Gao and Boss Wang were often away from the plant for days at a time, trying to woo new customers, but the bosses usually returned with long faces and short tempers. Workers had started to gossip—there were rumors that the factory was in financial trouble. The bosses had already laid off some of the young women on the assembly line, and they called the Tao family into work sporadically, when orders arrived. Only a half dozen technicians like Master Luo and Little Long were still working full-time.

After Little Long deciphered the envelope, I followed him to the factory lab, which was located next to the Machine room. Dressed in the Puma uniform, Little Long picked up his playbook—a loose-leaf notebook filled with dozens of rings taped in rows, their colors changing incrementally from page to page. Next to each ring, Little Long had inscribed the dyeing formula and an English name. These descriptions sounded exotic: a red ring, for example, was labeled as "Sellan Bordeaux G-P." Little Long didn't speak the foreign language, but he had copied long lines of inscriptions from other sample books:

Padomide Br. Yellow 8GMX
Padocid Violet NWL
Sellanyl Yellow N–5GL
Padocid Turquoise Blue N–3GL
Padomide Rhodamine

"I already know how to make the pink and the blue," he said. "But now I have to do the brown." He cut off a piece of the strap and compared the color to other browns in the book, trying to gauge the formula. Then he took out three powdered dyes: blue, yellow, and red. He poured each powder into a beaker and weighed them on a balance scale. He wrote down the ratios on a new page in his notebook. "This will take more blue and yellow, less red," he said. He heated water, mixed in the powders, and tried the resulting dye on a few rings. He checked the color against the strap—too light. More blue, more red. He tried again: still too light. It took three times before he got a match. "There are Big Masters in Guangdong who can just look at a color once and immediately know the formula," he said. "They work for the big Hong Kong companies; a Big Master like that makes tens of thousands of yuan every month. I'm nowhere near that level."

The sudden downpour had stopped and now the air felt muggy. Outdoors it was over one hundred degrees Fahrenheit, and here in the lab, with the burners and the machines, it was even hotter. After the initial round of dyeing, Little Long had taken off his uniform top, like a playground athlete who's finished the first game and wants to get serious. Finally I did the same, and both of us stood sweating in the lab, watching the rings spin in an industrial mixer. Virtually all the factory men went shirtless in summer.

Little Long was in his early twenties, and he was the only person in the plant who was not Han Chinese. He was Miao, an ethnicity that's native to parts of southwestern China, and culturally related to the Hmong of Laos and Vietnam. Little Long's skin was a shade darker than the Han Chinese, and his face was subtly different, almost girlish: he had full lips and high cheekbones. He was good-looking and slightly vain, especially when it came to his hair. He grew it past his shoulders, dyeing it a shade of red so bright it's best described in chemist's terms: Sellan Bordeaux G-P. When Little Long wasn't busy, he spent much of his time flirting with the Tao sisters and the other girls in the factory.

He had come from a poor farming village in Guizhou Province. His family's main crops were tea and tobacco, and after finishing the eighth grade Little Long had migrated to Guangdong. Initially he worked for a textile plant, and then he found a job at a bra factory that specialized in exports. "Each country has its own characteristic," he told me once. I expected him to embark on a series of sweeping generalizations, the kind of conversation that's common in villages. But Little Long's worldview was far more empirical: he saw foreign lands through a tight network of straps and rings. "The Japanese like to have little flowers on their bras," he continued. "They like that kind of detail. The Russians don't like that—they don't want flowers and little patterns. They just want bras to be plain and brightly colored. And big!"

Little Long was attentive, and in the bra factories of the south he had learned to specialize. After starting on the assembly line, he moved to the chemistry lab, where he picked up techniques of dyeing. He studied the trade from Big Masters; it was skilled work and the pay was good. In Lishui he had been hired for 2,500 yuan per month, more than three hundred dollars. But he wasn't satisfied with this status. On the unpainted plaster wall of his dorm room, he had inscribed a sentence:

A PERSON CAN BECOME SUCCESSFUL ANYWHERE;
I SWEAR I WILL NOT RETURN HOME UNTIL I AM FAMOUS.

In the bra ring factory, resident workers often wrote inspirational phrases on their walls. This particular sentence—a Mao Zedong quote—was Little Long's mantra. Years ago he had read it in a self-help book, and he adopted it as a guiding philosophy. His goal was to save enough money from factory jobs to eventually return home and start a business. Sometimes he talked about raising rabbits to sell to restaurants, and he also had an idea for marketing wholesale goods to small shopkeepers. These plans were vague; it was all in the distant future, and right now his top priority was concentrating on his work and saving money. He avoided taking trips home during vacations, and whenever his will began to flag, he thought of his mother back home on the farm. She was the only family member still in the village—Little Long's father and two siblings had all migrated to coastal regions. "I think about my mother when I'm tired," he said. "If I'm discouraged, I remember that she has to be alone." Recently he had written a song in her honor, and he had thought about singing it to her over the phone, but he was afraid of making her cry. Instead he inscribed the verses in his diary:

Lots of people say your life is hard,
But you smile and say that as long as you have us, you're never
    sad . . .

Little Long kept his diary in a spiral notebook. It also contained a copy of a long letter he had written to a former girlfriend, as well as pages on which he had practiced writing the Latin alphabet, in an attempt at self-education. Throughout the notebook he had copied aphorisms and mottos, some of which also appeared on his dormitory wall. In big characters above his bed was the phrase: "Find Success Immediately." Another wall read: "Face the Future Directly." And he also inscribed the title of one of his self-help books: "Square and Round."

Like many young people in factory towns, Little Long was a great consumer of inspirational literature. One of his favorites was *Square and Round*, a best-seller in China that explains how to function in modern society. The title comes from a traditional phrase—squareness represents a person's internal integrity, whereas roundness is the external flexibility necessary to deal with other people. The author adapts this classical notion to the intense competitiveness of today's boomtown society, with unsettling conclusions: much of the book describes how to lie profitably, manipulate co-workers, and generally behave like a post-Communist Machiavelli. There's a section on the best way to request something from a boss (first, ask for something unrealistic, so the rejection creates a sense of obligation). Another chapter tells how to cry effectively in front of a superior (don't overdo it). There's advice on how to keep friendship in perspective. ("If you and your best friend get along very well, then you are true friends for now. But if there is one million dollars' worth of business to be done, and if you don't kick him aside or he doesn't kick you aside, then you have mental problems.")

In addition to *Square and Round*, Little Long often turned to a Chinese copy of *The Harvard MBA Comprehensive Volume of How to Conduct Yourself in Society*. "I'm not mature enough," he told me. "Somebody as young as me needs help, and this book can provide it. If I have some kind of problem, I don't have anybody that I can talk to—I'm lonely in that way. But books like this give me ideas about how to handle situations." He also relied on *A Treasured Book for Success in Life*, and another one of his favorites was *A Collection of the Classics*. This book features foreign-themed stories, and Little Long was particularly impressed by a chapter about John D. Rockefeller. According to *Collection of the Classics*, the oil tycoon took his lunch every day at the same local restaurant, where he always left a one-dollar tip. After a period of weeks the waiter finally said, "If I were you, I wouldn't be so miserly as to give such a small tip." Rockefeller shot back, "Because of such thinking, you're only a waiter." The *Collection of the Classics* concludes with a moral: "A great many people can't become rich, and a major reason is that they spend money freely." Another chapter features Jesus Christ, although this particular parable isn't one that appears in the Bible. In the Chinese book, a man who tries to help others only makes things worse, and finally Jesus tells him to cut it out. That's the Messiah's message—accept the world as it is. "In our real world, we often think about the best way to act, but the reality and our desires are often at odds," explains the moral. "We must believe that accepting what we have is the best arrangement for us."

Little Long had a naturally sweet disposition, and from this odd cocktail of books he drew a lesson of equanimity. That was the most important thing he learned from all the great teachers: Confucius and Jesus, Rockefeller and Mao. "I want to be persistent," he told me. "I don't want things to frustrate me or make me angry." He wrote his slogans on the dormitory wall, and he made a point of never complaining about overwork—in his opinion, people in factories gripe too much. He wanted to be at peace with himself, and he wanted to get along with others. "In a group you need to be flexible," he said. "It's about balance, about trying to get along, trying to find the right path." Little Long's words could have come straight from a Daoist text, and the same is true for the parable about Jesus: it echoes the classical phrase *Wu wei er wu bu wei*, "By doing nothing everything will be done." It reminded me of my experience as a teacher of English literature in Sichuan, where my students often interpreted Western classics in a Chinese way. Even as foreign materials pour into China, and young people seek out new influences, their instincts often remain deeply traditional.

For his part, John D. Rockefeller inspired Little Long to switch cigarette brands. After reading about the difference between a waiter and an oil baron, Little Long decided to be more thrifty. So he quit smoking Profitable Crowd cigarettes and began buying a brand called Hibiscus. Hibiscus are terrible; they cost a cent and a half each, and the label immediately identifies the bearer as a peasant. But Little Long was determined to rise above such petty thinking, just like Rockefeller. Every time he smoked a pack, he saved 37.5 cents, and money like that was bound to add up over time. Someday he'd have enough to fulfill Mao Zedong's prophecy on the dormitory wall:

> A PERSON CAN BECOME SUCCESSFUL ANYWHERE;
> I SWEAR I WILL NOT RETURN HOME UNTIL I AM FAMOUS.

IN LISHUI, I OFTEN found myself talking about the outside world, although I never met a foreign buyer or investor. There wasn't much reason for them to come to the development zone, which was home to relatively few factories funded by overseas investment. And a remote place like Lishui tends to make things that are a step or two removed from the finished product. Rings are shipped elsewhere to be attached to bras; pleather eventually becomes handbags or car seats in bigger Chinese factories. Other goods are sold in bulk in Yiwu, a Zhejiang city whose wholesale malls attract hordes of foreign buyers. But such people don't bother traveling to Lishui, and whenever I drove around the city, glimpses of the foreign tended to be odd and slightly disorienting. The first gym to open downtown was called The Scent of a Woman. In the development zone, the Geley factory turned out crates of Jane Eyre light switches. A block away, at the front gate of Lishui Sanxing Power Machinery Co., Ltd., the owners had posted a huge sign that was supposed to be in English. But they had written the letters from right to left, the way the Chinese traditionally do with characters:

DTL, .OC YRENIHCAM REWOP GNIXNAS IUHSIL

And yet the people in Lishui—the migrants, the bosses, the entrepreneurs—made many products bound for the outside world, and they liked to talk about foreign things. They searched out self-help books with supposed American themes, and their curiosity was boundless. When I met somebody like Little Long, his energy and determination reminded me of other places, other times. This was China's version of the Industrial Revolution: rural people were moving to cities, and they had a gift for self-invention that rivaled anything in Dickens. And they practiced a no-holds-barred version of capitalism that would be recognizable to any American historian. At the bra ring factory, when I heard the tale of how Liu Hongwei memorized and copied the Machine, I thought of Francis Cabot Lowell, who performed the same trick in the early 1800s. Back then, the United States was the upstart society, and the British carefully guarded the designs for their water-powered Cartwright looms. But Lowell visited the mills of Manchester under false pretenses, and he used his photographic memory to rebuild the machinery in Massachusetts, where his company became the foundation for the American textile industry.

The sheer pace of change in China also has similarities to boom times in the United States. During the nineteenth century, when the first wave of American urban development swept westward, European visitors were amazed to see new settlements spring up as if overnight. Their sense of wonder resembled the way outsiders now feel in China, where development zones turn into instant cities. But the longer I stayed in Lishui, watching the factory district come to life, the more I noticed key contrasts. It wasn't simply a matter of a different age, a different culture—the fundamental motivation for settling a new city was also different. And there was a distinct narrowness to the groups of pioneers who showed up in a Chinese boomtown. Back when many American towns had been founded, the first wave of residents typically included lawyers, along with traders and bankers. A local newspaper often began printing while people still lived in tents. The first permanent buildings were generally the courthouse and the church. It was certainly a tough world, but at least there was some early sense of community and law.

In a Chinese boomtown, though, it's all business: factories and construction supplies and cell phone shops. The free market shapes all early stages of growth, which is why entertainment options appear instantly but social organizations are rare. No private newspapers, no independent labor unions—such things are banned by the Communist Party. Religion might flourish at the individual level, but institutions are weak; in Lishui's development zone nobody built a church or temple. There weren't any law firms or nonprofit organizations. Police and government cadres were almost as rare—they showed up only when there was some opportunity for profiteering.

On the Jinliwen Expressway, my first encounter with authority occurred in July of 2006, when I received a speeding ticket. It was fully automated: I didn't learn about the fine until I returned the Santana to the Prosperous Automobile Rental Company. Their computer showed that I had been photographed while driving ninety-six kilometers per hour in an eighty-kilometer zone. The fine, a total of about twenty-five dollars, was deducted directly from my deposit.

After that first violation, the floodgates opened wide, and I collected tickets in factory towns all along the expressway. One camera caught me outside of Qiaotou, the button town, and then I got fined in Jinhua, famous for producing underwear. The most tickets I received in a single day was three. Once in Lishui I got nailed twice in less than an hour. I was not a reckless driver, and my prior record had been spotless—in five years with a Chinese license, I never had a violation until I went to Zhejiang. But the authorities in the south were quick to figure out the entrepreneurial potential of speed traps. They posted cameras at confusing intersections, and on the expressway they set up radar guns in places where the speed limit suddenly dropped without reason or warning. Local drivers memorized the locations, and I did my best to do the same, but there was already so much to think about. For one thing, I had to watch out for bosses in their Audi A6s, driving a hundred miles per hour and then slamming on their brakes right before a radar camera. I never saw a live cop on that highway.

"It's a good business for the police," the manager at Prosperous Automobile told me, whenever I complained about another fine. And he was right: police officers invested as private stockholders in radar

COUNTRY DRIVING | 357

cameras, which paid dividends. If a Zhejiang cop contributed six thousand dollars to an expressway speed trap, he collected 7.5 percent of the proceeds from each ticket. Investors were limited to four per camera, and rookie cops weren't allowed to purchase a share until they had accumulated a certain amount of seniority. High-ranking officers could buy into multiple cameras. There was a lottery system that determined which cops got which locations on the expressway. This industry even had a corps of private moneylenders, because people knew it was safe to loan money to a cop who was buying into a speed trap. Like so many aspects of boomtown life, it wasn't exactly lawless—in fact there were strict rules that governed police investment. But these were the rules of hierarchy and profit, not law and order.

Each speeding ticket added points to a driver's record, and finally I accumulated so many that I was required by law to take a remedial driving course. But the manager at the car rental company told me it wouldn't be necessary if I made a personal visit to the Lishui police station. At the station, an officer called up my outstanding violations on a computer. He printed out a series of forms and instructed me to pay at the Bank of China, which was conveniently located across the street. The most recent tickets came to a total of about sixty dollars.

"What about the points?" I asked.

"I erased them," the officer said. "As long as your fee goes through, it won't be a problem."

At the bank I joined a special line dedicated to traffic violations. A half dozen yuppies were already waiting, and one by one we made our way to the front, where a clerk efficiently handled our money. It was February; a big English banner in the lobby said "Merry Christmas." That same week I noticed a new sign on the expressway:

DRIVE SAFELY!
26 PEOPLE HAVE DIED ON THIS ROAD!

BY THE END OF July, the factory still had only four customers, and they had accumulated over a million bra rings in storage. The Machine stood silent for days at a stretch, and now the factory was clearly in serious trouble. They stopped calling the part-time assembly-line workers, and they slashed the salaries of all high-level technicians. Little Long's wages were cut by 40 percent; Master Luo's salary was reduced by half. This violated the men's contracts, and in theory they could have complained to the local labor bureau, but Chinese workers rarely take such a step. They generally have little faith in government—"You have to handle these things yourself," as Master Luo often said. He told me that for the time being he'd be patient, and if things didn't turn around he'd search for another job.

Master Luo had worked with bra rings for so many years that he dreamed of them at night. When he slept, he saw rings coming off the Machine's conveyor belt, and he had visions of piles of rings waiting to be sorted and bagged. His nightmares usually featured long pointless arguments with bosses. Once, while we were chatting in the Machine room, Master Luo described the dream that had woken him up the night before. "We had just gotten a shipment of nylon powder and it wasn't any good," he said. "But Boss Wang said it was fine. I said, no, it won't work. He said it was fine. I said, no, you're talking farts!"

In the factory world, Luo was the kind of person known as a *Da Shifu*, a "Big Master." He was only in his late thirties, but twenty-three of those years had been spent working in plants across China. And like virtually all masters of his generation, he had grown up on a farm. His parents raised cotton outside of Songzi, a small city in central China's Hubei Province. In the late 1970s, rural schools were terrible, and Master Luo didn't receive much formal education. "We had only two textbooks," he remembered. "Chinese and mathematics. That was it." By the start of middle school, he was still functionally illiterate, but his parents decided to stop paying school fees. "They said they needed money, so it would be better if I went out to work."

In 1984, at the age of fourteen, he found a job in a toy factory in Hunan Province. He worked there for a year, sending home much of his twenty-five-dollar-a-month salary. Soon he made his way to Shenzhen, the special economic zone in the far south that began to boom in the 1980s. For a while, Master Luo worked in a textile factory, and then he changed jobs again. It became his pattern: over the course of a decade, he jumped from city to city, factory to factory, product to product. He manufactured screws in Hubei, and he worked in a paint plant in Xinjiang. He made plastic bowls in Guangzhou. He did trade in Yunnan Province, near the Burmese border; and he worked in a toy factory in northeastern Heilongjiang, near Siberia.

But eventually he returned to Shenzhen and the other cities of the far south. Years later, he spoke most fondly of this region, because in Shenzhen he attended private classes during the late 1980s. "The class started at eight o'clock, and we used to hurry over right after finishing our shift at the factory," he remembered. "The class cost five yuan and it was forty-five minutes long. They covered electrical wiring, machine tooling, welding—anything that's useful. The teacher was from Beijing; he was retired and he was really good. The class was in a room about this size, but there were more than two hundred people every night. It was packed because that teacher had such a good reputation."

Back then, Master Luo worked sixty hours a week, but he still found time to attend night school. The financial investment was significant— he earned only five hundred yuan per month, and yet he was willing to spend five yuan every time he attended a lesson. In development zones, private schools and tutorials are common, because motivated workers know they can rise from the assembly line. During his twenties, in his spare time, Master Luo also improved his reading and writing, until finally he became fully literate. In Shenzhen he passed a state-administered exam that granted him a vocational high school diploma.

Apart from his native intelligence and determination, Master Luo had few natural advantages. He had grown up in poverty, and he wasn't good-looking by Chinese standards. He was short, and he had freckles, which are considered blemishes in China. He had a heavy brow and a long nose; his teeth were bad. But there was an openness to his expression, and he smiled easily, with soft lines of age fanning out across his temples. He had the air of somebody who's experienced a great deal without becoming too cynical, and over time he became the factory worker I knew best. His vision was broader than most—he had the instinctive curiosity of the self-educated man. And as a Big Master he often found himself positioned between ownership and labor. In the city of Shantou, he had helped manage workers as well as machinery, and the experience left a deep impression.

"I took care of all the registration forms at the factory, and I noticed that many workers couldn't write," he said. "There are still so many uneducated people in China! But you know, sometimes these people are very smart. In Shantou I knew a man who worked as an elevator operator at the Blue Sky Hotel. He hadn't gone to school, and he couldn't read or write, but he was naturally intelligent. Once, the hotel's generator broke and the electricians couldn't fix it. After they failed, the elevator operator said to the boss, 'Let me look at it.' The boss said, 'You don't understand something like this.' But finally he let him try and the man fixed it within an hour. After that, the boss gave him more responsibility, and then another boss hired him for 2,800 yuan per month. This worker, he was from Sichuan, and he was very honest. He said, 'I can't read or write, how can I make that much money?' The boss said, 'I don't care as long as you understand things.' Eventually another boss hired him for four thousand. He basically couldn't write his name, but he could fix anything. He couldn't explain it, but he could do it."

In the Shantou suburb called Chaonan, Master Luo made his own rise in the factory world. During the late 1990s, he found a job at Shangang Keji, one of the early plants to manufacture bra rings. Master Luo learned to repair the Machine, and by 2002 he earned nearly two hundred dollars every month, an excellent wage. Meanwhile, other Chaonan bosses heard about the profits from bra rings, and one of them came calling. Initially the boss didn't say anything about a job, but he invited Master Luo to dinner at an expensive place called the Peace Restaurant. "We had crabs, squid, and lobster," Master Luo remembered. "And he ordered the kind of beer that's eighteen yuan per bottle. They gave me Chunghwa cigarettes. Afterward we went to a coffee shop and then to karaoke. We did this three times, and then the boss said, 'Can you help me?' He said his current master was bad and he needed somebody who understood the business."

Years later, Master Luo could still rattle off intricate details from the times he had been wooed by competing bosses. He was like a former debutante: he told these stories wistfully, recalling every hotel, every res-taurant, even the dishes and the prices. After the second boss offered to double Master Luo's salary, he accepted, and soon that company was successful, too. When the next one came calling, Master Luo's status had risen, and thus the courtship became more elaborate. "We went to eat at the Golden Garden Hotel twice," he said. "We also went to the Aus-picious Garden twice, and then once at the Golden Dragon, and once at the Golden Beautiful City." By the time Boss Gao and Boss Wang entered the picture, they represented the fourth bra ring factory to hire Master Luo, and along the way his monthly salary had risen from less than two hundred dollars to more than seven hundred.

Whenever Master Luo left a company, he followed a set protocol. He didn't tell his current boss about the new offer, and he tried to col-lect any salary that was still owed to him. Then he asked for a few days' vacation, explaining that he had to attend to urgent family business in his hometown. Sometimes he left a few worthless belongings in the fac-tory dormitory, to make it look like he'd be coming back. And then he simply changed his cell phone number, started work at the new job, and avoided everybody from the old company. In Chaonan, he had done this three times, at three different bra ring factories, all of which were located in the same neighborhood.

"Don't people get angry about this?" I asked.

"Of course!" he said. "But by the time they figure it out, they can't do anything about it. That's why you can't tell them ahead of time. If you do, they'll try to find some way to make you stay, probably by with-holding salary or threatening you or something."

"What if the new job turns out to be bad and you want to go back?"

"Well, that's a problem," he said with a grin. He told me his last jump had been easier, because Lishui is located hundreds of miles from Chaonan. This allowed him to maintain the fiction that he might even-tually return to the old job. Every now and then, Master Luo popped his previous SIM card into a cell phone, used the old number, and tele-phoned the former boss, explaining that unfortunately he was still in Hubei because of a serious illness in his family. This was the kind of solution that's propagated in Chinese self-help books like *Square and Round*—if a lie works, fine; otherwise just burn the bridges. Nobody thinks long-term in a development zone, and nobody looks backward. "Going to a new job is like gambling," Master Luo explained. "You leave and you hope that the new factory does well. If it doesn't, then you probably can't go back to the old job and the old life. What's in the past stays in the past."

LISHUI WAS THE FIRST place where Master Luo gambled and lost. Boss Gao and Boss Wang gave the technician a raise from his previous job, and they promised more money if the factory succeeded. But after they ran into financial problems, they reduced Master Luo's salary, and then they stopped paying him at all. Perversely, this was the most effective way of preventing him from jumping to another job. If they continued to give a lower salary, he'd probably abandon the factory, but he was less likely to leave if he was owed significant cash. All summer long, at the end of every month, Boss Gao and Boss Wang made excuses and promises, hoping their debt would keep Master Luo in Lishui. They were desperate not to lose him—he was the only employee who understood the Machine.

In development zones in southern China, summer is often a sluggish time. For many factories, the production schedule picks up in the fall, to prepare for the Christmas buying season in America and Europe. But weather also has something to do with the annual slowdown. Most Chinese factories lack air-conditioning, and summers in the south are brutal; it's hard to imagine anything worse than laboring on a pleather assembly line in mid-July. Workers become languid and bosses lose their motivation; construction crews seek out shade. When I visited Lishui that summer, work on Suisong Road had slowed to a near halt. The sidewalk remained unfinished; piles of paving stones baked in the sun. A malaise seemed to have settled over the district, reducing everybody to half speed.

At the bra ring factory, the product wasn't tied to Christmas schedules, and their problems went far beyond uncomfortable weather. The bosses looked tense and tight-lipped, and Master Luo said they were bickering about investment. Originally both Boss Wang and Boss Gao had agreed to fund the factory fifty-fifty, and each was supposed to contribute 750,000 yuan, about $90,000. But neither paid the full promised amount, and during summer each of them waited, unwilling to be the first to spend more. According to Master Luo, family-run factories are often trouble. "It's better to have a partnership between friends," he said. "With a friend you can speak more directly. With a relative, people are more sensitive, and they get angry easily."

The fundamental problem, though, seemed to be a complete lack of system. The factory had no management board, no investment schedule; nobody cared about legal contracts or predefined protocol. The bosses had funded almost entirely with cash, which raised the stakes and created tensions within families. They had sketched the blueprints for their factory in one hour and four minutes. Their most critical machinery had been designed according to the memory of a former peasant with a middle-school education. There wasn't the slightest hint of a formal business plan. The future customer base depended upon the hopeful distribution of Wuliangye *baijiu* and Chunghwa cigarettes. It was hardly surprising that by July the factory's most liquid assets consisted of a million bra rings packed in plastic bags.

If anything, it was amazing that they had gotten this far. The most educated person in the factory was Boss Gao, who had attended a couple years of trade school. The majority of employees lacked any formal training, and all of them, from top to bottom, had grown up on farms. Boss Gao and Boss Wang came from rice-growing families; Master Luo had been born on a cotton plot. Old Tian, the man in charge of underwire, had once farmed rice. Little Long's parents grew tea and tobacco. The Taos knew wheat and soybeans. The secretary—she was essentially an accountant, because she handled the books—had grown up in pear country. A former resident of an orange plot worked the metal punch press. Somehow all these agricultural products had been left behind, and the former peasant labor now manufactured two inedible objects: razor-thin underwire and bra rings that weighed half a gram each.

Almost every Chinese factory tells a similar story. People might lack formal education, but they find themselves in situations where they're forced to learn on the job. Most important, there are plenty of them out there. Of the nation's 1.3 billion citizens, 72 percent are between the ages of sixteen and sixty-four. In modern history, the nation has never enjoyed such a high percentage of able workers, and it's never been easier for them to leave the countryside. Roads are better; migrant networks are well established; the old Communist *hukou* registration system has become so lax that people can go wherever they wish. And all of them have been toughened by the past—workers are resourceful and motivated, and entrepreneurs are fearless. The government's basic strategy has been to unleash this human energy, trusting the market to build new towns like Lishui.

But there are limits to how far individuals can go on sheer will-power. Even with a product as simple as a bra ring, there's a point at which a lack of systematic structure and formal education causes problems. And the bigger question is whether Chinese companies can move beyond low-margin products, developing industries that require creativity and innovation. In the end, this is the greatest contrast between China's boom and the history of the western Industrial Revolution. In Europe and the United States, the rise of industry involved radical changes in thinking, and it happened partly because of a shortage of labor. In nineteenth-century America, for example, there was plenty of land and relatively few people; anyone who saved a few months' wages could move west and try farming. Agriculture and western expansion sapped the pool of able-bodied workers, so bosses made the most of limited labor. This need for efficiency inspired innovations that changed the world: the cotton gin, the sewing machine, the assembly line, the "American System" of standardization and interchangeable parts.

In today's China, though, there's little incentive to save labor. Each year the migrant population grows by another estimated ten million, and young people leave the countryside increasingly early. Formal schooling often seems irrelevant to students bound for the boomtowns, especially since traditional Chinese education offers little besides rote repetition and memorization. All of it—the high population, the lack of social institutions, the slowness of educational reform—combines to dull the edge of innovation. Inevitably, any nation is tempted to waste its greatest wealth, and in China this resource happens to be human. Master Luo's personal story was a triumph, but he was still making nothing more sophisticated than bra rings, and for every man like that, there were dozens of others who never made it so far.

WHEN THE LISHUI BOSSES first recruited Master Luo, he told them that he already had one child and planned to have another soon. They never met his wife or his first son; like many migrant workers Master Luo lived apart from his family. But he made sure the bosses knew about his personal obligations—this was an effective way to bargain for a higher salary. Boss Wang also had two children, so he was familiar with the bribes and fines necessary to deal with the planned birth officials.

Near the end of July, Master Luo requested permission to return to Hubei in order to attend the birth of his second child. But now the bosses were smart enough to turn his financial responsibility against him.

"You need to stay here," Boss Wang said. "It just wastes a lot of money to go home right now."

Master Luo explained that the factory wasn't busy, and he wouldn't be away for long; it was important for him to be there when his wife gave birth.

"You were there for the first one, right?" Boss Wang said. "That's all that matters. The first child is the exciting one. The second one isn't such a big deal. When my wife had the second child I wasn't nearly as excited."

For over a week they continued this conversation, in the slow-burn fashion of most development zone negotiations. There weren't any ultimatums, and nobody became angry or impatient; each man's voice remained as calm as if he were discussing last night's meal. But the conversation smoldered, day after day, and there were subtle signs of tension. Master Luo's face flushed and he no longer smiled as easily. Boss Wang became less free with cigarettes. These days he stuttered more often— the bad business weighed on him and now he had the added pressure of

Master Luo's request. In normal times, Boss Wang would have granted leave without a second thought, but he feared that Master Luo would take this opportunity to flee the factory. And his worries were well founded: in the past this was precisely the kind of family event that Master Luo had used as a pretext to switch jobs.

For the most part they negotiated in passing. The worker would say something; the boss would answer; neither made eye contact. Often it was so understated that I barely caught what they said. One morning, when I was in the Machine room with Master Luo, he turned to Boss Wang and I heard the word "salary." Boss Wang quickly looked away.

"L-l-l-later," he said. "Business isn't good enough right now."

"All I'm asking for is two months," Master Luo said. "You owe me three."

"C-c-c-can't do it."

"And all I want is to go for four days. Four days is enough."

"It's not p-p-possible. We might get new business any time."

With that, Boss Wang left the room, and Master Luo grinned at me. I had learned to be careful during this period—I watched myself around Master Luo. Not long ago, I had invited him to dinner at a restaurant on Suisong Road, where we drank a couple of beers and talked for two hours. The next day Boss Wang was full of questions for me: Where did you go with Master Luo last night? Why were you gone so long? And why are you always so curious about the factory? In other parts of China, during other writing projects, I occasionally had to reassure people that my stories wouldn't cause them political problems. But entrepreneurs in southern Zhejiang didn't worry about things like that. Their only fear involved business: they worried that I might be an undercover competitor hoping to start a bra ring factory of my own. After noticing Boss Wang's nervousness, I showed him a copy of one of my books, and I printed out published stories from the Internet. I told him the truth—I had no interest in poaching Master Luo, and I liked writing so much that I wouldn't give it up for all the bra rings in Zhejiang.

In the factory, the negotiations continued all the way until eleven o'clock in the morning of July 27, 2006, which was when Master Luo learned that his son had been born. He received the news on his cell phone, via text message from a relative. The baby had been delivered by C-section; the mother was expected to remain in the hospital for two or three days. And all at once the factory conversation made progress. Boss Wang agreed to grant leave, and he paid one month's back salary. They still owed two months' wages, an amount that they calculated would be adequate to ensure Master Luo's return. He immediately went out and bought a train ticket to Hubei. He was scheduled to leave in the middle of the night, and if there weren't any delays he'd meet his son before the baby was three days old.

That evening, before Master Luo's departure, I took him to a celebration dinner in downtown Lishui. We rode in my rented Santana, and Master Luo commented that it was the first time he'd left the development zone in three months. For dinner he chose a Sichuanese restaurant, where we ate spicy eel and Chongqing chicken and *mapo* bean curd. It wasn't nearly as elegant as the places he recalled from Chaonan days—the Golden Dragon, the Golden Beautiful Garden—but Master Luo was pleased.

"I wish I were still in Guangdong," he said. "If I were, I'd buy a lottery ticket, because this is a lucky day. In Guangdong they sell the Hong Kong lottery tickets, but you can't buy them here."

I asked him how he would handle the planned-birth officials. When migrants violate the policy, they often have children away from their place of registration, but Master Luo's child had been born in his hometown. He had told me his older son was there, too, and now he paused for a moment, thinking about my question. Finally he said, "It won't be a problem."

"Will you have to pay a fine?"

"It won't be a problem," he said again. "It's already been handled."

He changed the subject and raised his glass; we drank to the health of his newborn son. Master Luo beamed and commented once more that he wished he could buy a Hong Kong lottery ticket. He was owed serious money; he worked at a factory on the verge of bankruptcy; he had just missed the birth of his son. But from his perspective, on that summer evening, he was the luckiest man in all of Lishui.

III

FOR MORE THAN A YEAR I HAD TRAVELED REGULARLY to southern Zhejiang, until the place started to feel like another home. I enjoyed driving the new expressway, gazing out at the familiar scenery along the Ou River, and I always stopped to see the same places, the same people. In Lishui they built a new hotel called the Modern Square, and I negotiated a special rate with the managers, who let me stay for twenty dollars a night. A few blocks away I joined the gym called The Scent of a Woman. It was the only real gym in downtown Lishui, and it was open to both men and women; the managers told me they had chosen that name because it sounded nice. None of them had seen the American movie with the same title. In fact the gym smelled strongly of pleather, because all the machines were brand-new.

When the weather was good, I went for long runs in the hills south of town, through terraces of tangerine groves. The fruit in this region is wonderful—that's another reason I enjoyed spending time there. I found a decent Sichuanese restaurant and a first-rate noodle shop, and I explored the towns along the expressway. I liked having regular routines, and I liked the boomtown rush, the energy that comes from so many people on the move. And there was invariably something surreal about these trips to the south. Whenever I flew from Beijing and the plane touched down, a text message immediately appeared on my cell phone:

*Welcome to the home of one of China's ten most vital economies:
Wenzhou. Here in the pioneering hometown of "Daring
Trailblazers, Harmonious Citizens," the Wenzhou City Municipal
Communist Party Committee sincerely hopes that you find
friendship, business opportunities, and success.*

On one flight I met Mao Zedong. It was the first Beijing-Wenzhou departure of the morning, the 7:30 Air China special, and the moment I got to my seat I fell asleep. As usual, the flight was full of businessmen and cadres. While they were boarding I dozed fitfully, and at one point I half awoke and saw, as if through a fog, a passanger who bore a remarkable resemblance to the Chairman. But I dismissed it as a dream, at least until the plane took off and I heard two flight attendants talking.

"The actor who plays Chairman Mao is back there!" one of them said.

"Which row?"

"Twenty-five!"

He had the middle seat, wedged between two Wenzhou businessmen, who had conked out like nearly everybody else on the flight. But the actor who played Chairman Mao was completely alert. He wore a neat gray suit, a red tie, and stage makeup—his face glowed with unnatural brightness. His teeth gleamed, too, and his hair had been dyed black and brushed away from his forehead, the way Mao used to do it. He even had a prosthetic mole on the left side of his chin. Every time somebody walked past on their way to the bathroom, they did a double take: Mao Zedong, sitting in economy class, seat 25E.

After we landed in Wenzhou, a bus transferred all passengers from the plane to the terminal. The bus was even more crowded than the plane, and I found myself pressed against Chairman Mao. I introduced myself and gave him a business card; he fished one of his own out of a pocket. It listed no fewer than seven official titles:

*Jin Yang, The Actor Who Plays the Role of the Great Leader
Mao Zedong*

Director, Phoenix Cultural and Artistic Center
Director-General, China International Film Company, Ltd.
Vice-Manager, Beijing Strong and Prosperous International
*   Martial Arts Cultural Development Company*
Business Director, Beijing Film Research Institute
Honorary Director, Zhonghua Societal University Film Institute
High-Level Advisor, China Red Dragonfly Group
Chief Inspector, China Red Dragonfly Business and Cultural
*   Center*

He was traveling to Wenzhou in order to film a miniseries for China Central Television. They planned to tell the story of an incident from the 1940s, when the Red Army clashed with Japanese invaders in Zhejiang. Jin Yang said that for the past decade he had played the Chairman in movies and television shows. He smiled when he read my business card.

"Oh, you're a journalist," he said. "There was a famous American journalist named Edgar Snow who was friends with Chairman Mao."

I was well aware of Edgar Snow, whose history is a cautionary tale to any Missouri native who writes about China. Back in the 1930s, Snow had been a favorite of Mao and Zhou Enlai's, and eventually the American came to swallow much of their propaganda whole. During the Great Leap Forward, when tens of millions of Chinese starved to death, Edgar Snow toured the nation and reported that rumors of a famine were untrue. But here in Wenzhou I was much more curious about the story behind Jin Yang. How had this man been discovered? What had he been doing before he became the Actor Who Plays the Role of the Great Leader Mao Zedong?

But every time I asked a question, he responded with some anecdote from the Chairman's life. He told me he was from Changsha—Mao's actual home region. When I inquired about his former career, the actor said, "You know, the most famous photograph of Chairman Mao was taken by Edgar Snow."

"I've heard that," I said. "But what were you doing before you became an actor?"

"That's the photograph they always use for the young Mao," he continued. "It was reproduced in so many places in the fifties and sixties!"

Our bus lurched unsteadily toward the Wenzhou terminal; the vehicle was packed with people shouting into cell phones. But Jin Yang's smile was as steady as the plastic mole that clung to his chin. It was the same benevolent gaze that he had maintained throughout the flight, as if in fact he was still the leader of the nation, and not a passenger stuck in the middle seat on the early-morning special to Wenzhou. I kept trying to figure out his background; I studied the business card and asked about his position with the "Beijing Strong and Prosperous International Martial Arts Cultural Development Company." "Do you participate in martial arts?" I asked, and he smiled serenely and said, "Yes, I do. And Chairman Mao always emphasized the importance of physical activity! Did you know that he made a famous swim across the Yangtze River?" He told me again that he came from Changsha. He remarked that Edgar Snow's book had first introduced the Chairman to the West. With every secondhand anecdote, the smile seemed creepier, until at last I abandoned the conversation. Was this man completely insane? Did he really believe he was Mao Zedong?

At the terminal I picked up my bag. Before leaving the airport, I stopped to use the men's bathroom. It was empty except for Mao Zedong. He stood at the first urinal, and I heard him speak softly, as if to himself. "*Meiguo jizhe, Meiguo jizhe,*" he said. "American journalist, American journalist." I decided to occupy the urinal that was farthest from Chairman Mao. As quickly as possible, I went about my business, zipped up, and left without a word. He still wore the same benevolent smile, standing alone in the bathroom, muttering happily to himself.

AT THE BRA RING factory, the summer malaise ran through August, and then it finally ended with the appearance of deep coffee. In September, a new customer ordered over one hundred thousand rings, all of them dyed the same color. After months of inactivity, Little Long was suddenly busy; his laboratory was full of test tubes containing a shade of dark brown. In his color book it was identified as "deep coffee." The new customer was a bra assembly plant in southern Zhejiang, although Little Long and Master Luo didn't know much about the company. The bosses usually gave employees few details about customers, for fear that they would jump to another job with information about potential buyers. In this case, the bosses told Master Luo only that the new customer was involved in export, which meant that the rings needed to be of the highest quality. As for the final destination, Master Luo didn't know—it must have been some country with an appetite for brown underwear.

That same month, another new customer made a major order, and now the whole factory began to move. For the first time since spring, two metal punch presses were in operation, and the Machine rumbled eight hours a day. The Taos returned en masse: both sisters, the father, and a cousin were called in to work on a daily basis. The factory rehired a few of the assembly-line women who had been laid off, and Boss Wang told me that September was the first month in which income exceeded expenses. Eleven months had passed since they first designed the plant, and they were still a long way from recouping their investment, but finally the business was profitable.

Over the summer, the factory dormitory had acquired its youngest resident. Boss Wang's wife and two-year-old son often lived in the building for weeks at a time, and now the place also became home to Master Luo's newborn baby. Before the child was even two months old, his mother, whose name was Cheng Youqin, had taken him across China, traveling more than twenty hours by bus. In the dormitory the family lived together in an unfinished room on the third floor. They had a simple wooden bed, a hot plate, a few cooking utensils, and a cardboard box where they stored their clothes. Apart from that they had almost no possessions. Cheng told me proudly that the baby could already sleep through the sound of the machinery.

On the fiftieth day after the birth, I invited the family out to dinner. In China, people often mark such days, with a baby's hundredth being particularly important. We met in the dormitory; Master Luo was smoking a Profitable Crowd cigarette while he changed his son's clothes. The baby's head had been shaved recently, because of the heat in the factory, and he had his mother's pretty eyes. Fat cheeks, full lips, a nose that could have come from Buttontown: this was a good-looking child. Master Luo put him in my arms.

"How's his big brother doing?" I asked. I assumed the older child was still in the village, being cared for by grandparents or other relatives. But the moment I asked the question, Master Luo's face fell, and his wife gave him an uncomfortable look.

"There's something I should tell you," Master Luo said slowly. "This is actually our first child. When Boss Wang and Boss Gao hired me, I told them I already had a son so I could ask for a higher salary. I didn't want to lie to you, but they were around when we were talking. I was afraid they'd overhear, so I never told you the truth. I should have told you before I left, but I didn't. I'm sorry."

I told him not to worry. In any case, the phantom child had already returned to haunt Master Luo once, when Boss Wang refused to let him go home for the birth of his real child. At that time, the boss had insisted that the event wasn't important, because it was a second birth. I asked if now he knew the truth.

"No," Master Luo said. "It's too late to tell him now. I just act like there's another boy at home."

I hardly considered it a lie, because such stories are so common in boomtowns. When people negotiate with bosses, they find any advantage they can, and I understood the value of a nonexistent child. Even now he might still play a role. If Master Luo decided to quit the Lishui job and find something else, he could create a phantom sickness for the phantom child, and that would give him reason to ask for leave.

ON SUISONG ROAD, WE met a friend of Master Luo's, an entrepreneur who sold cheap clothes from a nearby stand. He said a new hotpot restaurant down the block was celebrating its grand opening. At hotpot places, diners sit around cauldrons filled with oil and spices, and a gas flame heats the stuff to a boil. Customers cook the food themselves, dropping raw vegetables and meat into the oil, and often the main ingredients are pig intestines and other innards. Much of the appeal is social: it's a good meal for drinking beer, and restaurants are always steam-filled and noisy, the way Chinese people like it on a night out. Hotpot is also the last meal to which I would take a baby celebrating his fifty-day anniversary, but nobody was asking me for child-care advice.

The appearance of the restaurant marked another stage in the neighborhood's progress. Hotpot isn't cheap, and it appeals to the middle-class of the development zone, the managers and the technicians. This was the second hotpot joint to open on Suisong Road within a month, and the entrance had been decorated with flowers to mark the occasion. They were setting off fireworks, too—the moment we sat down, the restaurant owner ignited a strand outside the door. The baby's eyes flickered with the sound of the explosion, but he didn't cry. At our table, we fired up the pot, and Master Luo and his friend lit Profitable Crowd cigarettes. Soon the child's porcelain skin glistened with sweat; his cheeks turned beet-red; his eyes looked slightly dazed. I was the only man in this restaurant who wasn't smoking. But the baby's expression remained calm, and at last I decided to stop worrying. He had already had fifty days to toughen up, and in a development zone that's an eternity.

Near the entrance of the restaurant, at a big round table, eight men were finishing their meal. They must have arrived early in the evening, and it was clear that they had been drinking hard. One of them hectored the waitress, complaining loudly about the food, and the restaurant owner hurried over. He was a young man in his thirties; his wife helped him run the place. He tried to appease the customer, offering apologies, but the other men chimed in loudly. At last the boss gave them a discount, along with a free round of beers, but the men's voices continued to rise.

In China it's common for people in restaurants to complain about food. The Chinese can be passive about many things, but food is not one of them; I suppose this is one reason they've ended up with a first-rate cuisine and a long history of political disasters. Nevertheless there was something unusual about the scene at the hotpot restaurant. Offering a discount and free drinks is an extreme measure, and generally it reduces a party to quiet grumbling. But this group continued to shout and carry on. They called the owner back for another tongue-lashing, and they yelled at his wife, and then they insisted on speaking with the chef. The poor man stood there, wide-eyed in a dirty white smock, while one of the drunks shook a finger in his face. He complained about the oil and the cuts of meat; he said the vegetables weren't fresh. The restaurant was quite small and the other diners watched this scene intently. After the party finally left, the place was quiet for a minute and then the drunkest man burst back through the door, like a villain in a horror film. He shouted one last string of complaints before his buddies pulled him out for good.

After it was finished, the owner came to our table. "I'm sorry about the disturbance," he said. "But you have to understand they weren't really angry about the food!" He explained: it had all been planned by the boss of the other hotpot restaurant down the street. The competing boss had paid the men to have an early meal, get drunk, and make a scene. The goal was to ruin the grand opening, and the owner hadn't recognized the stunt until it was too late.

He was earnest and soft-spoken, and he went from table to table, explaining the situation. But it was hopeless: Chinese complaints are highly contagious, sweeping through crowds like a bad germ. It has something to do with the group impulse, and people can't seem to help themselves—if they see others behaving a certain way, they immediately catch the vibe. And here in the hotpot restaurant it happened at our own table. Master Luo commented that the place wasn't very clean, and his friend remarked that the vegetables didn't look so great. The broth was too salty; there wasn't enough meat. It was low quality, too—they made this complaint while steadily dunking food into the oil and eating it with relish. That's one thing about Chinese food criticism: it never interferes with the appetite. By the end of the meal, Cheng Youqin was even denigrating the tea. The baby was the only one with nothing bad to say—he remained calm as ever, inhaling secondhand smoke and sweating like a little pig in the hotpot fumes.

After the unsatisfactory food had been completely devoured, Master Luo's friend dipped his chopsticks in beer and shoved them into the baby's mouth. The little guy wrinkled his face—the most expressive he'd been all evening. This encouraged the friend to embark on a series of reflex tests. He swung his hand as if to strike the baby, stopping just short of the button nose; the child remained unfazed. "He doesn't really see it," the man explained. "At this age they can't see very well."

"He can, too!" Cheng said.

"No he can't!" The man swung his fist again: no reaction. "See, I told you!"

No mother likes to see her child maligned, and Cheng quickly came to the defense. She jabbed her chopsticks within an inch of the baby's face—at last he blinked. "See!" she said triumphantly. "His eyes are good!"

"But he doesn't see *this*!"

"Yes, he does!"

"Watch this—he won't react."

"He does, too! You just have to do it like *this*!"

"Actually, I'm getting a little hot," I said. "Do you think we could leave now?"

On our way out, the owner gave us fifty yuan in coupons, by way of apology. "I won't go back there," Master Luo said, once we were out on Suisong Road. "The food's terrible." But he carefully folded the coupons and put them in his pocket. Outside, the air was cooler, and the baby stopped sweating. His eyes remained unblinking, calm as ever, ready for anything the next fifty days might throw at him.

WHENEVER I FOLLOWED THE expressway from Wenzhou to Lishui, I stopped in small towns along the way. A number of them had been planned in conjunction with the highway: at every exit, new neighborhoods were being built, and sometimes a whole settlement appeared in what had formerly been farmland. One of the exit towns was called Shifan, and it was located about ten miles south of Lishui. I first visited Shifan before the expressway had even opened, when the town was still a construction site full of unfinished streets and scaffolded apartment blocks. A billboard stood at the head of the main street:

CHERISH THE TANKENG DAM,
SERVE THE PEOPLE WHO WILL BE RELOCATED HERE
THE FIRST STAGE OF MOVING WILL BEGIN IN:
32 DAYS

The sign had tear-away numbers, and sheets of paper from previous days still lay on the ground beneath the billboard. There was a 5 here, a 4 there, a crumbled 3 nearby: countdown to a new community. When I wandered down the main street, a man carrying a hammer approached me. "Are you here to buy an apartment?" he said. I told him no, I was a journalist on my way to Lishui. "Oh, you're a journalist," he said. "Are you looking for people who are unhappy about the dam?"

Those were the first two things I was offered in Shifan: empty apartments and unhappy people. I learned that it was one of a number of exit towns that were being built because of a hydroelectric project called the Tankeng Dam. The dam is located on the Xiao River, high in the mountains west of Lishui; construction will require five years of work and a total investment of over six hundred million dollars. Upon completion, the new reservoir will submerge ten towns and eighty villages, and over fifty thousand people must be relocated. All of these facts were printed on information billboards near the construction site, but apart from that it was hard to learn much about the Tankeng Dam. Few articles about the project had appeared in Zhejiang newspapers, and not one word had been published in the foreign press. The most remarkable thing about the Tankeng Dam was that fifty thousand people could be displaced in virtual silence, at least as far as the media was concerned.

Chinese dams are so common that they often don't receive much attention, and domestic media is typically prevented from criticizing such projects. With air pollution an increasing concern, the government needs alternatives to coal-burning power plants, and hydroelectric is often the first option. This is especially true in a place like Lishui, which has high mountains, plenty of rainfall, and dreams of becoming a major industrial center. The region is already famous for its dam-building, and local electrical needs are only going to increase. In the development zone, a government official told me that industry currently accounted for 70 percent of Lishui's total consumption of electricity. This statistic was for the whole administrative region, which includes smaller towns and countryside. The percentage was so high because of all the heavy industry and mechanized manufacturing, but it also reflected low living standards. In the United States, in contrast, the industrial sector uses only one-third of the nation's total power.

Inevitably, the Lishui standard of living will rise as the initial investment in infrastructure and industry pays off. In the first six months after the expressway opened, the number of Lishui households buying an automobile doubled in comparison to the same period a year earlier. People were moving into bigger apartments, like the Riverside development owned by the Ji family. In the northern part of town, another real estate company was building White Cloud, the city's first neighborhood of stand-alone villas. Each White Cloud home came with a driveway and a garage—managers told me proudly this was another first for Lishui. But larger homes were bound to put more pressure on the city's power grid, which already relied heavily on electricity purchased from other parts of China. The Tankeng Dam was an attempt to reduce such dependence, and it had the advantage of being located high in the mountains, where people were poor and less likely to resist a resettlement.

The largest town in the affected region was called Beishan, with a population of about ten thousand. In the fall of 2005, when it came time to move the residents, the government consulted a fortune-teller, who determined that the twenty-third day of the ninth lunar month was the most auspicious moment to demolish the place. On the morning of the twenty-third, I drove my rented Santana westward toward Beishan. The unnamed road was narrow, and it followed the path of the Xiao River, where the fast-flowing channel was braided around boulders that marked the valley floor. Occasionally a fisherman waded along the banks, but the Xiao is too shallow for boats and these regions are lightly populated. It's a hard country for farming, too: rice paddies lie in the flatlands beside the river, but the mountains are too steep for terracing. This rugged countryside seems to have nothing in common with the factory districts of Wenzhou, but in fact the city is less than fifty miles away as the crow flies. And these landscapes helped shape the business instinct of southern Zhejiang. Centuries ago, the mountains drove people to a life of trade along the coast, and more recently the natives learned to direct their entrepreneurial energy toward manufacturing. Now at last they have returned to the hinterlands as dam builders, hoping to create more power for their factory towns.

All along the road stood billboards for Red Lion Cement. There were few other advertisements, and most settlements were tiny and poor, but the road itself was full of traffic. A steady stream of vehicles poured down from Beishan: big Liberation trucks, beaten-up flatbeds with wooden rails, tricycle tractor-carts sputtering behind two-stroke engines. They carried crates and cupboards and stacks of furniture; dirty old mattresses had been lashed to the sides of trucks. They passed blue government signs that had been posted beside the road:

FINISH BUILDING THE TANKENG DAM
BENEFIT THE FUTURE GENERATIONS

OFFER THE TANKENG DAM AS A TRIBUTE TODAY
BENEFIT THE GENERATIONS OF TOMORROW

Most vehicles heading in the same direction as me belonged to profiteers of one sort or another. Cement mixers rumbled toward the dam, along with flatbeds carrying work crews. Scavengers drove empty trucks: demolition sites always provide plenty of bricks, wood, and metal that can be recycled. There were cadres in black Audi A6s, and cops, too—more police than I had ever seen in rural Zhejiang. Along the way to Beishan, I passed the location of the dam, where another billboard noted that the project would require a total of 164,000 cubic meters of cement. That was Red Lion Cement's stake in this region, and most work was yet to come; the retaining wall was nothing but a sliver of scaffolded structures edging into the river. Up above, the scarred hillside marked the location of the future dam—a huge groove in the mountains, running from one side of the valley to the other, like a massive puzzle waiting for its final piece.

I had visited Beishan once before, when the town was still thriving, but today the place was unrecognizable. A countdown billboard stood on the main street, a counterpart to Shifan's sign. Here in Beishan the numbers had reached double zero, and demolition crews were finishing off the heart of the former downtown. Government-appointed teams wore white coveralls, and they went from building to building, checking for last residents. For the destruction itself they relied primarily on freelance scavengers. In Lishui's development zone, market forces built a whole community, with factories and shops rising simultaneously; and here the profit motive was equally efficient at demolishing Beishan. There were tiles on the roofs, bricks in the walls, copper beneath floors—all of it could be sold. And so the crews passed quickly through town, like locusts in a fertile field, leaving only desolation in their wake.

It took ten minutes to drive to the former center of town, because of backlogged trucks carting off materials. At last, after fighting the traffic inch by inch, I pulled over and simply listened. In the factory towns, mechanical noises rule the day, but here in Beishan the demolition was mostly done by hand. Boards were ripped apart; nails were torn from walls; cement was smashed with sledgehammers. I heard the percussion of one scavenger destroying a wall—*rip, tear, smash; rip, tear, smash*—and then a final *thud* followed by nothing. That emptiness was Beishan's destiny: the valley would never become home to the rhythms of the factory floor or the voices of nighttime workers. Instead it was bound for the stillness of the reservoir, the hush of walled water, and beneath fathoms of silence this place would die.

IN THE DEVELOPMENT ZONE, foliage appeared in the span of two days during November of 2006. That was the same month government work crews finished installing the sidewalk tiles on Suisong Road, where they even posted trash cans. Previously, as entrepreneurs built the place, garbage was allowed to accumulate in the gutters, but now the city instituted regular pickup. They started a public bus service to downtown, too, and work crews made their way along the development zone streets, installing nursery-grown camphor trees that were already eight feet tall. The trees appeared at intervals of every fifty meters, as regular as assembly-line stations. And all at once there was greenery in the factory district—a reminder that little more than year earlier, before the mountains had been blown up and the machinery had been installed, this region had been entirely rural.

A few days after the trees appeared, one of the girls who worked on the Machine's assembly line celebrated her sixteenth birthday. Her name was Ren Jing and she was originally from a village in Anhui Province, not far from the hometown of the Tao family. Like the Taos, the Ren family migrated en masse: both parents, two daughters, and a son. The parents ran a fruit and vegetable stand that catered to workers, and the eldest daughter sold bootleg video disks. At the bra ring factory, Ren Jing worked alongside Tao Yuran, the older of the Tao sisters; they sorted rings as they came off the Machine's assembly line. All three factory girls usually spent time together in the evenings, when the work shifts were finished and their parents were busy with their stands. This was one reason the girls enjoyed their work routines—at night they were usually unsupervised.

On the evening of the birthday, they didn't get off the assembly line until eight o'clock, because the factory was working overtime to process an order from another new customer. The Tao sisters bought Ren Jing a cake with frosting that said, in English, "Luck for You!" Ren Jing's sister took time away from selling video disks and prepared a seven-course dinner. She was nineteen years old, and tonight she cooked grass carp, cubed chicken, cauliflower, and lotus root. They ate in the Ren family home, which consisted of a rented room in a house that once belonged to a local farmer. The place had cement walls and a rough tile floor; crates of oranges and apples covered most of the floor space. The girls sat on their parents' bed, enjoying the banquet and toasting each other with shots of Sprite and Coca-Cola.

They had purchased bottles of Double Deer beer for the men. The older Ren sister's boyfriend was there—he had just finished a twelve-

hour shift at a pleather plant—and Old Tian came from the factory.
Old Tian was the foreman on the underwire assembly line, where he
monitored Tao Yufeng, the fifteen-year-old who had lied about her age
during the factory's first hiring. Tonight the girl targeted Old Tian as
soon as the beer was uncapped.

"Old Tian, drink a glass," she said. She topped off the man's shot
glass with beer and filled her own cup with Sprite. They both drank,
and Yufeng immediately followed with a refill.

"Drink again," she said sternly.

"Wait a minute," Old Tian said. "I need to rest."

"Drink it!"

"Wait."

"Now! Drink it now!"

The moment the glass was empty she poured another.

"Now it's your turn," she said, pointing to Ren's boyfriend. "Make
him drink. I want him drunk so he can't boss me around at work tomorrow morning."

"I won't boss you around!"

"Make him drink!"

After the boyfriend obliged, she turned to me. "You go next," she
instructed. "Make Old Tian drink." I didn't hesitate—I knew better than
to get in the way of Yufeng. From the moment she lied her way into
the job, Yufeng had established herself as a force of nature in the factory.
She had a young, boyish face, with chubby cheeks and short-cropped
hair, but she had more attitude than all of the adult workers combined.
Nobody else was nearly as fast with underwire, and she refused to be
intimidated by the bosses. Once, when Boss Wang told Yufeng there
wouldn't be any work for a few days, she cursed him and stormed out
of the factory. "That g-g-girl has a temper," he said mildly, after she was
gone. Like the other men at the plant, he seemed more bemused than
anything: nobody knew how to handle a woman so young and yet so
sharp.

In particular, Old Tian was no match for the girl. He barely weighed
one hundred pounds, with a gentle, elflike face, and he lived according
to a two-sentence motto: "Pass Every Day Happily! A New Day Begins

from Right Now!" This had been his catchphrase ever since he first set out from rural Sichuan in the mid–1980s. Back then, he earned a good living as a wristwatch repairman, setting up stands on the streets of development zones. Soon, however, he found himself overtaken by the pace of progress. In the early 2000s, cell phones suddenly became cheap enough for even low-income consumers, who also used the devices to tell time; Old Tian's trade in wristwatches became obsolete. Like so many people in China, he learned that it was impossible to be complacent with new knowledge; he had already shifted from farming to watches, but now it was time to learn something else. He took it all in stride, the eternal optimist: *A New Day Begins from Right Now!* In the Wenzhou region he found jobs as a factory technician, eventually specializing in the production of underwire.

He earned a good wage, roughly a third of which was spent on lottery tickets. In China, the state-run Welfare Lottery funds social programs, and Old Tian contributed more than his share. The man was obsessed—he kept track of winning numbers, writing them across the walls of his dormitory room. He slept in a windowless chamber on the first floor, where the bare plaster walls had been covered with his motto about passing days happily, along with dozens of mysterious lottery calculations:

$$95 \ 1.3.17.20.21.24 + 16$$
$$97 \ 1.5.9.13.15.33 + 14$$
$$97 \ 11.14.15.20.26.27 + 12$$
$$98 \ 6.7.10.11.15.23 + 16$$
$$99 \ 7.12.18.23.24.27 + 5$$

Every worker in the plant nursed some secret dream for the future. Yufeng told me that eventually she wanted to start a shoe factory, and Little Long talked about raising rabbits or doing wholesale trade. Master Luo had a business idea that involved drying lotus root and selling it shrink-wrapped in northern China, where it doesn't grow naturally. Once, when Old Tian was fiddling with the factory's machinery, I asked him what he would do if he got lucky and won the lottery. He smiled and pointed at the underwire. "I'd make this," he said. "I'd start my own business making it." He was the only person in the factory who aspired to do exactly what he already did. In China, that's a pipe dream, as unlikely as winning the lottery: to live in complete confidence that your trade will never become obsolete.

At the birthday party Old Tian's face quickly turned red from the beer. Yufeng bullied him into a few final shots before relenting, and he sank onto the bunk bed in the corner of the room. The girls started talking about factory jobs. They mentioned the rumors that working with *pige*, or pleather, causes birth defects, and Yufeng said shoe plants are better.

"They have toxic fumes, too," Ren Jing said. "It's the same problem."

"The fumes aren't the same," Yuran, the older sister, corrected her. "The problem with shoes is that they use a type of glue that's bad for you. But it's not as bad as the *pige* fumes."

Yuran was only seventeen, but she was worldly when it came to factories; this was her third assembly-line job. Previously she had made shoes and dress shirts. Ren Jing, the birthday girl, had technically come of legal working age only today, but she was already onto her second job. At the age of fourteen she had started as a seamstress in a low-end garment factory. "They paid by the piece," she told me. "This job is better, because I get paid by the hour. It's more relaxed."

"I liked the clothes factory where I used to work," Yuran said. "The boss was really nice. One night we had to work late, because of an order, and he came and brought drinks for all of us. Nobody asked him to do that."

"Boss Gao wouldn't do that."

"Boss Gao is too cheap."

"The boss at the clothes factory cared about the workers."

"Boss Wang is nice. He's just too worried all the time."

"Look at Old Tian!"

The girls laughed—the tipsy foreman had fallen asleep on the bunk bed. The cake had all been eaten, and a small pile of gifts sat on the table: a toy pig, a little cow, a floppy cloth dog. Ren Jing loved stuffed animals, and like all the girls she sometimes seemed younger than her years. They never mentioned boys, at least not in mixed company, and they obeyed their parents with a readiness that would have been unimaginable to an American teenager. But in other ways they were remarkably mature. In the United States, few girls could prepare a seven-course banquet for a sweet sixteen birthday party, and almost certainly such an event would not feature a fifteen-year-old bullying her assembly-line foreman into drinking too much. But some teenager qualities are the same everywhere, and once the Anhui girls started talking, their faces lit up and they couldn't have been happier. For an hour Ren Jing sat with her friends, chatting about old jobs and new bosses and which factories are the best.

ONE EVENING THAT FALL, while driving from Wenzhou to Lishui on the new expressway, Boss Gao lost control of his car. It was pitch-black and raining hard; he was going faster than eighty miles per hour. On a curve, he hit a patch of water and locked the brakes, and then he hydroplaned. He was driving his aptly named Buick Sail. The car spun a full three-sixty, skidded across the highway, and slammed into a guardrail. Many sections of the Jinliwen Expressway are elevated, and often the road is bordered by cliffs, but Boss Gao was fortunate in the location of his accident—the guardrail held. It was nearly midnight and the road was empty. Afterward, when the car came to a stop on the shoulder, Boss Gao smoked a State Express 555 until his nerves calmed. But the damage to the car was relatively minor, and he was able to continue driving to Lishui.

Both bosses still had homes near Wenzhou, and they made the round-trip journey two or three times a week. To some degree it was an issue of machine quality: in the factory, something always seemed to be breaking down, forcing them to return to Wenzhou to get the right part or repair. In the past, neither boss had driven much and the open road unsettled them. It was expensive, too—each round trip cost roughly twenty-five dollars in highway tolls. And that autumn, almost immediately after the factory became profitable, the bosses began to talk about moving the whole operation closer to their hometowns.

Some of it was simply the eternal restlessness of the development zone. People in such places become accustomed to moving and adjusting; their instinct is always to tinker. And often a little success proves to be more unsettling than satisfying. After the bosses began to earn money, they became obsessed with cutting costs. Their staff of twenty employees was overstretched, and often the crew worked late into the evening, but the bosses refused to hire new people. They complained about rent, because their factory space was so big. Their initial plans for the business had been overly ambitious; they had hoped to make a major expansion within six months. But after a year the growth had proven to be smaller than expected, and much of the empty space on the top floors was wasted.

Whenever the bosses discussed important business between themselves, they spoke in their local dialect, so the workers wouldn't understand. And they rarely gave anybody a sense of their plans. But during the fall they asked Master Luo how much time he would need, in the event of a factory transfer, to disassemble the Machine and put it back together again. He told them it would take ten days total. After that, they didn't ask him any more questions, and he couldn't tell whether they were serious about the possibility of moving. He believed they wouldn't try something like that before the end of the year, because business was just starting to boom and a transfer involved risks. But Master Luo admitted that after all the years he'd spent in Chinese factory towns, he still couldn't predict the snap decisions of a boss. People rarely planned carefully, especially in a place like Zhejiang. From Master Luo's perspective, the region was even more chaotic than Guangdong, where he spent so many years. "They build things differently there," he told me. "It's more logical. In Guangdong the first thing they do is build the road, and then they build the factories. But here it's the opposite. They build factories first and then they worry about finishing the roads and everything else."

At the end of autumn, Master Luo decided that it was best for his wife and baby to return to her hometown in Guizhou Province. He wasn't sure if the factory was going to move, and the bosses were still withholding part of his salary; there was a chance he'd make a job search after the Spring Festival holiday. In either case, mobility would be crucial, and such things are harder with a small child. Like so many migrant families, they decided to live apart until Master Luo's job situation was more stable.

Cheng Youqin packed up as much as she could carry, and she took their new Canon digital camera. This was the family's most valuable possession—after the baby's birth, they spent one hundred and fifty dollars on the camera. With all of her bags and the baby, Cheng left from the Lishui bus station, eventually transferring to a train to Guiyang, the capital of Guizhou Province. It was an overnight journey and they arrived before five in the morning. At the Guiyang train station, a friendly young woman approached Cheng and asked where she was going. The friendly woman said she knew somebody with a van that was also headed in that direction, and she offered a good price, so Cheng accepted. Her hometown was in the countryside outside of Guiyang, more than an hour away, and usually she had to connect with a couple of public buses in order to get there.

She followed the young woman outside the train station, but once she saw the vehicle she became nervous. It was dingy and cramped, the kind of minivan known as a "breadbox." Three people waited inside, and two of them were heavyset men who smoked cigarettes and didn't say much when Cheng approached. She thought about turning around and waiting for a public bus, but it was so early and the long journey from Lishui had left her tired. Her son still slept peacefully in her arms. At last she decided to enter the breadbox van and hope for the best.

They drove through Guiyang and into the countryside. The other four people all knew each other, but they didn't say much, and the farther they went, the more this silence unnerved Cheng. Guizhou is a poor, remote province, with stunningly rugged scenery, and soon they had left the last settlements of the Guiyang suburbs. Along an empty stretch of road Cheng noticed a strong chemical smell; suddenly she felt dizzy. The breadbox van pulled over to the side of the road. After that, events occurred as if through a haze: the men demanded her money, valuables, and cell phone; they threatened to kill her and the baby if she didn't cooperate. Cheng had the equivalent of one hundred and twenty dollars in cash, which she handed over, along with her cell phone. They asked for her earrings and she took them off. But she didn't tell them about the digital camera, which she had hidden at the bottom of a bag of baby supplies. Even when the men asked again about valuables, threatening to kill them both if she lied, she denied there was anything else.

The thieves left Cheng and her baby by the side of the road. It was early morning, and the air was wet and cold; Cheng still felt disoriented. She believed she had been drugged—recently there had been reports of thieves using chemicals to knock out victims. Fortunately, a farmhouse stood not far from the road, and Cheng stumbled there with the baby in her arms. The elderly couple who answered the door took Cheng in, gave her something to eat, and let her use their phone. The first thing she did was try to call every friend and relative whose number had been programmed onto her cell phone. After stealing a phone, Chinese thieves sometimes go through the memory bank, calling numbers with a story about a terrible accident. They claim the phone's owner is so badly injured that she can't speak, and she needs a medical procedure immediately; doctors won't treat if they're not paid in advance. If relatives fall for the story, the thieves convince them to wire money immediately.

Cheng had heard about such scams, so she tried to remember every number possible, and she called Master Luo to ask for any others. For half an hour she telephoned relatives and friends, explaining what had happened and warning them about the scam. Then she noticed that the baby was still asleep. Usually he woke up by this time in the morning, but today he seemed groggy, and Cheng called Master Luo again in a panic. He told her to bathe the baby immediately, scrubbing hard in case he had been contaminated with some drug.

In the farmhouse, the elderly couple ran a bath and the baby woke up. Afterward he seemed fine, and Cheng observed him carefully over the coming weeks. But he remained as calm and happy as ever, and she believed that the chemicals hadn't done any harm. The next time I saw her, she told me that she was certain the thieves would have murdered her if it hadn't been for the baby. She was proud that she had tricked them about the digital camera—even under duress, she had protected the family's most valued possession.

As the child grew older, his face began to resemble Master Luo's. The boy had the same long nose, heavy brow, and gentle smile. Maybe someday he would also share Master Luo's quiet manner, the air of experience without cynicism, but that remained to be seen. In the first four months of the child's life, he had traveled twice across China, lived in a factory dormitory, and served as a pawn in salary negotiations. He had witnessed the hotpot complaint scam and he had dodged the stolen phone trick. He had been drugged and robbed. His given name was Wen, which means "Cultured." Master Luo had chosen that character because he dreamed that someday his son would become an educated man.

MASTER LUO NEVER WROTE any slogans on the wall of his dormitory room. He didn't read self-help books, and he had no interest in religion. He disliked Mao Zedong, believing that the leader had caused China to waste thirty years, but he admired Deng Xiaoping for his pragmatism. After more than two decades in factory towns, Master Luo's life philosophy could be summed up in a single sentence: "If you have a problem, you have to take care of it yourself." It's common to hear people talk like this in development zones. The ones who succeed generally do so through their own talent and effort, and they neither expect nor receive support from the government, labor unions, or anybody else. A worker on the rise is rarely inspired to join the Communist Party, because such status is irrelevant in the factory world. There is one legal labor group, the government-run All-China Federation of Trade Unions, but in Lishui I never met a worker who had turned to this organization for support. In fact, the only evidence I saw of union activity consisted of streetside entertainments. Once a month, the All-China Federation of Trade Unions showed a movie on a portable screen in Suisong Road, free for everybody, and each year they hosted a big karaoke contest for workers. Apart from that, I never encountered the union during my trips to Lishui.

In factory towns, the most common attitudes toward the government range from scorn to complete disinterest. Many people complain about official corruption, but they tend to do so in abstract terms, because they have little direct contact with cadres. It's similar to the speeding tickets on the expressway: if drivers were pulled over and hassled by cops, or extorted in some heavy-handed way, they might be infuriated. But the authorities know better, and usually they find strategies to earn money without making it too personal. For the most part, citizens tolerate it; sometimes they're even patronizing. One factory boss described his bribes in terms of public service. "You need to make them feel like they're important," he told me. "You need to give them cigarettes, give them banquets—give them a little face. If they don't have these things to do, they'll just sit in an office all day long. Think about what it's like for them; they don't get to start businesses or do interesting things. Their lives are so boring!"

When people do turn to the government for assistance, it's usually a sign of desperation. During my drives along the expressway, the dam relocation towns were the only places where residents sometimes spoke hopefully of getting something from cadres. And these were by far the most depressing settlements I ever saw in Zhejiang. Most were located on lonely sites near some highway exit, and they had all the dusty feel of a new boomtown without the energy. In these construction sites, nothing ever seemed to get finished: I visited Shifan, the exit town south of Lishui, over a period of more than two years and never saw the main street completed. It began the same way as every other new town, with the same pioneer shops—China Mobile, construction supplies, home furnishings. They sold floor tiles and faucets, and there were plenty of goods for finishing an apartment. But over time the main street never reached the next stage of growth, where restaurants flourish and streetside entertainments appear. Shifan didn't have a chance to come to life, because there wasn't any major industry nearby.

It was a drive-by town, and it received nothing but drive-by work. Occasionally some big-city factory owner came in on the expressway and offered locals a chance to earn some extra money. Once, I stopped by and dozens of older women were sitting in the street, chatting idly while they sewed plastic beads onto strips of cloth. The work had been commissioned by a Wenzhou shoe factory, which paid twelve and a half cents per embroidered strip. Eventually they would be attached to the tops of children's shoes. A couple of months later, I made another visit to Shifan and saw people sewing beads onto headbands. Then there was a period during which everybody assembled tiny lightbulbs for electric signs. After that, they made cheap cotton gloves for a couple of months.

The most ambitious Shifan industry involved online video games. A group of young men purchased computers, set up high-speed Internet connections, and began playing World of Warcraft for profit. World of Warcraft is the world's most popular online game, and players build characters by accumulating virtual treasure. The game is so widespread that markets have developed in which these prizes can be bought and sold for real money. In America and Europe, players might be too busy to spend much time on the game, but they're happy to pay somebody else to do the grunt work of developing a character. It's called gold farming: essentially, the outsourcing of entertainment. For a time, the young men in Shifan made good money; they played World of Warcraft in shifts, twenty-four hours a day, selling the points to players in Germany. But then the game's administrators cracked down on the practice, shutting down accounts in China, and finally the Shifan players gave up on their venture. They sold their computers and headed off on the expressway, looking for work in Wenzhou and other places. For most young people in the exit towns, that was the obvious solution to the lack of opportunity: they left.

But there was also a small corps of people who had been embittered by the Tankeng Dam project and now sought justice. During the resettlement, authorities had promised compensation according to the type of home and farmland of each resident, and people were given discount prices on new apartments in Shifan and the other exit towns. The degree of detail was remarkable: if a person's former house had been made of brick, he received 220 yuan per square meter; if it was wood, the price was 180. Each stove was reimbursed at a set rate. A fee of 480 yuan covered transport costs. Any resident employed in a full-time job received another 480, to compensate for missed workdays during the move. If they had orchards, every individual fruit tree was noted, evaluated for maturity, and reimbursed accordingly. On the average, compensation came to over ten thousand dollars per resident, but often the actual amount was reduced by corruption. Virtually everybody in Shifan grumbled about the resettlement, and some had become so angry that they prepared official requests for justice.

Their goal was to contact a higher level of government. Like many traditional Chinese citizens, they had a deep-rooted faith in authority, believing that corruption was primarily a local issue. They visited Hangzhou, the provincial capital, where they waited in line at special offices, hoping some official would notice. I never heard of anybody in Shifan receiving justice from such a visit, but they kept trying. And almost every time I stopped in town, I was approached by somebody who wanted to tell the story of his case. I explained that I wrote books to be published overseas, and it wasn't possible for me to print something in Zhejiang, but people wanted to talk anyway. Probably they just needed somebody to listen: often I sat for an hour while a displaced farmer flipped through his resettlement book. Inevitably he knew it all by heart, every detail, every injustice—his house had been brick but he had been paid only for wood, or the floor space had been miscalculated, or tangerine trees had been marked as young when in fact they were mature. These conversations made me feel helpless, because only a functional local press could deal with such issues, but Zhejiang journalists had been told to stay away from the dam. In a drive-by town, I felt like a drive-by journalist, listening to sad stories before I got back on the expressway.

It was particularly depressing because in a way the system worked well. It didn't necessarily make people happy, and it certainly wasn't fair, but it was extremely functional. The government was smart enough not to resettle all the dam refugees in one place, which could have been a political disaster; instead they scattered them in exit towns all along the expressway. And they created lots of little rules that distracted people from the larger issues. They measured square meters and they counted trees; they quantified the difference between brick and wood. It gave an air of legality and due process to the whole affair, when in fact it was fundamentally flawed. There should have been public meetings about the dam; the press should have played a role; people should have been in a position to own the land they had farmed for generations. New towns like Shifan should have been located near industry, where people could find work. But these were rarely the issues that came up in conversations, because locals were so obsessed with the minutiae.

In the early stages of the project, there were demonstrations in Beishan. Locals told me that officials hired thugs to beat up a few organizers, and there were rumors that one man had been killed. In the end, the authorities were able to quell the unrest without much trouble. Such flare-ups are common in China—during the year that Beishan was demolished, the Ministry of Public Security reported 87,000 "public-order disturbances" nationwide. Every year, a similar statistic comes out of China, and it always seems staggering. But in fact the number of protests is irrelevant; all that matters is the target. If people were calling for the downfall of the Communist Party, or complaining about the fundamental structure of land-use laws, that might be a serious problem. But it's a very different issue when somebody is upset because his home has been measured at 100 square meters instead of 150. In China, virtually all complaints occur at this level: they're intensely local and individual. And it also matters who does the protesting. In rural areas, where the worst abuses occur, talented people tend to migrate. If a capable individual happens to stay behind, like Wei Ziqi in Sancha, there's a good chance he ends up involved in the local power structure, perhaps as a Communist Party member. This is another way in which the system is functional: there are plenty of pressure valves to redirect the energies of potentially dangerous people.

For the most part, capable Chinese have learned that there's no point in overt political activity, but this doesn't mean they're powerless. The degree of social mobility is higher than in most developing countries, and talent and hard work usually pay off—this is clear from the experience of people like Master Luo. But such folks rely on the government for virtually nothing. They find agency elsewhere: they pay for private training courses; they learn to use *guanxi*; they switch jobs on their own. They negotiate hard with bosses, using any advantage they can find. If they're relocated to a dead community, they simply leave. With so many options and so much movement, it doesn't make sense to get involved in a doomed battle against the cadres.

In Shifan, most petitioners I met seemed desperate. They tended to be less educated than the average resident, with worse job prospects, and often they had had poor luck as migrants. Many of them had been traumatized—during the course of protesting, they had been threatened in some manner. All of these factors made it even less likely that they would succeed, but they kept trying, because they had been pushed beyond the pale. And only once did I meet a protestor who impressed me as highly competent. He arranged a meeting carefully, through a mutual acquaintance, and the first thing he did was ask to see my government-issued journalist license. Nobody in an exit town had ever done that before.

"To be honest, I would prefer to talk with somebody else," he said. "I really want to speak with the Columbia Broadcasting System or the British Broadcasting Corporation."

I respected that—he wanted TV time, not some lousy print journalist. But on that day I was the only option at hand, so we chatted for an hour. He complained that nobody knew exactly how the Tankeng Dam had been approved and funded, and there were rumors of private investors who stood to profit from any electricity that was generated. "If they build something like this, we need to know why," he said. "We need to know who the investors are. But the main reason I oppose it is that the government didn't offer anything to the people. It's not enough to give us money and apartments. How are people going to earn a living in this place? Look outside—there's nothing here. In Beishan we had a good location for doing business, because it was a center for people from other villages in the region."

It was the first time I had met a local who seemed concerned with the fundamental issues behind the dam, and he had refused to accept his cash settlement out of principle. He was well dressed and he carried an expensive cell phone; I asked how he supported himself. "I do business," he said. "I have shops in this area, including one here."

I asked him what the shops sold.

"Floor tiles," he said.

He had rejected the government payoff, and he was trying to get the story into the press, but meanwhile he profited from the construction work that occurred in the exit towns. I wasn't about to blame him for hedging his bets—at least he was trying to figure things out, and perhaps someday more Chinese people like him would find a way to press fundamental issues. Maybe the education system would improve, and citizens would gain a broader vision that could be combined with their practical skills. In the development zone I was most heartened by signs of individualism—ways in which people had escaped the group mentality of the village, learning to make their own decisions and solve their own problems. But it would take another major step for such personal lessons to be applied to society-wide issues. Perhaps the final motivation would be economic—often I sensed that China needed to reach a point where the middle and upper classes felt like the system prevented them from succeeding. But that hadn't happened yet, not even in the exit towns, where there was still good money to be made from floor tiles.

AT THE BEGINNING OF November the bosses decided to move the bra ring factory. They didn't say when the transfer would happen, or where they were going, and they probably didn't know themselves. Periodically Boss Gao headed to the expressway in his Buick Sail, returning a day later to confer quietly with Boss Wang. Master Luo believed they were still searching out a new site, most likely near Wenzhou, but even he didn't know for certain. And it was characteristic of the bosses to keep such information quiet. If they announced a moving schedule, the lower-wage workers would either demand raises or immediately look for new jobs. With business still improving, the bosses couldn't afford to lose labor, so they simply said that they would move sometime in the distant future.

Boss Wang made one initial foray into negotiations with Mr. Tao. By this point, Mr. Tao had established himself as the spokesman for roughly one-quarter of the factory's workforce: himself, his two daughters, the Tao cousins who occasionally did part-time work, and Ren Jing, the sixteen-year-old who was also from Anhui Province. Boss Wang despised dealing with the man, but there was nothing he could do about it, and the girls were valuable workers. One day he asked Mr. Tao if the family would be willing to move.

"Where to?" Mr. Tao said.

"N-n-not sure yet," Boss Wang said. His stutter always emerged when he dealt with Mr. Tao. "But it won't be very far."

"Well, then I'm not sure either," Mr. Tao said. "You have to tell me where, and then I can answer." Boss Wang wasn't willing to give more information, and that was as far as they got—nothing more than a spark, but that was how the slow-burn negotiations always got started.

Nobody else in the factory could bargain like Mr. Tao. In the evenings, after the assembly-line work was finished, he managed the family's dry goods stand, and he was good at that, too. He stocked hundreds of books and magazines, and dozens of cheap goods; he knew every price by heart. Unlike some shopkeepers, he didn't joke around or feign friendship with potential customers. He intimidated people: with his height and ramrod posture, he made for a formidable bargainer. But he was known for having good judgment, and other local shopkeepers sometimes turned to him for advice.

The Tao stand was located on a small alley that connected to Suisong Road. Most alleyway entrepreneurs had come from Anhui Province, and there was a degree of camaraderie, despite the fact that they were all in competition. Over the months, some had expanded into real shops, and one couple had opened a storefront directly across from the Taos. The couple had a ten-month-old son whose features were strikingly different from most Chinese. The baby had light wispy hair that was almost blond, and his eyes were grayish. He had fair skin—locals called him "the Little Foreigner." In the evenings I sometimes sat with Mr. Tao, and the neighbors joked, "Hey, he could be your baby!" It made me uncomfortable when they talked this way. Occasionally in China I saw a child who looked different; it wasn't surprising in a country that had always been more ethnically diverse than people imagined. After centuries of movement and migrations, there were all sorts of genes floating around, and sometimes an unusual characteristic appeared in a child. These kids always received a lot of blunt attention—the baby in Lishui was still too small to understand, but I imagined that someday he would tire of these remarks.

His parents had never gotten along. The Taos told me they had bickered from the moment they arrived in the development zone, and one evening that November they erupted into a vicious public argument. As usual, the disagreement concerned money. In Chinese families, it's more often the man who is profligate, spending money on cigarettes and *baijiu* and banquets, and this was the point of contention for the Anhui couple. For five minutes they faced off, shouting at each other in the middle of the alley, and then the husband stalked away. Long after he was gone, his wife remained apoplectic, screaming into the distance. She was heavyset, with dark peasant features; it was hard to guess where the baby's fairness had come from. In all my trips to the Taos' stand I never saw this woman smile.

Tonight she yelled for a quarter of an hour, and then she began to set fire to the store's stock. She took a few cardboard packages of nylon socks, stacked them like kindling in the alleyway, and got a cigarette lighter. She left the baby on the shop's cold cement floor, where he began howling. Soon thirty people gathered to watch, but they didn't have the usual mood of a street crowd. For the most part, Chinese arguments and fights serve as public entertainment, but tonight nobody was smiling or laughing. They looked shocked, and finally a man in a factory uniform stepped forward.

"Don't do that," he said. "That's bad. Just go back inside; he's already gone."

The shopkeeper flung off his arm and kept struggling with the lighter. She was so angry that it took her a while to get the flame to catch a corner of the cardboard. By now the baby was red-faced and wet with tears.

"Don't let him cry like that," somebody else said. "He's too small!"

But the shopkeeper ignored them. She flicked the lighter again, igniting another package. Without a word Mr. Tao stepped into the alley.

As always, he was completely decisive; he didn't bother talking to the shopkeeper, who paid him no mind. Mr. Tao picked up her baby and carried him across the alley to his own stand.

Soon a heavy acrid smell filled the air. The socks were the cheap kind that sell for a few cents a pair, and they burned poorly, giving up thick black smoke. The woman stepped back into her shop, studying the shelves. The crowd began to murmur.

"Don't let her burn something else."

"She should just forget it!"

"Leave it alone!"

Mr. Tao held the baby so he couldn't see his mother, and he gave him a plastic Spiderman toy from the dry goods stand; at last the child stopped crying. The fire was still smoldering, but the shopkeeper couldn't seem to bring herself to add to it. The dispute had started over money, and even in her rage she still clung to her thriftiness: she had chosen the cheapest socks to ignite. And now she sat down heavily in the shop entrance, face furious, staring straight ahead. A few people in the crowd laughed uneasily, and finally they started to disperse. Somebody stamped out the fire. At last Mr. Tao walked across the alley and offered the woman her child.

She shook her head curtly. The baby began to cry once more, but his mother refused to look at him, and Mr. Tao had no choice but to return across the alley. Over the next forty-five minutes the baby became increasingly frantic. Mr. Tao's wife held him for a while, and then she passed him to me, and I passed him back to Mr. Tao. All of us tried to talk softly and calm him down, but it was hopeless; he screamed and his little head shone red beneath the fair hair. Whenever somebody approached the mother, she ignored them. She had failed to control her husband, and the bonfire had been an embarrassment, and now she directed the last of her rage at the only person she could overpower.

We stood with the baby until after nine o'clock, when the Tao sisters showed up. They had just finished an overtime shift at the factory, and Yuran, the oldest girl, immediately took the screaming baby. Yuran was only seventeen, and she had just worked an eleven-hour day, sorting out pink and purple bra rings, but now she took this new challenge in stride. She cooed at the baby and bounced him gently; at last his exhausted eyes began to close. The first time Yuran took him across the alley, his mother refused. Yuran waited patiently, baby on her hip, and then she tried again. She never said a word—she simply held the baby toward the woman. And finally, nearly two hours after the scene had started, the woman accepted her child. Together they disappeared into the back of the shop.

The next time I saw Yuran, I asked if there had been a problem when the shopkeeper's husband finally returned. She shook her head: he'd come back late that night and nothing happened. Yuran had a young, girlish face, but often her words seemed old. "They do this kind of thing all the time," she said. "It's just the way they are. Some people like to fight."

SOUTH OF LISHUI THE government had already started building another highway. Eventually it would connect with the Jinliwen Expressway, and the new road would run southwest past the development zone and into the countryside. The project was still in its early stages; work crews were blasting tunnels through the cliffs. Apart from the demolition sites, the region was mostly quiet, and sometimes, when I wanted a break from the development zone, I took a drive in that direction. A few years from now the factory towns would begin to rise, but for the time being this area remained peaceful farmland.

One of the expressway's future exits would be near a place called Dagangtou, which is less than twenty miles from Lishui. In the past, Dagangtou was a small fishing village on the Da River, where an old stone weir had been built many centuries ago. The village has a cobbled main street lined with traditional houses of wood and tile, and the city government identified it as the perfect location for a "green industry." Because of Lishui's early reliance on pleather factories, the cadres were looking for ways to encourage cleaner business, and in Dagangtou they decided to start an artists' commune. Their goals were twofold: painters would produce marketable work, and after the expressway was finished the place would also attract tourists. The only thing lacking was a vibrant arts community, which the government intended to attract in the exact same way that they attracted industry. In the development zone, factories received tax breaks for their first three years of residence; in the artists' commune, any painter who moved to town received discounted rent for the first three years. If it worked for pleather, why couldn't it also work for art?

The cadres named their project the Ancient Weir Art Village, and they claimed to have modeled it on the Barbizon, the nineteenth-century movement that first developed near the forest of Fontainebleau in France, where artists gathered to paint rural scenes and peasant subjects. In the Barbizon spirit, the Lishui government commissioned a series of landscapes of the surrounding countryside. They built a gallery to display these paintings, and not long after it opened I made a visit. I wandered through the gallery, gazing at scenes from the region: a bucolic stretch of the Da River, a quiet hillside of tangerine groves, a picturesque cluster of traditional peasant homes. Most paintings were heavily influenced by French Impressionism, with muted colors and soft light; some of the details even seemed European. One picture featured three languid cows, an animal I never saw in Lishui. Another painting used Van Gogh–style brushstrokes to depict a tangerine tree. There was a Monet-inspired scene of a local chaff fire. In the gallery's main room, out of twenty-six landscapes, only one included a human figure. It was exactly how Lishui would look if it were located in France and had no people.

The Ancient Weir Art Village had just opened, but its promise of free rent had already attracted eleven art companies. Most of these small businesses employed painters who created European and American cityscapes destined for the overseas market. They had been trained in art schools across Zhejiang, and a number of them specialized in reproducing portraits of Venice. One of the biggest local companies was called Hong Ye, where a manager told me that they dealt with a European buyer who wanted a thousand paintings of Venice every month. Back in Europe, these canvases were sold to tourist shops, hotels, and restaurants. There was also a good market for paintings copied from the work of Dutch Masters. Chinese artists called these scenes Helan Jie, "Holland Street," and usually it took them a little more than a day to turn one out.

At a gallery called Bomia, I watched a woman named Chen Meizi work on a "Holland Street." The scene featured cobblestones, a horse-drawn cart, and a building she referred to as "the tower." When I told Meizi it was actually a church, she said she had suspected as much but wasn't certain. She estimated that she had already painted this particular scene thirty times. Her other most common subjects were Saint Mark's Basilica and the Doge's Palace, although she didn't know the names of either building. Like other local artists, she referred to Venice as Shui-cheng, "Water City." Originally she had grown up on a farm in another part of Zhejiang, and I asked how she first became interested in art.

"Because I was a terrible student," Meizi said. "I had bad grades and I couldn't get into high school. It's easier to get accepted to an art school than a technical school, so that's what I did."

"Did you like to draw when you were little?"

"No," she said.

"But you had natural talent, right?"

"Absolutely none at all!" she said. "When I started, I couldn't even hold a brush!"

"Did you study well?"

"No. I was the worst in the class."

"But did you enjoy it?"

"No. I didn't like it one bit."

To my eye, Meizi seemed technically quite capable; her paintings looked good. But she spoke of her work without the slightest sentimentality. Chinese people tend to be blunt about such matters, especially if they're from the countryside, and often it's refreshing. A young American who doodles for an ad company might expound on creativity and inspiration—if only the company would let me follow my muse! But Meizi had no use for any of that. She was a petite, pretty woman with a raspy voice; she wore a white painter's smock and laughed at many of my questions. She never painted anything for fun—when I mentioned the possibility, she looked at me like I was crazy. She mocked the Barbizon concept; as with most young migrants, the last thing she wanted was rural tranquillity, and she had moved to Dagangtou strictly for the free rent. I asked which of her paintings she liked the best, and she said,

"I don't like any of them." She had a similar response when I inquired if she admired the work of any famous artists, like Monet and Van Gogh. "I don't have a favorite," she said. "That kind of art has no connection at all with what we do."

She lived with her boyfriend, another artist named Hu Jianhui, and together they ran the Bomia gallery. They had hired a couple of young art school graduates to work with them. Every month or so, Jianhui packed up a bundle of paintings and took a train to Dongguan, a city in the far south. Dongguan has a market that specializes in such paintings, and most of Jianhui's customers came from Europe and Russia. They paid according to size: an 8 x 10 usually went for $6.25, a 12 x 16 was $12.50, a 30 x 40 was $45.11. In the average month, Meizi and Jianhui earned a total of a thousand dollars, which is excellent money for Lishui. Among technicians in the factory world, only a Big Master can earn so much.

One afternoon I hung out in their studio while they painted. The conversation turned to taste, and Jianhui talked about things he noticed from the art market. "Americans prefer brighter pictures," he said. "They like scenes to be lighter. Russians like bright colors, too. Koreans like them to be more subdued, and Germans like things that are grayer. The French are like that, too."

Meizi flipped through a book that displayed sample landscapes, and she pointed to a clumsily exotic scene of palm trees on a beach. "Chinese people like this kind of picture," she said. "It's stupid, something a child would like. Chinese people have no taste. French people have the best taste, followed by the Russians and then the other Europeans, and the Americans are after that. We'll do a painting and the European customer won't buy it, and then we'll show it to a Chinese person, and he'll say, 'Great!'"

Sometimes the artists received commissions in the form of photographs that were to be reproduced in oil paint. That week an American had sent a bunch of snapshots, and Meizi showed me one: a big white barn with two silos. I asked her what she thought it was.

"A development zone," she said.

I told her it was a farm. "So big just for a farm?" she said. "What are those for?"

I said the silos are used for grain.

"*Those* big things are for grain?" she said, laughing. "I thought they were for storing chemicals!"

Now she studied the scene with new eyes. "I can't believe how big it is!" she said. "Where's the rest of the village?"

I told her that American farmers don't usually live in a town.

"Where are their neighbors?" Meizi asked.

"They're probably far away, too," I said.

"Aren't they lonely?"

"It doesn't bother them," I said. "That's how farming is in America."

She showed me the rest of the photos, which consisted mostly of shopfronts and old buildings that appeared to come from an American small town. Meizi couldn't tell me anything else about the commission—it had come through a middleman who didn't want to reveal the final buyer. From reading the shop signs and checking online, I learned that all the featured buildings were located in Park City, Utah. At first I thought they must be connected with some local tourist campaign, but when I contacted people in Park City they had no idea that their homes and businesses were being painted in the Chinese Barbizon. Probably somebody had passed through northern Utah with a camera, taken some quick snapshots, and commissioned the paintings. Most likely they would be sold as decorations for hotel rooms or restaurants; the final destination could be anywhere in America or Europe.

The shop signs in the photographs caused the biggest headache for the artists, who didn't speak English. Meizi had painted a building with a sign in front: "Miners Hospital 1904." In her picture, the building looked perfect, but the sign now read: "Miers Hospital 1904." Meizi had turned another shop, "Fine Sheepskin Leather Since 1973," into "Fine Sheepskim Leather Sine 1773." A "Bar" was now a "Dah." Other pictures featured a "Hope Nuseum," one shop that sold "Amiques," and a "Residentlal Bboker."

There was part of me that preferred the new versions—who

wouldn't want to drink at a place called Dah? But I hoped the artists would do well with their commission, so I pointed out all the necessary corrections. After that, every time I went to Lishui I made a trip out to the Ancient Weir Art Village. I liked the quiet scenery and the peaceful village, which wasn't going to change until the expressway opened. On my visits I helped Jianhui and Meizi clean up misspellings, and they were always grateful; repeatedly they offered to paint something especially for me. "Just bring a picture," Jianhui told me. Finally I gave them a photograph of my childhood home in Missouri, where my parents still live. I could tell that Jianhui was careful with this commission, and he apologized when I came to pick it up.

"I'm sorry about that one part," he said. "I couldn't really see it clearly, so I didn't know what it was."

He pointed to the driveway beside the house. In the photograph, shade falls across the asphalt, obscuring the surface. I realized that Jianhui had never seen such an arrangement: Lishui's first neighborhood with private driveways was White Cloud, which was still under construction. I explained that many Americans park their cars on strips of asphalt beside their homes.

"Oh, now I understand," he said. "I couldn't tell if it was another street or something. I can fix it if you want."

In the painting he had broadened the asphalt so it now occupied a good half of the front lawn. For years, back in Missouri, my parents had resisted changing their old-fashioned driveway, believing the new two-car garages were excessive. But now Jianhui had done the widening work for them. I told him it was perfect except for one thing: no signature. The artists always left their work anonymous, because nobody in Europe wants to look at a painting of Venice and see a Chinese name, but I asked Jianhui to sign the canvas. I rolled it up and carried it on my next flight back to the States. My parents were thrilled, and they hung the gift in their kitchen. Every time I saw the painting, it reminded me of one of my favorite parts of Lishui, where the gentle countryside gave way to the Ancient Weir Art Village. But the painting also made me feel a little guilty, because Jianhui and Meizi had refused to accept any money for the commission. In all the time I knew them, that was the closest they ever came to painting for fun.

AT THE END OF November, the bosses finally made a decision about moving the factory. Boss Gao drove to Ouhai, a region west of Wenzhou where the expressway had recently opened a new exit. He found an empty warehouse that was large enough to contain the Machine and the metal punch presses, and he signed a rental contract with the owners. It was cheaper than the current arrangement, and after the lease had been signed, the bosses consulted a fortune-teller. His advice was unequivocal: the twenty-eighth of November was also the eighth day of the lunar month, and there's no better luck than double eights.

They waited until the twenty-sixth to tell the workers. As expected, most of the assembly-line women immediately quit, and Master Luo and the other technicians attempted to leverage the move into higher salaries. But the bosses were able to dismiss these requests one by one. The only remaining issue was whether the Taos and Ren Jing would transfer with the factory. Boss Wang waited until the morning of the twenty-seventh to approach Mr. Tao directly, and at once the negotiations flared up.

"Are you c-c-coming or not coming?" he said.

"Not coming!" Mr. Tao said. "My son is in school here. We can't just leave. And we have our business, too."

"You can do business there if you want."

"Easy for you to say," Mr. Tao said. "We're doing well here."

Before Boss Wang had approached, I had been chatting with Mr. Tao, who had been relaxed and good-humored. But now his body language completely changed: back straight, head up, chin thrust forward. Boss Wang tried again. "C-c-come try it for a while," he said.

"I need to be here to take care of my son."

"Well, then let the girls come." This in fact was Boss Wang's ideal solution: to keep the girls and drop Mr. Tao. But Mr. Tao responded quickly.

"They can't go alone," he said. "They're too young. Anyway, we signed contracts for the whole year. If you move, then you're breaking the contract."

"I'm not breaking any contracts! I'm inviting you to come."

"The contract doesn't say anything about going to another city. How can I move my whole family?"

"That's your business," Boss Wang said. "I'm offering you the same job. That's the contract."

"If I went to the labor bureau, they wouldn't see it that way." It was an idle threat—if indeed Mr. Tao were foolish enough to visit the labor bureau, and if by some miracle the cadres actually listened to a citizen complaint, their response would be to stop the fifteen-year-old Yufeng from working illegally. But the remark served its purpose: Boss Wang stormed off in frustration, and Mr. Tao seemed pleased. There was less than a day left to negotiate, but for a man like him that was plenty of time.

HE DISAPPEARED AT LUNCHTIME, off on some mysterious errand. After Mr. Tao had left the factory, Master Luo invited Yufeng and Ren Jing to lunch in his dormitory room. Old Tian joined them, and after the meal the men began to needle the girls.

"You don't have a bank account, do you?" Master Luo said to Yufeng.

"No."

"You're still giving all your money to your parents! At your age you should have your own account."

"They need my help."

"It helps more if you learn to be independent," he said. "Lots of people are independent at your age. In my village, everybody who goes out to work gets a bank account right away."

"Well, my village is different," Yufeng said. Her arms were crossed and she stared stubbornly at the floor. Beside her, Ren Jing was silent; her mother had already told her she couldn't go unless the girls were accompanied by Mr. Tao.

"You should open a bank account now," Master Luo said.

"Fine, I'll open one tomorrow!" Yufeng shouted. "Will you leave me alone?"

"I just think you should make decisions for yourself," Master Luo said softly. "If you have a bank account, then you can start buying things for yourself. In my village, when young people come home for the Spring Festival, they wear name-brand clothes and they have name-brand cell phones."

"People do that in my village too," Yufeng shot back. "I remember when a girl came back with a motorcycle. Everybody said she was successful."

"Well, that's what you should do. Or at least you should make your own decision."

"It's not my decision!"

"No, it's obviously not," he said. "You're letting your father decide for you. He doesn't want you to be independent. What are you going to do if you stay here?"

"I'll work in a shoe factory," Yufeng said.

"How much will you make?"

"I don't know."

"Do you think a shoe factory is going to hire you now, at the end of the year?"

The girl fell silent—she knew Master Luo was right. November is a bad time to look for factory work; most people wait until after the holiday to jump jobs. But it's also true that November is a bad time to find new employees, which was Master Luo and Old Tian's stake in this conversation. Moving the machinery was going to be an enormous project, and the last thing they wanted to do was train new workers. And Master Luo knew that inevitably he would end up in the middle of any negotiations—a typical role for a high-level technician.

Before leaving on his errand, Mr. Tao had made his terms clear. He demanded one thousand yuan a month for everybody: himself, his two daughters, and Ren Jing. The salary represented a raise of roughly 30 percent, and he also asked for free room and board. Boss Wang hadn't responded yet—he had his hands full with pre-move preparations. His wife had come to help, and she had brought along his three-year-old son. Whenever the boy stayed in the factory, he spent his days poking into machinery and causing trouble. He pinballed back and forth between the floors, constantly chased away by workers. They did this with relish—they seemed to view the child as a convenient scapegoat for any aggression they harbored toward the boss.

Now after lunch the child entered Master Luo's dormitory room. Master Luo grabbed a big cooking knife, rolled up his sleeves, and crouched low to the ground, muttering like a psychopath. The three-year-old froze, eyes wide.

"Uhhhh!" Master Luo grunted loudly, staggering toward the child. "Uhhh! Uhhhh!"

He swiped at the air with the knife; the child screamed and ran. His cries echoed as he clattered down the stairway. Soon he'd be down in the chemist's lab, where Little Long would find some creative way to drive him off. After Master Luo and Old Tian stopped laughing, they resumed their abuse of Yufeng.

"Where's all your money?" Old Tian said, teasingly. "You don't get to keep any of the money you make, do you?"

"She needs to learn independence," Master Luo said.

"I'd like to go," Yufeng admitted. "But if my father says I have to stay, then maybe I can find a job in a shoe factory and learn some technical skills."

"That's a joke!" Old Tian said. "You're not going to find a technical job at your age."

"Come with us," Master Luo said. "Learn to be on your own, and then next year you can go to Guangzhou or Shanghai, an exciting place like that." He told the story of his own first migration, when he had saved money and eventually made his way to Shenzhen. The girls had heard it all before, but nevertheless they fell silent, eyes bright as they listened to tales of the south.

BY SEVEN O'CLOCK BOSS Wang had offered seven hundred yuan. Mr. Tao held firm at one thousand—the difference came to thirty-eight monthly dollars per person, a significant sum. He was waiting at home when his daughters returned from work.

"Master Luo and Old Tian are bullying me," Yufeng complained. "They keep saying I should go out on my own."

"It doesn't matter what they tell you," Mr. Tao said.

"But I want to go!"

"You have to wait and see what the bosses say. Be patient."

"I want to go." Her father ignored her, and the girl raised her voice: "I want to go!"

"Be good," Yuran said. The older sister had a calmer personality, and often she kept Yufeng in line. "Don't start fighting," she said.

"But I want to go." Yufeng's voice was small now.

"Just wait," her father said sternly. "Everything will be fine if you wait."

AT EIGHT O'CLOCK MASTER Luo arrived. We had just finished dinner, and now all of us gathered close around the gas-powered burner: the two Tao girls, their father, his cousin, and me. The rented room was basically a shack with mud walls; cold November air blew in through the cracks. Master Luo distributed a round of West Lake cigarettes to the men, and the girls quietly left—they knew this matter was restricted to adults. During dinner Mr. Tao and his cousin had talked idly about history, the way people do in the countryside, and now they continued the conversation.

"The Ming started strong, but then they got weaker," the cousin said.

"That's always true," Mr. Tao said. "It's the same way with a person. You get old, you get weak, and then you die."

"The Ming was when China got *really* weak," Master Luo said, slipping easily into the topic. "They were defeated by the Manchus. The Manchus were a minority, and yet they ruled for four hundred years. So few people ruling so many!"

"And then China stayed weak until Mao Zedong," Mr. Tao said.

From there we could have veered in any number of directions, but Master Luo brought us back on course. "Look, I want to give you what you want," he said to Mr. Tao. "I don't want to hire a lot of new people right now. You have to understand that I'm on your side." He paused to take another puff from his cigarette. "Boss Wang and Boss Gao say that they'll pay you each two thousand to work for the rest of the year. They'll give you a bonus if business is good, and then at Spring Festival they'll give each of you a red envelope. After Spring Festival they'll guarantee eight hundred per month. Boss Wang said he can't give you more."

The red envelope is a traditional Spring Festival gift, with money inside, but Mr. Tao was unimpressed. "I don't want to split up my family," he said. "It costs us money to do that."

"I know," Master Luo said. "I told him that if I have to find workers and train them, it's going to cost about five hundred per person. I told the bosses that your demands aren't so high."

"It doesn't include food and lodging?"

"It doesn't include food," Master Luo said. "They'll give lodging."

"I want both."

"I'm sorry, but don't forget they're offering the bonus and the red envelope."

"Red envelope or no red envelope; bonus or no bonus," Mr. Tao said. "All that matters is what's guaranteed. If they aren't paying for food and lodging, then they should pay seven yuan a day for living expenses. It has to be the same for everybody, including Ren Jing. She's my responsibility, just like the girls."

"I don't know what they'll say." Master Luo's hands were nervous; he folded a scrap of paper repeatedly. Now Mr. Tao's wife entered the shack and she joined the circle around the burner.

"When I started this job," Mr. Tao said, "I left a factory where I made four and a half yuan per hour. They told me I could make more here, which hasn't been the case. So I'm not going to move without a guarantee."

"I know it's a hassle," Master Luo said.

The woman spoke up. "Why bother?" she said. "We can send both of them to work in a shoe factory."

"We need to figure this out before we start talking about shoe factories," Mr. Tao said.

"For this period, two thousand is fair," Master Luo said. "And after the Spring Festival you'll get a guaranteed eight hundred."

"Things that happen in the future are things I can't control," Mr. Tao said. "'Guaranteed' is just another way to trick workers. Yufeng can do ten thousand pairs of wires in a day. Where are you going to find a new worker who's that fast?"

For the next forty-five minutes the conversation circled the room. The men chain-smoked West Lake cigarettes, complaining about the hassles of moving and hiring new workers; they agreed on the general untrustworthiness of Zhejiang bosses. But it took a long time before anybody mentioned a specific number again. "They have to pay each of us an extra hundred per month, before the holiday," Mr. Tao finally said. "Tell them the money is to cover living expenses." Master Luo nodded, put out his cigarette, and left the shack. He had been there for more than an hour.

BACK IN THE FACTORY, Boss Wang and Boss Gao were in the midst of negotiating with a moving crew. For days they had done nothing but haggle, and now they received the message from Master Luo.

"We should just pay them," Boss Gao said. "Who cares?" But he looked to his uncle for the final decision. Boss Wang thought for a moment—he was clearly annoyed to be dealing with Mr. Tao, even through an intermediary.

"Offer him fifty," he said. "Not one hundred."

"Is that the last offer?" Master Luo said. It was a difference of six dollars and thirty-seven cents.

"Tell him it's the last offer. I'm not going to give him what he wants."

MASTER LUO AND I walked back across Suisong Road. It was after 9:30 and the night had grown colder; he laughed bitterly at the routine. "I always have to do this," he said. "Every job, it's the same thing—the master has to be the middleman. Nobody wants to deal with each other directly. *Mafan!* All I want are reliable workers, but I have to do all this negotiating."

The Tao home was empty, so we continued to the family dry goods stand, where Yufeng and Yuran were handling the evening's customers. Usually their father was there at this time, but he had disappeared on another mysterious errand, and he wasn't answering his cell phone. Master Luo left a message with the girls, asking Mr. Tao to call, but he never did. The offer was still on the table when the night ended.

ON THE MORNING OF November 28, the eighth day of the lunar month, a day of good fortune and fine prospects, I awoke to a Volkswagen Santana with a flat tire. In over half a decade of driving in China, across all the bad roads and the half-built development zones, that was my first flat. I opened the trunk: no jack, no wrench. At the Wenzhou Prosperous Automobile Rental Company, you got an empty toolbox along with an empty tank; I was lucky they had included a spare. I telephoned a Lishui cabbie I had met in the past, and he arrived with his tools and changed the tire. While he was tightening the last bolt, he decided it was a good idea to stand on the wrench for better leverage. Before I could say anything, the bolt snapped—he sheared the head right off.

"*Mei shir*," he said. "No problem. It's tight enough—that tire sure isn't coming off!"

"But what if it gets a flat? How would I get that bolt off?"

He considered this in silence. "That would be a problem," he said slowly. "Maybe you shouldn't drive too fast."

I thought, *So much for the fortune-tellers.* The day had the angry look of pleather weather, with gray-streaked clouds sagging low above the development zone. At the bra ring factory, the bosses had hired a forklift, four Liberation trucks, and seven day laborers. The trucks were five-ton flatbeds with open backs, and one of them had already been loaded by the time I arrived. It was packed with cardboard boxes and pieces of machinery, and I asked Boss Gao what they planned to do if it rained.

"It can't rain," he said.

"It looks like it might."

"*Mei banfa*," he said. "There's nothing we can do about it."

Since early morning, Master Luo had been taking apart the Machine. He broke down the main assembly line into three sections, and they used the forklift to hoist the heavy steel frame onto a truck. They hauled out the metal punch presses and the underwire machinery. Old Tian and Little Long boxed up the finished bra rings: more than a million total, packaged into ninety-four cardboard crates. By that point, all the major equipment had been moved, and Boss Gao and Boss Wang picked through each floor like gleaners in the wake of a harvest. They salvaged the dirty carpet in the upstairs office; they gathered any scrap of metal that could be sold to recyclers. They unscrewed every single lightbulb in the factory. With a hammer, Boss Gao pounded out and pocketed nails from a pile of scrap wood. A little more than a year earlier, they had ordered the ten-dollar doors from the contractor, and now they took each one off its hinges. They stacked them flat like playing cards in the back of a truck. At midday a few heavy drops fell, and the bosses looked up in fear, but the weather held.

Mr. Tao showed up in the afternoon. For half an hour he stood there casually, watching the trucks get loaded. He didn't offer to help: as of now he was officially off the clock. During recent days, in addition to keeping the salary negotiations on slow burn, he had secretly embarked on a job search, finding an assembly-line position at the nearby Huadu pleather plant. Because of the reputation for toxic fumes, it paid better than most entry-level jobs: Mr. Tao stood to make fifty-nine cents an hour. In the evenings he'd be able to run the family dry goods stand. As for his daughters—all the talk about their youthfulness and the need for a chaperone had been nothing but a negotiating ploy. Mr. Tao had always known they were capable of surviving on their own, and now they were free to go.

Ren Jing made the same decision for herself. At the end, her mother panicked and pursued the girl all the way to the factory gate, begging her to stay. She was too young; this was only her second factory job; she needed to wait until next year! But Ren Jing was determined: she had packed a small bag with all her possessions, and she waited to catch a ride with one of the moving trucks. She said nothing and she refused to make eye contact with her mother. The woman pleaded until she burst into tears; the girl remained stoic. And finally the mother gave in, shouting, "Leave then, if you want to leave!"

She turned and walked stiff-legged across Suisong Road, crying hard. The moment she left Ren Jing's side, the girl broke down—she dropped her head between her knees and sobbed. For the next hour, mother and daughter stood on opposite sides of the street, crying. They were too angry to speak to each other, and they made no eye contact, but the mother refused to go. It's a Chinese tradition to see a loved one off to the final departure, and even in her rage the mother wouldn't turn her back on her child.

Finally Ren Jing's older sister arrived to ferry messages back and forth across Suisong Road. "She says you better be careful," she told Ren Jing, and the sixteen-year-old responded: "Tell her I'll be fine." Five minutes later, the sister returned: "She's crying; she really wants you to stay!" But Ren Jing held firm: "I'll call her when we get there tonight." It took a long time for the workers to load the third truck, and then Ren Jing climbed into the cab. At the end, after the mother's entreaties had been exhausted, she sent two hundred yuan across the street. She was still standing there, tears streaming down her cheeks, when the truck disappeared with her daughter.

Nobody cried at the Tao sisters' departure. Each girl packed a small suitcase, and they chattered excitedly as they made their way to the old factory, like American kids going off to college. Mr. Tao accompanied them to the gate but didn't linger. No hugs, no kisses—he was soldier-like until the end. Traditional farewells didn't matter to him; he had more important business to attend to. The last thing he said was, "You need to dress warmly. It's going to get cold, and you'll get sick if you're not careful. If you're sick, you'll have to spend money on medicine. So dress warmly, OK? Good-bye."

With that, he spun on his heel and marched off. At ten o'clock the last truck finally left the old factory. They drove to the new location, where everybody worked well past midnight, making sure that the equipment was unloaded and stacked safely indoors. They had moved it all—the Machine and the metal punch presses, the lightbulbs and the ten-dollar doors, the underwire and the million bra rings—in the span of a single day. Almost immediately after they finished the sky opened up and it rained like there was no tomorrow.

IV

―――

MY CHINESE DRIVER'S LICENSE EXPIRED IN THE SUMMER of 2007. By then, I had moved back to the United States, where I became accustomed to new road routines. In traffic I learned to drive slower, and the right shoulder no longer presented an option for passing. I kept my hand away from the horn. At intersections, when a light turned green, I had to suppress an instinct to immediately cut left across oncoming traffic, the way you do in China. I no longer worried about three-wheeled tractors, or long-distance buses, or black Audi A6s. I took my car to a garage where the mechanics don't smoke. Once, in Denver, a woman dented my back bumper, and we exchanged phone numbers instead of cash. Twice I was pulled over by the Colorado cops. Both times they let me off with warnings, telling me to drive a little slower and enjoy my day.

Near the end of the year I visited China. A friend told me there's a grace period for license expirations, so I went to Beijing's Public Safety Traffic Bureau and filled out all the forms. It couldn't have been easier; they gave me a new document that's valid until the year 2013. I caught a flight to Wenzhou, picked up a Volkswagen Santana, and turned the key in the ignition: red light. By then, I knew every gas station within a five-mile radius of the Prosperous Automobile Rental Company, so I drove to the nearest Sinopec. While I was filling up, two policemen pushed a patrol car into the station. The engine was off; they had it in neutral gear. I asked if the vehicle had broken down.

"No, it's fine," one of the cops said cheerfully. "We just ran out of gas!"

It felt good to be back. I headed north on the Jinliwen Expressway, cruising past the one-product towns: the jungle gyms of Xiaxie, the buttons of Qiaotou. In Lishui I spent a couple days driving around the development zone. The government had recently initiated a local project called the Eastern Expansion, which would quadruple the size of the existing factory district. They hoped to move into higher-tech industries, and the project would require an additional $900 million in investment, most of which would come from loans. This statistic was given to me by Wang Lijiong, the former tank driver and current director of the development zone. He told me that the Eastern Expansion would require the removal of another four hundred mountains and hills.

I remembered the explosion I'd witnessed in 2005, when the demolition crew was working near the bra ring plant. I drove back to the site, and the men were long gone; so was the mountain. In its place stood four new factories. One manufactured construction materials, another sold chemicals to DuPont, and the third produced polyurethane to be used by the pleather plants. The fourth factory had a big English sign: "Zhejiang Renli Environmental Protection Co., Ltd." It consisted of a long low building with a huge smokestack emitting billowing white clouds. Nearby, hundreds of rusty metal barrels had been lined up beneath a makeshift rain cover. A slogan decorated a wall:

IN ORDER TO PROTECT THE ENVIRONMENT,
EVERYBODY HAS RESPONSIBILITY

I wandered into the compound, where nobody minded that I was uninvited. A worker escorted me to an office, and a man in a dark suit handed me his card: Ye Chunsheng, vice president of Renli. He explained that Renli is a private enterprise that processes DMF, the poisonous solvent used in the manufacture of pleather. When Lishui's pleather factories complete a production cycle, they end up with DMF as a waste product, which they cart over to Renli. All the rusty barrels outside were full of the stuff, waiting to be processed.

"This facility runs twenty-four hours a day," Mr. Ye said. "We're the only company in China that does this. We have one facility in Wenzhou and one facility here."

I asked about the clouds of white smoke, and Mr. Ye assured me they were clean. "The government approved it all," he said. He offered me a cigarette and shook my hand; he invited me to come back any time. On the way out, I counted a total of six hundred and forty barrels of DMF. It occurred to me that only in China could you visit a mountain and then, two years later, find it replaced by something called the Renli Environmental Protection Co., Ltd.

THE BRA RING FACTORY initially did well after moving. Their new location was in Ouhai, the marshlands south of Wenzhou, where it had been announced that part of the region would eventually be cleared of all industry in order to create a green belt. In Chinese cities, such projects are early signs that an environmental consciousness is developing, but there's still a long way to go. In Ouhai, after the green belt plans were announced, people responded by moving in a lot of low-end factories that are heavy polluters. They figured that a doomed region temporarily enjoys less regulation, and rents are cheap, too. This was the main appeal for Boss Wang and Boss Gao—they saved a lot of money on their lease. Eventually they'd have to move again, but there wasn't much reason to worry about that now.

Within a few months of the transfer, a neighboring entrepreneur secretly approached Master Luo. The neighbor had noticed the bra rings were selling well, and he wanted to get into the business, so he offered Master Luo a stake in a new company. But Master Luo turned it down—he decided that Wenzhou people are too untrustworthy. "I learned that from working with these guys," he said. "If a Wenzhou boss makes a promise, you know he'll break it."

Nevertheless, the neighbor entrepreneur made an order with the Qingsui Machinery Manufacture Company, and soon there was another Machine in the Wenzhou region, cranking out bra rings. During one of my conversations with Master Luo, he told me that it would require only forty thousand American dollars for an outside investor to start such a business, so long as Master Luo was involved. He knew how to buy a Machine and assemble it, and he could find factory space. Workers were cheap. Master Luo mentioned that he had savings of his own to contribute to the forty thousand in start-up fees, and finally I realized what he was getting at. I thanked him, explaining that I wasn't cut out for business, especially not in China. But if I ever quit writing and decided to make brassiere accessories, there was nobody else with whom I could imagine partnering.

A few months later Master Luo left the bra ring factory. They had never paid him the promised salary, and they owed him nearly fifteen hundred dollars, an enormous sum in China—but at last he decided to cut his losses. He returned to the south, where he found another boss who wanted to get into the ring business. Master Luo helped the boss assemble two Machines, and sales were moving briskly when the global economic crisis struck. During the second half of 2008, the effects were felt in factory towns all across China. "Every day you heard about two or three companies going bankrupt," Master Luo told me. His own factory laid off workers, which was common during that period. Back in Wenzhou, Boss Gao and Boss Wang reduced their workforce by half. In the end, their factory survived, but it was a tough year.

Others in the region weren't so fortunate. In Lishui, real estate prices plummeted, and the Yintai real estate company, which had built the Riverside apartment complex that I visited, was suddenly in trouble. Much of their funding was private, but by the summer of 2008 they couldn't pay interest on these loans, and a panic swept through the investors. They all wanted their money back, but the company couldn't pay; one farmer became so distraught that he killed himself by drinking pesticide. The government investigated, and they uncovered what everybody had known for years—that Yintai had raised money illegally. All told, more than fifteen thousand people had made loans to the company, whose total debt exceeded 123 million dollars. Now that they couldn't pay, the government clamped down, seizing assets and arresting Yintai officials. The founder was thrown in jail, along with his sons; in 2009 they were still awaiting trail. Ji Shengjun, the young vice chairman of the board who had met me in his nightclub—dressed in Prada, accompanied by his bodyguard, drinking Old Matisse Scotch and green tea—could expect to spend years in prison. During the investigation of the Ji family, the government seized forty luxury vehicles, including a Ferrari.

But such major collapses were rare in China, which seemed to have weathered the crisis better than other parts of the world. They didn't have the same widespread problem with mortgages as the United States, because credit is much harder to come by for a Chinese individual. Even a worst-case scenario like Yintai didn't paralyze the system, because the loans were private rather than state-backed. Banks didn't fail: instead it was average people who lost their investments. And in China, where the nation's rise had depended largely on the initiative of migrants and small entrepreneurs, these same individuals now provided a buffer against economic crisis. They were emotionally prepared for the stress of a downturn: everybody had seen instability and hard times; they knew that opportunities come and go. In 2008, when factory workers were laid off, they usually returned to their villages and waited until things improved. The Chinese had picked up many new skills during the Reform period; they had become quick and resourceful and tough-minded. But they could also be patient—that was an old quality, as old as the countryside itself.

The central government responded to the economic crisis with another major road-building campaign. In 2008, they announced a two-year stimulus plan that would spend 586 billion dollars, of which nearly half would go toward roads, railways, and airports. Some critics wondered why more of these resources weren't directed toward Chinese schools; it could have been an opportunity to finally build an education system that better prepared people for innovative work. But the government preferred a time-tested solution: spend money on infrastructure, and teach the citizens to spend money of their own. In particular, they targeted rural regions, hoping to turn the hundreds of millions of Chinese farmers into bigger consumers. The State Council passed a resolution that, if implemented, would allow farmers to lease and trade—but not sell—their land-use rights. Some rural regions began to experiment with small mortgages and loans. The national government initiated a new campaign called "Electronic Appliances Go to the Countryside." They gave subsidies to rural residents who bought refrigerators, televisions, cell phones, and other goods. It was a boon for farmers, as well

as for the factory towns—it helped them reduce the backlog in warehouses.

In Lishui, these strategies seemed to work, at least initially. During
the middle of 2009, Director Wang Lijiong told me that he expected
the city's GDP to grow by at least 10 percent for the year. It was the
same story across the country—Chinese exports were down by 20 percent, but the national economy was still growing at a rate of about 8
percent. China had traded overseas consumers for the ones at home; the
sheer size of the nation made it possible. Even the car market did well,
especially after the government reduced taxes on new vehicles. In the
first quarter of 2009, for the first time ever, Chinese consumers bought
more motor vehicles than people in the United States.

During the heart of the economic crisis Luo Shouyun finally made
the transition from Big Master to Boss. For a quarter century, nearly
the entire span of the Reform period, he had worked for other people.
Having started out as an illiterate assembly-line boy, he had bounced
across the country, from city to city, factory to factory, rising at last to
become a skilled technician. He had dealt with unreliable bosses and
broken contracts, and he had manufactured so many bra rings that he
dreamed of them at night. But in 2009 he left all of that behind. He
started his own company, partnering with his nephew, and they set up
operations in the southern city of Foshan. They recycled—they purchased trash from overseas and converted it into raw materials for Chinese factories. The company specialized in high-grade plastic, and they
relied on Luo's technical skills to set up the machinery. By the middle of
the year they had a dozen employees, and Luo was making more money
than he ever had with bra rings. His wife worked with him, and their son
remained in Guizhou, living with relatives and attending nursery school.

He laughed when I referred to him by the new name: Boss Luo. "We
get trash from your country," he said. They received regular shipments
from the United States, Europe, and Australia, and most of it arrived
in good condition; he could recognize refrigerators and televisions and
even parts of cars. They separated the materials, processed the plastic,
and sold it to Chinese manufacturers. "Some of them use it to make
toys," Boss Luo said. "But we also have a lot of customers who make

refrigerators, televisions—the same things we get from the foreigners. It's all the same stuff, basically."

IN ZHEJIANG, THE TAO sisters and Ren Jing left the bra ring factory not long after the move to the Wenzhou region. That turned out to be another aspect of Mr. Tao's plan: he negotiated hard for a higher salary before the holiday, and then, once the bonus and the red envelopes were in hand, he pulled out the girls. All of them came back to Lishui, where together they found jobs in a factory that produced ashtrays. After Yufeng turned sixteen, and it was easier to find work at a big plant, they jumped to Huadu pleather, where they worked in quality control. They inspected the finished product, checking for defects, and with their approval the rolls of pleather were sent out to the great wide world.

During my last visit, I stopped at the Taos' one-room shack. Yufeng had just gotten off work, and she chattered happily about the job. "They pay overtime!" she said. "I make nine hundred a month, but with the extra hours it's usually about fifteen hundred." It was a high salary, about two hundred American dollars, which was more than double the earnings of an entry-level assembly-line worker. Yufeng told me proudly that the factory made *pige*, or pleather, of an unusually high quality: some of it was used for motorcycle seat covers and automobile interiors. "I like the boss," she said. "If we get tired and fall asleep, he doesn't get so angry. And if we work a really long day, he'll buy us fruit or some snack like that. It's fun."

She intended to stay at the pleather factory for another year or so, and then she'd use the family savings to go into business, probably with her father. They wanted to start a real shop—a place with a roof and doors, not just a stand in the street. "You can't stay very long at a *pige* factory," she said. "There's poison, and it's not good for you. It's better where we are in quality control, but it's still not healthy. You stay for one or two years and then it's time to leave. If it weren't for the poison it would be a great place to work."

Yufeng was about to turn seventeen. I had met her nearly two years earlier, when she applied for her first job with her sister's ID. Back then she had pudgy, boyish features, and she clutched the bra rings like casino chips and sold the boss a line about experience. But over the last twenty months she had grown into her stories. Her baby fat was gone, and all at once she had become pretty—she had high cheekbones, a delicate chin, and well-styled hair. Her nails were manicured, a rarity among factory girls. The village was two years gone and a world away; she said nothing about her grandparents or her former classmates. All she wanted to talk about was tomorrow—new jobs, new plans, new lives, everything that seemed promised by the thrill of rushing time.

ONE AFTERNOON I DROVE to the former site of the bra ring factory. On Suisong Road, the three-story building was still empty, although eventually Geley would probably expand into the space. They were in full swing, cranking out copper wiring and Jane Eyre light switches; a security guard told me that business was good. I asked if I could stop in the old factory space, and he said it wasn't a problem. I walked past the stone lions, the folding security gate, and the American flag. The owner's gold calligraphy still gleamed bright on the wall:

THE TREMORS OF THE FUTURE
ARE HAPPENING RIGHT BEFORE YOUR EYES

Inside the factory, the first thing I noticed was all the rings. Nobody had bothered to clean the place since the move, and they were everywhere: black rings, red rings, bent rings, broken rings. In the room where Yufeng used to work, twisted underwire lay thick as straw. There were empty Double Deer beer bottles, crumpled packages of State Express 555 cigarettes, and used rolls of packing tape. A dead plant in a broken vase. A chess player's pawn, an orphan chopstick. A tear-off calendar stuck on November 22. An empty diaper bag, a child's shoe. On the first floor, where Old Tian once slept, a string of lottery numbers stained the plaster:

95 1.3.17.20.21.24 + 16
97 1.5.9.13.15.33 + 14
97 11.14.15.20.26.27 + 12
98 6.7.10.11.15.23 + 16
99 7.12.18.23.24.27 + 5

There was writing everywhere workers used to live. They had written in pen, in pencil, in paint; their self-help slogans crisscrossed dirty walls. I made my way through the former dormitory, past all the mottoes:

FIND SUCCESS IMMEDIATELY

PASS EVERY DAY HAPPILY!
A NEW DAY BEGINS FROM RIGHT NOW!

FACE THE FUTURE DIRECTLY

A PERSON CAN BECOME SUCCESSFUL ANYWHERE;
I SWEAR I WILL NOT RETURN HOME UNTIL I AM FAMOUS.

A cool wind blew against the windows. The busy fall season had arrived, and most factories in the development zone were working hard. From outside I heard the rhythms of machinery—the rattle of glassmaking, the rumble of plastic molds, the whirr of wrapping wire. But there wasn't a single human sound, and for half an hour I stood alone, reading the walls of the empty factory.

ACKNOWLEDGMENTS

A DECADE AGO, WHEN I WAS LIVING IN COLUMBIA, MISSOURI, and finishing the first draft of *River Town*, I asked a neighbor if he'd take a look at the manuscript. I had heard about Doug Hunt's skill as an editor, but I never imagined how much I would come to depend on him. Over the course of ten years, he gave advice on virtually everything I wrote from China, and this book, like the others, was much improved by his sharp eye and good judgment. I'm sure that Doug had no idea what he was getting into back in 1999. (Nor did he realize that this Stewart Road *guanxi* would also lead to his giving editorial counsel for Ian Johnson's *A Mosque in Munich* and my wife, Leslie's *Factory Girls*.) All I can say to Doug is thanks—for patience and generosity, and mostly for friendship.

In Beijing a couple of close writer friends were willing to read an early draft of the book. Ian Johnson offered excellent advice, especially with regard to cutting. Michael Meyer helped me improve the book's focus—and over all the years, from Sichuan to Beijing, it's been wonderful to share the journey with a fellow Peace Corps alum. Another former volunteer, Mike Goettig, accompanied me on a couple of rough stretches of the driving trip. At home in Beijing, Travis Klingberg was always willing to discuss projects (as well as give good advice on covers).

I am deeply indebted to David Spindler's research. I've never known anybody as meticulous and dedicated, and he completely changed my concept of the Great Wall. He also proofread a draft of this book, for which I'm grateful. As for the broken kneecap—it was worth it.

I was fortunate to share my house in Sancha with Mimi Kuo-Deemer. In the early years it was a challenge to deal with local authorities, and I wouldn't have been able to negotiate these issues without Mimi's patience and good sense. And her friendship helped make Sancha such a joy. I'm also grateful for Mimi's help in fact-checking that section of the manuscript, and thanks to her and Aaron Kuo-Deemer, we still have a house in the village—I look forward to sharing it over the years.

When Wei Jia was ill, I depended heavily on three physicians in the United States: Ted Scott, Eileen Kavanagh, and Vincent P. Gurucharri. I also appreciated the help of Kathrine Meyers, who explained the complexities of blood testing in China. The expertise of these people was invaluable, but mostly I appreciated their generosity of spirit—despite busy schedules they responded quickly to all my questions. I wish that I could thank Dr. Gurucharri in person. But I would like his wife and daughters to know that even in the midst of his own battle with cancer, he took the time to think about a sick child in China.

ALL THREE SECTIONS OF this book were connected, in various ways, to projects at *The New Yorker* or *National Geographic*. At *The New Yorker*, during the years in which I researched these stories, I was fortunate to work with three great editors—Nick Paumgarten, Dana Goodyear, and Amy Davidson. I'm grateful that David Remnick's breadth of interest allowed me to write about such different subjects: village life, Chinese driving, Lishui artists, Chery automobiles, and the Great Wall of China.

At *National Geographic*, I worked with the photographer Mike Yamashita on the Great Wall story, and his enthusiasm, energy, and flexibility helped make that project so enjoyable. It was also great to work with Elizabeth Krist, whose interest in China pushed these projects forward. My long driving trip across the north would not have happened without the early faith of Oliver Payne at *National Geographic*. Ollie took an interest in my writing before I had published much, and he allowed me to embark on a road trip with an open mind—no planned itineraries, no pre-arranged interviews, no promised themes. He encouraged the same kind of spontaneity in Zhejiang. For a researcher hoping to spend time with people and places, this kind of support is invaluable, and it's hard to find in the current climate of journalism. Carolyn White at the magazine was also an early proponent of the Lishui project. And I'm deeply grateful for Chris Johns for devoting so much space to that story.

Many of my magazine pieces were illustrated with the distinctive photographs of Mark Leong. I'm especially glad that we shared the Lishui project—in addition to his ability with a camera, Mark is both observant and thoughtful, and he enriched my understanding of that corner of Zhejiang.

Without Helen Chang's help, I wouldn't have understood the classical Chinese of the old Sancha land contracts. Rania Ho provided maps of Beijing cloverleaf exchanges. Michael Dunne, managing director of the China office at J. D. Power and Associates, answered countless questions about the Chinese auto industry. Jiang Hong, now at the University of Hawaii, generously suggested people to meet in Wushenqi, Inner Mongolia. Dou Changlu at *The Wall Street Journal* gave me early driving tips, and Lily Song helped me keep various registrations current. I first became interested in Zhejiang because of former students who had migrated there, and they helped me in different ways: William Jefferson Foster did fact-checking in the province, and Shirley Zhao vouched for me at the Wenzhou Prosperous Automobile Rental Company. Cui Rong at *The Wall Street Journal* found background material on the factory towns. For fact-checking, I depended heavily on Kersten Zhang—I much appreciate her willingness to work overtime.

Many thanks to Angela Hessler, who in the course of her own empire building—the Rome of Cesare and Adriano—took time off to draw beautiful maps of the People's Republic. Birgitta gave good advice on covers, and throughout the years I benefited from the support of all the Hesslers and Gundys and Nybecks.

Over the course of three books at HarperCollins, I've had one editor, Tim Duggan. As a writer working from far away, it's helped enormously to have such stability and support. Jane Beirn has been a wonderful publicist, and Allison Lorentzen did a great job coordinating the various (and endless) edits of this book. And I'll always be grateful to my agent William Clark for reading an unsolicited manuscript back in 1999, and for taking such good care of everything that followed.

IT'S NOT EASY TO leave China after a decade. And it's especially hard to take a project on the road, which is how it had to happen—two displaced people, each of us with a book researched, driving around southwestern Colorado and looking for a place to write. But we found it and we survived; for whatever it's worth, two China books took shape atop Log Hill Mesa. It was inspiring to watch *Factory Girls* come to life, right in the next room; and it was just as inspiring to share these projects in China, discussing what we each learned on various research trips down to the south. For Leslie—with respect for the work, and joy in the writing.

I'm most deeply indebted to the people I wrote about in China. I have no way of thanking the folks I met on the road, the hitchers and the migrants and the generous villagers; but I hope this book captures some of their spirit. I suppose that renting a car in Beijing would have been an adventure regardless, but it wouldn't have been such a pleasure without Mr. Wang at Capital Motors. In Lishui, I was fortunate to meet Gao Xiaomeng and Wang Aiguo, and I appreciated their openness at the factory. The Tao family was always willing to spend time together, and most of all I'm grateful to Luo Shouyun for his friendship and hard-earned expertise. In Sancha I was blessed to know Wei Ziqi, Cao Chunmei, Wei Jia, and Wei Zonglou. Thank you for sharing your home; thank you for sharing your table; thank you for opening your hearts. Because of your kindness Sancha will always feel like home.

September 2009
Ridgway, Colorado

SOURCES

MOST OF *COUNTRY DRIVING* WAS RESEARCHED THROUGH personal observation, but in some sections I also relied on published sources and interviews with experts. I have not included footnotes, because most readers find them distracting in a work of narrative nonfiction (and most readers will be happy to ignore this section). But I want to make my sources clear for anybody who is conducting research of his own. I've organized references in order of appearance, listed by page number.

This is a work of nonfiction, and I've tried to be as accurate as possible. I haven't deliberately changed events, details, or chronology; any errors are accidental. I used real names throughout the book, with the exception of Wei Jia's elementary school classmates; the names of those children were changed.

This book was researched from 2001 to 2009, and during this time some important figures changed significantly. China's total number of migrants, as estimated by the National Bureau of Statistics, grew from 89.61 million in 2001 to 132.12 million in 2006. Today most experts believe the figure to be over 140 million. But these statistics should be considered rough estimates, given the difficulty of tracking and even defining migrants.

Currency exchange rates also changed during this eight-year period, so I have not used a flat rate for dollar conversions throughout this book. Instead I calculated them according to the exchange rate at the time of the reference.

BOOK I: THE WALL

Part I

5   *almost a thousand new drivers*: According to China's National Bureau of Statistics, the number of registered automobile drivers in Beijing increased by 300,000 in 2001.

5   *223. If you come to a road*: Chinese driving laws are national, and they are listed in the "Zhonghua Renmin Gongheguo Jiaotong Anquan Fa" ["The People's Republic of China Traffic Safety Laws"]. Driving examinations are similar from place to place, but there are slight regional variations. I researched training methods and testing in the city of Lishui, in Zhejiang Province. The Lishui Public Safety Traffic Bureau provided me with a copy of their official study booklet, which lists questions that appear on the exam. The study booklet is entitled "Lishui Shi Qiche Jiashiren: Like Peixun Fuxi Ziliao" ["Lishui City Automobile Drivers: Scientific Training Review Materials"]. All quoted exam questions come from this study booklet.

7   *"The Chinese Automobile Driver's Book of Maps"*:

> *Zhongguo Qiche Siji Dituce*. Beijing: Zhongguo Ditu Chubanshe [Sinomaps], 2001.

8   *By 1931, more than two dozen places*: For background on how the Chinese converted ancient city walls into roads:

> Campanella, Thomas J. "'The Civilising Road': American Influence on the Development of Highways and Motoring in China, 1900–1949." *The Journal of Transport History* 26, no. 1 (March 2005): pp. 78–98.

9   *modernizers turned their attention to the Great Wall*: For the Chinese plan to convert the Great Wall into a highway:

> Lei Sheng. "Changcheng Zhu Lu Zhi Feiwu Liyong" [Using Waste Material to Build a Road on the Great Wall]. *Shenbao Qiche Zengkan* [Shenbao Automobile Supplement] 76 (May 12, 1923): pp. 2–3.

> Liu Huru. "Changcheng" [Great Wall]. *Xuesheng Zazhi* [Students' Magazine] 18, no. 3 (March 1931): pp. 75–76.

13   *the Ming dynasty avoided building the Great Wall*: For the influence of feng shui beliefs on wall construction near the Ming tombs:

> Hong Feng. "Longquan Yu Zhi Shifo Si Duan Bian Chengyin Tijie" [Notes on Contributing Factors to the Lack of Great Wall From Longquan Valley to Stone Buddha Temple]. *Zhongguo Changcheng Bowuguan* [China Great Wall Museum] 21, no. 1 (2006): pp. 52–63.

15   *The first major construction campaign*: For the history of the American Red Cross road-building campaign, see the article by Thomas J. Campanella: Ibid.

16 *similar to the United States in 1911*: According to China's National Bureau of Statistics, there were 9,939,600 passenger vehicles in 2001; this figure includes cars and buses, but not trucks. According to *The Statistical History of the United States*, there were 618,727 registered automobiles in 1911, for a ratio of 152 people for every car. By 1912, it had dropped to 106. (There were no registered buses at that time.)

22 *there isn't a single scholar at any university in the world who specializes in the Great Wall*: Arthur Waldron, now at the University of Pennsylvania, researched the Great Wall during the early part of his career, but he has since moved to other subjects. Julia Lovell at Cambridge University published *The Great Wall: China Against the World, 1000 BC–AD 2000*, a broad historical survey that describes, in part, cultural interpretations of the wall. Apart from that project, Lovell has not specialized in the Great Wall.

23 *In the eighteenth century, Western explorers and missionaries*: For background on Western confusion about the history of the Great Wall:

> Waldron, Arthur. *The Great Wall of China: From History to Myth*. Cambridge: Cambridge University Press, 1990.

23 *claimed that the Great Wall is visible to the human eye from the moon*:

> Warwick, Adam. "A Thousand Miles Along the Great Wall of China." *National Geographic* XLII, no. 2 (February 1923): pp. 114–43.

27 *China had about one-fifth*: The figures in this paragraph come from the National Bureau of Statistics.

29 *use of headlights was banned*:

> United Press International. "Light in China." January 4, 1984.

34 *"They come like hurricanes*: This quotation is from Han Anguo, the minister of censorship in 134 BC. It can be found in:

> Jagchid, Sechin, and Van Jay Symons. *Peace, War, and Trade Along the Great Wall: Nomadic-Chinese Interaction through Two Millennia*. Bloomington: Indiana University Press, 1989. Page 60.

34 *"is like attacking a shadow"*: This quotation comes from the Han dynasty official Zhufu Yan in 200 BC. Also found in Jagchid and Symons, page 57.

34 *"covetous for grain"*: This quotation is from the Book of Han, a history completed in AD 111. It can be found on page 33 in Arthur Waldron's book about the Great Wall. Other quotes in this section are from my interviews with Waldron.

35 *the Chinese response*: The material in this section, which concerns the various strategies employed by the Ming in their attempt to manage the nomads, comes from the research of the independent historian David Spindler. Spindler's project on the Great Wall is ongoing, and most of his findings have yet to be published. He gave me an introduction to his work over the course of many interviews and several journeys to the Great Wall near Beijing. For background

on Spindler's methodology and conclusions about the Wall, see my magazine profile of him:

Hessler, Peter. "Walking the Wall." *The New Yorker*, May 21, 2007.

37   *a major tremor in 1556*:

Chen Genyuan. "Ming Dai Guanzhong Da Dizhen Dui Shanxi Wenwu Zaocheng de Pohuai" [Damage to Shaanxi Cultural Relics from the Ming Dynasty Guanzhong Earthquake]. *Shoucang* [Collection], August 2008.

53   *the Ordos Desert*: For the relationship between the Ordos Desert and the Great Wall, see Arthur Waldron: Ibid.

54   *more than one-fourth of China's land suffers from desertification*:

Jia Xiaoxia. "Desertification: A Growing Threat in China." *Down to Earth: The Newsletter of the United Nations Convention to Combat Desertification* 19 (December 2003): p. 2.

55   *any benefits of willow planting would be short-lived*: For background on Wushenqi (also written as Uxin Ju) and environmental issues in the Ordos:

Jiang Hong. "Grassland Campaigns in China's Collective Era: Socialist Policies and Local Initiatives in Uxin Ju, a 'Pastoral Dazhai.'" *China's Embedded Activism: Opportunities and Constraints of a Social Movement*. London: Routledge, 2008. Pages 89–110.

———. "Reading China's Environmental Crisis: 'Mao's War Against Nature' Continues." *China Scope* (September/October 2007): pp. 3–16.

———. "China's Great Green Wall Proves Hollow." *The Epoch Times*, July 30, 2009.

Part II

62   *In 1924, Sun Yat-sen*: For the history of Sun Yat-sen's correspondence with Henry Ford, and the Chinese switch to the right-hand side of the road, see Thomas J. Campanella: Ibid.

63   *a book called* Beijing Jeep:

Mann, Jim. *Beijing Jeep: A Case Study of Western Business in China*. Boulder, Colorado: Westview Press, 1997.

64   *Volkswagen and General Motors made more profits*: For information about profit margins for foreign automakers, I relied on interviews with Michael Dunne, currently managing director of the China office at J. D. Power and Associates. Dunne also provided me with the history of the City Special, as well as background on Chery Automobile Co.

65   *the government of Wuhu*: For information about Chery, I interviewed a number of workers and company officials in Wuhu, including Lin Zhang, the general

manager for Chery's International Division, and Yin Tongyao, the company president. The company's strategy of asking forgiveness rather than permission was explained to me by Chu Changjun, the Communist Party Deputy Secretary of the Wuhu Economic and Technological Development Area. I also spoke with John Dinkel and other foreign consultants and partners. For more information, see my article about Chery:

> Hessler, Peter. "Car Town." *The New Yorker*, September 26, 2005.

65　*one step away from the complacency that comes with happiness*: There are various and often conflicting explanations of the spelling of Chery's name. Here I've relied on what company officials told me in Wuhu.

79　*In Genghis Khan's military*: For background on Genghis Khan and the rise of the Mongols:

> Weatherford, Jack. *Genghis Khan and the Making of the Modern World*. New York: Three Rivers Press, 2004.

81　*Yin Geng's words*: Many of these quotations are from David Spindler's unpublished research. He has published an article about Altan Khan and the "Raid of the Scorned Mongol Women":

> Spindler, David. "A Twice-Scorned Mongol Woman, the Raid of 1576, and the Building of the Brick Great Wall." *Ming Studies* 60 (Fall 2009).

100　*earliest known maps*: For a discussion of the earliest known Chinese maps, and the impact of Pei Xiu, see the following article. (In English sources his name is often rendered as Pei Hsiu.):

> Hsu, Mei-Ling. "The Han Maps and Early Chinese Cartography." *Annals of the Association of American Geographers* 68, issue 1 (March 1978): pp. 45–60.

100　*cartography developed out of astronomy*: For background on the history of Western cartography, and contrasts in development with Chinese mapmaking, I interviewed Patricia Seed, a historian at the University of California, Irvine. Her article provides an introduction to early European maps of Africa:

> Seed, Patricia. "The Cone of Africa . . . Took Shape in Lisbon." *Humanities* 29, no. 6 (November/December 2008).

113　*for Lu Xun*:

> Roberts, Claire, and Geremie R. Barmé, editors. *The Great Wall of China*. Sydney: Powerhouse Publishing, 2006. Page 24.

113　*"more like a river than a barrier"*:

> Waldron, Arthur. "Scholarship and Patriotic Education: The Great Wall Conference, 1994." *China Quarterly* 143 (September 1995): p. 846.

115　*we stuck the severed heads*: This quotation is from David Spindler's research.

121   *"Time seems to have lost all power"*: For background on Aurel Stein in China:

> Walker, Annabel. *Aurel Stein: Pioneer of the Silk Road*. Seattle: University of Washington Press, 1998.

BOOK II: THE VILLAGE

Part I

138   *Even as far back as the seventeenth century*: For background on the book culture of imperial China:

> Rawski, Evelyn Sakakida. *Education and Popular Literacy in Ch'ing China*. Ann Arbor: The University of Michigan Press, 1979.

139   *texts from the late Ming dynasty*: This detail comes from David Spindler's research.

145   *in AD 1615, a crew of 2,400 soldiers*: David Spindler has transcribed and studied the tablet above Sancha; these details are from his research.

152   *118 boys born for every 100 girls*:

> "Rising Sex-Ratio Imbalance 'A Danger'." *China Daily*. January 23, 2007.

168   *estimated that more than one million Chinese had been infected with H.I.V.*: At the time of Wei Jia's illness, the Western media carried many reports of unsanitary donor practices in China, and people feared that the country was on the verge of a major epidemic. In 2001, a United Nations report estimated that over one million Chinese had been infected, and they warned of a possible figure of twenty million by 2010. The Chinese government, on the other hand, estimated that there were only 840,000 H.I.V. and AIDS cases in 2003. In the following years, it became clear that the epidemic was not as widespread as many believed. In 2006, the figures were actually reduced: the Chinese government, working with the World Health Organization and the United Nation's AIDS program, estimated that the total number of Chinese H.I.V. and AIDS cases was 650,000. For reference, see the articles below:

> Rosenthal, Elisabeth. "China Now Facing an AIDS Epidemic, A Top Aide Admits." *The New York Times*, August 24, 2001.

> Yardley, Jim. "New Estimate in China Finds Fewer AIDS Cases." *The New York Times*, January 26, 2006.

Part II

187   *average net income for rural people increased by 11 percent*: This and the other figures in this section come from "The Rural Land Question in China," an excellent introduction to rural issues. This paper also gives a concise history of rural land policies since the Revolution. It was prepared by a number of Chinese

and American academics who worked in conjunction with the Rural Development Institute. For background, I also spoke with two of the authors of this report, Zhu Keliang and Ye Jianping.

> Zhu Keliang et al. "The Rural Land Question in China: Analysis and Recommendations Based on a Seventeen-Province Survey." *New York University Journal of International Law and Politics* 38, no. 4 (Summer 2006): pp. 761–839.

188 *sixty-six million farmers lost their land*: This figure is from a recent summary of China's rural issues, which also includes an analysis of proposed policy changes:

> Cheng Li. "Hu Jintao's Land Reform: Ambition, Ambiguity, and Anxiety." *China Leadership Monitor* 27 (Winter 2009).

188 *average rural household consisted of 4.55 people*: Figures in this section are from Zhu Keliang et al.: Ibid.

192 *paving 119,000 miles of rural roads*: These figures, and the comparison with the previous half century, were given at a government press conference I attended in Beijing: "The Highlights of National Expressway Network Plan," presented by Zhang Chunxian, Minister of Communications, on January 13, 2005.

192 *in 2003, nearly half a million Beijing residents acquired their driver's licenses*: Total figure was 480,000, according to the National Bureau of Statistics.

193 *looked almost exactly like the Chevy Spark*: For the controversy regarding the Chery QQ, I spoke with Chery officials and also Timothy P. Stratford, general counsel for General Motors' China Group.

193 *dropped by 8.8 percent*: This figure comes from the People's Bank of China, and was reported by *The New York Times*:

> Bradsher, Keith. "G.M. to Speed Up Expansion in China." *The New York Times*, June 8, 2004.

193 *leaped by 80 percent*: This figure is from an interview with Yale Zhang, director of emerging markets vehicle forecasts at CSM Asia.

195 *fewer than one in five used a loan*: see Bradsher, Keith: Ibid.

203 *Falun Gong*: For background on the rise of Falun Gong, and the crackdown:

> Johnson, Ian. *Wild Grass: Three Stories of Change in Modern China*. New York: Pantheon Books, 2004.

204 *hundreds of believers died in custody*: This was the figure generally reported by foreign newspapers during the period when the Wei family began to engage in business. Today, estimates are even higher; Amnesty International says that over two thousand believers have died in custody. For a more recent newspaper report:

> Jacobs, Andrew. "China Still Presses Crusade Against Falun Gong." *The New York Times*, April 27, 2009.

Part III

225 *"Build New Countryside"*: For background on this campaign, see Cheng Li: Ibid.

229 *"Preserving the Progressiveness"*: For background on this campaign:

> Yardley, Jim. "China Attacks Its Woes With an Old Party Ritual." *The New York Times*, March 9, 2006.

231 *One volume was entitled "A Textbook for Urbanizing the Countryside"*:

> "Tuijin Nongcun Chengshihua Duben" [A Textbook for Urbanizing the Countryside]. Huairou Qu Shizheng Guanli Weiyuanhui [Huairou District Municipal Administration Committee]. July 2005.

233 *cigarettes are even subsidized*: This detail and the other facts about smoking in China are from my interview with Yang Gonghuan, deputy director general of the Chinese Center for Disease Control and Prevention.

268 *Trouble can start within the Party itself*: For background on village elections, and the ways in which dissent sometimes occurs, I spoke with Kevin J. O'Brien, a political scientist who specializes in China at the University of California, Berkeley. See also:

> O'Brien, Kevin J., and Rongbin Han. "Path to Democracy? Assessing Village Elections in China." *Journal of Contemporary China* 18, no. 60 (June 2009): pp. 359–378.

BOOK III: THE FACTORY

Part I

281 *officials announced plans*: Details about China's highway project, and Zhang Chunxian's comments about Condoleezza Rice, are from the government press conference I attended on January 13, 2005 (see previous reference).

282 *the Jinliwen Expressway*: Background on the new road came from He Jiongwei at the Lishui City Department of Communications.

284 *the town had 380 factories*: Details about Qiaotou's button production came from Ye Zhengxiang, chairman of the Qiaotou Button Association. The Wuyi Printing Association gave figures for Wuyi's playing card production. Other figures came from the Wenzhou Educational Toy Association, the Wenzhou Shoe and Leather Association, the Wenzhou Smoking Paraphernalia Association, the Shengzhou Neckties Industry Association, and the Datang Textile Socks Industry Company.

291 *nearly 80 percent of all Wenzhou entrepreneurs*: Details on the educational level of Wenzhou business people, and local economic statistics, are from:

> Lu Haoting. "Millionaire School." *China Daily, China Business Weekly*, January 23, 2005.

292 The Jews of the East:

> Ye Jiandong. *Dongfang Youtairen: 50 Wei Wenzhou Shangren de Chuangye Gushi*
> [The Jews of the East: The Commercial Stories of Fifty Wenzhou Entre-
> preneurs]. Beijing: Renmin Ribao Chubanshe [People's Daily Press], 2002.

293 *a survey of local male millionaires*:

> "Wenzhou Qiyejia 2.14 Qinggan Shenghuo Diaocha" [Valentine's Day
> Survey of the Love Life of Wenzhou Entrepreneurs]. *Caifu* [Fortune
> Weekly, a supplement of the newspaper *Wenzhou Dushibao*] 138 (Febru-
> ary 14, 2006): p. 17.

305 *Yang Xiaohong*: He was the director of Lishui's Economy Trade Committee.
307 *Long-term exposure to DMF causes liver damage*:

> Redlich, Carrie A., et al. "Liver Disease Associated with Occupational Ex-
> posure to the Solvent Dimethylformamide." *Annals of Internal Medicine*
> 108, issue 5 (May 1988): pp. 680–86.

> Also see the Office of Environmental Health Hazard Assessment's "Chronic
> Toxicity Summary: N,N-Dimethylformamide," December 2000.

Part II

343 *annual per capita GDP*: This figure, and the statistics about Lishui infrastructure,
are from Yang Xiaohong, director of Lishui's Economy Trade Committee.
344 *infrastructure investment*: This figure, along with the statistic about real estate, is
from the local Lishui newspaper:

> Lan Yan. "Wo Shi Jingji Baochi Jiao Kuai Zengzhang" [Our City Main-
> tains a Relatively Fast Rate of Growth]. *Chuzhou Wanbao* [Chuzhou
> Evening News], July 28, 2006, p. 5.

352 Square and Round: For background on this self-help book, see:

> Chang, Leslie T. *Factory Girls: From Village to City in a Changing China*. New
> York: Spiegel & Grau, 2008.

355 *Francis Cabot Lowell*: For background on Lowell, see the introduction to:

> Eisler, Benita, editor. *The Lowell Offering: Writings by New England Mill
> Women (1840–1845)*. New York: W. W. Norton & Company, 1998.

356 *speeding ticket*: Background on radar tickets in Zhejiang came from interviews
with local police officers.

Part III

378 *70 percent of Lishui's total consumption of electricity*: This figure is from director
Yang Xiaohong.

378   *number of Lishui households buying an automobile*:

> Zhang Qiao. "Mei Qian Hu Jumin Jiating Goumai Yong Qiche 20 Liang"
> [For Every Thousand Households, 20 New Cars Were Purchased]. *Chu-*
> *zhou Wanbao* [Chuzhou Evening News], July 27, 2006.

393   *87,000 "public-order disturbances"*: "China Handles 87,000 Public Order Distur-
       bance Cases." *People's Daily*, January 20, 2006.

400   *Ancient Weir Art Village*: For background on the Dagangtou artists' commune, I
       referred to the local government proposal "Guyan Huaxiang Huibao Cailiao"
       [Report on the Ancient Weir Art Village], as well as:

> Lan Weirong. "Lishui Huaxiang Chuangzuo Jidi Zai Quan Sheng Shao Jian"
> [The Lishui Artists' Village Creates a Unique Base in the Province].
> *Chuzhou Wanbao* [Chuzhou Evening News], November 29, 2006.

Part IV

419   *the Yintai real estate company*: For background on the Yintai case:

> Zhang Daosheng. "Lishui Yintai Fanchan Feifa Jizi An Wancheng Jiezi Hu
> Zhaiquan Shenbao Shenhe" [Creditors' Rights Are Declared in the
> Yintai Real Estate Illegal Fund-Raising Case]. *Xinhua*, March 4, 2009.

> Dong Bishui. "Zhejiang Fangchan Shang Da Guimo Mingjian Rongzi Ju
> Kui 8 Yi Sun Ji 3 Wan Renci" [Large-scale Privately Invested Zhejiang
> Company Loses 800 Million Yuan and Damages 30,000 Investor
> Units]. *Zhongguo Qingnian Bao*, September 23, 2008.

> Jiang Dongliang. "Feifa Jizi Zhi Huan" [The Anxiety Over Illegal Fund-
> Raising]. *Faren*, February 2, 2009.

420   *two-year stimulus plan*:

> Barboza, David. "China Unveils Sweeping Plan for Economy." *The New*
> *York Times*, November 9, 2008.

420   *targeted rural regions*: For background on the role of rural consumers in the stim-
       ulus plan, as well as proposed changes to rural land-use laws, see Cheng Li,
       "Hu Jintao's Land Reform" (referred to earlier).

421   *national economy was still growing*:

> Barboza, David. "Economy in China Regains Robust Pace of Growth."
> *The New York Times*, July 17, 2009.

421   *Chinese consumers bought more motor vehicles*:

> Bradsher, Keith. "China Influence Grows with Its Car Sales." *The New York*
> *Times*, April 21, 2009.